☐ A135A SCOTTY MOORE'S GIBSON L5 GUITAR, #A18195

This is believed by many to be one of the most important guitars in the history of Rock & Roll. Throughout Elvis' early years, Scotty Moore was the well-known guitar player who backed up Elvis both in live performances and on recordings. Indeed, this guitar was played on Elvis' last two Sun Records recordings "Mystery Train" and "Baby, Let's Play House". The guitar was used on Elvis' first #1 selling record - "Heartbreak Hotel" on the RCA label. Following that smash hit, the guitar was featured on "Hound Dog", "Lovin' You", Baby, I Don't Care" along with many others.

This Gibson guitar was used in Elvis' 1950's movies as well as his 1950's television appearances including The Ed Sullivan Show, Steve Allen, Milton Berle and the Dorsey Brothers.

ESTIMATE ON REQUEST

☐ B191A ELVIS PRESLEY'S "SPEEDWAY"
BLUE JACKET WITH WHITE STRIPES

This blue "shirt type" jacket with two vertical
white stripes down the left side was worn by
Elvis during the filming of *SPEEDWAY* in 1968.
In this film, which co-starred Nancy Sinatra,
Elvis wears the shirt while singing a song to a
young girl and her family.

A scene from this part of the film was used as
the cover photo for the multi-million selling LP
"ELVIS' CHRISTMAS ALBUM".

Other photos depicting Elvis in this jacket
appear in many Elvis books and printed
memorabilia.

$20,000 - 25,000

PHOTO OF SCOTTY MOORE, THE L5 GIBSON GUITAR AND ELVIS

☐ B17A ELVIS PRESLEY'S RED SHIRT FROM *SPINOUT*

This red shirt was worn by Elvis throughout the filming of *SPINOUT* in 1966. Elvis wore the shirt while singing songs and in numerous scenes from the beginning to the end of the film.

A photograph of Elvis wearing this shirt appeared in the memorial edition of the The Commercial Appeal, Memphis' leading newspaper published the week of his death. Other photos of Elvis in this shirt were widely used for publicity purposes.

$12,000 - 15,000

☐ B236A ELVIS PRESLEY'S 1962 CENTURY CORONADO SPEED BOAT

Please note: Photographs of this boat were unavailable at press time. The boat will be at the preview.

☐ C235A ELVIS PRESLEY'S CONCERT BELT

This large white belt with brass studs, chains and encircled stars was owned and worn by Elvis

$12,000 - 15,000

☐ • A90A ELVIS PRESLEY'S WHITE KNABE GRAND PIANO #70545. The history of this piano is as follows:

1930's to 1957:   Used in Memphis' Ellis Auditorium & Performance Hall from the early 1930's until replaced in 1957 when the facility was refurbished. The piano was played during this time period by such great musicians as W.C. Handy, Duke Ellington, Count Basie, Cab Calloway and others.

1957:   Jack Marshall, owner of a music store in Memphis, obtains the piano. Elvis finds out about the piano and obtains it for his new home in Memphis, Graceland. Elvis has the Knabe Baby Grand refinished to his personal specifications and oversees the work on an almost daily basis. The work is performed at Jack Marshall's Music store because Elvis knows and trusts Jack Marshall, who is also the pianist for the Blackwood Brothers Gospel Quartet. Ron Blackwood, a member of the singing family and at the time a student in high school in Memphis, is hired by Jack Marshal to hand strip and refinish the piano for Elvis.

1957 - 1969:   The piano stays in the Music Room at Graceland. It is played constantly by Elvis and friends, frequently being used for practice sessions, friendly "sing along's" and untold numbers of jam sessions by Elvis and visiting celebrities to Graceland. The piano became one of Elvis' most loved, personal musical instruments.

1965:   Elvis allows photographers from the Memphis newspaper into Graceland to photograph the interior of Graceland for the first and only time. During the session, Elvis was pictured several times standing at and playing this piano. Photos from this session have appeared in Memphis newspapers several times over the years.

1969 - 1976:   Priscilla gives Elvis him a new gold-leafed piano for their anniversary. The white Knabe is put in storage.

1976 - 1981:   In 1976 Vernon Presley, in a house cleaning measure, sells the piano to Ted Sturges, owner of Sturges Recording Studio. Over the next five years, the piano is used during the recording of over fifty albums by various artists including Jerry Lee Lewis.

1981 - 1990:   Jimmy Velvet buys the piano and displays it in his museum until 1990, when the piano then returns to private hands.

1990 - Present: The Knabe Grand Piano, serial #70545, has remained in private hands.

10/1996 through 2/1997:   Mr. C.B. Coltharp, whose family-owned piano business has serviced and maintained the pianos of Graceland for almost 40 years, performs a total refurbishing of the piano. Referring to old photos and records, Mr. Coltharp matches exactly, the specifications originally given by Elvis. The entire process takes almost 5 months.

ESTIMATE UPON REQUEST

Looking back on the twentieth century, one man - perhaps more than any other - influenced the course of popular culture. That man's name was Elvis.

The artifacts in this auction document his life.

Looking back on the twentieth century,
one man - perhaps more than any other -
influenced the course of popular culture.
That man's name was Elvis.

The artifacts in this auction
document his life.

ELVIS PRESLEY:

THE OFFICIAL AUCTION
FEATURING ITEMS FROM
THE ARCHIVES OF GRACELAND

ELVIS PRESLEY:
THE OFFICIAL AUCTION FEATURING ITEMS
FROM THE ARCHIVES OF GRACELAND

AUCTION	Friday, October 8, 1999 Saturday, October 9, 1999 Sunday October 10, 1999
HOURS	Friday, October 8: 1:00 PM, Session 1 - The 50's (starting with Lot A1) Saturday, October 9: 1:00 PM, Session 2 - The 60's (starting with Lot B1) Saturday, October 9: 7:00 PM, Session 3 - The 60's (starting with Lot B200) Sunday, October 10: 1:00 PM, Session 4 - The 70's (starting with Lot C1)
AUCTION LOCATION	MGM Grand Hotel & Casino Las Vegas, Nevada
PUBLIC PREVIEW	Tuesday, September 28 - Thursday October 7, 1999 10 AM - 11 PM Daily
PREVIEW LOCATION	MGM Grand Hotel & Casino, Las Vegas, Nevada
ABSENTEE BIDS	Please refer to the Introductory Section of this catalogue
ADMISSION	This Catalogue admits one to the auction and two to the preview. Preview admission for non-catalogue holders: $5
CATALOGUE	$40; $45 by Priority Mail in the United States; $70 Internationally
PRINCIPAL AUCTIONEER	Arlan Ettinger
GUERNSEY'S	A division of Barlan Enterprises, Ltd. 108 East 73rd Street, New York, New York 10021 Telephone: 212-794-2280 Fax: 212-744-3638 Web: www.guernseys.com

GUERNSEY•S

MGM GRAND.

HARRY N. ABRAMS, INC., PUBLISHERS

ISBN 0-8109-2942-2

Harry N. Abrams, Inc.
100 Fifth Avenue
New York, NY 10011
www.abramsbooks.com

Published in 1999 by Harry N. Abrams, Incorporated, New York. Printed in the U.S.A.

CONTENTS

TERMS & CONDITIONS

This catalogue, as amended by any posted notices during the sale, together with the purchaser's registration statement, is Guernsey's and the consignor's entire agreement with the purchaser relative to the property listed herein. The following conditions of sale are the only terms and conditions by which all properties are offered for sale. The property will be offered by us as the agent for the consignor unless the catalogue indicates otherwise. By bidding at auction, whether present in person or by agent, by written bid, telephone or by other means, the buyer agrees to be bound by these Conditions of Sale.

1. All properties are sold as is, and neither we nor the consignor make any warranties or representations with respect to any lot sold including but not limited to the correctness of the catalogue and glossary or other description of the origin, physical condition, size, quality, rarity, attribution, authorship, importance, medium, provenance, exhibitions, literature or historical relevance of the property, and no statement anywhere, whether oral or written, shall be deemed such a warranty or representation. All sizes listed are approximate. Prospective bidders should inspect the property before bidding to determine its condition, size, and whether or not it has been repaired or restored. WE AND THE CONSIGNOR DISCLAIM ANY AND ALL WARRANTIES, EXPRESSED OR IMPLIED, INCLUDING BUT NOT LIMITED TO THE IMPLIED WARRANTY OF MERCHANTABILITY OR FITNESS FOR ANY PARTICULAR PURPOSE. NO WARRANTIES ARE MADE THAT ANY OF THE MERCHANDISE COMPLIES WITH ANY APPLICABLE GOVERNMENTAL RULES, REGULATIONS OR ORDINANCES OF ANY KIND OR NATURE WHATSOEVER. Neither Guernsey's as agent nor the consignor is responsible for any faults or defects in any lot of the correctness of any statement as to the authorship of any origin, authorship, date, age, attribution, genuineness, provenance or condition of any lot.

2. A premium of 15% on any amount bid up to $50,000 will be added to the purchase of all lots in the sale. On bids in excess of $50,000, the premium is 15% up to $50,000 and 10% thereafter. This premium is payable by the purchaser as part of the total purchase price. Guernsey's also receives a commission directly from the consignor.

3. We reserve the right to withdraw any property before the sale.

4. Unless otherwise announced by the auctioneer, all bids are per lot as numbered in the catalogue.

5. We reserve the right to reject any bid. The highest bidder, acknowledged by the auctioneer, will be the purchaser. In the event of a dispute between bidders, or in the event of doubt on our part as to the validity of any bid, the auctioneer will have the final discretion whether to determine the successful bidder or to reoffer and resell the article in dispute. If any dispute arises after the sale, our sale records are conclusive. Although in our discretion, we will execute other order bids or accept telephone bids as a convenience to clients who are not present at auctions, we are not responsible for any errors or omissions in connection therewith.

6. If the auctioneer decides that any opening bid is below the value of the article offered, he or she may reject the same and withdraw the article from sale, and if having acknowledged an opening bid, he or she decides that any advance thereafter is insufficient, he or she may reject the advance.

7. On the fall of the auctioneer's hammer, title to the offered lot will pass to the highest bidder acknowledged by the auctioneer, subject to fulfillment by such bidder, of all the conditions set forth herein, and such bidder thereupon a) assumes full risk and responsibility thereof, but not limited to, insurance, fire, theft, removal and storage or damage from any and all causes, and b) will pay the full purchase price thereof or such part as we may require. In addition to other remedies available to us by law, we reserve the right to impose a late charge of 1 1/2% per month of the total purchase price if payment is not made in accordance with the conditions set forth herein. SHOULD A BIDDER BE ACTING ON BEHALF OF ANOTHER PURCHASER, IT SHOULD BE KNOWN THAT BIDDERS ARE PERSONALLY AND INDIVIDUALLY RESPONSIBLE FOR ANY OBLIGATIONS OF THE PURCHASER SET FORTH IN THE TERMS AND CONDITIONS OF SALE. If any applicable conditions herein are not complied with by the purchaser, in addition to other remedies available to us and the consignor by law, including, without limitation, the right to hold the purchaser liable for the total purchase price, we at our option may either, a) cancel the sale, retaining as liquidated damages all payments made by the purchaser, or b) resell the property at public auction without reserve, and the purchaser will be liable for any deficiency costs including handling charges, the expenses of both sales, our commissions on both sales at our regular rates, reasonable attorney's fees, incidental damages, and all other charges due hereunder. In the event that such a buyer pays a portion of the purchase price for any or all lots purchased, Guernsey's shall apply the payment received to such lot or lots that Guernsey's, in its sole discretion deems, appropriate. In the case of default, purchaser shall be liable for legal fees and expenses. In addition, a defaulting purchaser will be deemed to have granted us a security interest in, and we may retain as collateral security for such purchaser's obligations to us, any property in our possession owned by such purchaser. We shall have the rights afforded a secured party under the New York Uniform Commercial Code with respect to such property and we may apply against such obliga-

tions all monies held or received by us for the account of, due from us to, such purchaser. At our option, payment will not be deemed to have been made in full until we have collected funds represented by checks, or, in the case of bank or cashier's checks, we have confirmed their authenticity. Upon collection of funds, purchaser shall receive a bill of sale for the concerned items of merchandise.

8. Lots marked with • immediately preceding the lot number are offered subject to a reserve, which is the confidential minimum price below such a lot will not be sold. We may implement such reserves, by bidding on behalf of the Consignor. In certain instances the Consignor may pay us less than the standard commission rate where a lot is "bought in" to protect its reserve. Where the Consignor is indebted to us or has a monetary guarantee from us, and in certain other instances where we may have an interest in the offered lots, we may bid to protect such interests. Guernsey's shall act to protect the reserve by bidding through the auctioneer. The auctioneer may open bidding on any lot below the reserve by placing a bid on behalf of the seller. The auctioneer may continue to bid on behalf of the seller up to the amount of the reserve either by placing consecutive bids or by placing bids in response to other bidders.

9. Unless exempted by law, the purchaser will be required to pay Nevada and local sales tax or any applicable compensating use tax of another state on the total purchase price. Deliveries outside the state may be subject to the compensating use tax of another state. Where duty or collection is imposed on Guernsey's by law, it will require payment of these taxes.

10. These Terms and Conditions of Sale as well as the purchaser's and our respective rights and obligations thereunder shall be governed by and construed and and enforced in accordance with the laws of the State of New York. By bidding at an auction, whether present in person or by agent, order

bid, telephone or by other means, the purchaser shall be deemed to have consented to the exclusive jurisdiction of the State of New York, with exclusive venue in the county of New York.

11. We are not responsible for the act or omissions of carriers or packers of purchased lots, whether or not recommended by us. Packing and handling of purchased lots by us is at the entire risk of the purchaser. In no event will our liability to a purchaser exceed the purchase price actually paid.

12. Estimates provided in this catalogue do not represent any opinion or guarantee of actual value or ultimate sale price. Actual prices realized for items can fall below or above this range. They should not be relied upon as a prediction or guarantee of the actual selling price. They are prepared well in advance of the sale and are subject to revision.

13. Should any disputes arise pertaining to purchases at this auction or any other matters relating to the auction, such disputes shall be brought in the courts of the State of New York. Venue shall be within the County of New York.

14. We and the consignors make no representations and warranties as to whether the purchaser acquires any copyrights, including but not limited to, any reproduction rights to the property.

15. Elvis, Elvis Presley, Graceland, King of Rock 'n' Roll and TCB are Registered Trademarks with USPTO. The rights of publicity to the name, image and likeness of Elvis Presley are exclusively owned by Elvis Presley Enterprises, Inc. All rights are reserved. Copyright © 1999 EPE. No copies of photographs, catalogue descriptions or other written material in this catalogue may be reproduced in any manner without the express written permission of the copyright holder(s) listed in this catalogue.

REMOVAL OR SHIPMENT OF PURCHASES

Inasmuch as Guernsey's does not permanently reside at the MGM Grand Hotel & Casino (the auction site), it is essential that items are either 1) paid for immediately after the conclusion of the auction (items can be paid for and removed at any time during the three session event) and immediately removed; 2) paid for on **October 11, 1999** and removed from the MGM Grand at that time; or 3) paid for immediately, making arrangements for the removal of the items by your designated shipper and alerting Guernsey's of your intent. To facilitate shipping, Spartacus Movers / White Glove Transportation, a firm that Guernsey's has worked with satisfactorily for many years, will be on site should you wish to avail yourself of their services. Guernsey's takes no part in any transactions between you and this firm; their presence at the auction is merely a convenience for interested purchasers. In some cases, there may be savings of sales tax by the use of a recognized, licensed transport company. Should your wish to contact the aforementioned shipping firm to discuss the possibility of working with them, their telephone is 718-706-8888.

IN ALL CASES, PURCHASED ITEMS MUST BE REMOVED (BY YOU OR A SHIPPER) NO LATER THAN 3:00 PM, OCTOBER 12 UNLESS OTHER SPECIFIC ARRANGEMENTS HAVE BEEN MADE WITH GUERNSEY'S IN ADVANCE.

About the auction lots and their descriptions...

Lots

In most auctions, a lot consists of a single item. The word "lot" therefore is at times confusing to the person who imagines that multiple items are being referred to. In <u>this</u> auction, many of the lots <u>do</u> have multiple elements. This reflects Graceland's attempt to offer unprecedented material and offer it in such a way as to make that material truly exceptional to its new owner.

Descriptions

In this catalogue, we have divided most descriptions into two parts. The first part provides factual information necessary to envision what a lot actually consists of. The second part of the description attempts to define the <u>significance</u> of the lots as they relate to the life and career of Elvis Presley.

Estimates

At the end of each lot description will be a pair of numbers.* These represent the <u>estimated value</u> Guernsey's and the experts at Graceland believe the lot to be worth. These estimates are offered as a range such as $600 - 800. (*In a few instances, a very special item may not have an estimate but rather will include the suggestion that interested parties contact Guernsey's for the estimate.) The potential buyer should be aware that an estimate is just that; it is not a minimum. MOST ITEMS IN THIS AUCTION ARE BEING OFFERED WITHOUT PRE-SET MINIMUMS.

Lot Numbers

The lots in this auction have been divided into three categories based primarily on their age. The categories are as follows: the 1950's (including a few items from the 1940's), the 1960's and the 1970's. Auction sessions have been divided to reflect these categories.

Dot

When a dot (•) appears in front of a lot number, it means that that lot has a pre-set minimum under which that lot cannot be sold. *The minimum is substantially lower than the printed low estimate.* Very few items in this auction have minimums.

Square

When a box (□) appears in front of a lot number, it means that that lot has been consigned by a consignor other than Graceland. In preparing for this auction, Guernsey's has received many offers of items people have asked us to place into the auction. Never forgetting for a minute that this is *the auction of archival items from Graceland*, the auction house nevertheless has considered these additions seriously. When an item seems so special as to potentially warrant inclusion in the auction, the auction house has brought the item to the attention of Graceland. If Graceland agrees with Guernsey's assessment as to the special nature of the item, then - and only then - will the item be accepted into this auction. Only a very few items have passed this rigorous scrutiny.

Participating in the Auction

Bidding and Pre-Establishing Credit

In an effort to facilitate your rapid removal of items immediately following the auction, you can pre-establish credit with Guernsey's. Having done so, you need only write a check for the amount of your purchase (assuming it is within the range of your credit line) and you can remove your purchases. The easiest way to accomplish establishing credit is to provide an Irrevocable Letter of Credit from your bank stating that they will guarantee your check up to an indicated amount. Such letters normally have a time limit and therefore, for this auction, a 14 business day limit from the first day of the auction would be appropriate. The bank letter should include the bank officer's name and telephone number and should indicate that the letter is for Guernsey's auction of Elvis Presley material. The letter should be addressed to Barbara Mintz, Vice President of Guernsey's and, of course, indicate the limit to which checks can be written.

YOU CAN BID AT THIS AUCTION WITHOUT PRE-ESTABLISHING CREDIT. You can use the bidder registration form inserted loosely in this catalogue (which can be mailed or faxed to Guernsey's) or fill out a similar form when you arrive at the preview or auction. Without pre-establishing credit, unless you pay with cash or a bank check or certified check, your purchases will be held until you personal check clears. In such case, you will be responsible for the cost of shipping.

Absentee Bidding

Although all are welcome to attend the auction in person at the MGM Grand, it is clear that many may wish to participate as Absentee Bidders. To facilitate absentee bidding, one may bid by filling out the Absentee Bid Form on the following page and mail or fax the Form to Guernsey's (address information on title page) prior to the auction. One can also bid by telephone during the actual by contacting Guernsey's well in advance of the actual auction dates to arrange for this method of bidding.

Internet Bidding

One can bid as an absentee bidder on the Internet through Icollector at www.icollector.com. Bidding on the Internet begins well in advance of the "live" auction, with leading Internet bids entered into the "live" auction at the MGM Grand.

Admission and Seating at the Auction

This catalogue will serve as admission to the auction. Due to the anticipated popularity of the Elvis auction we think it fair to assume that a large audience will be in attendance, therefore, the auction will be restricted to those who individually acquire the catalogue. Fortunately, seating at the MGM Grand Hotel & Casino (the auction site) is extensive, capable of holding many more people than would be accommodated at most normal auctions. Seating at the MGM Grand will be in two forms: FOR THOSE REGISTERING IN ADVANCE AS A BIDDER AND PRE-ESTABLISHING A LINE OF CREDIT, RESERVED SEATING WILL BE MADE AVAILABLE. TICKETS IN BIDDERS NAMES WILL BE DISTRIBUTED AT THE AUCTION. For those wishing to attend the auction but not participate in bidding, seating will be on a FIRST-COME, FIRST-SERVE BASIS in the large, unreserved section. (Both bidders and non-bidders are still required to purchase the catalogue for admission to the auction.

Previewing

Previewing of all the items to be included in the auction will commence September 28th and continue daily through October 7th, the day before the first auction session. Previewing hours daily are 10 AM to 11 PM. The catalogue serves as admission for two people to the preview; preview admission for non-catalogue holders is $5 per person.

Post-Auction Prices

If you wish to receive post-auction prices, please send to Guernsey's a self-addressed legal-sized #10 envelope with 32-cent stamp affixed, and labeled "Elvis Presley Post-Auction Price List" and you will receive same within six weeks after the auction.

ABSENTEE BID FORM

GUERNSEY'S
108 East 73rd Street
New York, NY 10021
Telephone: 212-794-2280
Fax: 212-744-3638

Date_____

I desire to place the following bids for the auction entitled "Elvis Presley: The Official Auction Featuring Items from the Archives of Graceland," to be held on October 8th, 9th, and 10th, 1999. The bid is to be executed by Guernsey's up to but not exceeding the amount specified below. The bids are PER LOT. All bids will be executed and are accepted subject to the "Terms and Conditions" printed in the catalogue of this sale. Please see "Information for Absentee Bidders" on the preceding pages and note that a buyers premium as described in the Terms & Conditions of this catalogue will be added to the hammer price as part of the total purchase price. It is recommended that you telephone us after mailing of faxing bids for confirmation of our receipt.

Name_____

Address_____

Telephone_____

Signature_____

NOTE: A "Letter of Guarantee" from an officer of your bank clearly stating the maximum amount which your bank will hold funds to cover your personal check must accompany this order bid. In lieu of this letter, a certified check made payable to Guernsey's for and amount equal to 15% of your total bid will serve as a deposit. This deposit to be refunded on all unsuccessful bids.

Bank_____ Contact_____

Account Number_____ Telephone_____

Lot Number	Catalogue/Description	Top limit of bid in $ not including buyer's premium

(Please print or type. For additional bids, please duplicate this form.)

(Bid is per lot number as listed in the catalogue.)

12

ABSENTEE BID FORM

Lot Number	Catalogue/Description	Top limit of bid in $ not including buyer's premium

(Please print or type. For additional bids, please duplicate this form.)   *(Bid is per lot number as listed in the catalogue.)*

Thank You

The staff at Guernsey's feels particularly honored to have been chosen to create this unprecented auction. Clearly, the event could not have been produced without the substantial help of many people. With apologies to those we may inadvertently omit, we would like to sincerely thank the following:

GRACELAND

Lisa Marie Presley
Jack Soden
Greg Howell
Debbie Johnson
Pat Mullins
Todd Morgan
David Beckwith
Carol Butler
Carrie Stetler
Carol Drake
Katie Wimbish
Angie Marchese
Sheila James
Phoebe Neal
Michele Desrosiers
Kelly Hill
Jennifer Burgess
La Vonne Gaw
Ronny McElhaney
Wayne Campbell
Dave Nicar
Mark Carroll
Bill Barmer

MGM GRAND

Bill Hornbuckle
Richard Sturm
Don Welsh

DISTINGUISHED CONTRIBUTORS

Sam Philips
Bernard Lansky
Jerry Osborne

CONSULTANTS

John Heath
Alexandra Garalnick

THERE ARE MANY THINGS ABOUT MY FATHER, ELVIS PRESLEY...

that so many others and I can admire eternally. He rose from humble beginnings and when the realizations of his dreams and aspirations exceeded all that he had imagined, it gave others hope - a new awareness of their own potential, whatever challenges they might be facing in life. With his success came the accolades and respect he deserved. However, the fame also brought with it a harsh kind of scrutiny and judgement that no on e should have to experience. The truth of his artistry and his character always rose above this. It always will. HIs place in our musical and cultural history, and in so many hearts, will always be secure.

One of the very special aspects of Elvis Presley's character was his generosity of spirit. He expressed it with benefit concerts and charitable donations that were well known by the public. But most of what he did for others was done quietly, without publicity. My father never once forgot what it was like to want, to need, to do without. He spent most of his life bringing happiness to others, endlessly giving to those around him. It is one of the things that I admire most about him.

In his own tradition of giving, we have created the Elvis Presley Charitable Foundation to do good works for the community and to honor my father's memory in ways that I know would make him very proud. Nothing we have done through this foundation would have pleased him more than our commitment to fund the building and operation of Presley Place, a transitional housing program designed to bring homeless families the helping hand, the skills and the guidance they need to break the cycle of poverty.

The Elvis Presley Auctions will make Presley Place and other worthwhile endeavors possible. I thank you for your support of our efforts and I hope you enjoy this rare glimpse into the private archives at Graceland.

Sincerely,

Lisa Marie Presley
Elvis Presley Enterprises, Inc.,
and The Elvis Presley Charitable Foundation

Thoughts from the Director's Chair

To continue Elvis' Presley's tradition of generosity and to honor his memory, *Elvis Presley Enterprises, Inc.* created them *Elvis Presley Charitable Foundation*. This foundation has quietly supported numerous charities through the years, especially focusing on arts, education and children's programs. Now, it has committed to its greatest endeavor of all - the creation of *Presley Place*, a transitional housing development in Memphis, Tennessee. The first goal of the Elvis Presley Auction is to generate enough funds to meet the foundation's initial $1.4 million commitment to the building of *Presley Place* and to support its ongoing operational needs. Any other possibilities for use of auction proceeds by our company or by our charitable foundation will be determined only after this commitment to *Presley Place* is met.

Presley Place will provide homeless families up to one year of rent-free housing, child day care, job training and counseling, financial guidance and other tools to help them break the cycle of poverty and gain self-esteem and independence. Phase One of *Presley Place* will be a 10 - 12 unit residential facility which could be in operation as early as the fall of 2000. It is the next in a series of similar developments that have been created and managed by the Metropolitan Inter-Faith Association (MIFA) in Memphis, all under their widely acclaimed Estival Communities program. A special added feature for the *Presley Place* edition of Estival Communities will be the Elvis Presley Music Room, where the youngsters of *Presley Place* and the other Estival properties may enjoy access to musical instruments and instruction and participate in special related programs.

In addition to our charitable foundation's quieter efforts, we wanted to select a major commitment that would establish the identity and purpose of the Elvis Presley Charitable Foundation more widely. We wanted that choice to reflect our deep sense of appreciation and respect for Elvis

Presley's own feelings and personal history and one that would be a source of pride to everyone who ever admired him. More than anything we wanted our choice to lead to a meaningful contribution to peoples' lives in Elvis' hometown and be one that we could feel with perfect certainty ELvis Presley himself would approve of with all his heart. We found all this in MIFA's Estival Communities program.

All of us with *Elvis Presley Enterprises* and the *ELvis Presley Charitable Foundation* are proud to work with MIFA in creating *Presley Place*. We felt that placing a selection of very special items from the vast archives of Graceland at auction would be an exciting way to raise funds and awareness for Presley Place. We also knew that it would be a means of sharing with the world many fascinating new glimpses into the life and career of our century's most beloved entertainer.

Jack Soden
Chief Executive Officer
Elvis Presley Enterprises, Inc.

The death of Dr. Martin Luther King, Jr. in 1968 plunged the city of Memphis and his dream into darkness. A group of religious leaders rekindled that dream, putting their faith into action to bring hope, independence and dignity to all Memphians. Since that humble beginning, the Metropolitan Inter-Faith Association has offered a hand up to hundreds of thousands of our mid-South neighbors in need. With the support of many generous donors and thousands of dedicated volunteers, MIFA empowers homeless families, unlocks the potential of our youth, extends a hand of hope to the working poor, supports the independence of our frail elderly and develops strong support communities. MIFA makes a difference because we bring together people of different faiths, races and ages who have a common dream . . . to make Memphis a better place to live.

MIFA's ever changing, always innovative methods of empowering homeless families have grown from 15 years of identifying the needs of homeless families and finding new and different ways to serve them. MIFA has taken these years of experience and learned how to provide housing and services to homeless families efficiently and effectively in order to help them achieve independence and self-sufficiency. To understand where the program has grown to today, you must examine where and how it began.

In 1984, MIFA began serving homeless families through the Emergency Homes for Families program. The program was unique for its time because it served intact families (men, women and children) in apartment housing (as opposed to shelters). At the time the program was initiated, the agency's limited knowledge of homeless families led the staff to design a program for families experiencing a one-time crisis, thereby making 30-60 days of emergency housing a sufficient response. However, program participants experienced a high rate of recidivism, causing MIFA staff to analyze the low rate of success. This analysis revealed the following:

1) Most homeless families are not victims of a one-time crisis, but instead have experienced months, or even years, of instability;
2) Most homeless families lack basic independent living skills;
3) Most homeless parents lack job skills, a consistent work

history or even a high school education;
4) Most homeless families are dealing with psychosocial issues such as addiction, domestic violence, and depression;
5) Most homeless families have serious credit problems which prevent them from obtaining permanent housing; and
6) Most homeless families have preschool children and are unable to work or attend school without quality day care.

In response, MIFA redesigned its service delivery to homeless families and opened the Estival Place Life Skills School in September, 1991. This program combined twenty new units of transitional housing with a service center designed to address the issues listed above. This new model of transitional housing provided housing for up to 12 months along with a comprehensive set of services to guide the families toward self-sufficiency. Today our multi-site program is known as Estival Communities and the supportive services provided include:

- A Child Development Center serving 59 children ages 6 weeks to 13 years old.
- Weekly Life Skills Classes addressing topics such as money and household management, parenting and child development, employment readiness, credit issues and many others.
- Case Management. Each family is assigned a case manager to help them identify the events that led to their becoming homeless in order to learn the skills necessary for self-sufficiency. Any needs that cannot be met by the case management staff on-site, such as counseling or legal issues, are referred to partnering agencies to ensure that all the families' needs are met in a timely and effective man-

ner.
- Financial Responsibility. Case Managers help each family develop and maintain a personal budget, teaching them to pay back debts, save money and live within their means. Families leave Estival Communities on a much more firm financial footing than when they came, having repaid an average of $1,000 in back debt and saved an average of $1,100.

Another innovative aspect of the program which began in 1991 and continues today is the savings component. Families are not charged a fee, or rent, but they are required to deposit 30% of their income into a MIFA savings account. The funds are returned to the family when they graduate from the program. Savings funds are typically used to pay for first month's rent, security deposit and in some cases, down payment towards the purchase of a home. With a maximum length of stay of twelve months, this allows the graduate to make their first steps towards independence, instead of seeking further assistance from MIFA or other social service or public agencies.

The primary purpose of the program is to combine quality housing with comprehensive educational services, thereby creating a life skills school which teaches participants how to live stable and independent lives. The program seeks to improve the physical, mental and spiritual health of all participants. After seven years of service to over 400 families, this program has achieved measurable success as demonstrated by the fact that 85% of families served have obtained permanent housing and maintained their housing for at least two years. This is due in part to the fact that the employment rate doubles from 35% at program entry to 72%

at the time of move-out. The innovative educational features of Estival Place, combined with the documented success of the program, inspired Tipper Gore to declare the program to be "a model for the nation" during her visit in 1995. The program was also recognized in 1997 by the Department of Housing and Urban Development in their National publication Spotlighting What Works.

In spite of the success of Estival Place, there is still a tremendous need for housing for homeless families in Memphis. Program staff often must turn away families due to a lack of space. Estival staff make referrals to other emergency shelters, but there is no other facility in Memphis which offers the same combination of quality, long-term housing with comprehensive supportive services.

To address this need, MIFA has recently expanded to 66 units of transitional housing, providing comprehensive services to all residents. Twenty of the new units comprise Idlewild Court, a new development built in partnership with Idlewild Presbyterian Church. This complex includes a classroom with a teaching kitchen. After this expansion, the program name was changed from Estival Place to Estival Communities to encompass the numerous campuses and various services provided.

Estival Communities will expand further with proceeds from the Elvis Presley Auction. Funds from this auction will make possible the construction of Presley Place, a new campus of Estival Communities containing 12 units of transitional housing for homeless families! Elvis himself spent a portion of his childhood in public housing when it was truly transitional and not a way of life. Elvis never forgot about the struggles his family went through, as evidenced by his annual tradition of distributing checks to fifty or more local charities. Today, through the Elvis Presley Auction, his legacy of generosity continues as a new generation of families will be given the opportunity to achieve their own measure of success at Presley Place.

MIFA's Estival Communities will continue to grow and evolve to meet the ever changing needs of homeless families. This vital expansion would not be possible without partners such as the Elvis Presley Charitable Foundation. Through their generous donation, they are helping to guide homeless families on the pathway to independence.

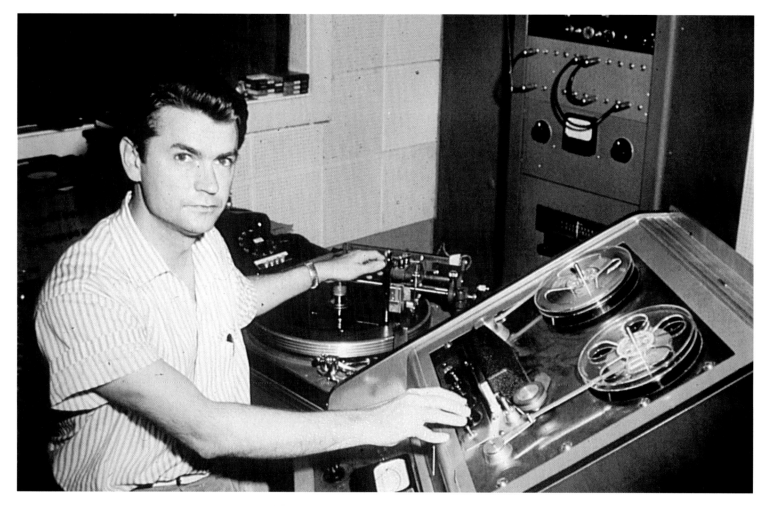

From the Founder of
Sun Records...

TO THE GREATEST FANS ON EARTH
- ELVIS PRESLEY FANS -

Yes and to non-Elvis fans (if there dare be one) you have the opportunity to have ownership of one or more mementos that in one way or the other intersected the life of the World's Most Beloved Entertainer and most assuredly the best known person of the Twentieth Century.

With the love, respect and close friendship I had with Elvis throughout his all too short life I am pleased that Priscilla and Lisa Marie are making this occasion possible.

There could be nothing that would be please Elvis more - the cause (MIFA)* for which the funds received on this occasion shall be a continuum of his love of helping others. That was always a hallmark of the soul of this most unusual man!

The authenticity of each of the items offered and conveyed is singularly the most important aspect of your acquisition. Coming from the authority of Graceland, Lisa Marie and Priscilla that validity is certainly assured.

Please know I have no monetary interest in this offering in any way whatsoever, nor am I being paid to express my personal sentiments herein. It is simply that I am proud to participate in something I know Elvis would want shared with those that meant so very much to him: Helping others and the phenomenally loyal following of his, *then and now!*

Priscilla and Lisa Marie, you could not have made better choices than all the wonderful staff of caring people at Graceland. We are proud of you and may God's riches in love abide.

Sam Phillips

Sam Phillips is Founder and Owner of the legendary Sun Record Company that discovered and started the careers of ELvis, Johnny Cash, B.B. King, Carl Perkins, Jerry Lee Lewis, Ike Turner, Howlin' Wolf, Roy Orbison, and Charlie Rich to name his most prominent proteges through which he changed the face of music around the world. Among the numerous lifetime achievement awards he has received, Sam was the first non-performer inducted into the Rock and Roll Hall of Fame.

*MIFA - A non-denominational charity that deals with all phases of human misfortune and suffering, ie: food pantries, housing, seniors, parenting assistance, memorials, emergencies, meals, clothing, etc. to name just a few of its unparalleled arms of help and assistance.

Clothier to the King

By Bernard J. Lansky

I looked up one day and saw this young man looking at the displays in the window of our menswear store on Beale Street in Memphis.

I had seen him before. I knew enough about him to know he worked as an usher at Loew's State theater on Main Street, just around the corner. I didn't know his name.

But, I get ahead of the story of how Lansky's became known as Clothier to the King.

Actually, as my brother and I started out just after coming home from the Army in World War Two, we sold military surplus goods. The war was over. People were looking for inexpensive clothes. They could come into our shop and drop down fifty cents and walk out of there with a cap or something. For a dollar ninety-five, they could get a fatigue shirt or fatigue pants. All of this is a far cry from the reputation we were to build within the next decade on Beale.

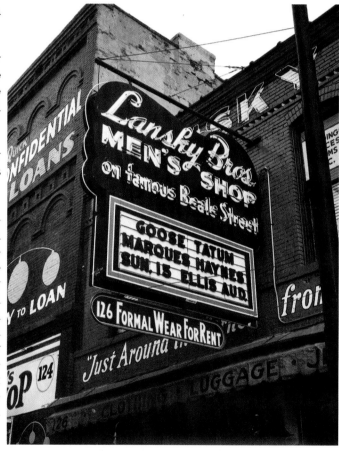

When the surplus era began phasing out, we switched to high-fashion menswear and all the merchants up and down Beale, and around the corner on Main Street, were looking at us with raised eyebrows.

High fashion? On Beale? Are you crazy or something?

But we had seen a void in the Memphis market. Practically everyone was selling the same plain old things everyone else was selling. No one was selling really high fashion

clothes. I mean, we carried nothing but the finest. That's what the kids of the late Forties, early Fifties wanted. And we gave it to them.

Now, back to that young man eyeballing the haberdashery in our window.

I walked outside to greet him and told him, "Come on in and let me show you around."

He said, "I don't have any money. But when I get rich, I'm going to buy you out."

I had no idea what his name was, but I told him, "Do me a favor, will you? Just buy from me. I don't want you buying me out."

And that's how Elvis Presley began shopping at Lansky's and via our connection with Elvis and a flood of other well-known artists, that's how we earned the reputation of Clothier to the King.

Elvis started out buying things in a pink and black combination. After his early records on the Sun label began making him a local hero, all the kids were swarming down to Lansky's on Beale because they wanted pink and black, just like Elvis wore.

We had everything they wanted. Black pants with pink shirts with big high collars; the row collars with the big sleeve; with three button sleeves; and with big sleeve cuffs. Something

different. They were looking for something different, and we gave it to them.

We knew what this young man should be wearing when he went on stage, on television, things like that. We knew he should be wearing something different from what other entertainers were wearing. So we started him out with big shirts, peg pants, half-boots of patent leather. He would also come into the store and buy fly clothes. This was with the rolled up collars.

He would watch TV and see those gangsters wear-ing those big hats – we called them Dobbs hats. I think we sold them for twenty-five, thirty dol-lars. They would cost a hundred and a half today. Elvis would call and say, "Mr. Lansky, send me over a half-dozen of them hats. And send some over for the other guys, too." So everybody in the group – they later became known as the Memphis Mafia – got a hat.

Elvis was a dynamite young man. What he did for us . . . well, he was a great public relations man for us. Anybody asking him where he got his clothes, he would answer, "I got them from Lansky's on Beale."

Once he hit it really big, he came in more often and, no, he never bought me out. Every time he dropped by he wanted something different. We outfitted him for his appearances on

the Louisiana Hayride. We outfitted him for the Ed Sullivan and Dorsey Brothers shows on TV. Knowing he was going on the Sullivan show, I sold him a coat with a velour collar. That was a real shock, that and his pegged pants and patent leather half-boots.

And despite how tremendously big he became – you know RCA/BMG has named him Artist of the Century – he was the nicest guy you would ever want to meet.

It was always "Yes, sir, Mister Lansky."

And I would tell him, "Mister Lansky is my father. I'm Bernard."

And he would reply, "Yes, sir, Mister Lansky."

And that never changed.

And when he came in on a shopping spree, if you happened to be in the store when he was there and you wanted something you liked, he'd buy it. He didn't care who it was or what it was. He bought it for them.

We sold to quite a few well-known entertainers: B.B. King, Jerry Lee Lewis, Johnny Cash, Carl Perkins, Rufus Thomas, Bobby Blue Bland, Charlie Rich.

For years Rufus would go on stage and show off his clothes and say, "Ain't I clean? Lansky's." Rufus introduced Walking the Dog and Do the Funky Chicken to the world.

When we went to the markets, we were always on the lookout for something different for Elvis, because Elvis would put them on and walk out on the streets and he was going to be our advertising, our billboard.

People would ask, "Elvis, where are you buying your clothes?" And he would say "Lansky's." We did a lot of mail order sales because of him. He was a real sharp dresser. Real neat. His clothes looked great on him. He was clean as Ajax. I mean, really nice. We would get new merchandise in and we would load it into a truck and I would have my son drive it out to Graceland for Elvis to look at. When the truck came back, it was empty. Elvis had taken all of it.

I still remember his size. At that time it was a 42 coat with a 32 waist, a size 10 1/2 boot. He wore a medium shirt – 15 1/2 by 34 shirt.

We knew what Elvis concerts were like, filled with screaming women. When he first started throwing scarves into the audience, those were scarves we got for Elvis.

When Elvis came into the shop, I would treat him like a baby. Put clothes on him. Stand him in front of a mirror. Marked his clothes (for alterations). And I would say, "Elvis, this is what you want, right here. This is what I've got for you." And he would start laughing, and then buy it.

He walked into the store one day and said, "Come look what I've got." Outside, he showed me a German Messerschmidt car, saying it had been given to him by RCA Victor, his record label then.

I said, "Elvis, that's a nice one. When you get tired of it, I want it. That's mine."

He laughed. And thirty days later he gave me the car.

I still have it.

And I still have all those wonderful memories of when Elvis was a Number One customer and a Number One walking billboard for Lansky's, which soon became known as the Clothier to the King.

(The site of Lansky's at 126 Beale is now occupied by Elvis Presley's – Memphis nightclub / restaurant. Lansky can be found just around the corner in a high fashion shop in the lobby of the history Peabody Hotel.)

Bernard J. Lansky

THIS JUST IN:
ELVIS PRESLEY IS UNIQUE!

Okay, so that's not a genuine news bulletin. But let's look a little deeper into this overused – and worse yet, misused – word "unique."

To righteously qualify as "unique," whatever it is that is being so described must stand alone; must have no equal; and must be the one and only of its kind

.

Unquestionably, all of those qualifying factors apply to Elvis Presley. Now let's turn our attention elsewhere.

Right under the company name on the Guernsey's letterhead are the words: "The Unique at Auction." I doubt when first written, its author could have known how prophetic this catchy line would be.

In light of Graceland's decision to have Guernsey's auction 2,000 or so cherished valuables from their archives, the jaw-dropping realization of that brief statement and reference to "the unique" hits with a real wallop.

Informal usage notwithstanding, what is "unique" should have no modifiers, and with this event there are none. Treasures like these from the Presley estate are not rather unique, or somewhat unique – they are flat out unique, period.

For example, as the successful bidder for Elvis Presley's personal 1956 address book, you are assured of having the only copy of this particular item in existence.

Same goes for the (May 25) 1956 Detroit concert lot. Here you have not only the original concert publicity placard –

itself indescribably rare – but Elvis' own copy of the original contract wherein he agreed to perform in the Motor City at the Fox Theatre.

How many other times have you seen a 1950s concert poster offered along with a copy of the actual contract for that performance? Probably never. I do know that in 36 years of dealing with Elvis collectibles, this is the first time I have seen such a package deal.

Imagine having these two eye-popping documents framed side-by-side, hanging on your wall. Now you're talking some real rock and roll history.

But, as they always say on those late-night infomercials: "Don't call yet – there's more!"

Document lovers (and I am one) will drool over some of the other momentous contracts in this collection. There are fascinating ones for various singing engagements – from shows as early as 1955 and into the mid-'70s. Among these are three deserving of special attention: the 1968 "NBC-TV Special"; the 1973 "Aloha from Hawaii" satellite TV show; and Elvis' attendance-shattering 1970 appearance at Houston's Astrodome.

Apart from the contracts and numerous other pieces of entertainment business-related correspondence, Presley collectors will also covet the examples of his handwritten letters and notes found in this sale. Having Elvis' autograph is great, make no mistake about it, but owning an entire page, or more, in his own hand is quite exceptional.

Whether a hand-drawn sketch of a football play , or Elvis' own song notes and tracks listing for the 1960 "His Hand in

Mine" sessions, there is something uncommonly exhilarating and highly personal about such artifacts. Because you know that in one moment in time the man himself put pen to paper and created this piece of history – and now it can belong to you.

On those few and far between occasions in the past when just one Elvis letter or contract has surfaced for sale, the bidding was very competitive. This is because the number of collectors seeking personal Presley items far outstrips the number of such items available, at any price.

Until now. What with 2,000 or so Elvis relics in this Graceland Archives sale, it will not be one and done. Anxious buyers will have chance after chance to take home something unimaginably special. An acquisition that for many of us becomes the single most astounding collectible we possess.

For those drawn to the investment potential of collectibles, the news is also very good. As with investments of any kind, history is the best teacher. And while acknowledging there have been few sales involving items of the type found in this sale, enough precedents exist to establish a growth history.

Prices for Elvis Presley's belongings have skyrocketed in the past 20 years, with increases averaging across the board a whopping 100 fold. It's true! Things selling for $100 in 1979 may now fetch $10,000, and in some cases closer to $20,000. The crystal ball is always cloudy and there are no guarantees; however, good students of history usually learn from it. Buy first because you love the item, but buy also being confident that your investment is a prudent one.

One pattern we have observed repeatedly is that auction items of this pedigree rarely, if ever, sell for the same or less than their buyer paid. This axiom seems to hold true regardless of how much it may have appeared the buyer overpaid at the time. With each new sale it seems a new minimum price is created, and the cycle just continues on and on.

Adding substantially to the worth of the merchandise in this sale is its legendary source. Having appropriate documentation stating that something came directly from Elvis Presley's Graceland will forever ensure its authenticity, making it more attractive should you ever choose to resell.

In conclusion, if we agree that "unique" really means "standing alone; having no like or equal; unrivaled; unparalleled; and the one and only of its kind," this extraordinary offering is clearly unique – as is the distinguished gentleman it honors.

JERRY OSBORNE

Aside from being an avid collector of Elvis Presley records and memorabilia for over thirty years, Jerry Osborne has been producing Elvis record price guides and reference books since 1977. Jerry has also published numerous Elvis periodicals and, since 1965, been a regular contributor of Presley-related features to countless music publications.

Elvis and Jerry met and became friends in 1967, a time when both men lived in Memphis. Jerry had been a dee jay since 1962 and had established a reputation as one of the most pro-Presley jocks in the country.

Guernsey's is honored
to be conducting
this unprecedented auction
at the fabulous
MGM Grand Hotel and Casino
in Las Vegas, Nevada.
For a preview of the MGM Grand,
please turn to page 286.

MGM GRAND.
THE CITY OF ENTERTAINMENT.

Offering state-of-the-art
auction facilities
on the Internet...Icollector.

To bid online
for items from this remarkable
Elvis Presley auction,
log on to
www.icollector.com

To learn more about Icollector,
please turn to page 290.

icollector
www.icollector.com

THE FIFTIES

A1

A1 ELVIS' 6TH GRADE REPORT CARD

Double-sided faded white "Pupil's Report Card" from Tupelo Junior High School in Tupelo, Mississippi. Sixth grade report card for the 1946-1947 school year issued to "Elvis Pressley"[sic]. Card listed Elvis as promoted to the 7th grade. Signed in pencil on back by Vernon Presley. 8 x 4 1/2 inches

Front side of card lists "School Citizenship Ratings" with grades from "1" (excellent or superior) to "4" (very poor) for "Reliability," "Cooperation," "Industry," and "Courtesy" for each of the six grading periods. Elvis apparently got off to a rocky start with grades of "3" (poor or inferior)in Reliability and Industry, and grades of "2" (medium or ordinary) for Cooperation and Courtesy for the first grading period. But he got straightened out by the end of the year with all "1"s for the final grading period. The back of the card has regular subject grades. Elvis was strong in Spelling, earning straight A's for the year. He also did well in Music (of course) and Phys. Ed., with a mixture of A's and B's. Elvis struggled with Geography and Arithmetic, getting all D's for the former and a mix of F's and D's for the latter. Elvis' grades for English, Reading and Penmanship were a mixtures of A's, B's, C's, and D's. Elvis' final grades for the year were: Reading-C, English-C, Spelling-A, Penmanship-B, Arithmetic-D, Geography-D, Music-A and Phys. Ed.-A. He is listed as being absent 4 1/2 days out of the 180 day school year. Elvis is remembered by Tupelo classmates as a loner who didn't really fit in, though his passion for music was noticed even this early on. The Presley family would leave Tupelo for Memphis in the fall of 1948. $15,000 - 20,000

A2 PRESLEY FAMILY DAIRY STORE RECEIPT

Receipt from Carr Myers Dairy Company in Tupelo, Mississippi. This particular receipt is for 32 quarts of sweet milk and 96 quarts of buttermilk. The receipt is dated June 1, 1947, and is made in the name of "Mrs.V. Presley." This represents a purchase made by the Presley's while they were living in Tupelo. The total bill comes to $21.33. 2) A list of groceries bought on account dated July 1, 1947. Receipt lists thirty-four items and the amount each cost. Paper is brown with black lines

and numbers. Two Union carpenter cards issued to V. E. Presley dated August 29 and September 5, 1942. Cards are a cream color with brown lettering that say "Carpenter Local No. 2183 Tupelo, Miss. Fee for August is listed as $18.00, and $14.00 for September. On the left side of each card is a list of each month of the year. "Pd-in full" is written in pencil on the September card. Two paid stubs issued to Vernon E. Presley [sic]. First receipt is from the J.A. Jones Construction Co., Inc. in Grenada, Mississippi dated August 1, 1942 for a net amount of $44.05. Second receipt is from the Ferguson-Oman Co., in Aberdeen, Mississippi dated August 29, 1942 for the net amount of $69.30. Photograph included. 7 1/2 x 5 3/4 inches buttermilk receipt. 5 1/4 x 3 1/2 inches "on account" receipt. 2 1/4 x 4 1/2 inches Union Cards. 3 1/3 x 8

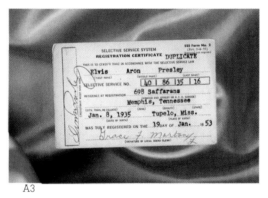

A3

1/4 inches pay stub/J.A. Jones. 3 3/4 x 7 3/4 inches pay stub/Ferguson-Oman

This receipt is for a months supply of sweet milk, and buttermilk. They were bought the summer after Elvis graduated from sixth grade during the time the Presley's lived at 1010 North Green Street. Gladys was occasionally working for Reed Brothers clothing factory, and Vernon was driving a delivery truck. It was hard times for the Presley's, and their favorite food was buttermilk and corn bread. Food they bought was the typical southern food that Elvis loved so much, and also what they could afford at this time since they were very poor. Grocery list consisted of peas, tomatoes, milk, bread, salt meat, crackers, cheese, and baloney. Vernon worked many odd jobs including delivery and carpentry work. $1,200 - 1,500

A3 ELVIS' DRAFT CARD

Double-sided white card stock "Selective Service" card, dated January 19, 1953 and signed in blue ink by Elvis Presley. Card issued to Elvis Aron Presley at 698 Saffarans in Memphis, Tennessee. Lists birth-date of Jan. 8, 1935 and birthplace of Tupelo, Miss. Back of card lists personal information: brown hair, green eyes, height of 5'11" and weight of 150. Selective Service number "40-86-35-16." 2 1/2 x 3 3/4 inches.

Elvis filled out this Selective Service card about a week after his 18th birthday. Then a senior at Memphis' Humes High School, Elvis and his family had moved to the Saffarans Street address from the Lauderdale Courts housing projects just a week earlier. Elvis, by then a major star, was called for his pre-induction physical on January 4, 1957, in order to determine his status for the draft. On December 19, 1957, Elvis, now 22 years old, was notified that he'd been inducted into the Army. The next day, after picking up his draft notice in person, Elvis stopped by Sun records and talked to reporters, calling his impending Army service a "duty I've got to fill and I'm going to do it." On Christmas Eve 1957 Elvis wrote to the Memphis Draft Board requesting a deferment in order to finish filming his latest film for Paramount, "King Creole." Elvis asks for the deferment so that "these folks will not lose so much money, with all they have done so far." Two days later the Draft Board granted Elvis a deferment until March 20, 1958. Elvis reported for duty on March 24, 1958 and was taken to Fort Chaffee in Arkansas for processing and then sent to Fort Hood in Texas. Elvis shipped out to Germany in September 1958. The Army had considered putting Elvis in its "Special Services" division to take advantage of his celebrity, but both the Colonel and Elvis insisted that he receive no special treatment, and Elvis' Army stint was relatively conventional.

$10,000 - 15,000

A4 "STAGE SHOW" APPEARANCE AIRPLANE INVOICE AND PAYCHECKS

Blue invoice from Travel, Inc. for four one way air tickets from Atlanta to New York, and four one-way tickets from New York to Charleston. Tickets were for Elvis Presley, W.P. Black, D.J. Fontana and W.S. Moore. Invoice totals 343.88. Attached is original yellow check from the account of All Star Shows made out to Travel, Inc. for $343.88. Signed by Colonel Tom Parker. Three yellow checks from the account of All Star Shows made out to Scotty Moore, Bill Black and D.J. Fontana. Moore and Black received $145, while Fontana received $50. Checks are signed by Thomas Francis Diskin. 7 x 8 1/2 inches invoice. 3 x 8 1/4 inches travel check. 2 5/8 x 6 inches paychecks.

On March 17, 1956, Elvis made his fifth appearance on the Dorsey Brother's "Stage Show." The show aired on CBS following the "Jackie Gleason Show." Elvis, clad in black shirt, white tie and mohair coat, rocked the audience with "Blue Suede Shoes" and "Heartbreak Hotel," which was quickly climbing its way up the national charts at the time. After this appearance, Elvis and his band flew to Charleston, South Carolina to perform at the County Hall.

$8,000 - 10,000

A5

A5 AN ASSORTMENT OF CHRISTMAS CARDS TO ELVIS FROM CELEBRITIES

Liberace:1968 card with imprinted name and logo, color photo of Liberace, and envelope. Gracie and George Burns: 1965 card with name imprinted; envelope included. Don Ho: 1968 card with signature and personal note; envelope included. Sonny and Cher: with name imprinted. Jerry Lee Lewis and Kay Martin: 1963 card with signature; envelope included. D.J. Fontana and family: 1963 card with name imprinted; envelope included. Edward Byrnes: 1960 card with name imprinted; envelope included. Rick Nelson family: 1969 card with signatures and photograph of Matthew, Tracy, and Gunnar; envelope included. Bob Hope and family: 1970 card with family members' head shots superimposed on a space theme background; envelope

A5

included. Also a 1960 card from Bob and family with plastic record inside that carries a holiday greeting; envelope included. Lyndon and Lady Bird Johnson: imprinted; with envelope. Mae West: card with name imprinted and rendering of the star on front. Jayne Mansfield and family: 1960 photograph of Jayne, with weight-lifter husband holding up the family; envelope included. Jackie Gleason: red velvet card with name imprinted. Lawrence Welk: 1967 card with name imprinted; calendar included with photo of Welk on back. Connie Francis: 1960 card with with signature and Connie's photo inside; envelope included.Ina and Gene Autry: 1969 card with name imprinted; envelope included. Larry Geller and family: with signature. Charlie Rich family: 1964 card with name imprinted; envelope included. Hal and Martha Wallis: name imprinted; envelope included. Blackwood Brothers: imprinted. Chet Atkins: imprinted. Robert Mitchum family: imprinted; note inside from Elvis to Bob and family (probably written by the Colonel). Red Skelton and family: imprinted. Kingston Trio: 1964 card with name imprinted; card folds into envelope. Dave Clark: 1969 card with signature Hedda Hopper: photo card imprinted "Merry, Merry" Hedda Hopper Bobby Darin: with signature

Elvis maintained his contact with many celebrities in the film and music industry.

$7,000 - 8,000

A6 BOOK JACKET FROM "THE ELVIS PRESLEY STORY"

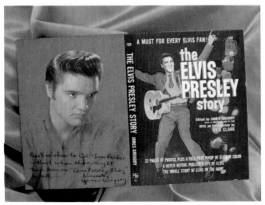

A6

Book jacket from "The Elvis Presley Story," written by James Gregory with an introduction by Dick Clark. Back cover features a picture of Elvis in a red shirt on a red background and is signed by James Gregory, the book's editor, to Col. Tom Parker. The cost of the book was 35 cents. 6 1/2 x 9 "

Elvis Presley is one of the most written about people in popular music, however, few books were actually written during his lifetime. This is a color proof of a book jacket for one of the earlier Elvis books.

$1,200 - 1,400

A7 LAYERED PUBLICITY PHOTOGRAPH OF ELVIS PRESLEY

Publicity photograph of Elvis Presley on a red background wearing a light blue jacket over a black collared shirt. Photograph has four cellophane overlays, each with a different color tint - black, blue, red, and yellow. 13 3/4 x 10 3/4 inches.

This is the color-separated artwork to be used for an Elvis Christmas card.

$2,000 - 2,500

A8 AUTOGRAPHED CELEBRITY PHOTOGRAPHS

Thirty-four celebrity photographs all signed to the Colonel or Mrs. Parker, except one, which is signed to Elvis from Deacon Jones. Most are black and white; Jacques Cousteau is in color. Deborah Kerr, Jayne Mansfield, and Joan Collins: framed together in brown wooden frame. Bob Hope: in wooden frame; to "The Original Snow-Man". Deacon Jones: signed to Elvis "A great artist". Nat King Cole. Marlon Brando Dick Gardner: signed "To the man with the strongest heart in Hollywood.".Danny Kaye: signed "I like Elvis, too.". Pat Boone: one of Pat alone and one of Pat with the Colonel; "You'll never know how thrilled I was to have you at my opening selling Elvis pictures.". Frank Sinatra: rendering of the star. Ernie Borgnine: two photos; one signed "To Colonel Tom Parker--the best star-maker in the business"; the other signed "I'd sure like to have you for my manager!". Perry Como, Debbie Reynolds: signed "Sending two gracious, lovely people all my warm wishes." Jacques Cousteau William Holden Red Skelton: "A great guy, a good friend and master showman." Jim Ed, Maxine, and Bonnie Brown: "One of the very nicest people we've ever had the pleasure of knowing." Milton Berle: "You're the greatest." Raymond Burr Slim Whitman: "Proud of our relationship an starting my career in 1948." Peter Lawford: "One of these days I'm going to hustle you for something." Yul Brynner Spencer Tracy Walter Winchell Ray Milland Arthur Godfrey Hal Wallis: "Who can make a 'snow job' a pleasure." Harey Carey Tom Jones: "A man even the Welsh would appreciate."

A small sampling from A8

Sylvester Stallone. 10 x 8 inches most photos. 15 x 12 inches Bob Hope in frame. 18 1/4 x 37 inches Kerr, Mansfield, and Collins. 7 x 5 inches Perry Como.

The Colonel made many friends throughout his career and while helping Elvis gain stardom. These are just a few of the celebrities who respected him as a person . . . and as a "star maker."

$3,000 - 4,000

A9

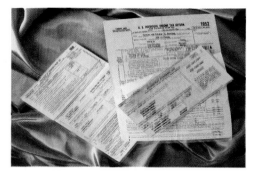

A11

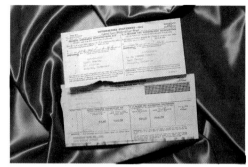

A12

A9 COLONEL PARKER'S PHONE LIST

Two pages typed on "Thomas A. Parker Exclusive Management" stationery, with handwritten additions and corrections. In clear plastic sleeve. 11 7/8 x 9 1/8 inches.

This is a personal phone list from the Colonel's Madison, Tennessee office, and can be dated from the 1960s. Among the names and numbers on the list are: Milton Berle, Joseph Hazen, Hal Wallis and Eddy Arnold. This document gives an excellent view of the Colonel's business universe.

$1,400 - 1,600

A10 THANK YOU LETTER TO TOM PARKER FROM GENE AUTRY

Letter to Col. Tom Parker from Gene Autry thanking him for sending pictures taken at the Knickerbocker Hotel. Autry also thanked the Colonel for suggestions he made about the Checkerboard Jamboree. Autry sent his regards to "the gang." Although the letter was dated September 20, 1950, Autry explained in a handwritten note in blue ink at the bottom of the page that the letter had been misdirected when it was sent to him to be signed. He redated the letter November 1, 1950. Autographed photo of Gene Autry with Colonel Parker included. 10 1/2 x 7 1/4 inches.

Gene Autry, well-known country singer, knew Colonel Parker from his Nashville connections. The Colonel represented Eddy Arnold, and Autry often toured with Arnold for various shows.

$800 - 900

A11 VERNON & GLADYS' INCOME TAX RETURN FOR 1952 AND 1958

Two copies of Vernon & Gladys' four page 1040 income tax return and W2's for 1952. One copy is handwritten and the other is typewritten. Return shows that between Vernon and Gladys they earned $3,336.88 for the year. Elvis is listed as a dependent and their address is 698 Saffrans. Attached are two W2's, one for Gladys from St. Joseph Hospital for a net earning of $70.30; the other is for Vernon Presley from United Paint Co. for a net earning of $2781.18. Both copies are on a standard withholding form, beige in color with brown lettering. Vernon's W2 is torn on the left bottom side. Also attached is a adding machine tape with the total amount of income, deductions, and amount due on the tape.

One page 1957 Income Tax return for Vernon & Gladys. Total income is $16,419.97, and their address is listed as 661 Madison Avenue. Attached to return is a typewritten list of the different sources of their income plus taxes withheld. Paper shows wages listed as $11,026.95 from Elvis Presley, $21.51 from Paramount Pictures, $2,750 from Gladys Music, Inc., $21.51 from Paramount Pictures, and $2,600 from Elvis Presley Music, Inc. Total tax withheld was $2,204.09. Attached to the 1957 return is a 1958 Declaration of Estimated Income; estimated 1958 income tax was listed as $3,500.
Also attached are five W2 forms; first one is Vernon Presley's from Elvis for the amount of $11,026.95; second one is for Gladys from Paramount Pictures for $21.41; third one is for Vernon Presley from Gladys Music, Inc., for $2, 750; fourth one is for Vernon Presley from Paramount Pictures for $21.51, and the last one is for Vernon Presley from Elvis

Presley for $2,600. 11 x 8 1/4 tax returns. 3 3/4 x 8 inches W2 (Gladys). 3 1/4 x 7 inches W2 (Vernon). 7 3/4 x 3 inches adding tape. 11 x 8 1/4 inches wage statement. 3 3/4 x 8 inches estimate form. 3 1/2 x 8 inches W2 forms (5).

In 1952 the Presley's were very poor, however by 1956 Elvis' career began to take off. It was always his dream to support his family, and in 1957 on the tax returns it shows that he did contribute heavily to their income (and would for the rest of their lives).

$1,000 - 1,500

A12 ELVIS PRESLEY'S 1953 WITHHOLDING STATEMENTS

Two withholding statements from 1953 when Elvis worked for Precision Tool Co., and M.B. Parker Company. Both are Memphis companies. 3 3/4 x 8 inches Precision Tools. 3 1/4 x 7 inches M.B. Parker.

Many of Elvis' relatives worked at Precision Tools, therefore, it was only natural that he would work there in the summer of '53 after graduation from high school. Precision Tools made artillery shells, and Elvis was only employed for a few months. Elvis found a job with M.B. Parker through the Tennessee Department of Employment Security during the early months of 1953. Elvis did assembly line work; taking heads off flame-throw regulators, replacing "O" rings, then putting the heads back on.

$1,000 - 2,000

A13 LETTER FROM EDDIE CANTOR TO TOM PARKER

Dated January 6, 1953, letter on "Eddie Cantor" stationery and signed by the singer: "How nice to receive your very gracious letter. And those Eddy Arnold string ties! I'm liable to be the best dressed old man in show business."10 1/2 x 7 1/4 inches.

Eddie Cantor, one of the most beloved American vaudeville entertainers, became a Hollywood star in the thirties. He received an Academy Award in 1956 for distinguished service to the film industry.

$200 - 300

A14 PRECISION TOOL CO. PAY STUB

A pay stub issued to Elvis Presley from Precision Tool Co., Inc. in Memphis. Dated September 9, 1953. Shows 54 hours worked during the pay period, with $61.00 earned, $21.00 of which was overtime. $4.50 was deducted from income taxes. Photograph included. 3 1/2 x 6 3/4 inches.

Elvis graduated from Humes High School in May of 1953. After a brief temporary job with a machine shop and several failed job interviews, Elvis began working at Precision Tool, a local shop that manufactured shells for the Army. Elvis worked at Precision Tool with his cousin Gene Smith, and stayed at the job through March, 1954.

$4,000 - 5,000

A15 GRAND OLE OPRY POSTER ON SCRAPBOOK PAGE AND EARLY COLONEL PARKER WESTERN UNION TELEGRAM

Large rare Grand Ole Opry poster attached to a page from Colonel Parker's 1954-55 scrapbook. Poster is white with brown lettering, advertising the Grand Ole Opry Show. Lineup includes Hank Snow, The Duke of Paducah, and special added attraction Elvis Presley with Bill and Scotty. Show billed as "The Biggest Jamboree of the Season." Three newspaper clippings on front of scrapbook page advertise the Hank Snow Show for February

16th. Also included is one blue felt badge with the words "Victor RCA Caravan" attached with pins. Back of scrapbook page holds 14 articles and ads about the shows. January 23, 1955, Western Union telegram to Fire Chief of Tyler Texas from Col. Parker's office. Telegram announces an upcoming event at the Grand Ole Opry with Hank Snow,

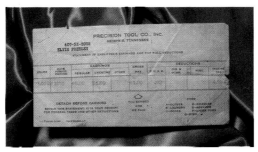

A14

A15

Duke of Paddock, and Elvis Presley. January 23, 1955, telegram from Colonel Parker to the principal of Monroe High school, Monroe, Louisiana, confirming auditorium availability for the Hank Snow Grand Ole Opry Show with Elvis added to the lineup. Western Union telegram from Colonel Parker to Rinaldi Printing regarding a rush order for Elvis

Presley Show in Camden Arkansas, February 21, 1955. 5 3/4 x 8 inches Fire Chief and Monroe principal telegrams. 10 x 8 inches Colonel Parker to Rinaldi Printing telegram. 24 1/2 x 19 1/2 inches scrapbook page. 42 1/2 x 28 1/4 inches poster.

This Grand Ole Opry Poster is a rare piece of early advertising by the Colonel for his Grand Ole Opry shows. The telegrams represent some of the earliest bookings of Elvis made by Colonel Parker; in fact, the Colonel had only been working with Elvis for about a month. However, Elvis did not perform in Tyler, Texas as indicated in the telegram of January 23, 1955. Instead he played at Odessa, Texas, and his performance at Monroe marked the beginning of his growing importance to the show.

$10,000 - 15,000

A16 ELVIS PRESLEY WESTERN UNION MONEY ORDER MESSAGE

Elvis sent this Western Union Money Order Message on November 26, 1954, to his father, Vernon Presley. The address on the telegram shows the Presley's address at 462 Alabama Street, Memphis,TN. Elvis sent the money order from Houston, Texas with the following message: "HI BABIES HERES THE MONEY TO PAY THE BILLS. DONT TELL NO ONE HOW MUCH I SENT I WILL SEND MORE NEXT WEEK. THERE IS A CARD IN THE MAIL. LOVE, ELVIS" Photographs included. 5 3/4 x 8 inches.

This telegram was sent the day after Elvis had performed at the Houston Hoedown on November 24 - 25, 1954. The reaction to Elvis' appearance was good, and he was held over by "popular demand". Biff Collie felt the nature of his act was the same he had observed in Memphis in that his repertoire was limited, and he did not sing slow songs. Although it was obvious to Mr. Collie that Elvis was just learning the ropes, he felt he had star quality. Telegram was sent to Vernon and Gladys; Elvis always kept in touch with his family when he was on the road.

$3,000 - 4,000

A17 EARLY REQUEST FOR ELVIS TO PERFORM

Typed letter to "Mr. Presley" dated December 3, 1954, from the Hyatt F.H.A. (Future Homemakers of America) Chapter, in Fields, Louisiana. The letter states that Elvis and his band were listed among two other bands as possibilities to play at an F.H.A fund raiser, and asks if he and the band could come in February or March. Also questions whether Elvis would require a fee or would be satisfied with a portion of the funds raised at the function. 11 x 8 1/2 inches letter.

This was during the time Elvis was managed by Bob Neal. Elvis never played Fields, Louisiana.

$500 - 700

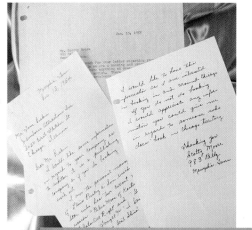

A18 "THERE ARE FEW OUTLETS FOR HILLBILLY ENTERTAINERS IN THIS AREA."— CORRESPONDENCE BETWEEN SCOTTY MOORE AND TOM DISKIN, 1954-1955

Two page letter, handwritten in black ink and dated December 13, 1954. Sent from Scotty Moore in Memphis to Tom Diskin at Jamboree Attractions in Chicago. One copy page typed reply from Diskin to Moore, dated January 13, 1954. Photograph included. 9 x 5 1/2 inches letters from Moore. 11 x 8 1/2 inches letter from Diskin.

Moore writes: "I would like some information in regard to your company as to whether it is a publishing company or if you do booking... I am the personal manager of Elvis Presley, a Sun recording Star who has two current hit records "Blue Moon of Kentucky" b/w "That's All Right" and "Good Rocking Tonight" b/w "I Don't Care if the Sun Don't Shine." I would like to have this information as I am interested in booking in and around Chicago. If you do not do booking I would appreciate any information you could give me in regard to someone who does booking in Chicago territory. Thank You, Scotty Moore, 983 Belz, Memphis, TN." Diskin responds: "Thank you so much for your letter

regarding your artist and while we are a booking and promotion agency I don't have anything at present where I could place your artist. There are few outlets for hillbilly entertainers in this area around Chicago. Kindest Regards, Tom Diskin."

At the time Moore's letter was written the guitarist was acting manager of the group; Elvis wouldn't sign with Bob Neal until January 1, 1955. Tom Diskin was booking the Chicago area for Colonel Parker and sent this rejection letter to Moore without the knowledge that the Colonel had seen Elvis perform just two days earlier in Texas, and was interested in the young performer. Two days after Diskin sent this letter he and the Colonel would see Elvis perform at the Louisiana Hayride, and the Colonel would first speak to Bob Neal about becoming involved with Elvis' career.

$2,000 - 2,500

A19 SIGNED "PERSONAL APPEARANCE CONTRACT"

On Colonel Parker's specially designed "Personal Appearance Contract" form, containing several black and white photographs of Elvis, his named printed twice in pink and the slogan "The Nation's Only Atomic Powered Singer." Contract signed in blue ink by Elvis Presley and promoter Lee Gordon is for a string of ten shows March 29-April 7, 1957, for which it is stipulated that Elvis will receive $100,000. 36 1/2 x 8 5/8 inches.

This tour consisted of shows in St. Louis; Fort Wayne, Indiana; Detroit; Buffalo; Toronto; Ottawa and Philadelphia. A show in suburban Montreal was canceled due to civic concern and pressure from local Catholic officials. The Canadian shows on this tour comprise Elvis' only concert performances outside of the United States. This was also the tour in which Elvis often wore his famous gold lame suit.

$12,000 - 15,000

A18

A20 1954 JAMBOREE ATTRACTIONS CONTRACT FOR SHOWS IN INDIANAPOLIS

One-page, two-sided contract dated November 22, 1955. The Indianapolis contract was for Elvis with Scotty, Bill, and one other musician to appear on the Hank Snow Show on December 4-7, 1955. Contract is signed by Col. Tom Parker and Elvis Presley. A handwritten note attached to the contract is written in blue ink on pink Elvis Presley Enterprises notepaper indicating a $500 deposit and a $500 payment at the end of the series. 11 x 8 1/2 inches contract. 6 x 4 inches pink note.

The Hank Snow Show played at the Lyric Theater in Indianapolis. When Hank failed to make the first show due to bad weather, Elvis took over for him. Others on the bill included Mother Maybelle and the Carter Sisters and comedian Rod Brasfield, who was a regular on the Grand Ole Opry.

$5,000 - 7,000

A21 ELVIS' FIRST SCREEN TEST - TRAVEL AND LODGING RECORDS

Yellow check #273 made out to Travel, Inc. from All Star Shows for $256.64 and signed by Colonel Tom Parker. Blue Travel, Inc. memo dated March 21, 1956 for 2 one-way tickets from Nashville to Los Angeles for Col. Parker and Oscar Davis for $256.64. White American Airlines passenger coupon for Mr. E. Presley from Idlewild to Los Angeles; stamped March 16, 1956. Two white American Airlines passenger coupons for Colonel Parker and Oscar Davis; stamped March 21, 1956. Ruled ledger paper titled "Elvis Presley Screen Test, Hollywood, Calif.; March 26, 27, 28, 1956" and listing travel expenses for the Colonel and Davis. Memo on white stationery with letterhead "Hollywood Knickerbocker Travel Service"; dated March 24, 1956 and showing receipt of $82.50 from O. Davis, covering plane fares to and from Las Vegas. Blue Travel Inc. memo dated March 27, 1956 for 4 one-way tickets from Shreveport to San Diego for Elvis and his band on April 1 for $401.28. Six pages of hotel bills from the Warwick Hotel in New York City for the night of March 24, 1956. The rooms were for Tom Disken, D.J. Fontana, Scotty Moore, Bill Black, Elvis Presley, and Gene Smith. The

prices of the rooms were $7, except for Elvis' which was $15. 3 x 8 1/4 inches check. 3 1/4 x 6 1/4 inches coupons. 7 x 8 1/2 inches blue memos. 11 x 8 1/2 inches ledger paper and white memo. 6 7/8 x 6 7/8 inches hotel bills.

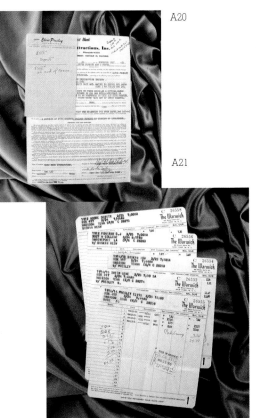

A20

A21

On March 21, 1956, the Colonel and Davis flew to Los Angeles to prepare for Elvis' screen test. Meanwhile, Elvis and his band played on the Dorsey Brothers Stage Show on March 24 in New York. They stayed at the Warwick Hotel. It was Elvis' sixth and final appearance on the show. "Money Honey" and "Heartbreak Hotel" were two of the featured songs. He planned to sing "Blue Suede Shoes," but because Carl Perkins, who wrote and performed the famous song, had recently been injured in an automobile accident, Elvis declined to perform that tune. Elvis flew to Los Angeles on March 25, while his band drove back to Memphis. The screen test with Hall Wallis at Paramount Studios began the next day and took three days to

complete. Elvis flew back to Memphis on the 28th, and he and his band headed to Shreveport for his final appearance on Louisiana Hayride. On April 1, they again boarded a plane for San Diego to begin preparation for their upcoming appearance on the Milton Berle show two days later.

$3,000 - 4,000

A22 MOCK-UP HANK SNOW STATIONERY

Hand sketched mock-up of potential letterhead for Hank Snow made for Colonel Parker and signed by "Ed". The stationery features Hank Snow's picture at the top with the label "The Singing Ranger" above, and "There's no Business like SNOW Business" below Snow's picture. The bottom line of the stationery reads "Exclusive Management: Col.Thomas A. Parker" 11 x 8 1/2 inches.

On January 1, 1955, the Colonel became the manager of Hank Snow and they combined Jamboree Attractions under the banner of Hank Snow Enterprises. However, by 1956 this partnership had been dissolved.

$800 - 1,000

A23 NOTES FROM MAE AXTON

Note signed by Mae Axton on April 29, 1955 showing Tom Diskin received bill posting for ad in Jacksonville show for $17. Note typed to Colonel Parker on paper torn from a notebook and signed by Mae Axton for her services rendered for Hank Snow Jamboree Attractions at Orlando and Daytona Beach show dates (July 26 and 31, 1955). The payment amounted to $150. 11 x 8 1/2 inches April note. 9 x 6 inches typed note.

Mae Boren Axton, a high school English teacher, worked for the Colonel to publicize those whom he managed during the Andy Griffith tour in Florida in the summer of 1955. This was her first introduction to Elvis, the rising star. She later talked Elvis into listening to (and finally recording) "Heartbreak Hotel."

$250 - 300

A24 1955 ANDY GRIFFITH SHOW ITEMS

Five sample tickets from the Andy Griffith show held in July 1955 in various locations in Florida: 1 ticket (reserved) from July 26 in Orlando at City Auditorium. 1 ticket (general) from July 27 in Orlando. 1 ticket (general) from July 28-29 in New Baseball Stadium in Jacksonville. 1 ticket (child's) from July 30 in Peabody Auditorium in Daytona Beach. 1 ticket (general) from July 31 in the Armory in Tampa. Handwritten and typed copies showing gate receipts on Andy Griffith shows of July 28-29, 1955 in Jacksonville, Florida. Net gain shows $8,048.83. In a copy of a letter written on June 9, 1955 to DJ Happy Ison of radio station WORZ in Orlando, Florida, Colonel Parker discusses the upcoming July tour of the Andy Griffith show, slated to play in Orlando July 26-27. Lineup includes Mr. Griffith, Marty Robbins, and Elvis Presley. The Colonel asks Happy to handle details correctly.

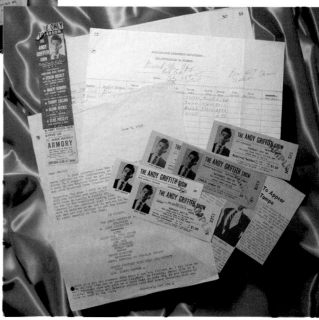

A24

Advertisement for the Andy Griffith shows in Tampa newspaper and article highlighting the upcoming show. Both mention Elvis Presley on the bill. The ad says: "By popular demand, Elvis Presley, with Scotty & Bill." Article headline says: "Deacon Andy Griffith to Appear on Hillbilly Program in Tampa." Photographs included. 2 1/4 x 5 inches tickets 8 1/2 x 11 inches box office receipts 11 x 8 1/2 inches letter 7 3/4 x 1 3/4 inches ad 6 x 5 1/2 inches news article

This Florida tour was headlined by Comedian Andy Griffith, who later became a TV star--and movie star in "A Face in the Crowd." Others on this tour included Marty Robbins, Jimmie Rodgers Snow, and Ferlin Huskey. Elvis later appeared with Griffith on the Steve Allen Show.

$4,000 - 5,000

A25 TELEGRAMS FROM COLONEL PARKER REGARDING HIS FIRST ELVIS BOOKINGS

Western Union telegram from Colonel Parker to George Daniels in Roswell, New Mexico, on January 24, 1955. Message requests that show in Roswell be changed to two shows on Monday, February 14. Lineup includes Hank Snow and Elvis Presley, among others. Western Union telegram dated January 25, 1955 from Colonel Parker to Mrs. D. J. Branhard in Longview, Texas. Message asks if she has any interest in sponsoring a show in Odessa for February 17. Lineup includes Hank Snow, the Duke of Paducah, and Elvis Presley, among others. 10 x 8 inches Daniels telegram. 5 1/2 x 8 inches Branhard telegram

Lubbock, Texas, on February 13, 1955, became the site of the first booking of Elvis by the Colonel, rather than Bob Neal. The Roswell, New Mexico, show took place the day after that. In Odessa, the show ultimately was performed on February 16, and the Hank Snow show--and Elvis--played in San Angelo on the 17th.

$3,000 - 4,000

A26 EARLY TELEGRAMS AND MEMOS TO AND FROM COLONEL PARKER

January 25, 1955, Western Union telegram from Col. Parker to Bob Neal of WMPS Radio, Memphis. Telegram announces first show Elvis did with Col. Parker. January 23, 1955, telegram from Pappy to Colonel Parker regarding Presley's Antonio date, and possible Waco booking. Memo to Bob Neal from Tom Diskin, regarding Elvis Presley Show dates with Hank Snow, Duke of Puducah, Charline Arthur, and Jimmy Rodgers Snow in February of 1955. In the memo Bob Neal is advised to instruct Elvis Presley to meet with Tom Diskin "before 3:00 pm in Roswell, New Mexico". The memo goes on to detail the tour which includes Abilene, New Mexico; Odessa, Texas; San Angelo, Texas, and Monroe, Louisiana. Telegram also notes that the February 20 show will also have a different line-up,

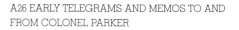

A26

which Elvis will be advised of "in plenty of time." Diskin also notes in the telegram that he is working on interviews for Elvis. Photograph included. 5 3/4 x 8 inches Colonel to Bob Neal. 5 3/4 x 8 inches Colonel to Pappy Telegram 7 1/4 x 8 1/2 inches Memo between Bob Neal/Tom Diskin.

Colonel Parker sends telegram to Bob Neal and Pappy Covington (Louisiana Hayride) regarding upcoming dates. "Have Presley contact Tom Diskin at Roswell leading hotel on February fourteen not later than three pm for interviews on radio and show schedule." Handwritten memo from Tom Diskin to Bob Neal with booking suggestions for Elvis. "The dates starting February 20th will be a different line-up and he'll be advised in plenty of time. Best regards. I'm going to work on interviews for Elvis - that will be good for him. Tom Diskin."

$1,000 - 2,000

A27 ELVIS PRESLEY AND SCOTTY MOORE LIABILITY INSURANCE APPLICATION

1955 application for liability insurance for Elvis and Scotty Moore. Insurance was to cover a 1955 Cadillac, and a 1956 Plymouth station wagon. Cars were to be used for business. Document shows Elvis living at 1414 Getwell, and that Scotty Moore had been in a previous accident. Application shows that Elvis had tried and failed at obtaining auto liability insurance in Tennessee sixty days prior to this application. Photograph incl. 11 x 8 1/2"

This policy was written when Elvis lived at Getwell, and covered a 1955 Fleetwood Cadillac that had a black top and a pink bottom. Later the top would be changed to white, and given to GLADYS' in 1956. The car is presently in Elvis Presley's Car Museum. The Plymouth station wagon was for Elvis' parents. The insurance form states that the cars will be used for travel to and from shows, and that both he and Scotty will be using the cars 50% of the time. The accident Scotty Moore had on September 2, was with a pick-up truck, but was not his fault.

$1,000 - 2,000

A28 TELEGRAM TO GRELUN LANDON FROM TOM DISKIN

Western Union telegram dated September 7, 1955 to Grelun Landon at Hill & Range Music in New York from Tom Diskin regarding latest tour. Lineup included Hank Snow, Louvin Brothers, Presley, and Cowboy Copas, playing Norfolk, Roanoke, Asheville from September 11-16. Then playing without Snow in some North Carolina locations and Kingsport, TN, from September 13-22. Message ends: "Blow up Presley--make it fabulous.". 5 1/2 x 8 inches.

This early tour for Elvis held significance in that it established his presence in the southern East Coast area. These engagements took place before his RCA contract, so Sun Records was still distributing his records.

$700 - 900

A29

A29 ARTHUR GODFREY TALENT SCOUTS AUDITION CORRESPONDENCE

Western Union telegram sent March 7, 1955, to Colonel Parker from the William Morris Agency in New York: "Could Elvis Presley 'addition' Godfrey Talent Scouts Wednesday March 9th. 501 Madison Avenue. 2:30 PM. If not advise if can audition week later. Wire. Sender is waiting may we have an answer at your convenience." Copy of a March 8, 1955 typewritten letter from Col. Parker to Harry Kalcheim of the William Morris Agency. The correspondence centers on ideas for CBS television shows to feature Hank Snow and possibly Elvis Presley. Letters to Bob Neal and Elvis Presley from Tom Diskin dated March 11 and 16, 1955 concern-

ing arrangements for Elvis' audition with the William Morris agency for the Godfrey Show. The audition was scheduled for March 23, 1955 in New York City. Letter to Col. Tom Parker from Harry Kalcheim of the William Morris Agency dated March 29. The letter regarding Elvis Presley states that the talent scout people (Godfrey) "showed no interest whatsoever in him." Photograph of Arthur Godfrey with Colonel Parker; signed by Godfrey. 5 3/4 x 8 inches telegram. 11 x 8 1/2 inches Parker's and Diskin's letters. 8 x 8 1/2 inches William Morris letter. 8 x 10 inches photo.

Elvis Presley was not under the Colonel's management at this time, but still tied to Bob Neal. However, the Colonel was the one trying to get him on the Talent Scout program.

$5,000 - 6,000

A30 EARLY COLONEL PARKER TELEGRAMS

Telegram from Colonel Parker to Louie Buck at WSM radio in Nashville instructing him to announce Elvis as a "special added attraction" to a show that already included the Duke of Paducah, Mother Maybelle, and The Carter Sisters. This telegram is one of the earliest examples of Elvis' name mentioned in the Colonel's correspondence. Western Union telegram from Colonel Parker to Charley Stewart, dated January 31, 1955, regarding a reservation for an auditorium in Little Rock. Photograph included. 10 x 8 1/4 inches Louie Buck telegram. 5 1/2 x 8 inches Charley Stewart telegram.

Telegram to Louie Buck at WSM is in regards to an upcoming attraction with Elvis, which was to be broadcasted on Sunday in February of 1955.

$1,500 - 2,500

A31 LUBBOCK, TEXAS CONCERT TELEGRAMS.
1955

Telegram dated February 3, 1955 from Bob Neal to Col. Tom Parker at the Francis Motel in Monroe, LA. The telegram confirmed bookings of Elvis in Lubbock, Texas, on February 13, 1955 for $350; Little Rock, Arkansas, on February 20 for $350; and two extra dates for $200. 5 3/4 x 8 inches.

Bob Neal and Colonel Parker were both setting up booking dates at this time. During the Lubbock show on February 13, Buddy Holly appeared on the lower part of the bill as "Buddy and Bob."

$1,200 - 1,500

A32 EARLY TELEGRAM TO ELVIS
PRESLEY FROM COLONEL PARKER

Western Union telegram sent February 5, 1955 from Colonel Parker to Elvis at the Louisiana Hayride in Shreveport. The telegram details the initial bookings for Elvis' first tour with the Hank Snow All Star Jamboree, from February 13 - 22, 1955. Col. Parker writes "Give my best to Pappy-Horace Logan" and informs Elvis that the next day's show in Memphis is a "complete sellout." Photograph included. 10 x 8 inches.

This telegram documents one of the earliest (possibly the earliest) connections between Colonel Tom Parker and Elvis Presley. The stretch of shows Colonel Parker refers to in the telegram— beginning with an Elvis headlined show in Lubbock on February 13, and picking up with the "Hank Snow All Star Jamboree" on February 14 in Roswell—constitutes the first official involvement by Colonel Parker into Elvis Presley's career, the beginnings of one of the most famous associations in all of American culture.

The sold out show in Memphis that the Colonel refers to are a pair of performances on February 6 at Ellis Auditorium. This show was booked by then Elvis manager Bob Neal and in between the afternoon and evening performances a sort of summit meeting was held to discuss Elvis' career. In attendance were Neal, Sam Phillips, Colonel Parker, Parker's assistants Tom Diskin and Oscar Davis, and Elvis and Scotty Moore. This was the first meeting between Colonel Parker and Sam Phillips, and may have been the first time Elvis and the Colonel physically met. The "Pappy" Colonel Parker refers to is Pappy Covington, who was the booking agent for the Louisiana Hayride. Horace Logan was the Hayride's director. Elvis first performed as part of the Louisiana Hayride on October 16, 1954.

$1,500 - 2,000

A34

A33 LETTERS FROM TOM DISKIN, 1955

On Jamboree Attractions letterhead, Tom Diskin wrote to Mr. Fogle on February 8, 1955, enclosing a contract for Elvis' upcoming show in Lubbock, Texas, on February 13, 1955. He invited Mr. Fogle to be his guest at the show. The letter was signed, "Fraternally, Tom Disken.". On Jamboree Attractions letterhead, Tom Diskin wrote a letter to Mr. Thompson with an enclosed contract for a show at "the Auditorium" in Little Rock. The show, on February 20, 1955, featured Elvis and the Carter Sisters. Mr. Diskin hoped that Mr. Thompson, his wife, and his family would be able to attend the show as their guests. The letter was signed,

"Fraternally, Tom Diskin.". 8 1/2 x 5 1/2 inches both.

At the show in Little Rock, Elvis met Mother Maybelle Carter and her daughters, Anita and June. Later he would tour with them frequently.

$800 - 1,000

A34 LETTER FROM TOM DISKIN REGARDING
ELVIS PRESLEY'S PROMOTION IN MONROE, LA.

In a letter dated February 8, 1955, Tom Diskin wrote to Bell Captain Jack Hammonds at the Frances Hotel in Monroe, Louisiana. He sent records along with the letter in hopes that Hammonds would distribute them to local disc "jockies" to promote Elvis (especially with high school kids) before his arrival in Monroe on February 18. 78 rpm record: "Baby Let's Play House" and "I'm Left, You're Right, She's Gone". 11 x 8 1/2 inches. 10-inch diameter record.

This is just one of the many examples of the Colonel and his staff working hard to help Elvis' music become recognized early in his career.

$1,000 - 1,500

A35 LETTER FROM WILLIAM MORRIS
AGENCY TO COLONEL TOM PARKER
REGARDING A NEW ARTIST NAMED ELVIS
PRESLEY

Original one page typed letter dated February 10, 1955, from Harry Kalcheim of the William Morris Agency to Col. Parker. "In connection with Presley, I am sorry I evidently mislaid the picture. Could you send me another one? He sounds like a good prospect......" 11 x 8 1/2 inches.

This is an example of the early interest in Elvis. Harry Kalcheim felt Elvis had an unusual voice.

$800 - 1,000

A36 CORRESPONDENCE REGARDING EARLE ELVIS TOUR DATES

Letter dated February 20, 1955, to Tom Parker from A.V.Bamford regarding the ability to use "Alvin" Presley during April and wanting to know the price for one date. Western Union telegram sent February 23, 1955, from the Colonel to Bamford. Parker informs Bamford that he solely represents Elvis Presley, not Bob Neal. Another Western Union telegram sent February 23, 1955, from the Colonel to Bamford asks what cities in Texas Bamford has in mind and whether he wanted Hank Snow for a coast guest appearance at some of the "big shindigs." Letter dated February 24, 1955, from Bamford back to the Colonel regarding lining up Elvis and possibly Snow. 11 x 8 1/2 inches letters. 5 3/4 x 8 inches and 10 x 8 inches telegrams.

In this example of his early business dealings, the Colonel corresponds with A.V. Bamford, a promoter of country western shows. Elvis is still unknown in many areas (perhaps why is name is misspelled), and the Colonel is trying to get him more widely recognized. Elvis is still under Bob Neal's management, providing part of the confusion, and still distributed by Sun Records, limiting his distribution area.

$1,500 - 1,800

A37 LETTER FROM TOM DISKIN REGARDING GRAND OLE OPRY TOUR

On March 28, 1955, Tom Diskin wrote to the Special Service Officer at Camp Gordon in Augusta, Georgia, regarding the May touring of the Grand Ole Opry show. His hope was to present the show at Camp Gordon. The tour lineup included Hank Snow, Slim Whitman, the Carter Sisters, and Elvis Presley. 11 x 8 1/2 inches.

This is one example of Tom Diskin, under the Colonel's direction, trying to set up "gigs" for the Hank Snow tour, which included Elvis' appearances. The tour never played Augusta in 1955, but Elvis performed on March 20 and June 27, 1956 at the Bell Auditorium.

$800 - 1,000

Left: A36

Below: A39

A38 HANK SNOW ALL-STAR JAMBOREE SHOW DOCUMENTS, MAY 7, 1955

Two page lease on blue paper, dated April 25, 1955. For the use of the Municipal Auditorium in New Orleans for one performance of the Hank Snow All-Star Jamboree on May 1, 1955. Rental of the facility was $330 and is leased to Colonel Thomas A. Parker. Original carbon of one page typed letter from Col. Parker to Bill Stanley of WNOE radio in New Orleans, dated March 29, 1955. Letter is regarding accommodations for Parker and Tom Diskin in New Orleans. The letter details the line-up for the Hank Snow All-Star Jamboree that was held May, 1. Elvis is listed as a special added attraction at the bottom of a line-up that also includes Hank Snow, Faron Young, the Wilburn Brothers and Mother Maybelle Carter and the Carter Sisters. Ticket number 2500 features a snapshot of Hank Snow and was good for general admission to any of three shows that were given that day. Ticket price is listed as $1.25 in advance and $1.50 at the box office. 14 x 8 1/2 inches lease. 11 x 8 1/2 inches letter. 4 x 5 inches ticket.

This show was opening night of a 21-day/20 town Jamboree tour, booked by Colonel Parker. It was the day after Elvis' fourth Sun single, "Baby, Let's Play House," was released. Elvis was set to close the first half of each show, and the reactions he drew were at near riot-level for many of the performances. On May 6 the tour played Birmingham, but Elvis returned to Memphis to attend then girlfriend Dixie Locke's junior prom.

$3,000 -4,000

A39 ELVIS PRESLEY, BILL BLACK, SCOTTY MOORE, DJ FONTANA WARDROBE MEASUREMENTS

Bill Black, DJ Fontana, and Elvis' measurements are written on Shamrock Hilton Stationery; Scotty Moore's measurements are written on note paper. The other measurements (of unknowns) are written on paper. Elvis' measurements: Suit: 40, Waist: 32, Shoes: 10 1/2, Shirt: 15 1/2. Three Bills from Squire's Clothes in Hollywood CA. Bill amounts: June 6, 1956: $199.85; June 7, 1956:$404.65, and June 8, 1956: $39.95. Photograph included. 6 x 3 3/4 inches stationery. 8 x 5 inches note paper. 3 3/4 x 2 1/2 inches notes. 2 3/4 x 6 inches bills.

June 6th and 8th bill for Colonel Tom Parker and E.M. Mott; June 7th bill for All Star Shows-Wardrobe; Stage Clothes for Elvis and band.

$3,500 - 5,000

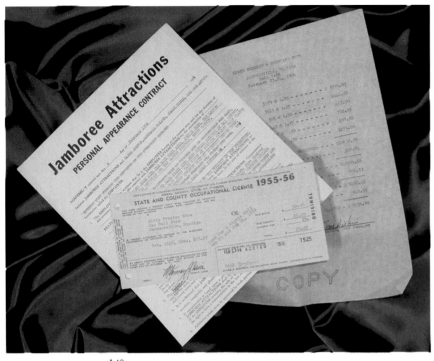

A40

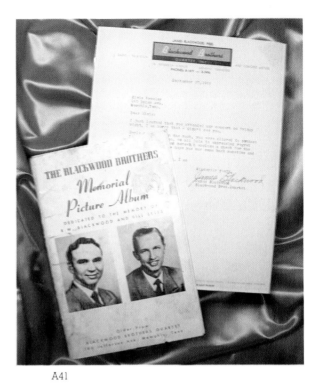

A41

A40 CONTRACT FOR ATLANTA APPEARANCE, DECEMBER 2, 1955

Letter dated September 19, 1955 from Cotton Carrier (WAGA in Atlanta) to Bob Neal to try to schedule Elvis for Atlanta's Sports Arena on December 2 for $300. If they agreed to amount, they were to send contracts. Memphis Federation of Musicians contract dated September 21, 1955 for Elvis Presley to play the Sports Arena in Atlanta on December 2, 1955 for 1 show. Contract signed by Cotton Carrier (employer of WAGA in Atlanta) and Bob Neal (who also signed Elvis Presley's signature). Letter (copy) dated September 21, 1955 to Cotton Carrier from Bob Neal accompanied the contract. Bob asks what else they need from Elvis Presley Enterprises before the event. Letter of September 24, 1955 from Cotton Carrier listing other radio stations and disc jockeys in the area. Postcard dated November 25, 1955 from Cotton Carrier mentions additional appearances they would like Elvis to make while in Atlanta. 11 x 8 1/2 " contract. 11 x 8 1/2 " letters. 3 1/4 x 5 1/2" postcard.

This show, booked by Bob Neal, was Elvis' first appearance in Atlanta. Held in the Atlanta Sports Arena, with a capacity of 3,000, the show was poorly attended due to insufficient advertising. Sun Records also lacked distribution in the Atlanta area, so Elvis' music had not been played much prior to the show. This was one of the Colonel's concerns--that Neal had reached too far and into too large a venue with Elvis' bookings, without preparing his audience.

$9,000 - 11,000

A41 JAMES BLACKWOOD LETTER TO ELVIS PRESLEY WITH "PICTURE ALBUM"

Typed on Blackwood Brothers pink and black letterhead and dated September 27, 1955. Blackwood expresses regret that on attending one of their recent concerts, Elvis was "allowed to purchase a ticket of admission." A check (not included) was enclosed to reimburse Elvis for the ticket charge.

Photograph included. Forty page black and white "Blackwood Brothers Memorial Picture Album" 11 x 8 1/2 inches.

The Blackwood Brothers gospel quartet was a favorite of Gladys Presley's, and they eventually sang at her funeral in 1958. The Memphis-based group was active during Elvis' teens and was based out of First Assembly of God Church on McLemore Avenue. Elvis began attending the church in January 1954, in large part because the Blackwoods were members and often performed at services. The Blackwoods sponsored a junior quartet called the Songfellows, which Elvis auditioned for and was turned down. Though Gladys loved the Blackwoods, Elvis and Vernon actually preferred the livelier Statesmen.

$1,000 - 1,500

A42 EARLY REQUEST FOR ELVIS PERFORMANCE

Typed letter to "Mr. Presley" dated December 3, 1954, from the Hyatt F.H.A. (Future Homemakers of America) Chapter, in Fields, Louisiana. The letter states that Elvis and his band were listed among two other bands as possibilities to play at an F.H.A fund raiser, and asks if he and the band could come in February or March. Also questions whether Elvis would require a fee or would be satisfied with a portion of the funds raised at the function. 11 x 8 1/2 inches.

This was during the time Elvis was managed by Bob Neal. Elvis never played Fields, Louisiana.

$500 - 700

A43 CONTRACT AND POSTER FOR BILL HALEY AND THE COMETS

Contract from Jolly Joyce Theatricals--and signed by Colonel Parker--dated August 29, 1955, for Bill Haley and His Comets. The group is scheduled to play various cities from October 10-17, 1955. Pay stated as $1,250 daily. This contract shows Colonel Parker's involvement in country music. White poster of Bill Haley and the Comets; red and blue lettering; blue photo of the group. Bottom reads "Of 'Shake Rattle & Roll' fame, 'Rock Around the Clock,' and 'Razzle Dazzle'" 11 x 8 1/2 inches contract. 22 x 14 inches poster

Elvis joined Haley on the Hank Snow Tour on October 16, 1955 in Oklahoma City. It was the first time Elvis worked with Haley. The poster for the event gave Bill Haley and Elvis Presley top billing, while Hank Snow highlighted the bottom half of the poster. Haley's popularity was at a "high" when they met, and Elvis hoped to learn from some of the "stardom."

$2,000 - 3,000

A43

A44 THE COMING OF THE 1953 DEAL - CORRESPONDENCE BETWEEN RCA AND THE COLONEL

Stephen Sholes of the A&R Department of RCA Victor wrote this letter to Colonel Tom Parker on October 27, 1955. The letter, written on RCA letterhead, discusses the deal between Sun Records and RCA Victor Records. Sholes was sorry that they were so far apart on the matter and hoped that they could agree on one of the previous RCA offers because, "these were the best deals we can offer." 11 x 8 3/8 inches

Stephen Sholes' department, A&R or Artists & Repertoire, picked the songs, got the producers etc. to make the records. RCA was trying to make a recording deal for Elvis at this time, but letter shows that they are not close in their negotiations. It took a few more weeks of steady negotiating with crafty Colonel Parker to make the contract a reality-- November 21, 1955. $1,200 - 1,500

A45 ANDY GRIFFITH SHOW LICENSE AND APPLICATION FOR PERMIT

Yellow State and County 1954-55 Occupational License from Duval County, Florida, dated July 27, 1955 and sold to All Star Jamboree for July 28 and 29 performances. Cost of license $75.25. White City of Jacksonville License attached; dated July 6, 1955; cost $187.50. State of Florida application for permit dated July 11, 1955. Signed by Colonel Parker, Unit Manager. Cost $1.50. 3 3/4 x 8 1/2 inches license. 14 x 8 1/2 inches show permit

The Occupational License was granted for the Andy Griffith Show on July 28-29, 1955 in Jacksonville. The State of Florida application applied for the All Star Jamboree performances July 25-31.

$5,000 - 7,000

A46 ELVIS' MOTOROLA TV RECEIPT

Original September 10, 1955, General Electric paid sales contract for a 21K34 Motorola TV for Elvis. Contract lists Elvis' address at 2414 Lamar. Total bill came to $292.32 with monthly installments of $12.18 beginning October 15th for twenty-four months. 7 1/2 x 4"

Address on contract is listed as 2414 Lamar, however, he had just moved to Getwell at this time. Contract is signed by Elvis Presley.

$2,500 - 3,500

A47 ELVIS PRESLEY'S FIRST RCA CONTRACT

Four page typed contract on RCA Victor letterhead, dated November 15, 1955 and signed in blue ink by H. Coleman Tily III of RCA, Elvis Presley, Vernon Presley (signing as Elvis' "father and natural guardian"), and Col. Tom Parker. Contract stipulates a payment of $35,000 to Sun Records to buy out their contract with Elvis, and a bonus payment of $5,000 to Elvis. The contract is for three years and would take effect on November 21, 1955, stipulating the production of eight record sides per year through the terms of the contract. There are two handwritten corrections in the contract: 1. A clause giving RCA exclusivity in marketing has been crossed out, and 2. Elvis' initial royalty rate of one cent per record for songs he owns a copyright of is crossed out and changed to one and a half cents. Both corrections are initialed by RCA legal representative Tily. 11 x 8 1/2 inches.

The deal that would forever change American popular culture didn't happen overnight. Its seeds were planted months in advance—by the concomitant increase in the intensity of Elvis Presley's success, Colonel Tom Parker's ambition and Sam Phillips' desperation. On August 15, 1955, after much courting, Elvis signed a contract naming the Colonel as "special advisor to Elvis Presley and [then manager] Bob Neal," in effect giving the Colonel authority to negotiate on his behalf. At the same time Sam Phillips' tiny Sun Records was having difficulty meeting demand for its rising star, and bankruptcy seemed imminent. By the late summer of 1955 a deal of some kind appeared to be inevitable. The Colonel had his sights set on RCA all along. As the only major record company attached to a corporation, RCA had deep pockets, and the Colonel had decade-long ties to the label through his management of RCA artists Eddy Arnold and Hank Snow. But, ever the shrewd operator, Colonel Parker didn't want RCA to take anything for granted, and continued to have discussions with other labels. In the early fall Sam Phillips sat down with Colonel Parker to talk details. He knew he needed to sell Elvis' contract but was still understandably reluctant to do so. The Colonel asked Phillips to name his price, and he did: $35,000 plus $5,000 to pay back royalties the label owed to Elvis. That number may seem small today, especially given what we know of Elvis' subsequent career, but in 1955 it

was more than had ever been paid for a performer's contract. It was an outrageous figure—the Colonel knew it and Sam Phillips didn't think it would be met.

Negotiations progressed well into the fall, with the Colonel getting a call from RCA executive W.W. Bullock on October 28 with a "final" offer of $25,000. The Colonel reportedly received the same offer from Ahmet Ertegun at Atlantic Records. The final deal was brokered by the Colonel on November 15 from his Madison, Tennessee office. In the end RCA assented and Sam Phillips got every penny he asked for. On November 21 a summit convened at Sun in Memphis to make the historic deal official— Colonel Parker and his assistant Tom Diskin came in from Madison, RCA representatives H. Coleman Tily and Steve Sholes flew down from New York, and RCA field representatives Sam Esgro and Jim Crudgington also made their way to Memphis. Awaiting this contingent were Sam Phillips, Bob Neal, Gladys and Vernon Presley and, of course, Elvis Presley himself. "DOUBLE DEALS HURL PRESLEY INTO STARDOM" went the Billboard headline.

This contract meant many things to many people. For Sam Phillips, for whom the decision was by far the toughest, it meant financial solvency. His little label was finally in the black and through the deal had acquired a reputation that promised to draw talent, and the resources to develop and promote that talent. The magnificent array of artists that followed Elvis through the doors of Sun is perhaps the greatest testament to the wisdom of Phillips choice: Carl Perkins, Jerry Lee Lewis, Johnny Cash, Roy Orbison, Charlie Rich. For RCA it was a tremendous gamble. They had just paid an unprecedented amount of money to sign a twenty year-old kid (Vernon had to sign the contract because Elvis was still a minor at the time.) who had never dented the pop charts.

For Elvis Presley it was the fulfillment of a dream. The poor boy from Tupelo who had watched movies and imagined himself in them, who had read comic books and made himself the hero, was now on the cusp of realizing his every ambition, even if some would later wonder at what Faustian price his incredible success was attained. But as much as the ramifications of this document meant

for Sam Phillips or RCA or even Elvis Presley himself— and its impact cannot be overstated on each count— it pales in comparison to what it meant for the country and its culture. When RCA paid $35,000 for Elvis Presley's contract it sent a message: That the largest of all record companies believed that a rock and roll performer could become as broad-based a star as Frank Sinatra. Before the RCA deal Elvis had been marketed as a country performer: He had won country music awards, his records had performed best on the country charts and he toured almost exclusively with country performers, such as on the Hank Snow Jamboree. But the sheer size of RCA's investment necessitated that Elvis be promoted as an all-market performer—country, pop and rhythm and blues. And, at least initially, RCA pushed Elvis into all of these markets without attempting to alter the sound or instrumentation that he used at Sun.

The invisible republic at the heart of Elvis' musical vision (remember the now immortal words spoken by the teenage boy upon first entering Sun Records: "I sing all kinds.") had been an artistic fact from the very beginning—the uniting of black and white, city and country, urbane sophistication and proletarian vitality. But the exposure granted by RCA made it a commercial fact as well. The democratic impulse behind rock and roll that had secretly manifested itself in the South for years was becoming a marketplace reality across the country, and a post-war youth culture with a surfeit of discretionary income had the buying power to turn this subculture into mass, and Elvis into a star. Before it may have seemed unlikely in a nation so divided that the many tributaries of American music, and the cultures they represented, could come together in one music and one man (though Elvis surely wasn't the only one making these connections tangible). It may have seemed unlikely that followers of Jimmie Rodgers and Nat King Cole, of Dean Martin and Ray Charles could so easily find common ground. The rise of Elvis Presley as a pop culture hero, perhaps no less than the Brown v. the Board of Education decision a year earlier, signaled a fundamental turn in American culture. The rest was history, and not just music history. This document is its foundation.

$100,000 - 150,000

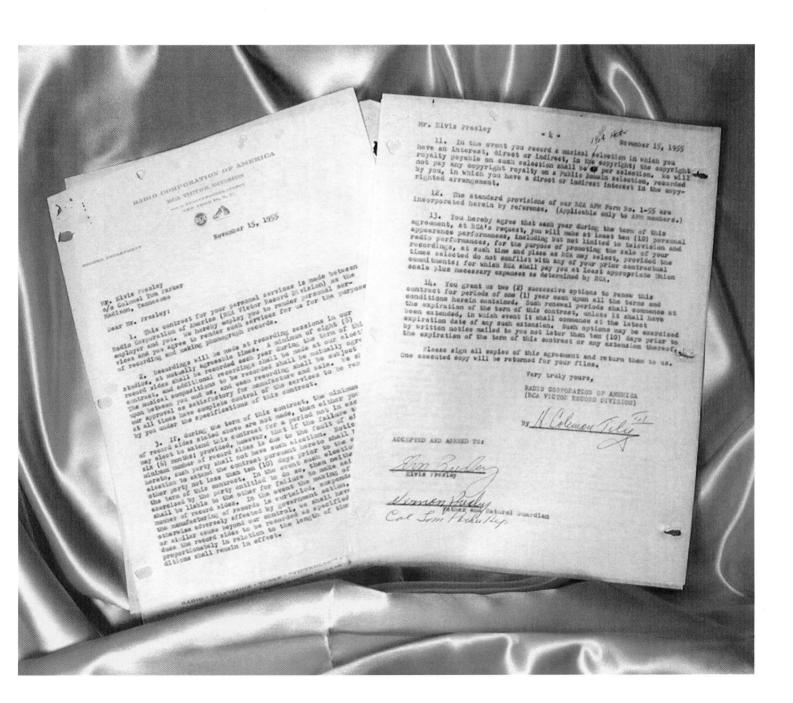

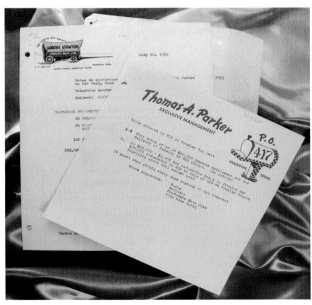

A48

State and County Occupational License from Orange County, Florida, dated July 21, 1955 and sold to All-Star Jamboree--Andy Griffith Show for the show on July 26, 1955 in Orlando. Cost of license $37.75. Receipt from DeVerner's Skillet in Daytona Beach, Florida, on July 30, 1955. Bill shows Andy Griffith show members had luncheon ordered, including 30 ham and cheese sandwiches, 24 iced Coca Colas, 24 assorted ice creams. The bill totals $31 and is signed by Tom Diskin. Newspaper advertisement for Daytona Beach Show. Handwritten note on Colonel Parker's stationery signed by Elvis. Note acknowledges payment received by Elvis from the Colonel for $750 for the Andy Griffith tour. Pencil note marked "paid 7/31/55." One blue ticket for Andy Griffith Show, July 30, stamped "Sample" 5 1/2 x 8 1/4 inches license. 9 x 7 inches DeVerner's receipt. 7 3/4 x 1 3/4 inches ad. 8 1/2 x 8 1/2 inches Elvis note. 2 x 5 inches ticket

The Andy Griffith Show played July 26-27, 1955 in Orlando, the 28th and 29th in Jacksonville, 30th in Daytona Beach, and ended in Tampa on the 31st. Elvis was well received, even to riotous extremes in Jacksonville, where the fans helped themselves to his clothing.

$1,500 - 2,000

A49

A51 RECEIPT FOR A RECORD PLAYER BOUGHT BY ELVIS

Original October 10, 1955, General Electric paid receipt for a CP 251 Magnavox record player bought by Elvis while he lived at 1414 Getwell. Total amount was $223.92 with monthly payments of $9.33 for twenty-four months beginning November 15th. Photograph included. 7 1/2 x 4 inches.

Signature on contract is that of Vernon's (his initial's are next to Elvis' name)

$500 - 700

A48 NOTES ON ELVIS PRESLEY MOVING FROM SUN TO RCA RECORDS

Notes dated July 22, 1955, on Jamboree Attractions letterhead, regarding a conference call between Parker, Bob Neal, Hank Snow, and Tom Diskin about Elvis Presley package deal proposition. Note dated 7/22/55 on Thomas A. Parker's older "Jamboree Attractions" stationery, regarding terms offered by RCA on Presley Contract. One term was a TV guest shot within sixty days signing of the contract with either Berle, Garroway, Producers Show Case, or Wide Wide World. Copy of an August 24, 1955 letter to Bob Neal from Georgene Keeney, Secretary to Col. Parker. Letter forwards contracts that need signing and states that Elvis must be at the New Orleans radio station WBOK on September 1 at 2 p.m. Photo incl. 8 1/2 x 8 1/2 " note .11 x 8 1/2 " notes on conference call and letter.

The Colonel's note from Jamboree Attractions is written on some of his older stationery. Elvis was still managed by Bob Neal at the time and the Colonel was trying to get more control. Since he had more experience than Neal, he was trying to establish a plan to help him succeed, including the transfer from Sun Records to RCA.

A49 CORRESPONDENCE BETWEEN BOB NEAL, COLONEL TOM PARKER, AND TOM DISKIN REGARDING ELVIS PRESLEY'S LATE ARRIVAL AT THE MISSOURI THEATER

Original letter dated October 26,1955, from Bob Neal to Col. Tom Parker regarding Elvis' late arrival for a show at the Missouri Theater. Elvis claimed he lost his pocketbook and this delayed him. However, Roy Acuff had refused to allow him to play and Bob Neal was asking advise on payment . Copy of October 28, 1955, letter to Bob Neal from Tom Diskin replying to first letter. Photograph included. 11 x 8 1/2 inches.

Colonel Parker agreed with Roy Acuff in not allowing Elvis to play, and would remind Elvis always to "be professional".

$1,000 - 1,500

$2,000 - 2,500

A52 BOB NEAL RECEIPT REGARDING RCA COMMISSION

A typed and signed receipt from Bob Neal written on stationery from the Peabody Hotel in Memphis. Dated November 21, 1955, detailing the receipt from Col. Parker of $653.62 in commissions from payments made to Elvis from RCA Victor and the publishing company Hill and Range. Photograph included. 9 1/2 x 6 inches.

November 21 was the day that Elvis' contract with RCA took effect. This receipt, found in Colonel Parker's records, shows Neal's cut of the deal being paid to him from the Colonel. In a sense, this document captures the beginning of the end for Bob Neal's association with Elvis. At the time the RCA contract was signed, Bob Neal was Elvis' manager—Colonel Parker wouldn't officially take control of Elvis' career until March, 1956—but the Colonel was clearly in the driver's seat.

$1,200 - 1,500

A53 TOMMY COLLINS' AND MARTY ROBBINS' RECEIPTS AND GRIFFITH SHOW TICKET

Letter typed on Thomas A. Parker stationery for payment received from Tommy Collins on Andy Griffith Show from July 25-31, 1955. Signed by Tommy Collins. Handwritten revisions included on side of receipt.Letter typed on Thomas A. Parker stationery for payment received from Marty Robbins on Andy Griffith Show from July 25-31, 1955. Signed by Marty Robbins and showing total amount due balance of $1,275 on July 31, 1955. Andy Griffith Show reserved ticket for July 30, 1955 at the Peabody Auditorium in Daytona Beach. 8 1/2 x 8 1/2 inches each receipt. 2 x 5 inches ticket.

Robbins and Collins both performed on the Andy Griffith Show tour. Robbins became a well-known country singer who influenced Elvis with many of his songs, including "You Gave Me a Mountain."

$1,200 - 1,500

A53

A54 ELVIS PRESLEY'S DEPOSIT SLIP FROM AUGUST 8, 1955, AND A CHECK ENDORSED BY ELVIS PRESLEY

National Bank of Commerce "new account" deposit slip from August 8, 1955. Total amount deposited, $1000.00. A check written on First American National Bank from Tom Diskin to Elvis Presley for $1800.00. Elvis' signature is on the back of the check. 8 3/4 x 3/ 3/4" Deposit Slip 3 x 8 1/4" check.

Check was for appearances from January 15 - 20, 1956. Pay was $300 per day.

$3,000 - 4,000

A55 "I FORGOT TO REMEMBER TO FORGET"/"MYSTERY TRAIN" RECORD AND LETTER

Copy of two page typed letter dated November 16, 1955. Written to Harry Kalcheim of William Morris Agency. Parker mentions the inclusion of a couple of Hank Snow records as well as Elvis' latest single, "I Forgot to Remember to Forget." The letter also details the division of Elvis' management duties between Col. Parker and Bob Neal. With original Sun single of "I Forgot to Remember to Forget" b/w

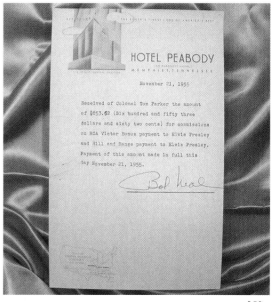

A52

"Mystery Train." 11 x 8 1/2 inches letter. 7 inches diameter record.

Just one day after Elvis has signed with RCA and five days before the contract will actually take effect, the Colonel is already working hard for his new client. At this point, Bob Neal is still technically Elvis' manager, but the Colonel makes clear exactly who is in charge, informing Kalcheim that Neal is handling "one-nighters" while he is exclusively handling "radio, television, motion pictures, endorsements, publishing and theatres."

$1,500 - 2,000

A56 CHECK TO GULF HILLS DUDE RANCH

Light green check dated August 2, 1956 and made out to Gulf Hills Dude Ranch for $310.84. The check is signed, E.A. Presley. Photograph included. 3 1/2 x 8 1/2 inches

Elvis and his entourage stayed at the Gulf Hills Dude Ranch in Biloxi, Mississippi, for about 3 weeks while he was visiting June Juanico, one of his girlfriends at that time. This vacation took place immediately before his Florida tour.

$2,500 -3,500

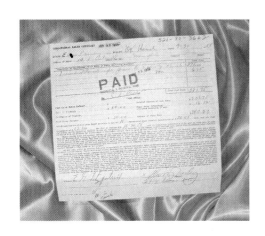

A57 ELVIS' RECEIPT FOR A USED STROUD PIANO

Two-sided receipt from O.K. Houck Piano Company, Inc. on Getwell in Memphis dated September 30, 1955. Elvis purchased a used Stroud Upright piano and bench for $275 plus tax totaling $281.75. With a trade in allowance of $50, Elvis was to pay the remainder in eleven monthly installments. A red ink stamp indicates that the debt was paid May 25, 1956. Signed in blue ink by Elvis Presley. 8 x 8 1/2 inches.

This is the first piano purchased by Elvis and his family after beginning his recording career.

$4,000 - 5,000

☐A58 ELVIS PRESLEY'S FIRST PIANO

The Aeolin Piano Company of Worcester, MA established in 1888 by William B. Tremaine, owned several piano companies including The Stroud Piano Company. This Stroud upright piano was manufactured in 1911-1912 and is comprised of a maple bridge, spruce soundboard, laminated hard rock maple pin block, constructional mahogany and maple back assembly, ivorine keys, maple action, sugar pine and spruce key levers, cast iron metal parts and carbon steel strings wrapped in copper wire. The serial number is 28059.

After Elvis graduated from Humes High School on June 3, 1953, he began working at M.B. Parker Machinists' Shop and eventually at the Precision Tool Shop. Making only fifty dollars a week, Elvis went with Barbara Pittman, a friend of the Presley's who also lived on Alabama Street and recorded for Sun Records, to O.K. Houck Piano Store located on 121 Union Avenue in Downtown Memphis to purchase his very first piano. The Stroud upright piano was in the used section of the store and Elvis financed the piano through a monthly payment plan. In January of 1954 Elvis attended the

Assembly of God church where the Blackwood brothers Quartet often performed and had been prominent members since 1950. Elvis was an avid listener of gospel music and the upright was a favorite of gospel groups. In the 1960's Elvis purchased a Kanabe Baby Grand piano and moved the Stroud upright piano to the back house of Graceland in a room occupied by Joe Esposito. Mrs. Christine Strickland, a cook for Elvis, was given the upright piano around the year 1966. In 1989 Mrs. Strickland faced foreclosure on her home and bankruptcy. Her only alternative was to sell her precious piano. Fortunately, when her story was made known to the press, kind acts of generosity allowed her to keep the prized piano. After her passing a few years later, her family sold the piano to the Memphis Music Hall of Fame Museum in July 1992 where it has been housed ever since.

$300,000 - 400,000

A59

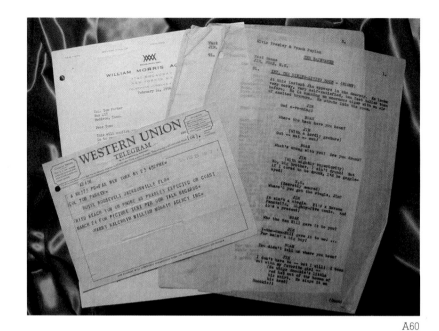

A60

A59 HANK SNOW JAMBOREE TICKETS, ROANOKE, VIRGINIA

Four rare, early Elvis, beige concert tickets for Grand Ole Opry Show on September 15, 1955, in Roanoke, Virginia. Three tickets are stamped "Roanoke Record Shop." Photograph included. 2 x 3 3/4 inches.

Elvis and his band played with the Hank Snow Jamboree on September 15. Billed as the Grand Ole Opry Show, the event took place at the American Legion Auditorium at 8 p.m. The show was sponsored by the Chamber of Commerce, with profits benefitting Midget Sandlot Baseball. Advance tickets were available at Roanoke Record Shop for $1.

$3,000 - 5,000

A60 ELVIS PRESLEY'S SCREEN TEST FOR HAL WALLIS

Two page test scene from "The Rainmaker" that was read by Elvis and actor Frank Faylan. The scene is of a conversation between characters "Jim" and "Noah" in which Jim reveals his engagement to his girlfriend "Snookie." One page typed letter on William Morris Agency letterhead, sent to Colonel Parker from Harry Kalcheim of William Morris. Dated February 24, 1956 and initialed in blue ink by Kalcheim. Letter concerns a screen test set up between Elvis and producer Hal Wallis for March 26-28. Letter details a six-year option that Wallis could pick up within 30 days of the screen test. Western Union telegram dated February 23, 1956, sent to Colonel Parker from Harry Kalcheim, regarding Elvis' arrival on the West Coast for the screen test. Photograph included. 11 x 8 1/2 inches letter. 5 5/8 x 8 inches telegram. 11 x 8 1/2 inches screen test.

This is Elvis' script for his first screen test, made for Hal Wallis at Paramount on April 1, 1956. He read for the male ingenue role of "Jim." Elvis was in Los Angeles for a performance on The Milton Berle Show on April 3. Though Elvis wasn't pleased with how this initial screen test went, he did sign a seven-year, three-picture contract with Paramount five days later, on April 6, 1956. Despite erroneously reporting in an interview that "The Rainmaker" would be his film debut, Elvis didn't get the part. Instead, Earl Holliman played Jim in a film that starred Burt Lancaster and Katherine Hepburn. Elvis' screen debut would come in "Love Me Tender" later that year. Being an actor was as much an ambition of Elvis' as being a singer, and this screen test was the being of a film career that, in terms of commercial success and time spent, rivaled his music career. Elvis would go on to act in 31 feature films, starting with "Love Me Tender" later that year.

$3,000 - 5,000

A61 "HEARTBREAK HOTEL" CONTRACT AND LETTER

Letter dated January 18, 1956 from Buddy Killen of Tree Publishing Company, Inc. stating that he had enclosed (spelled "inclosed") a copy of the contract on "Heartbreak Hotel." The four-page contract, dated November 16, 1955, named Mae Boren, Tommy Durden, and Elvis Presley as the composers of Heartbreak Hotel. This contract sold, assigned, and transferred all rights on the song "Heartbreak Hotel" to the Tree Publishing Company, Inc. Pages of the letter and the contract are faded in color. Photograph included. 10 1/2 x 7 1/4 inches letter. 11 x 8 1/2 inches contract.

It was November 10, 1955 and Elvis was attending the fourth annual Country Music Disc Jockey's Convention in Nashville, Tennessee. Elvis was busy enjoying his new-found status, meeting people in the business, attending parties, getting introduced to girls, and excitely spreading the news of his imminent contract with RCA which Colonel Parker was still hashing out. Elvis was completely uninterested in discussing business matters, content to leave that up to the Colonel and Bob Neal. Mae Boren Axton, however, had business to discuss with him. Mae was a promoter from Jacksonville, Florida who had previously worked with the Colonel and Elvis. From the moment she arrived at the convention, she persisted in trying to persuade Elvis to listen to a new song, promising that it would be his first million seller. Finally, Bob Neal was able to convince a reluctant Elvis to take a few minutes to listen to the song. In the hotel room, Mae played "Heartbreak Hotel" for Elvis for the first time. Upon hearing it Elvis exclaimed, "Hot dog, Mae, play it again." He loved it. She played it for him over and over, and before he left the room,

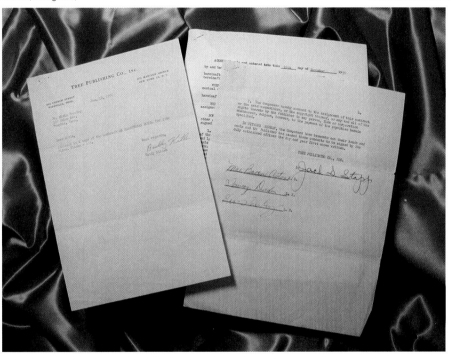

Elvis had the song memorized. He told Bob and Mae that night, "That's gonna be my next record." The song had an almost morbid twist to it, having been written after Tommy Durden showed Mae a story from a Miami newspaper about a man who committed suicide. The headline read, "Do You Know This Man?" He had no identification on him, but left a suicide note simply stating, "I walk a lonely street."

Mae was stunned by the story and told Tommy, "Everybody in the world has somebody who cares. Let's put a Heartbreak Hotel and the end of this lonely street." In less than 30 minutes, Mae and Tommy wrote "Heartbreak Hotel," complete with bellhops whose tears kept flowing and a desk clerk dressed in black. January 10, 1956 marked Elvis' first RCA recording session, held at the RCA studios in Nashville. Backing Elvis up were Scotty Moore on guitar, Bill Black on bass, D.J. Fontana on drums, Floyd Cramer on piano and Chet Atkins on guitar. Gordon Stoker, Ben Speer and Brock Speer provided the backup vocals. Elvis kicked off the session with Ray Charles' "I've Got a Woman"

before moving into "Heartbreak Hotel." Chet Atkins was so impressed by Elvis' performance that he called his wife telling her to come to the studio immediately. "I told her she'd never see anything like this again, it was just so damn exciting." After just a few takes of "Heartbreak Hotel," Elvis had the song nailed and his first gold record was in the bag. The first time Elvis performed "Heartbreak Hotel" on the Louisiana Hayride, Scotty Moore said, "That damn auditorium down there almost exploded. I mean, it had been wild before that, but it was more like playing down at your local camp, a home folks-type situation. But now they turned into - it was different faces, just a whole other... That's the earliest I can remember saying, 'What's going on?'" Just 17 days after the recording session, "Heartbreak Hotel" was released on January 27, 1956. "Billboard" described it as "a strong blues item wrapped up in his usual powerful style and a great beat." "Heartbreak Hotel" was unlike anything Elvis had done and unlike anything anyone had heard, possibly contributing the fact that it was not until March 3 that the song finally entered the charts.

The headline in "Billboard" on March 3 announced, "A WINNAH! Presley Hot as $1Pistol." In only seven weeks, "Heartbreak Hotel" reached #1 on the pop charts where it remained for seven weeks. It was also #1 for 17 weeks on the country and western chart, 13 weeks on the Country Juke Box chart, 12 weeks on the Country Disc Jockey chart, and made it to #5 on the rhythm and blues chart. By April it sold a million copies and "Billboard" listed it as the number one single of 1956. "Heartbreak Hotel" was the second record in history (the first being Carl Perkins' "Blue Suede Shoes") to reach all three "Billboard" charts. With "Heartbreak Hotel," Elvis made music history.

$40,000 -60,000

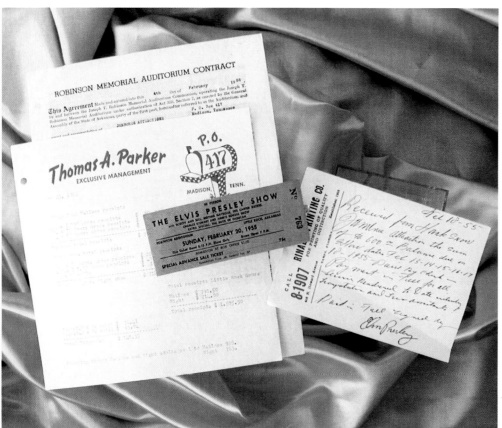

A62 ELVIS PRESLEY'S LITTLE ROCK
PERFORMANCE, FEBRUARY 1955 - CONTRACT
AND OTHER DOCUMENTS

Four-page contract between Robinson Memorial
Auditorium and Jamboree Attractions dated
February 4, 1955 for a performance on February 20,
1955. One page record of Little Rock receipts and
gross on Thomas A. Parker letterhead. Receipts
totaled $1,505.50. Handwritten receipt from Rinaldi
Printing Company dated February 18, 1955.
Signed by Elvis Presley. Original pink ticket for the
Elvis Presley Show on Sunday, February 20, 1955 at
the Robinson Auditorium in Little Rock, Arkansas.
Advance ticket sale price was 75 cents. 11 x 8 1/2
inches contract, 8 1/2 x 8 1/2 inches record of
receipts, 4 1/2 x 6 1/4 inches Rinaldi receipt, 2 x 5
inches ticket.

Elvis' Little Rock performance marked the beginning of a week-long Jamboree Attractions tour,
billed as the "WSM Grand Ole Opry" show. Elvis
was third on the bill behind Duke of Paducah, and
Mother Maebelle and the Carter Sisters. Some
consider the performances of this era to be the
golden age of Elvis shows, with each show being
fresh, rowdy, outrageous and spontaneous. Roy
Orbison who had seen Elvis several days before
his Little Rock performance described him as "a
real raw cat singing like a bird."

$8,000 - 10,000

A63 TRAVEL ARRANGEMENTS FOR ELVIS' FIRST
NATIONAL TELEVISION APPEARANCE

A check from Col. Parker to Travel, Inc. in the
amount of $215.38 to cover airfare for Parker and
Elvis from Nashville to New York for Elvis' first
national television appearance on "Stage Show."
Check number 208 from an account in the name of
All Star Shows is dated January 23, 1956. Two first
class airline ticket stubs dated January 24, 1956 for
American Airlines flight #148 from Nashville to New
York. One ticket is assigned to Col. Parker and one
to Elvis. Two receipts from Travel, Inc. in Nashville
for the purchase of the airline tickets. One receipt
dated January 23, 1956, one dated January 24, 1956.
Photograph included. 3 x 8 1/2 inches check. 3 1/4
x 6 1/4 inches ticket stubs. 7 x 8 1/2 inches receipts.

Elvis and the Colonel flew to New York (the band
drove) three days after Elvis appeared on the
Louisiana Hayride. Elvis made his national television debut on CBS' "Stage Show" on January 28 as
the first portion of a four show contract. The show
was produced by Jackie Gleason and hosted by
brothers Jimmy and Tommy Dorsey. Elvis wore a
black shirt, white tie and sports coat and performed
two songs, Big Joe Turner's "Shake, Rattle and Roll"
and Ray Charles' "I Got a Woman," which would
be included on his RCA debut album two months
later.

$2,500 - 3,000

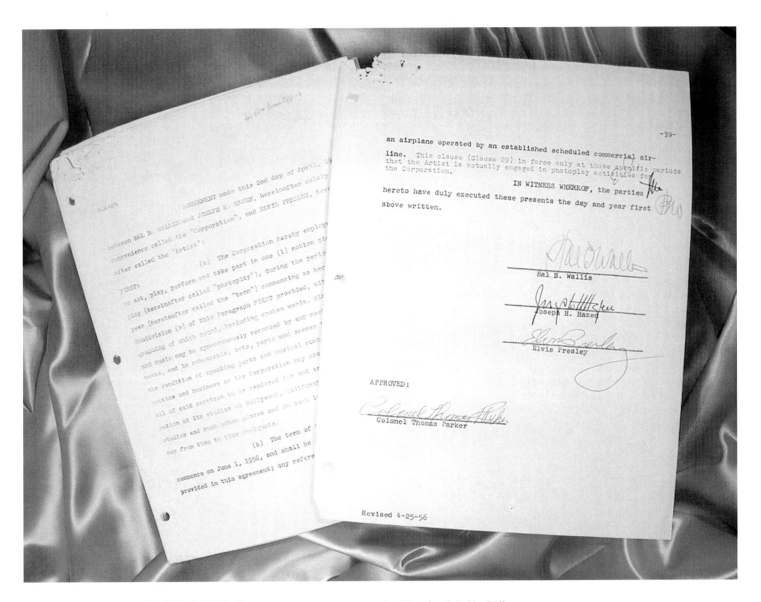

A64 ELVIS PRESLEY'S FIRST MOVIE CONTRACT WITH PARAMOUNT PICTURES

Elvis' original 1956 movie contract with Paramount Pictures. Agreement was made on the second of April, 1956, for a total of seven pictures. Terms of contract state that Elvis was allowed one "outside" picture a year. Contract was signed by Hal B. Wallis, Joseph H. Hazen and Elvis Presley. Terms of agreement to commence on June 1, 1956. Sheet music, on green paper, for "King Creole". 11 x 8 1/2 inches contract. 12 x 9 inches sheet music.

Under this contract Elvis filmed "Love Me Tender" in 1956 for Twentieth Century-Fox; "Jailhouse Rock" in 1957 for MGM; "Loving You" in 1957 for Paramount Pictures; and "King Creole" in 1958 for Paramount pictures. (Also included in lot is sheet music for "King Creole).

$40,000 - 60,000

A65 LETTER TO CAROLINA THEATRE MANAGERS REGARDING "THE ELVIS PRESLEY SHOW"

A two page typed letter dated January 13, 1956 from Harry Hardy to five theatre managers in the Carolinas giving instructions for the promotion of "Elvis Presley Show" tour dates from February 6-10. Contains a quote from Col. Parker which states "The manager that we think did the most successful job of promoting will be awarded a real Tennessee smoked ham with my compliments." Press release dated February 2, 1956 on peach-colored paper, issued by the Southern Radio Corporation in Charlotte, North Carolina. Promotes Elvis' newest release, "Heartbreak Hotel" b/w "I Was the One," as well as previous singles.Western Union telegram, dated September 10, 1956, to Harry Brand from Charles Einfeld regarding Movie to news' coverage of Elvis Presley's homecoming in Tupelo and his intentions of feeding the material to television. Brand forwarded this telegram to Colonel Parker with a typed note on Twentieth Century-Fox Film Corporation stationery. With two-page press release, white with red print. 14 x 8 1/2 inches letter. 11 x 8 1/2 inches press release. 5 5/8 x 8 inches telegram. 11 x 8 1/2 inches note. 11 x 8 1/2 inches press release.

This is an internal document from a theatre chain in the Carolinas, regarding promotional concerns for a string of Elvis Presley shows. This was the era of the movie palaces, and Elvis' performances on this tour would alternate with film shorts, mentioned in the telegram as well. The first press release, which is from the same tour discussed in the theatre managers letter, features an early photo of Elvis with long sideburns, taken prior to his stardom. The second press release features a black and white photo of Elvis—the same photo used on the cover of his RCA debut album—against a drawing of a red "broken" heart. Inside is an "Elvis Presley Story" biography.

$2,000 - 3,000

A66 LETTER TO ELVIS FROM HIS GRANDFATHER

Two page letter written on light green stationary in darker green ink. It is dated February 26, 1956, "Sunday Afternoon." The letter was from Grandfather Jesse and was written by Vera. The letter congratulates Elvis on his success and warns him not to overdo it. The envelope, addressed to 1414 Getwell and torn open at the side, spells Presley as "Presley," the spelling the grandfather and his wife used at that time. 18 x 6" letter. 4 1/8 x 6 1/2" envelope.

Jessie Presley, Elvis' paternal grandfather, divorced his wife, Minnie Mae, and moved to Louisville, Kentucky, where he worked at the Pepsi Cola plant. He married Vera Pruitt in 1957. Elvis didn't see Jessie for a long time; however, his grandfather came to his concert in Louisville in November 1971.

$1,000 - 1,500

A67 WESTERN UNION TELEGRAM TO COL. PARKER FROM GRELUN LANDON, AND A BOOKLET CONTAINING ELVIS PRESLEY'S JUKE BOX FAVORITES

October 3rd, 1956, four page telegram to Col. Parker (who was at the Beverly Wilshire Hotel) from Grelun Landon. Telegram is regarding motion picture songs, and a certain photographer involved in an upcoming song book titled "Elvis Presley Music." Landon is concerned with his relationship with the Col. , and is quoted as saying "Have been on Presley bandwagon since May of 1955 and with you all the way so am a little surprised that you would entertain motion of any circumvention of you or your staff on this close subject." Nine page original booklet titled "The Elvis Presley Album of Juke Box Favorites." Included: "Blue Suede Shoes," "I Was The One," "Tennessee Saturday Night," etc. Front cover has photograph of Elvis playing his guitar with white background and red border. 5 3/4 x 8 inches Telegram. 11 x 8 1/2 inches Booklet.

Grelun Landon worked for the publishing company "Hill and Range". The book they are discussing is a British edition of "Elvis Presley Music."

$1,000 - 2,000

A68 ELVIS' CORRESPONDENCE FORM THE "LOVE ME TENDER" PRODUCTION

Typed letter from Elvis on Twentieth Century-Fox Film Corporation letterhead. Elvis congratulated the customers of Bill Williams' restaurants. He told them to take a close look next time they were at a Bill Williams restaurant because they just might see him eating some delicious chicken. Typed letter from Elvis Presley to Mr. Laboe on Twentieth Century-Fox Film Corporation letterhead. Elvis wrote this while filming "Love Me Tender." He thanks his many friends for their patience and Mr. Laboe for everything he had done for Elvis. Typed letter from Elvis Presley to Mr. Marshall on Twentieth Century-Fox Film Corporation letterhead. Elvis wrote this while filming "Love Me Tender." He thanks Mr. Marshall for his support and hopes to see him in New York on October 28 when he would be there for the Ed Sullivan Show. Typed letter from Elvis Presley to General Sarnof on Twentieth Century-Fox Film Corporation letterhead. Elvis wrote this while filming "Love Me Tender." Elvis expresses his regret for not being able to attend Sarnoff's Anniversary dinner, but he includes an anniversary song he wrote for him. Photo album with 13 black and white photos of Elvis inside and color photos on front and back cover. 11 x 8 1/2 inches all documents

Letters were undated and unsigned because the Colonel took a tape recorder to the set of "Love Me Tender" and got Elvis to compose the messages of these letters. Then the Colonel typed up the letters.

$700 - 800

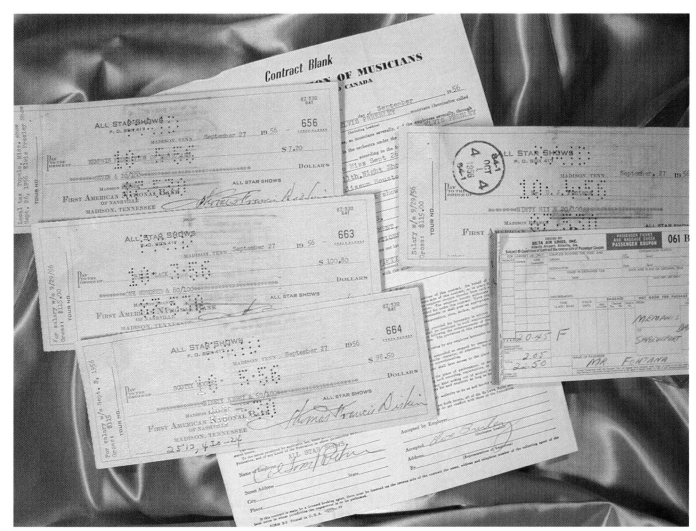

A69 ELVIS CONTRACT FOR THE TUPELO HOME-
COMING PERFORMANCE

American Federal of Musicians contract dated
September 15, 1956. The contract was for Elvis
Presley and the Blue Moon Boys Three (Scotty, Bill,
and D.J.) to appear at the Tupelo Fairgrounds on
September 26, 1956, and for several shows in Texas.
The contract was signed in blue ink by Col. Tom
Parker and Elvis Presley. Elvis was to receive
$1,000 per day or 50% of the profit, whichever was
greater. Delta airlines passenger coupon for D.J. to
fly from Memphis to Shreveport on September 29,
1956. All Star Shows checks from First American

National Bank for the Tupelo show. Made out to
Scotty, Bill, D.J., and Memphis Federation of
Musicians (for local tax); signed by Thomas Francis
Diskin. Scotty, Bill, and D.J. endorsed their salary
checks. Photograph included. 11 x 8 1/2 inches contract. 3 1/4 x 6 1/4 inches coupon. 8 1/4 x 3 1/8 inches
checks.

On September 26, 1956, Elvis returned to Tupelo,
Mississippi, the town where he was born and
reared as a young boy. His Tupelo homecoming
was thrilling for him and his parents, who still had
many friends in the area. The town proclaimed it

"Elvis Presley Day.". During the Mississippi-
Alabama Fair and Dairy Show, the enthralled
crowds waited at the Tupelo Fairgrounds for Elvis'
afternoon show, while the star and his parents
were escorted there by a force of police. The
Governor, who gave Elvis a scroll, attended, as did
the Tupelo mayor, who gave him a key to the city in
the shape of a metal-sculptured guitar. For the
evening show, fifty National Guardsmen were
added to the forty police already on duty. And that
crowd was wilder than the previous one.

$20,000 - 30,000

A70 SECOND "ED SULLIVAN SHOW" APPEARANCE EXPENSES

One sheet of plain paper listing check numbers, dates, amounts and description of expenses. Expenses included are salaries, tickets, plastic inserts for Elvis' upper teeth. and limo services. Original invoice from Robert E. Kinsman, D.D.S. for plastic inserts for upper anterior teeth for Elvis. Total bill is for $150.00, and dated October 9, 1956. Invoice from Travel, Inc., for four first class round trip rail tickets from Memphis to New York, dated October 22, 1956. Total bill is for $467.98. Original invoice from Travel, Inc., dated October 23, 1956, for two round trip air tickets from Nashville to New York; tickets for Colonel Parker and Tom Diskin. Total bill is for $215.38. Check attached to bill in the amount of $683.36, written on "All Star Shows" account, and signed by Thomas Diskin. Note is attached behind check charging the $467.98 to Elvis Presley payroll and expense fund. Copy of letter to Bill Black from Tom Diskin, dated October 22, 1956, regarding an enclosed check for $100.00 covering expenses for gas and oil for limo. Original check attached from "All Star Shows" account, and signed by Thomas Diskin. 11 x 8 1/2 inches Expense List. 11 x 8 1/2 inches Invoice/Kinsman D.D.S. 7 x 8 1/2 inches Invoice/Travel Inc. 7 x 8 1/2 inches invoice/Travel Inc. 3 x 8 1/4 inches Check. 3 1/2 x 6 inches note. 11 x 8 1/2 inches Check

This was Elvis' second appearance on the Ed Sullivan Show, and it was broadcast from the Maxine Elliot Theater on West 39th Street. At noon they had a rehearsal, and afterward Elvis held his first New York press conference. The "New York" times noted that Elvis was "polite, personable, quick-witted, and charming."

$2,000 - 3,000

A71 ORIGINAL LETTER TO ELVIS FROM TOM DISKIN REGARDING AN APPEARANCE ON THE ED SULLIVAN SHOW

January 3, 1956, correspondence on Thomas A. Parker letterhead to Elvis from Tom Diskin. Letter is advising Elvis of which songs he is to sing on the upcoming January 6th show. Elvis is advised to be prepared to sing a hymn or semi-religious song to impress the viewers. "Peace In The Valley" is suggested. Copy of letter is sent to Ed Sullivan. The date of January 3rd, 1956, is a miss-type; it should have been 1957. Original sleeve from Elvis' single "Peace In The Valley." Front cover is an upper body photograph of Elvis in the foreground, and a

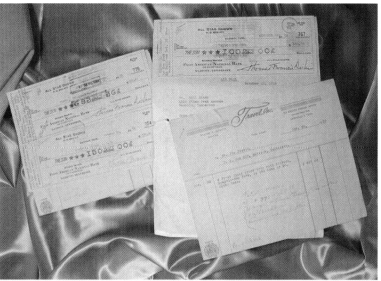

A70

peaceful valley scene behind him. In gold are the words "Gold Standard Series"; in blue are the word "Peace In The Valley," and in pink is the name "Elvis Presley." Photograph included.11 x 8 1/2 inches letter. 7 x 7 inches sleeve.

Elvis did sing "Peace In The Valley" for the show. He also sang "Don't Be Cruel", but he sang the song in the style that Jackie Wilson had performed it. Elvis admired Jackie Wilson and really liked his version of "Don't Be Cruel".

$1,500 - 2,500

A72 "ED SULLIVAN SHOW" APPEARANCE - BILL BLACK LETTER AND CAR EXPENSES

Original handwritten letter from Bill Black to Tom Diskin, dated from 1956. A Thomas Chevrolet invoice dated October 26, 1956, for car repairs on way to the Ed Sullivan Show. Total bill $55.98. 8 1/2 x 11 inches car repair. 10 1/4 x 8 inches letter.

The handwritten letter from Bill Black concerns various expenses, and a request to take the train to New York. However, they took the car instead which ended up breaking down along the way. Thomas Chevrolet invoice was incurred during the band's travel to New York for the Ed Sullivan Show. Elvis was not along since he had flown ahead to New York. The band drove the 1955 black and pink Cadillac which broke down in Pennsylvania.

$1,000 - 1,300

A73 WARWICK HOTEL BILLS

Five pages of charges from the Warwick Hotel from Oct. 27 - 31 in Clint Reno's name. Total bill $501.47 Six pages of charges from the Warwick Hotel for Colonel Parker and Oscar Davis from October 23 - 31. Check to Warwick Hotel for $502.13, signed by Tom Diskin, and a note that says bill was paid in the amount of $502.23 (ten cent difference in amounts).Photograph included. 7 x 8 1/2 inches Five page Warwick bill. 7 x 7 inches Bill for Parker and Davis. 3 x 8 1/4 inches check. 5 x 3 1/2 inches note

Hotel bill also includes Elvis' good friend, Nick Adams, and Gene Smith. Elvis used a number of fictitious names when he traveled, and Clint Reno (his character in "Love Me Tender") was one of them. The stay at the Warwick Hotel was during Elvis' second appearance on the Ed Sullivan Show.

$1,000 - 1,500

A74 "STAGE SHOW" - GOOD LUCK AND
CONGRATULATORY TELEGRAMS TO ELVIS

Western Union Telegram dated January 28, 1956 to
Elvis at CBS on Madison. Bernard and Guy
Lansky, of the Lanksy Brothers Men's Shop on Beale
Street, wish Elvis a successful future and tell him
they will be watching him that night. Western
Union Telegram with a pink flower, dated January
28, 1956, to Elvis from Oscar Davis and Tom Disken.
The telegram was delivered to Elvis at the Warwick
Hotel in New York City and congratulated him on
his sensational performance. Photograph included.
6 1/4 x 8 inches each.

On March 2, 1956 Colonel Parker informed his
attorney that both Bob Neal, Elvis' manager since
January 1955, and Hank Snow, the Colonel's business partner since the same period, were officially
severed from any business associations with Elvis.
Elvis made this trip to Nashville three days later
with his cousin Gene Smith. It has been speculated
that this trip was made in order to meet with
Colonel Parker and reaffirm his new management
agreement.

$4,000 - 5,000

sessions. Elvis had just returned to Memphis from
Nashville, where he was recording for RCA on
January 10 and 11. In the fifties, a person could
write a check on any bank just by crossing off the
bank's name and writing in the new name.

$2,500 - 3,500

A77 THE PRESLEY'S' HOMEOWNER'S
INSURANCE POLICY

Homeowner's insurance policy insuring Vernon
Elvis Presley, Gladys L. Presley, and Elvis Aron

A75

On January 28, 1956, Elvis performed on Jackie
Gleason's "Stage Show" at CBS studios. Because of
the miserable winter weather and Elvis' rather
unknown status in New York at this time, attendance at the show was poor.

$4,000 - 5,000

A75 ELVIS PRESLEY AMERICAN AIRLINES
COUNTER CHECK

Dated March 5, 1956 and signed in blue ink by Elvis
Presley. Payable to American Airlines in the
amount of $55.88. Photograph included. 3 x 8"

A76 POPLAR TUNES CHECK

Beige check dated January 13, 1956 and made out
to Poplar Tunes for $3.00. Check is signed, E.A.
Presley. "Union Planters National Bank", which is
printed on the check, is scratched through with
blue ink and "National Bank of Commerce Main
Office" is handwritten above it. 3 x 8 3/8 inches.

Poplar Tunes, known as Pop Tunes, was the popular spot to buy records in Memphis at the time.
Elvis frequented the store when he was in town,
especially for some of the evening record-playing

Presley in their home at 1034 Audubon Drive. The
policy, dated June 26, 1956, is with United States
Fidelity and Guaranty Company and counter-
signed by E.H Crump & Company A silver and red
E. H. Crump seal was placed on the policy. The
total premium is $445.50. The policy is two, two-
sided, long pages. Photograph included. 33 x 8 1/2
inches. 23 3/8 x 7 1/2 inches.

The Presley's bought their Audubon Drive home in
April 1956 and lived there until March 1957, when
the family moved to Graceland.

$1,000 - 1500

•A78 ELVIS PRESLEY'S
1956 LINCOLN CONTINENTAL MARK II

Above: Elvis, Natalie Wood and the Lincoln
Below: The Lincoln at Graceland today

The 1956 Lincoln Continental Mark II - the last of the hand built cars in American, only 3, 012 were built in n1956 and 1957. This vehicle features special hides imported from England, power windows, power brakes, power steering, refrigerated air conditioning, Town and Country station-seeking radio. It is powered by an overhead valve 90-degree V-8 engine of 368 cubic inches, delivering 285 horsepower at 4,600 rpm. and had a 10 to 1 compression ratio. His personal signature appears on the title of this automobile.

This Mark II was a project of William Clay Ford, grandson of Henry Ford. John Reinhart was the chief stylist for the Continental Mark II. Ford spared no expense to build a perfect automobile. This vehicle cost over $10,000 when a new Ford or Chevrolet was on the market for less than $2,000. Money alone couldn't buy this auto; a buyer had to qualify to be able to purchase it. Obviously, Elvis qualified!

Elvis Presley purchased this beautiful and sleek white automobile on August 6, 1956. Elvis had recently skyrocketed to fame and fortune, and this was the first of many luxury cars Elvis would acquire in the years to come. Elvis used this car to attend many personal appearance over the next few years. This hand built Lincoln Continental Mark II was reported to be Elvis' favorite car. He kept this special automobile at Graceland for twenty years and used it often when he was home. As a bachelor, Elvis escorted many young ladies in this handsome vehicle including Natalie Wood, pictured with Elvis above.

It was this automobile that Elvis was driving when he escorted Priscilla from the airport to Graceland for her visit at Christmas time. He also drove his Lincoln Continental Mark II from Memphis to Fort Hood where he began his basic training with the U.S. Army. Elvis was quite an automotive enthusiast. His generous spirit lead him to give the majority of the cars which he purchased to friends and family. There were only a few cars that were truly Elvis' favorites, vehicles which he kept and used through his career. This stunning 1956 Lincoln Continental Mark II can certainly be described as one of Elvis' great favorites.

ESTIMATE UPON REQUEST

A79
APRIL
1956
TOUR
FINAN-
CIAL

STATEMENT

One legal size, typed, original carbon copy of the financial statement sent by Thomas Parker management for expenses relating to the April 1956 tour. Included are Elvis' cash advances, pay, taxes, promotions, RCA royalties, expenses, and Col. Parkers commissions. Also included is payment for the Las Vegas engagement of April 23rd. Document signed by Vernon and Elvis, and is in the original envelope sent to Mr. and Mrs. Vernon Presley at 1034 Audubon Drive. 13 x 8 1/2 inches letter. 4 x 9 1/2 inches envelope.

April tour ran for two weeks with twenty-three shows from April eighth to the twenty-first. Elvis earned $21,679.04 for the twenty-three performances. Las Vegas engagement ran for two weeks, and during that time he met Johnnie Ray, and Liberace whose flamboyant style made a big impression on Elvis.

$7,000 - 9,000

A80 ELVIS' FOX THEATER CONTRACT, ATLANTA, MARCH 1956.

Western Union telegram dated March 6, 1956 to Colonel Tom Parker, confirming Elvis' appearances in Atlanta. Two-sided contract from the American Federation of Musicians dated March 8, 1956. The contract was for Elvis and ten additional musicians to appear in the Elvis Presley Show at the Fox Theatre in Atlanta, Georgia, on March 14 and 15, 1956. Payment was $2,000. The contract was signed in blue ink by Col. Tom Parker, Elvis Presley, and Tom Diskin. One-page contract for the

A79

Jordanaires for appearances at the Fox Theatre. Pay is $300. Contract signed by Col. Tom Parker, Gordon Stoker (of the Jordanaires), and Tom Diskin. Two Daily Box Office Report from March 14 and 15, 1956 when Elvis performed at the Fox Theatre in Atlanta, GA. Both of the reports are typed on white paper with a pink carbon copy behind it. Totals were $3355.15 on March 14, and $5424.35 on March 15. Letter dated March 19, 1956 from Frank Vinson, manager of the Fox Theatre, to Colonel Parker. He was shipping back blowups from the show. 5 5/8 x 8 inches telegram. 11 x 8 1/2 inches contracts and letter. 12 x 8 1/2 inches box office reports.

Elvis played Atlanta in December 1955, while he was under the management of Bob Neal. He performed before a small audience. Four months later, under the management of Colonel Parker, the crowds were much heavier for Elvis when he performed March 14 and 15 at the Fox Theatre. Rather than the $300 he received previously, he now took 50% of the profits. The box office reports were typical of the time, dividing the receipts into "white" and "colored" ticket holders and listing "Opposite Attractions," which were movies playing elsewhere in town. Elvis played three shows daily, with "Square Jungle," starring Tony Curtis, shown in between.

$4,000 - 5,000

A81 ELVIS IN MEMPHIS - LANSKY'S CHECK AND AMERICAN FEDERATION OF MUSICIANS LETTER

A81

White check dated March 9, 1956. The check was made out to Lansky Brothers Men's Shop for $103 and signed by E. A. Presley. Typewritten letter addressed to "Dear Sir and Brother" stating that a check was enclosed for $1.40 for Elvis Presley. The check was for an engagement at the Chisca Hotel on March 9, 1956. 28 cents were due to the side men. 3 x 8 inches check. 11 x 8 1/2 inches letter.

Elvis returned to Memphis for a few days from a road trip. On March 9, 1956, he bought some clothing at Lansky's, a local men's store that was one of Elvis' favorites shops. That evening, he appeared at the Chisca Hotel at a gig hosted by Dewey Phillips, well-known local DJ who helped promote Elvis' music. Sy Rose's Band performed as well.

$3,000 - 4,000

A82 EARLY COLONEL PARKER MEMOS AND CHECKS

These memos from the Colonel regard payment of musicians; checks, and receipts. First memo to Elvis Presley regarding the subject of "Payment of Band Members." Memo grants Colonel Parker to "maintain and direct salary for: Mr. Bill Black, Mr. Scotty Moore, Mr. D.J. Fontana." The accounts of the preceding to be maintained on behalf of and in the name of Elvis Presley. Bears signature of Elvis Presley. Following 3 correspondence pieces printed on memo stationery with checks to accompany. Check #849 made out to Mr. Bill Black for $115.00 for salary payment for the week of March 25 - 31. Check #850 for $110.00 made to D.J. Fontana for dates of Feb 26, March 3-9-10-31. Check #848 to Winfield Scott Moore for $115.00 for the week of March 25-31. Photograph included. 2 1/2 x 6 inches checks. 7 1/4 x 8 1/2 inches memos.

This is the first time terms were written out allowing Colonel Parker to take over financial arrangements for paying the band. All checks are written on the First American National Bank of Nashville, Madison, Tennessee, and all are signed "Thomas Francis Diskin". Each check is dated April 4th, 1956. Checks are from an account in the name of "All Star Shows".

$5,000 - 7,000

A83 NEW FRONTIER HOTEL DOCUMENTS

Six original documents from Elvis' 1956 engagement at the Frontier Hotel in Las Vegas. The first, a cash advance of $200.00 to Elvis for his Las Vegas

show at the Frontier. The second and third documents are salary check stubs to Elvis from the William Morris Agency for the performances ending April 29th, and May 6th, at the Frontier. Total pay was $7500.00 less $750.00 for commissions. The fourth document is a Western Union telegram to Tom Diskin from Phil Maraquin confirming acceptance of Presley Tours for show dates at the Frontier. The fifth document is a receipt from Hatch Show Print for color promotional prints. Total bill was $38.35. The sixth document is an original carbon letter on grey stationery with maroon letterhead, dated April 30, 1956. Correspondence is

regarding the "Musician's Protected Union" and payment of dues for appearance at the Las Vegas Hotel. 4 x 8 1/2 inches Telegram. 5 3/4 x 8 3/4 inches Print. 10 1/2 x 7 1/4 inches Letter. 8 1/2 x 3 1/4 inches Receipt. 3 x 8 1/4 inches Cash Advance.

Correspondence is in regards to the week ending May 6, 1956. *This engagement at the Frontier was Elvis' first Las Vegas appearance.*

$2,500 - 3,500

A84 CHECKS AND RECEIPT FOR VARIOUS EARLY SHOWS

Four yellow salary checks written TO SCOTTY Moore, Bill Black, D.J. Fontana, and Elvis. Checks are signed BY TOM Diskin, and represent payment in regards to the second Ed Sullivan Show on October 28, 1956. One yellow check written to the Jordanaires for $1000, and signed by Colonel Parker for October 11 - 14 shows in Texas. Receipt for $1000 payment signed by Gordon Stoker of the Jordanaires. Photograph included. 2 3/4 x 6 1/4 inches checks (4) 3 1/4 x 8 1/4 inches Jordanaire check3 x 8 1/4 inches receipt.

On October 28, Elvis received a polio vaccination as a public service announcement for the March of Dimes. When asked about his influence on teenagers he responds, "My Bible tells me what he sows he will also reap, and if I'm sowing evil and wickedness it will catch up with me. If I did think I was bad for people, I would go back to driving a truck, and I really mean this." While Elvis is attending the rehearsal for the show, the Colonel was handing out "Elvis for President" buttons. During Elvis' second appearance on the Ed Sullivan Show he sang "Don't Be Cruel," "Love Me," "Love Me Tender, " and "Hound Dog."

A84

$8,000 - 10,000

A85 TELEGRAM REGARDING ELVIS' FIRST NUMBER ONE HIT

Western Union telegram dated February 24, 1956. Sent to Col. Parker from Julian Aberbach of Hill and Range publishing company. Aberbach expresses happiness over Elvis reaching #1 in Billboard. Aberbach writes "Now exactly what I discussed is happening, and I am sure you know what I mean." With two page, red-tinted sheet music for "Mystery Train." 5 5/8 x 8 inches telegram. 12 x 9 inches sheet music.

Aberbach is referring to "I Forgot to Remember to Forget"/"Mystery Train," a Sun single re-released by RCA that hit #1 on Billboard's country chart on February 15, 1956.

$700 - 1,000

A86 BILL FROM CAFE DE PARIS AT 20TH CENTURY FOX

A bill from Cafe de Paris at 20th Century Fox for Elvis Presley in Dressing Room #6. Dated October 5, 1956 in the amount of $17.90. Photograph included. 8 1/2 x 5 1/2 inches.

At this time Elvis was on the set of "Love Me Tender," his first feature film. The bill was paid by Trude Forsher, who was the Colonel's secretary in Los Angeles.

$700 - 1000

A87 AUTOMOBILE INSURANCE POLICIES ON ELVIS PRESLEY'S '56 CADILLAC CONVERTIBLE AND '56 LINCOLN CONTINENTAL

Elvis Presley's automobile insurance policy on Elvis' 1956 Convertible Cadillac El Dorado with Public National Insurance Company and McElroy Insurance Agency . The policy was effective September 13, 1956 - September 13, 1957. This air conditioned Cadillac cost $10,000 at purchase. The total premium was $141.00. Automobile insurance policy on Elvis Presley's 1956 Lincoln

A86   A85   A87

Continental with Public National Insurance Company and McElroy Insurance Agency. The white was purchased for $10,668. The policy was effective September 13, 1956 - September 13, 1957. The total premium was $141. The policy is one page with two sides. 28 x 8 1/2"each.

Elvis and June Juanico flew to Houston to purchase the 1956 ivory-colored Cadillac on June 12, 1956. Visitors can now view it on display at Graceland.

$1,000 - 1,500

A88 CASH ADVANCE, INVOICE FOR PLANE TICKETS, LETTER FROM TOM DISKIN, AND A NEW FRONTIER HOTEL BILL

One cash advance of $250.00 written to Elvis on April 17, 1956. Travel Inc., invoice regarding a plane ticket for Elvis to Los Angeles via Tulsa on April 18th, 1956. Attached to invoice is an All Star Shows check for the amount of $106.37. Four passenger coupons from Travel, Inc., on Braniff airlines for Gene Smith and Elvis Presley. Two of the coupons are for travel from Corpus Christi to Waco, Texas, and the other two are from Waco, Texas to Tulsa, Oklahoma. Carbon copy of a letter on gray paper with maroon colored New Frontier Hotel letterhead, dated April 28, 1956. Correspondence is from Tom Diskin to booking agent James Denny regarding commissions for the Carter Sisters. Bill from the New Frontier Hotel. 3 x 8 1/4 inches Checks. 5 3/4 x 8 1/2 inches invoice. 10 1/2 x7 1/4 inches Letter 7 x 7 inches hotel bill. 6 1/2 x 3 3/8 inches travel coupons.

Elvis performed his sixteenth show in Corpus Christi on April 16, 1956. Immediately following the performance the building manager outlawed rock 'n' roll at the coliseum because a number of fans, and their parents, complained that the show was vulgar. Tom Diskin told the Colonel it was another act in the show that was guilty of the vulgar behavior. Elvis performed his seventeenth show the next day, April 17, in Waco, Texas.. He drove out to the field to the stage in his Cadillac. He told one reporter that his fame "happened so fast, I'm scared. You know, I could go out like a light, just like I came on."

$3,500 - 4,500

A89 DOCUMENTS FROM AMARILLO ENGAGEMENT

A three page invoice from capitol Hotel for April 13, 1956, with check from Tom Diskin attached for $76.04. One invoice from Garner-Randall motors for repairs to Elvis' 1954 cadillac limo which the band drove to the gig. Total bill is for $191.80. Copy of the American Federation of Musicians contract, dated April 4, 1956, for Amarillo, Texas engagement on April 13. Three green checks signed by Tom Diskin for Scotty Moore, D.J. Fontana, and Bill Black in payment for the April 8 - 14 performances. Fourth check is dated April 13, 1956 and endorsed by Elvis and Bill Black. 5 1/2 x 8 1/2 inches Hotel invoice. 3 x 8 1/4 Inches Check. 8 1/2 x 10 1/4 inches motors invoice. 8 1/2 x 11 inches contract. 6 x 2 3/4 inches (3) checks. 6 x 2 5/8 inches check

Elvis and his band played at the Municipal Auditorium IN AMARILLO, Texas. This marked the beginning of a two-day break in the tour, and Scotty Moore claimed the crowd noise became so loud the musicians could not hear their music.

$10,000 - 12,000

A90 ELVIS PRESLEY FILM CONTRACT WITH 20TH CENTURY FOX.

Two-page typed contract dated August 13, 1956 addressed to Elvis Presley in Hollywood. Amends and supplements an earlier contract between Elvis and 20th Century Fox from April 2, 1956. Signed by Elvis Presley and Joseph H. Hazen of 20th Century Fox. Photograph included. 11 x 8 1/2 inches.

Elvis' original contract with Wallis and Hazen of Paramount allowed Elvis to do outside movies, but under the condition that he notify them thirty days prior to the start of filming. This contract was drawn up because Elvis notified Wallis and Hazen of his intentions to do a film with 20th Century-Fox Film Corporation. The contract release Elvis to do the film "Love Me Tender." The filming of "Love Me Tender" began August 23, 1956, just ten days after this contract was sent. It was released in November 1956. It was the first of Elvis' 33 films and the only one in which he did not receive top billing.

$10,000 - 15,000

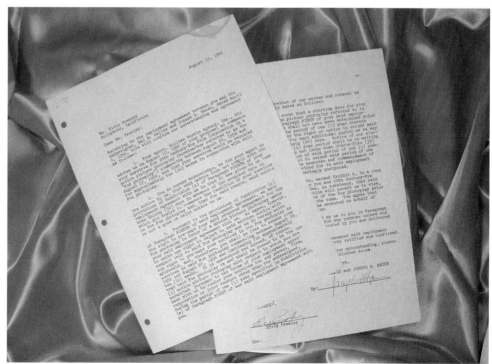

A91 MISSISSIPPI-ALABAMA FAIR & DAIRY SHOW—ELVIS RETURNS TO TUPELO

One page letter typed on Miss.-Ala. Fair & Dairy Show letterhead and signed by the show's President-Manager, J.M. Savery. Dated October 19, 1956. The letter thanks Elvis for his appearance at the September event and also expresses gratitude to Gladys and Vernon Presley, saying "it was certainly a privilege and pleasure to have them back home." One backstage pass for the show, on white card stock with yellow and blue print, issued to Tom Diskin from the account of Elvis Presley. Photograph included. 11 x 8 1/2 inches letter. 2 5/8 x 3 3/4 inches pass.

Elvis performed on September 26 in his birthplace of Tupelo, where the mayor declared it "Elvis Presley Day." Elvis arrived in Tupelo with his parents, then girlfriend Barbara Hearn and friend Nick Adams. He performed two shows before a crowd of 20,000, with a 14 year-old Wynette Pugh (later country singer Tammy Wynette) in the front row. This is the same festival that Elvis performed at as a 10 year-old living in Tupelo. On October 3, 1945 it was "Children's Day" at the Mississippi-Alabama Fair and Dairy Show and Elvis, then in the fifth grade, won 2nd prize at the children's talent show with the country weeper "Old Shep."

$7,000 - 9,000

A92 TOM DISKIN LETTER REGARDING TRAVEL TO "HEARTBREAK HOTEL" RECORDING SESSION

Two letters sent April 24 and June 15, 1956, to the manager of the Plains Aero Service for a refund on a chartered plane. Letters detail a flight that had Elvis and his band fearing for their safety. Total bill was $747.50. Original check to Plains Aero Service for $747.50 signed by Tom Parker. A refund of $223.60 was requested to cover the cost for them to fly the remainder of the way on American Airlines. Plane left Amarillo to Nashville for a RCA Victor recording session. Blue and pink letter from Plains Aero Service dated April 13, 1956. Photograph included. 11 x 8 1/2 inches letter. 3 x 6 1/2 inches. check. 7 3/4 x 5 1/2 inches letter/memo. 8 1/2 x 5 1/2 inches letter.

From this RCA Victor recording session "Heartbreak Hotel" went gold; also cut "I Want You, I Need You, I Love You".

$1,500 - 2,000

A93 SCOTTY MOORE LETTERS

These letters were written on EXTREMELY RARE Elvis Presley stationery (with Associates Scotty and Bill listed underneath) when he was part of the Louisiana Hayride. The letter, dated August 17, 1956, from Scotty Moore to Colonel Parker, is acknowledging receipt of a check and forwarding

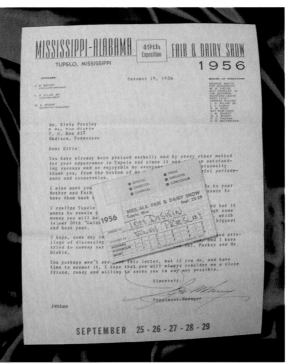

A91

invoices from a record session. Copy of a handwritten letter on loose leaf lined notebook paper dated December 28, 1956. Written to Tom Diskin from Scotty Moore confirming that travel plans have been received. Moore requests in the letter that travel expense checks be mailed so that Moore receives them by Wednesday January 2. Moore also requests that weekly checks for the week of

January 5 be held in New York. In a P.S., Moore requests that any mail also be brought to New York. Two-page interoffice memo dated 12/15/56, white with green lettering, written in pencil and ink, and elaborating on $1,000 Christmas bonuses for Scotty, Bill, and D.J. 11 x 8 1/2 inches 8/17 letter. 10 1/2 x 8 inches 12/28 letter. 7 1/4 x 8 1/2 inches memo.

Scotty Moore and Bill Black played with Elvis from the beginning recording sessions in July 1954. As Elvis became more famous and moved his career toward more films, Scotty and Bill felt they were missing their share of the financial success, so they quit the band in September 1957. Bill continued to work with Elvis after that on a per job arrangement until Elvis entered the Army in 1958. Scotty played with Elvis many his recordings until June 1968 and on his "68 Special."

$4,000 - 6,000

A93A JEWELRY STORE LETTER

Letter to Elvis Presley from Julius Goodman & Son in Memphis, Tennessee dated September 11, 1956. Addressed to Elvis Presley c/o Twentieth Century Fox Studio in Hollywood, California. Letter starts off congratulating Elvis for his great success. Continues to explain that they sold Elvis a horseshoe ring in previous months. The writer acknowledges newspaper reports that Elvis has a new girlfriend and suggests that if he needs an engagement ring he might return to Julius Goodman & Son. They have a 4-carat emerald cut diamond ring that is "reasonably priced." Ends by saying they would love a visit when Elvis is back in Memphis. Signed by Joseph A. Goodman. Photograph included. 10 1/2 x 7 1/4 inches letter.

The horseshoe ring referred to in the letter was raffled off at a July 4, 1956 concert Elvis performed at Russwood Park in Memphis.

$800 - 1,000

A94 ELVIS' FIRST LAS VEGAS TRIP - TELEGRAM AND CLOTHING RECEIPT

Western Union Telegraph Company receipt on beige paper, dated November 9, 1956. The telegraph for $1,000 was sent from Vernon Presley in Memphis to Elvis Presley at the New Frontier Hotel in Las Vegas, Nevada. Pink receipt with blue carbon from Jack Garn Men's Shop Ltd. in Las Vegas, dated November 10, 1956. Elvis paid cash for two pairs of slacks and 2 jackets for his wardrobe totaling $93.79. 4 3/4 x 7 inches telegraph. 8 1/2 x 5 1/2 inches men's shop receipt.

After Elvis' first visit to Las Vegas, he fell in love with the city and went there as often as possible. With his cousin Gene Smith and the Colonel's brother-in-law, Bitsy Mott, he boarded a train on November 8, 1956 from Memphis to Vegas. While on his 10-day vacation, he had Vernon wire him extra money, went shopping to expand his wardrobe, and saw Liberace in a show.

$1,500 - 2,000

A94A MILTON BERLE PROGRAM - DOCUMENTS FOR PURCHASE OF COPY OF THE SHOW

One original invoice from NBC Television Films dated September 21, 1956, for one sixteen millimeter print of Elvis' appearance on the Milton Berle show, June 5, 1956. Included is an All Star Show's check in the amount of $25.00 paying for invoice. 8 1/2 x 8 1/2" invoice. 3 x 8 1/4" check.

Elvis appeared twice on Milton Berle's program; once on April 3rd, and on June 5 (in Hollywood). He sang "Hound Dog," and "I Want You, I Need You, I Love You." This was the first time the Joranaires had backed up Elvis on Television. Berle presented Elvis two "Billboard" Triple Crown Awards for "Heartbreak Hotel" during this show.

$1,000 -1,500

A96

A95 RCA PROMOTIONAL CONTRACT

Two typed pages signed by Elvis Presley, Col. Tom Parker and RCA Vice-President and Operations Manager H.L. Letts. Dated October 26, 1956. Contract for an agreement between Elvis and RCA for Elvis to endorse RCA Victor "Victrola" phonographs. Contract stipulates that 50% of payments be made to Elvis Presley and 50% to the Elvis Presley Fan Club in Beverly Hills. Victorola phonograph included. 11 x 8 1/2 inches.

Fan club payments are specified to go through Hank Saperstein, Colonel Parker's merchandising manager who also supervised the fan Clubs.

$8,000 - 10,000

A96 "ELVIS PRESLEY SPEAKS!"

Black and white magazine with glossy color cover. Sixty-six pages, approximately 100 photographs. Text written by Memphis "Press-Scimitar" reporter and Elvis confidant Robert "Bob" Johnson. Photos taken by Memphis "Commercial Appeal" photographer Robert Williams. Published by Rave Publications, copyright 1956, at a cover price of 25 cents. Includes typed memo dated November 15, 1956, sent to Tom Diskin from Hill and Range representative Grelun Landon about the publication of the magazine. 10 1/4 x 8" magazine. 7 1/4 x 8 1/2" memo.

This was one of the very first Elvis Presley fan publications. The magazine's cover includes "Elvis Says" quotes: "I've thought I've been in love, but mostly I've played the field. I enjoy dating more than anything. Is that wrong?" and "I like a girl who's fun to be with, who enjoys just going out and looking around."

$800 - 1,000

A97 TELEGRAM FROM COLONEL TOM PARKER REGARDING LYNCHBURG, VA SHOW

Western Union Telegram dated March 5. Sent by Col. Tom Parker to Allen Harvey at Harvey's Motel in Lynchburg, Virginia. Telegram outlines conditions and payment for upcoming Elvis Presley Show. 10 x 8 inches.

Perhaps Allen Harvey was unhappy with the Colonel's terms because this show in Lynchburg never developed.

$ 300 - 500

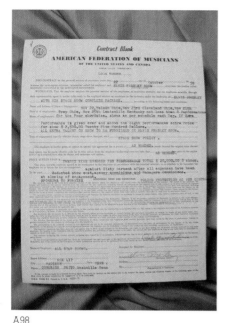

A98

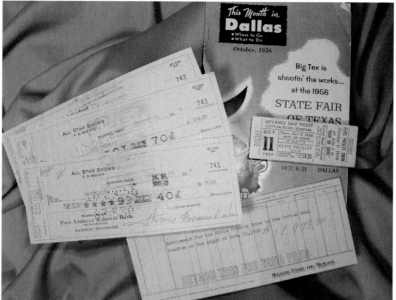

A101

Elvis had signed his contract with RCA on November 15, 1955 and it was set to go in effect on November 21. The first letter, from Kalcheim to Parker note of congratulations on the Elvis/RCA deal. The letter to Fuller from Kalcheim announces that Elvis' "TV affairs" have been put into William Morris' hands by the Colonel and inquires about Elvis making an appearance on an NBC TV show. The third letter, from Kalcheim to the Colonel, updates the Colonel on Kalcheim's dealings with NBC. Elvis would in fact make his national television debut on CBS, on the Jackie Gleason-produced "Stage Show" in January of 1956. It would first appear on NBC that April on Milton Berle's show.

$1,000 -1,500

A98 OHIO/KENTUCKY CONTRACT

One page typed contract on American Federation of Musicians letterhead. Signed by Elvis Presley. Contract dated October 22, 1956 for eight performances and four show dates for "The Elvis Presley Show" in Ohio and Kentucky between November 22 and November 25. Contract stipulates payment of $2,500 per show. 11 x 8 1/2 inches.

On the last show covered by this early contract, November 25 in Louisville, Kentucky, Elvis visited with his estranged grandfather Jesse D. Presley, Vernon's father, who was working at a Pepsi bottling plant in Louisville. Elvis bought his grandfather a new car on this day.

$5,000 - 7,000

A99 HANK SNOW LETTER TO BILL BULLOCK

Original letter, on Hank Snow Letterhead, sent to Bill Bullock at the Record Department of RCA New York. Letter asks for suggestions regarding Elvis setup, and an attempt at a better deal with Sun Records. 11 x 8 1/2 inches.

Hank Snow was a partner with the Colonel at this time, and the Colonel was pitching Bullock on a possible deal for Elvis with RCA.

$1,000 - 2,000

A100 WILLIAM MORRIS LETTERS REGARDING THE SIGNING OF ELVIS PRESLEY TO RCA

Two one-page typed letters on William Morris Agency stationery, sent to Colonel Parker from Harry Kalcheim of William Morris. One letter dated November 18, 1955 and hand-initialed in blue ink by Kalcheim with a handwritten note at bottom. One letter dated November 25, 1955 and hand-initialed in blue ink by Kalcheim. One page typed letter on William Morris Agency stationery, sent to Sam Fuller of NBC from Harry Kalcheim and dated November 23, 1955. In the Fuller letter, Kalcheim writes, "RCA just tied up a youngster, Elvis Presley, a sensational singer very much on the order of Johnnie Ray." Photograph included. 11 x 8 1/2 inches letter #1. 11 x 8 1/2 inches letter #2. 8 x 8 1/2 inches letter #3.

A101 DALLAS CONCERT PAYCHECKS, TICKET, AND PROGRAM

Three salary checks written on All Star Shows for Bill Black, Scotty Moore, and DJ Fontana for week ending 10/20/56. Checks are dated 10/19/56, and signed by Tom Diskin. All three checks have an unreadable note in the upper left hand corner. Original, yellow with red/black print, ticket. Five page program booklet with advertisements, and two references to Elvis; one includes a brief paragraph about Elvis. 3 x 8 1/4 inches checks. 4 x 1 9/16 inches ticket. 9 x 5 3/4 inches program.

During this concert Elvis drove onto the football field in an open convertible. There were so many flash bulbs going off, someone remarked that it looked like war.

$5,000 - 7,500

A102 HOTEL NEW FRONTIER BILL AND CHECK TO ELVIS PRESLEY

Bill dated May 9, 1956 from the Hotel New Frontier in Las Vegas, Nevada, for Elvis and his group from April 22 to May 7. Bill is a 2-week accounting of expenses incurred there during a 2-week stay, including room charges, laundry, restaurant, and phone calls. A check dated May 5, 1956 is made out to Elvis Presley and signed by Thomas Francis Diskin on his All Star Shows account. The amount is $150 for car expenses for his trip from Las Vegas to Memphis. Check is from the Madison Branch of First American National Bank and cashed by the Bank of Las Vegas for the New Frontier Hotel Corporation Casino Exchange Account. Photograph included. 6 3/4 x 7 inches and 10 x 6 inches bills. 3 x 8 1/4 inches check.

Elvis first appeared in Las Vegas for a two-week engagement at the New Frontier Hotel's Venus Room. Billed third on the lineup, he appeared behind Freddy Martin and his orchestra and comedian Shecky Greene. The audiences definitely were older crowds and not as taken with Elvis' music. On Saturday, April 28, the Colonel arranged for a teenagers' matinee for $1, which included admittance to the show and a free soft drink.

$6,000 - 7,000

A103 FLAMINGO HOTEL BILL AND CHECK FOR PAYMENT

Three page hotel bill from the Flamingo Hotel, San Antonio, Texas for Clem Reno (Elvis Presley), Nick Adams, and Gene Smith for the nights of October 14th and 15th, 1956. Room rate is $33.00/night. Total bill comes to $105.59. Original check dated October 15, 1956, from All Star Shows in the amount of $105.59. 8 1/2 x 7 inches bill. 3 x 8 1/4 inches check.

Appearances were held at the outdoor Bexar County Coliseum. They stayed at the Flamingo Hotel in rooms 107, 108 and 109.

$1,000 - 1,500

A104 1956 FLORIDA TOUR CONTRACT AND LICENSE

Original August 3, 1956, American Federation of Musicians contract for Elvis and band, signed by Elvis. Contract is to cover August 3 through the 12th performances in Miami, Tampa, Lakeland, St. Petersburg, Orlando, Dayton and Jacksonville Florida, plus New Orleans LA. Original State and County Occupational License is also included for August 8, 1956 show in Orlando. Total cost of license was $37.75. 11 x 8 1/2".

During their engagement at Jacksonville Florida, Elvis was warned by Maron Gooding to tone down his stage show. In response, Elvis went on stage and wiggled his finger, and the audience went crazy.

$8,000 - 10,000

A105 ELVIS PRESLEY STATIONERY

One sheet of blank, pink "Elvis Presley" stationery with RCA Victor/Elvis Presley letterhead at bottom and a photo of Elvis in the top left corner. Typed "drawing account" records on back, hand-dated August 11, 1956, for expenses for Elvis' 1956 Florida tour. 11 x 8 1/2 inches.

This rare stationery lists the address of Colonel Parker's office in Madison, Tennessee, and was printed immediately after Elvis' RCA signing.

$800 - 1,000

A106 NOTE TO COLONEL TOM PARKER FROM JACK PAAR

Typed note to Colonel Tom Parker from Jack Paar. Noted dated July 10 and is on "Tonight" NBC

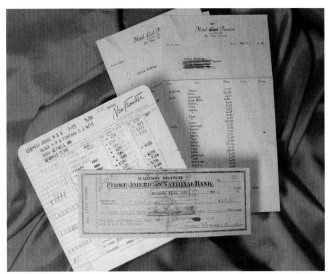
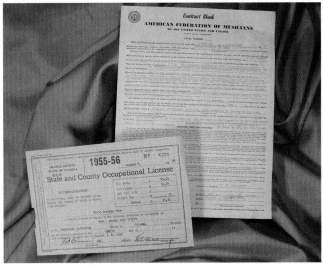

A102
A104

Television letterhead. Paar states that it was wonderful to hear from Colonel Parker and that if he ever comes on the show he would be one of "the more colorful characters around." Writes that he can be reached at the Hotel Algonquin. Signed in blue ink, "Jack." 8 3/8 x 5 1/2 inches.

Jack Paar was the original "Tonight Show "host. The Hotel Algonquin was where literary elite stayed and lunched in New York City.

$200 - 300

A107 ELVIS PRESLEY'S PERSONAL APPEARANCE CONTRACT FOR HOUSTON COLISEUM

Contract for Elvis Presley and his Variety Show Vaudeville Acts to play the Houston Coliseum on October 13, 1956 and the San Antonio Coliseum on October 14. Contract lists payment as $15,000 against 50% of the gross receipts after taxes. Colonel Parker reserves the right to substitute other talent, if necessary, but not Elvis. Western Swing Enterprises sponsors the show and the contract is signed by their president, A.V. Bamford, and Colonel Tom Parker. A large photo of Elvis singing and playing his guitar fronts the contract with the words Personal Appearance Contract at top and Elvis Presley in salmon-colored lettering and "The Nation's Only Atomic Powered Singer" underneath. Twenty six black-and-white photos of Elvis border three sides. 38 x 8 1/2 inches

The booking agent for this performance, A.V. Bamford, once worked out of Nashville so he and the Colonel were friends; later he relocated his business to Hollywood. Elvis performed two shows--4 p.m. and 9 p.m.-- on October 13. Elvis was coming from a performance in Waco and arrived late for his first show. He was greeted by 8,000 screaming fans, mostly teenagers, for that show, and the same amount for the second show. Even before the performances, organizers were having problems keeping fans in line. Elvis appeared in San Antonio the next day at 3 p.m. and 8 p.m. shows to similar frenzied crowds at the Bexar County Coliseum.

$9,000 - 11,000

A108 CONTRACT FOR JACKSONVILLE, FLORIDA SHOWS, FEBRUARY 23-24, 1956

Contract dated February 9, 1956 between Jamboree Attractions and Jacksonville show sponsors, Glenn Reeves, Marshall Roland, Frank Theis, and Mrs. Mae Axton. Occupational License from Duval County, Florida, 1955-56. Cost $75.25. Copy of a ticket sales sheet showing amount of tickets sold and totals. Net balance for the shows was $8536.90. Signed by Tom Diskin, tour manager. 4 tickets for early 1956 Jamboree Attractions. 14 x 8 1/2" contract. 3 3/4 x 8 1/2" license. 11 x 8 1/2" ticket sales sheet. 1 x 2 inches tickets.

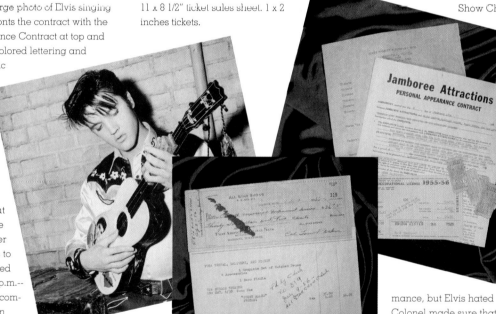

A108

A109

The Jamboree Attractions Shows played Jacksonville, Florida, on February 23 and 24, 1956. After the show on February 23, Elvis collapsed from exhaustion. The doctor recommended that he needed to slow down. He did, however, appear in the show on February 24, which was the same day he learned he would have a screen test with Hal Wallis at Paramount Studios.

$6,000 - 8,000

A109 STEVE ALLEN SHOW INSTRUMENT RENTAL

A109 STEVE ALLEN SHOW INSTRUMENT RENTAL

Receipt from Carroll Musical Instrument Service of New York City, in the name of Mr. C.E. Crumpacker of RCA Victor Corporation, and dated June 30 ,1956. Order # 3654 is for the rental, delivery and pickup of "One Complete Set of Matched Drums and Accessories, One Bass Fiddle". To be delivered to Hudson Theater on Saturday at 6:30 for noon use. In quotes is the name "Steve Allan" and below that is printed "Presley" (not in quotes). Total comes to $36.05. Instrument rental for Elvis' appearance on the Steve Allan Show. Bill has notes to indicate the bill was "pd by check no 319 July 9-56- All Star Show Check". All Star Show check # 319 also included in the amount of $36.05. Dated July 9, 1956. Check signed by Colonel Tom Parker. 3 x 8 1/4 inches check. 7 1/4 x 8 1/2 inches bill.

Due to previous bad press, Elvis was asked to perform on the "Steve Allen" show in a tuxedo, and sing to a hound dog. Not only was the dog extremely upset during the performance, but Elvis hated the whole idea. The Colonel made sure that for any engagements after this show Elvis would have total control over both wardrobe and song selection.

$1,500 - 2,500

A110 ELVIS PRESLEY'S 1956 ADDRESS BOOK

Black hard bound address book with gold E.P. initials on the front cover. Inside are white pages with gray lines and the alphabet on maroon tabs separated by yellow pages. Some of the names and address listed are: Anita Wood, Nick Adams, Colonel Tom Parker, Jean Smith, Alan Fortas, George Klein, Yvonne Lime and Piper Laurie (names crossed out), and many more.

$20,000 - 30,000

A111 CHARLOTTE, NORTH CAROLINA SHOW DOCUMENTS, 1956

Two copies of the Gross Receipts Tax for performance of June 26, 1956. One copy of the box office statement showing sales of show. Original contract of American Federation of Musicians, signed by Elvis on June, 18th, for the concert on the 26th. One original, with copy of an invoice, from WAYS radio for thirty-two one minute announcements. Total bill is $152.24. *memorabilia. 11 x 8 1/2 inches Tax receipt. 13 x 9 inches Box Office statement. 11 x 8 1/2 inches Radio invoice. 11 x 8 1/2 inches contract.

It was during Elvis' concert in Charlotte that he mentions the blues singer Arthur Crudup and how greatly he admires him. "I used to hear old Arthur Crudup bang his box the way I do now, and I said if I ever got to the place where I could feel all old Arthur felt, I'd be a music man like nobody ever saw."

$7,000 - 8,000

A112 LETTER TO MR. & MRS. VERNON PRESLEY FROM THE *COMMERCIAL APPEAL*

Typed letter written on The Commercial Appeal letterhead (well-known Memphis newspaper) and dated October 20, 1956. Correspondence is addressed to Mr. and Mrs. Vernon Presley at 1034 Audobon Drive in Memphis from James D. Kingsley of The Commercial Appeal's Tupelo Bureau. Kingsley notes he has enclosed an album of photos from Elvis' "Homecoming Celebration at Tupelo". There is a mention of his pleasurable experience of working with Elvis that day, and goes on to request an autographed Elvis photo to Witt Presley of the

Tupelo Fire Department. He has enclosed two photos - one of his wife and one of his secretary - for Elvis to sign. The P.S.: "I hope your son shall always be as considerate of the press as he was September 26". Original envelope and photograph included. 11 x 8 1/2 inches letter. 4 1/4 x 9 1/2 inches envelope.

This is just one of many examples of the praises of Elvis Presley.

$400 - 500

A113 WESTERN UNION TELEGRAM FROM COLONEL PARKER TO VERNON PRESLEY

One page original Western Union telegram from Colonel Parker to Vernon Presley dated April 17, 1957. Correspondence mentions a sixteen millimeter machine Elvis received from RCA for Christmas, tunes Elvis wishes to record , and a mention of an award for "Don't Be Cruel." 10 x 8 1/2 inches.

Elvis loved to watch movies at home so the Colonel suggested to RCA that a sixteen millimeter machine would be ideal for a Christmas gift. In order for Elvis to get publishing credits, arrangements had to be made in advance of the recording sessions, therefore songs needed to selected in advance.

$250 - 300

A114 "LOVING YOU" WARDROBE LETTER FROM NUDIE'S RODEO TAILORS

Original signed correspondence dated December 4, 1956 to Col. Parker. This one page typed letter requests complete measurements on Elvis for the Paramount movie "Loving You." Measurements are written in pencil at bottom of page. Photo of Nudie attached. 10 1/2 x 7 1/4 inches letter. 8 x 11 inches Photograph

Elvis' measurements are listed at the bottom of the letter in pencil: waist 32", Pants Length 32 1/2", Hat 7 1/4", Shoe 10, Shirt 15 1/2", Suite 40, And coat 40.

$3,000 - 4,000

A115 LETTER FROM TOM DISKIN TO BOB NEAL REGARDING RECORDING SESSION PLANS

Letter on Colonel Parker's letterhead dated January 5, 1956, to Bob Neal from Tom Diskin. Diskin relays a letter from a Mr. Shoals who plans to arrive in Nashville on Sunday, January 8, and would like to record with Elvis the following morning, and continue on until Wednesday. Diskin requests from Neal, Elvis' arrival time in Nashville for the recording session so he may advise Mr. Shoals. 11 x 8 1/2 inches letter.

Correspondence is regarding Elvis' first recording session with RCA in Nashville. Colonel Parker's letterhead is unique and rare and includes "Hank Snow" imprinted name and address.

$800 - 1,000

A116 MERCHANDISING CORRESPONDENCE, 1956

In a letter to Elvis dated October 20, 1956 Hank Saperstein, of Special Projects, Inc., Merchandising Directors for Elvis Presley Enterprises, explains his reasons for sending accounting sheet and payment for all monies received and deposited to date. Listing is titled "Cash Receipts--From Inception to Date" and lists 21 licensee companies and amounts, including Aristocrat Leather ($1,000), Majestic Stationery ($5,000), and Faith Shoe Co. ($5,000). Totals include $7,566.36 due William Morris Agency, and net amount due to Elvis and the Colonel, $11,548.62. Bronze-colored statue of Elvis singing with his guitar; unbreakable styrene plastic. Photograph included. 10 1/2 x 7 1/4 inches letter. 11 x 8 1/2 inches listing. 8 1/2 inches statue.

In the summer of 1956, Hank Saperstein, a California merchandiser, became exclusive merchandising and "exploitation" manager for Elvis products. Exploitation was a term used frequently at the time for finding the best exposure for stars. Saperstein had been successful with Lassie, the Lone Ranger, and Wyatt Earp. He started with 29 products, such as belts, scarves, statuettes, and lipsticks, and his campaign began full force with the release of "Love Me Tender."

$1,500 - 2,500

A117 MEMPHIS COTTON CARNIVAL ITEMS

Nine American Federation of Musicians contracts for May 13-19, 1956 for Memphis Cotton Carnival. Contracts for: Elvis Presley and the Blue Moon Boys, dated April 30, with signature. Hal and Ginger Wallis, two contracts dated April 17, with signature. George Morgan and his Candy Kids, dated May 1, with signature. Grand Ole Opry Show (9 musicians), dated May 1, no signature. Maybelle, Helen, and Anita Carter and Don Davis, dated May 1, with Maybelle signature. June Carter, two contracts dated May 1, no signature. Charley Stewart, dated May 13, with signature. Brown envelope addressed to Royal American Shows; from Colonel Parker and Jamboree Attractions. Handwritten notes on back. Western Union telegram dated April 9 to Col. Parker from Bob Neal: "Please advise talent on May 15 show so I can start promotion." Western Union telegram dated April 10 to Col. Parker in Wichita Falls, Texas, from Carolyn Asmus in Madison, Tennessee. Message regards papers Elvis is sending the Colonel and that Elvis needed to speak to him. 10 x 8 1/2 inches contracts. 9 x 12 inches envelope. 5 3/4 x 8 1/8 inches telegrams.

The Cotton Picking Jamboree starred as part of Memphis' 22nd annual Cotton Festival or Carnival. Elvis only performed on its opening night, May 15, 1956. He and Hank Snow shared top billing at Ellis Auditorium to a crowd of about 7,000. Some of Elvis' show stopping tunes included "Hound Dog" "Long Tall Sally." The Carters, George Morgan, and the Willises played at the Tent Theater and offered their best in country shows.

$9,000 - 11,000

A118 COLONEL PARKER STATIONERY

Thirteen piece packet of Colonel Parker stationery, envelopes, mailing labels and note paper. In varying sizes. One eight-piece set of "Thomas A. Parker Exclusive Management" stationery, envelopes and mailing labels. Blue and red print with the Colonel's covered wagon logo. One three-piece set of "Boxcar Enterprises" stationery, envelope and mailing label. With black print with the train boxcar and double-six dice logo. One sheet of RCA Victor stationery that reads "From

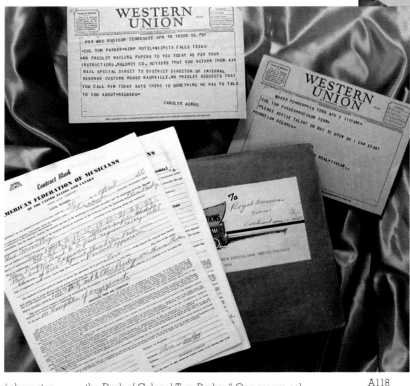

the Desk of Colonel Tom Parker." One cream-colored note pad with a watermarked photograph of Colonel Parker on each sheet.

$500 - 700

A118

A117

A119 WESTERN UNION TELEGRAM TO COLONEL TOM PARKER REGARDING AN ED SULLIVAN OFFER

Original 1956 Western Union telegram to Col. Parker regarding three offers for Elvis to appear on the Ed Sullivan Show. Show dates scheduled for September 5, and October 28, 1956, and January 6, 1957. Photographs included. 10 3/4 x 8 1/2 inches.

Ed Sullivan was once quoted as saying that he would never allow Elvis on his show. However, after seeing him on the Steve Allen Show he changed his mind. In fact, when Elvis did perform on the Ed Sullivan Show, Mr. Sullivan told the audience, "This is a real decent, fine boy." One of the terms for Elvis' appearance on the Ed Sullivan show was that he would have complete control over his wardrobe and song selection. This was in direct response to his performance on the Steve Allen Show were he was made to wear a tux and sing "Hound Dog" to a hound dog. Elvis absolutely hated that performance.

$3,000 - 4,000

A120 TELEGRAMS AND LETTER REGARDING ELVIS PRESLEY'S APPEARANCE ON THE STAGE SHOW

One beige Western Union telegram to Steve Yates from Colonel Parker dated December 15, 1955 with specifics about Elvis' appearance on the Stage Show. Three beige Western Union Telegram between Col. Tom Parker and Steve Yates dated February 2. The telegrams discuss arrangements for Elvis' appearance on the "Stage Show" in March 1956. Photograph included. Tom Parker wrote to Steve Yates of Yates Artist Corporation on March 5, 1956. He enclosed a check for $500, Yates' commission on Elvis' four appearances on the Jackie Gleason show. Written on official Colonel Parker stationery. 10 x 8 inches telegrams. 11 x 8 1/2 inches.

A120

A122

Steve Yates booked Elvis on the Stage Show. He had already appeared once, and the show management wanted to add six additional shows at $15,000, with an option for seven more.

$2,000 - 2,500

A121 TELEGRAM TO COLONEL TOM PARKER FROM ELVIS PRESLEY, 1956

Western Union telegram to Colonel Parker from Elvis Presley dated November 9, 1956 from Greenriver, Wyoming. Message related that Elvis will be in Los Angeles for his appointment. "Am stopping over in Las Vegas for a few hours. Hope the DJ Convention is going well. Wish I could have made it as I did last year." It was signed: "Elvin" Presley. 6 x 8 inches.

Elvis never performed in Wyoming, so the telegram must have been routed through there back to the

Colonel. He did, however, arrive in Las Vegas by train from Memphis on November 9. He remained in Vegas until November 12, when he rented a car to drive to Los Angeles. The DJ convention he mentions was always held in Nashville in the fall. Elvis had attended the previous one in 1955. That's were he became reacquainted with Mae Axton, who introduced him to her song, "Heartbreak Hotel."

$700 - 900

A122 TELEGRAM FROM THE LANSKY BROTHERS WITH SIGNED CHECK FROM ELVIS

Western Union telegram dated October 28, 1956. Addressed to Elvis Presley and Dewey Phillips at "The Ed Sullivan Show" from Memphis clothing merchants Bernard and Guy Lansky. One check written to "Lansky Bros. Men's Shop" in the amount of $46.33, dated June 1, 1956 and signed in blue ink

"E.A. Presley." Photograph included. 5 3/4 x 8 inches telegram. 2 3/4 x 6 1/8 inches check.

The Lansky brothers write: "WATCHING YOUR SHOW IN DALLAS TEXAS ATTENDING BIGGEST MENS FASHION SHOW IN COUNTRY, ALSO PICKING YOUR NEXT SHARP OUTFIT. IF POSSIBLE TO MAKE CASUAL REMARK ABOUT LANSKY BROTHERS MENS SHOP ON FAMOUS BEALE STREET WOULD REALLY APPRECIATE IT" Elvis began shopping at Lansky's on Beale as a teenager and continued to patronize the shop through out his life. This particular telegram was sent to Elvis as he was preparing for his second appearance on "The Ed Sullivan Show." (See introductory article in this catalogue written by Bernard Lansky.)

$3,000 - 4,000

A123 TUPELO HOMECOMING TELEGRAMS

One Western Union telefax (2 sheets) sent September 22, 1956 to Elvis in Beverly Hills from M.C. Dougherty, Community Development Foundation President in Tupelo. Message states that Chamber of Commerce has luncheon planned on September 26 to honor Elvis' homecoming. "You will not be exposed to the public. . . Your mother and father have been invited. Reply stating number in your party." Second telegram taken by telephone for Vernon or Mrs. Presley at their Audubon Drive address. Dated September 26, 1956. Message regards arrangements for police escort into Tupelo. Photograph included. 4 1/2 x 6 1/2 inches 9/22 telefax. 6 x 8 1/2 inches 9/26 message.

Elvis played Tupelo, Mississippi, on September 26, 1956, his first return to the town where he grew up.

$400 - 500

A124 ELVIS PRESLEY FAN CLUB PACKAGE

One page typed letter on Special Projects, Inc. stationery, dated December 20, 1956. Sent to Col. Parker along with a sample of the package sent to those making inquiries about Elvis Presley Fan Club. Fan club package contains: The original typed copy of a one page letter on "Elvis Presley" stationery with a stamped Elvis Presley signature. Two double-sided sheets on blue paper, one with advertisements for Elvis Presley souvenirs on both sides, the other with advertisements for Elvis Presley souvenirs on one side and and a typed version of "The Elvis Presley Story" bio on the other. One Special Order Blank on blue paper. One Elvis Presley Fan Club membership card on yellow card stock (this sample made out to "Mr. Tom Diskin" in Madison, Tenn.) One pink Elvis Presley Fan Club return envelope. One white envelope from Elvis Presley Fan Club postmarked December 19, 1956 from Beverly Hills, California. 11 x 8 1/2" letter; 8 1/2 x 5 1/2 " Fan Club letter; 5 1/2 x 5" blue sheet #1; 8 1/2 x 5 1/2" blue sheet #2; 5 1/2 x 3 1/2" order blank; 3 1/4 x 6 1/4" membership card; 3 1/2 x 6" return envelope; 3 5/8 x 6 1/2 " envelope.

Fan club letter reads "But between the movies, records, TV and personal appearances, they've got me hopping around like a jack rabbit being chased around like a hound dog," and has a full body photo of Elvis in top left corner. Souvenirs for order include a 7 1/2 inch plastic statuette ($1.00), an "intimate message" on a "Special Gold record" ($.50 each), an 8 x 10 glow-in-the-dark photo ($1.00) and "Elvis Presley Lipstick" ("Keep me always on your lips!" $1.00 each). Special Projects, Inc. was a Beverly Hills based firm that was owned by Hank Saperstein and that began managing Elvis Presley merchandise in 1956. Saperstein also handled administration for the Elvis Presley National Fan Club.

$2,000 - 3,000

A125 ELVIS PRESLEY: AMERICA'S ONLY ATOMIC POWERED SINGER

Telegram from the Colonel in New Mexico to Harry Kalcheim (of the William Morris Agency), dated April 13, 1956. Colonel discusses the success of the Albuquerque shows, noting that they were covered by the London Daily Mirror. In regards to Elvis' Las Vegas Booking, Colonel suggests using the same

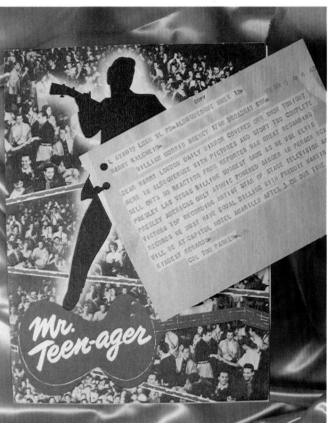

A125

billing of "Elvis Presley America's Only Atomic Powered Singer" and points out that Elvis must be given equal billing with Freddie Martin. Notes that they will be stopping at the Capitol Hotel in Amarillo. Also included is a rare black, white, and purple "Mr. Teenager" booklet. 5 3/4 x 8 inches telegram. 12 x 9 inches booklet .

The telegrams were sent right before Elvis played Las Vegas for the first time. Colonel Parker used the phrase "Elvis Presley America's Only Atomic

Powered Singer" for a Las Vegas billboard. "Mr. Teenager" booklet was never approved by the Colonel, therefore there was only about twenty-five made making this book very rare.

$4,000 - 5,000

A126 "JAILHOUSE ROCK" PRINT

Case containing Elvis' personal 16 mm print of "Jailhouse Rock." Case is brown with metal corners, a handle on one end and a horizontal and vertical buckled strap. 15 1/4 x 15 3/4 inches film case.

The 1957 M-G-M production "Jailhouse Rock" was Elvis' third feature film and one of his most popular. Elvis plays Vince Everett, a young man who serves 14 months in prison for manslaughter and becomes a rock and roll star after his release. The film features a fabulous slate of Leiber and Stoller songs and the famous "Jailhouse Rock" production number.

$2,000 - 3,000

A127 LETTER REGARDING "LOVE ME TENDER" STATUE OF ELVIS PRESLEY

Letter dated October 16, 1956 to Tom Diskin from Harry Kalcheim of the William Morris Agency on official agency letterhead. Note reads: "We called the 20th Century Fox publicity department and they advised that they have not planned anything except the unveiling of the 'statue' of Elvis on the marquee of the Paramount Theatre on October 28th . . . ." Photograph included. 8 x 8 1/2 inches.

"Love Me Tender," Elvis' first film, premiered in New York City at the Paramount Theatre in Times Square on November 15, 1956. The theater unveiled a 40-foot statue of Elvis on top of its marquee on October 28 to announce the opening of the film and promote the actor. Richard Egan and Debra Paget starred with Elvis in this picture.

$900 - 1,000

A128 PERSONAL APPEARANCE POSTER AND
CONTRACTS FOR FOX THEATRE IN DETROIT,
MICHIGAN

An American Federation of Musicians typed contract, drafted on May 1, 1956 to employ thirteen musicians, including Elvis, for a performance at the Fox Theatre in Detroit, Michigan on Friday, May 25, 1956. Poster (printed on cardboard) of performance at the Fox Theatre. 8 1/2 x 10 13/16 inches contracts, 14 3/16 x 22 inches poster.

 A list of all thirteen musicians is typed on the reverse of the agreement in this order: Elvis Presley, Bill Black, Scotty Moore, D.J. Fontana, Rick Flame, Jerry Ross, Wayne Ford, Marty Scatina, Bob Allen, Gordon Stoker, Neil Matthews and Hoyt Hawkins. This contract was formalized and signed by the William Morris Agency and drafted on May 8, 1956. The contract stipulates payment as $6,000 plus 70% of gross admission receipts in excess of fifteen thousand dollars for three stage shows to be performed on Friday, May 25, 1956 at the Fox Theatre in Detroit, Michigan. Other provisions state that the $6000 is to be paid upon execution of the contract and the balance, "if any," after the engagement. Additional clauses include, "Employer will furnish Employee a certified copy of box office statement immediately following conclusion of the engagement. Employee to furnish and pay for one hour stage show. Employer to furnish and pay all other costs and expenses including but not limited to eighteen musicians, stage hands, not

less than $2500.00 for advertising and, additionally, Employer agrees that there will be a new first run motion picture photoplay presented during this engagement." Also included in the agreement is Elvis' authorization to sell souvenir programs and song books during the performance. The contract is signed by Colonel Tom Parker, on behalf on Elvis, in blue ink.

Accompanying these original contracts, is an original poster of that performance at the Fox Theatre which features an intense Elvis pictured full-body and centered. Elvis was scheduled to perform three times at 4:00, 7:00 and 9:45 PM all on the same day. Tickets to the performance for all seats were $1.50. This cardboard poster seemingly was sent through the mail (in a single folded state) as on the reverse side it features the handwritten address of Co. Tom Parker, Box 417, Madison, Tennessee. It has a return address of Fox Michigan Corporation, 2211 Woodward Avenue, Detroit, Michigan. It has four cancelled 3 cent stamps and a Detroit postmark dated May 10, 1956.

This poster is generally believed to be the only surviving example of its kind known to exist, making it the rarest of the rare. The combination of this valuable poster with the original contracts for the performance promoted in the poster represents a truly extraordinary lot.

$20,000 - 30,000

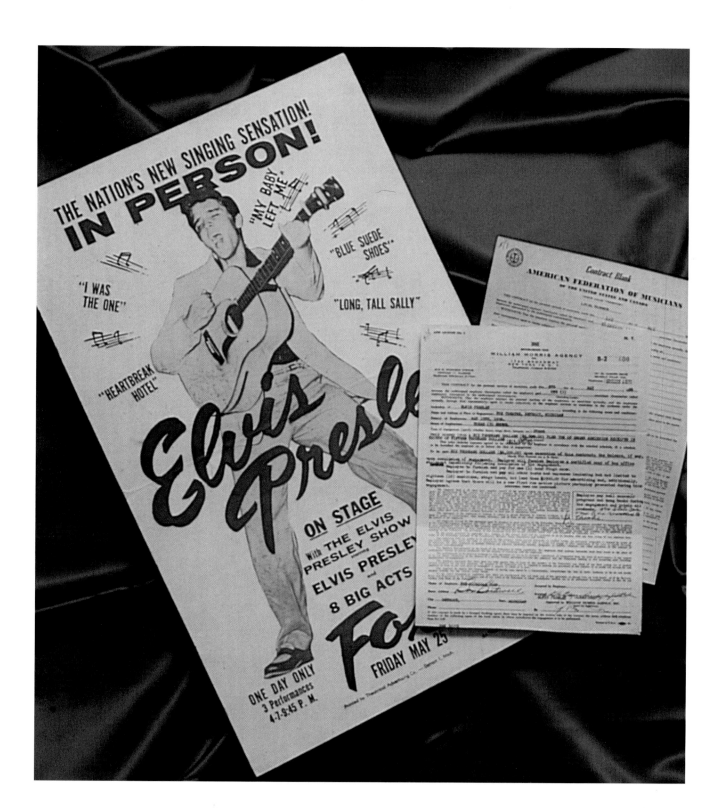

A132

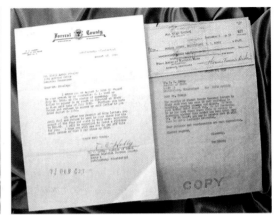

A131

A129

A129 NOTE FROM STEVE ALLEN SHOW TO COLONEL TOM PARKER

Dated July 20, 1956, note written on "Steve Allen" letterhead: "Many thanks for your letter of July 12th . . . and for sending the wonderful saddle for Stevie." Signed "Steve Allen." Photograph included. 10 1/2 x 7 3/8 inches.

Allen sent this note soon after Elvis' appearance on his July 1, 1956 show. Elvis sang his famous rendition of "Hound Dog" to a nervous basset hound who sat beside him.

$800 - 1,000

A130 WESTERN UNION TELEGRAMS REGARDING EARTHQUAKE IN CALIFORNIA

Western Union telegram from Alan White, KLUV radio, to Elvis Presley. "Where are you now living, your fans are twice as desperate to reach you fearing you may have been hurt in the earthquake. Please put them at ease at once and us too we are bushed, Gratefully= Alan White MGR Radio KLUV and limited staff". Elvis responds with a Western Union Telegram on February 15 (or 25) 1957, saying he appreciated the concern, and that he went without harm during the storm and earthquake. States

that he is working very hard on his new picture "Loving You" and goes on to send his thanks." Photograph included. 6 1/2 x 8 1/2 inches telegram. 4 1/2 x 6 1/2 inches telegram

The earthquake was so minor some of Elvis' friends did not even know about it until reading of it in the paper. $500 - 700

A131 SPEEDING TICKET CORRESPONDENCE

One page typed letter from T.C. Hobby, Justice of the Peace in Hattiesburg, Mississippi to Elvis Presley, dated August 22, 1956. Original carbon copy of one page typed letter from Tom Diskin to Hobby, dated August 28, 1956. One All-Star Shows check, dated September 6, 1956, made out to Hobby and signed by Diskin. 11 x 8 1/2" letters. 3 x 8 1/2" check.

Hobby's letter concerns an unpaid speeding ticket Elvis received on July 30, 1956. Hobby writes that if Elvis does not pay the $19.64 fine that he will be compelled to make a court appearance. Diskin's letter explains that Elvis receives almost 20,000 letter a week and that it takes a while to sort through them. He assures Hobby that the matter will be handled. Check for $19.65 has note reading "Charge Presley Acct. Mississippi Ticket."

$1,500 - 2,500

A132 ELVIS MURAL BILL

One page typed letter from Tom Diskin to "Photomammoth" in Hollywood, dated April 26, 1956. One All-Star Shows check made out to Photomammoth and signed by Diskin. One receipt from Photomammoth. Photograph included. 11 x 8 1/2 inches letter. 2 3/4 x 6 inches check. 8 x 8 1/2 inches receipt.

Documents relating to the purchase of a twenty foot high Elvis mural that was displayed at the New Frontier Hotel in Las Vegas. Elvis played a two-week engagement at the New Frontier's "Venus Room" starting April 23, 1956. These shows marked Elvis' first appearance in Las Vegas.

$1,500 - 2,000

A133 ELVIS PRESLEY'S LOVE SEAT

Two love seat. Diamond and striped pattern in orange and green.

These love seat were in the TV room at Graceland prior to the 1974 redecoration. Elvis and his friends would gather in the TV room to watch movies while helping themselves to refreshments from the wet bar and soda fountain.

$8,000 - 10,000

A134 ELVIS PRESLEY'S SOCIAL SECURITY CARD

Elvis Presley's social security card. Printed in black: *Elvis A. Presley*, 2600 Poplar Bldg. Suite 516, Memphis, TN 38112. 3 1/4 x 1 3/4 inches

Elvis' social security card, found in Vernon Presley's office, is signed by Elvis Presley in blue ink. His social security number is 409-52-2002.

$12,000 - 15,000

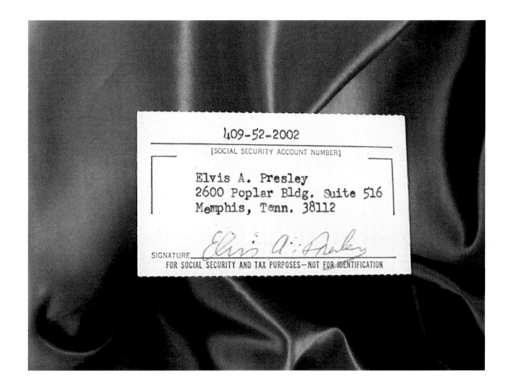

A135 COAT HANGER AND BOX TOP FROM LANSKY BROTHERS'; CHECK TO LANSKYS FROM E.A. PRESLEY

One wooden coat hanger from Lanskys of Memphis; Lansky logo appears at the top of the hanger. Box top from Lanskys; cardboard with white and gray stripes, and numerous "Lansky Bros. Men's Shop" logos scattered about. Original check dated July 24, 1956, to Lansky Bros Men Shop for $500.00; check is signed by E.A. Presley. Lanskys Brothers' Men's store was located at 126 Beale Street and catered to mostly the black clientele. Their stock included flashy, bold-colored items favored by musicians. Elvis bought many of his first stage clothes, including the pink and black suits from Lanskys. The Lanskys once traded a buying spree with Elvis for a three-wheel Messerschmidt motorcycle, which they still own.

$4,000 - 5,000

A136 "HOUND DOG/"DON'T BE CRUEL" ACETATE

Double-sided acetate. 10 inches diameter.

Released in July 1956, "Don't Be Cruel" spent 27 weeks on the Billboard singles chart and was the first of three Elvis singles to hit #1 on the pop, country and R&B charts. It has been estimated that total sales of the "Don't Be Cruel"/"Hound Dog" single exceed nine million copies. The two sides of the single fought each other up the chart in 1956, at one point simultaneously holding the one and two spots on Billboard.

$1,500 - 2,500

A137 SETTLEMENT STATEMENT FROM JANUARY 31, 1957

One page original settlement statement, typed on Elvis Presley letterhead, dated January 31, 1957. Earnings include; a bonus payment, weekly pay from January 25, earnings from Elvis Presley Music, and traveling expenses for RCA recording session. Total amount of earnings are $5,513.22. 14 x 8 3/4 inches.

Settlement statement is typed on rare and unique stationery. On statement "Elvis" is spelled "Elbis".

$350 -450

A138 TICKET FOR ELVIS' PERFORMANCE, FEBRUARY 15, 1956

Original light blue admission ticket for Elvis Presley Show on February 15, 1956 at Walter M. Williams High School Auditorium. Ticket price was $1 in advance and $1.25 at the door. This ticket is marked "refunded" and is from Elvis' personal files from the Graceland office. 2 x 4 3/4 inches.

Justin Tubb, a country singer who toured with Elvis in 1956, said of him, "When he walked offstage, he would be just soaked, just drippin. He worked hard, and he put everything he had into it, and everything he did worked, because the audience just didn't care -- we had never seen anything like it before."

$2,000 - 3,000

A139 LETTERS TO ELVIS AND VERNON PRESLEY IN GERMANY

Air Mail Special Delivery Settlement Statement #63, dated June 16, 1958: earnings for "Jailhouse Rock." Check for $4,254.68 was sent along with the statement from Colonel Parker to Vernon Presley. Air Mail Special Delivery envelope included. Air Mail Special

A137   A136   A138

Delivery Settlement Statement #81, dated June 30, 1958: earnings from RCA. Check for $1,000 sent along with the statement from Colonel Parker to Vernon Presley. Air Mail Special Delivery envelope included. Letter dated November 18, 1958 addressed to Vernon and Elvis signed by the Colonel. Letter on Thomas A. Parker wagon letterhead and announces that "20th Century Fox is also picking up the new deal I worked on the past 8 months." Colonel also discusses promotions that he was working on. Original Thomas A. Parker envelope included. Addressed to Vernon Presley

at Hilberts Park Hotel in Bad Nauheim, Germany. Included is a news clipping by Frank Sparks titled, "Elvis Disappoints Fans with Overseas Romance." Letter dated May 19, 1959 addressed to "Elvis, Vernon and all" and signed, "Tom Diskin." Letter discusses publicity for Elvis. Letter Dated May 19, 1959 addressed to Elvis and Vernon and signed, "Col.." Letter concerns Anita's upcoming plans to visit Elvis in Germany, and several business matters. Original Thomas A. Parker envelope included. Typed on front is, "Elvis and Veronon Presley (Personal)Personal)Personal)" Back is stamped in blue ink an announcement for Elvis in "Loving You" and "King Creole." 11 x 8 1/2 inches settlement statements and letters. 5 1/2 x 8 1/2 inches. May 19 letter. 7 x 4 1/4 inches news clipping. 4 1/8 x 9 1/2 inches envelopes.

Elvis may have been out of the country, but Colonel Parker was bound and determined that Elvis would not be forgotten. The Colonel worked diligently on promotions, deals, and contracts while Elvis was in the Army to ensure that he had a healthy, still blooming career to come home to. These letters reflect the unwavering commitment that the Colonel had for Elvis and his career. A deal that Colonel Parker worked out during this time "brings the outlook for Elvis in a pretty solid picture for his future." He got Elvis "a couple hundred thousand dollars more for the first Wallis and Fox pictures when Elvis comes out plus a percentage."

$4,000 - 5,000

A140 PADDOCK SWIMMING POOL CONTRACT FOR GRACELAND

Original three page swimming pool contract for Graceland dated April 16, 1957. The Paddock Company of California was contracted for $7,510.00. Photograph included. 14 x 8 1/2 inches.

This is the same pool that is at Graceland today.

$1,500 - 2,500

A141   ORIGINAL SCORE OF "I'M ALL SHOOK UP"

Beige sheet music for "I'm All Shook Up" by Otis Blackwell. "SMASH" is written in pencil across the top. Telegram dated February 8, 1957 From Otis Blackwell. Telegram reads "JUST HEARD ABOUT YOUR NEW PICTURE. BABY, SURE WOULD LIKE TO DIG YOU IN PERSON." Also included is sheet music for "Paralyzed." 12 1/2 x 19 inches.

Otis Blackwell submitted "All Shook Up" among other songs for Elvis' consideration. "SMASH" was written on the sheet music after the song was reviewed, indicating that Elvis and team immediately recognized it as an hit. Elvis recorded "All Shook Up", the third artist to do so, in January 1957. It entered the Billboard's Top 100 chart at #25, but was number one by its third week and stayed there for eight weeks. "All Shook Up" stayed on the charts for a total of 30 weeks, more than any other Elvis single. It was in fact, a "SMASH."

$2,500 - 3,000

A142 - No Lot

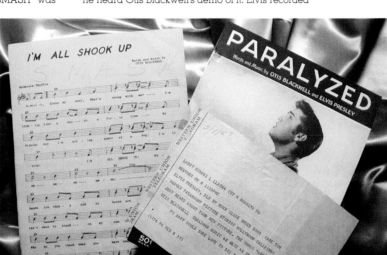

A141

A143   "DON'T BE CRUEL" GOLD RECORD

Framed award. Gold, 45 rpm record of "Don't Be Cruel" with black RCA label with RCA victrola and dog logo. Record on green velvet background and above a gold plaque reading, "To Col. T. Parker... million seller, 1956." Frame is silver painted wood. Taken from Colonel Parker's personal collection. 16 x 14 inches framed award

Elvis fell in love with "Don't Be Cruel" the first time he heard Otis Blackwell's demo of it. Elvis recorded the song in July, 1956. "Don't Be Cruel" had a seven-week stay at number one on "Billboard's" Top 100 chart. This was the first of three Elvis songs to reach number one on all three "Billboard" charts. It is estimated that "Hound Dog/Don't Be Cruel" sold over nine million copies. In addition to being one of Elvis' most successful songs, it was also one of Gladys Presley's favorite by her son.

$20,000 - 30,000

A144   "(NOW AND THEN THERE'S) A FOOL SUCH AS I" GOLD RECORD

Framed award. Gold, 45 rpm record of "(Now and Then There's) A Fool Such As I" with black RCA label with RCA victrola and dog logo. Record on green velvet background and above a gold plaque reading, "To Col. T. Parker... million seller, 1959." Frame is silver painted wood. Taken from Colonel Parker's personal collection. 14 x 16 inches framed award

Elvis recorded "(Now and Then There's) A Fool Such As I" while on leave from the Army in June 1958. This song had been a favorite of Tom Diskin's since the days when he and the Colonel managed Hank Snow and he recorded it. Elvis' version had a 15-week stay on "Billboard's" Top 100 chart, peaking at number two. More than one million records were sold.

$15,000 - 20,000

A145   "I WAS THE ONE" GOLD RECORD

Framed award. Gold, 45 rpm record of "I Was the One" with black RCA label with RCA victrola and dog logo. Record on green velvet background and above a gold plaque reading, "To Col. T. Parker... million seller, 1957." Frame is silver painted wood. Taken from Colonel Parker's personal collection. 14 x 16 inches framed award

"I Was the One," backed with "Heartbreak Hotel," was Elvis' first release of new material with RCA. The single, released on January 11, 1956, had a 16-week stay on "Billboard's" Top 100 chart, peaking at number 23. Elvis sang "I Was the One" during his fourth appearance on "Stage Show" and during his final performance on the "Louisiana Hayride."

$5,000 - 7,000

A146 JOKE PERSONAL APPEARANCE CONTRACT

A large photo of Elvis singing and playing his guitar fronts the contract with the words Personal Appearance Contract at top and Elvis Presley in salmon-colored lettering and "The Nation's Only Atomic Powered Singer" underneath. 26 black-and-white photos of Elvis border three sides.This contract is filled with bogus information about an agreement "between Colonel Thomas A. Parker for the services of Elvis Presley (party of the first part) and Colonel Howard Strickling (party of the unimportant part), press agent for Metro-Goldwyn-Mayer Pictures, the stuffed-lion studio, and Col. Strickling's entire staff of assistants, without whom he would be unable to snow all the visiting dignitaries." 38 x 8 1/2"

The Colonel always played the jokester, even in his business dealings. This contract is an example of his wit and how he got his point across in that manner. The Colonel developed his Snowmen's League as his private club of celebrities. The group had no meetings, cost nothing to get in, and $10,000 to get out. It was all just his take on "snowing" folks, a combination of selling and conning them.

$8,000 - 10,000

A147 ELVIS' PERSONAL "LOVE ME TENDER" FILM AND ACETATES

Case containing Elvis' personal 16 mm print of "Love Me Tender." Case features red and white label reading: "'Love Me Tender,' 20th Century Fox, Producer: David Weisbert, Director: Robert Webb, Released 1956." Acetate case with four acetates from the film, including the songs "Love Me Tender," "There's a Leak in This Old Building," "Poor Boy," "We're Gonna Move" and "Let Me." Also includes a song list. Cases are brown with metal corners, a handle on one end and a

horizontal and vertical buckled strap. 15 1/4 x 15 3/4 inches film case. 15 x 15 inches acetate case.

This 1956 Twentieth Century-Fox production was Elvis' first feature film. Filming began in late August, 1956, when Elvis was just a week past 21. "Love Me Tender" was the only film in which Elvis did not receive top billing. This Civil War era period film ran up production costs of just under $1 million, and recouped those costs within three days of its release. Acetates include three versions of "Love Me Tender."

$5,000 - 7,000

A148 CORRESPONDENCE FROM RCA TO COLONEL PARKER, AND TWO RARE ORIGINAL COVER SLEEVES FOR "DON'T BE CRUEL," AND "HOUND DOG."

Letter dated August 20, 1956, on RCA letterhead: To Colonel T.A. Parker at the Hollywood-Knickerbocker Hotel in Hollywood, CA. The letter reads: "Dear Colonel: Starting with this week, we are using the new sleeve. Notice DONT BE CRUEL is the featured tune. Best Regards. Sincerely, W.W. Bullock"Correspondence on RCA letterhead dated February 1, 1957, from W.W. Bullock about the sales

A148

of "Don't Be Cruel," and "Hound Dog." Bullock notes sales to date of $4,600,000 with sales in the past week of about $7,000. Also mentions that "It might make it and then again it might not." Writes of an award and the possibility of presenting it to Elvis on any upcoming tv appearances. Does not want this reward to go without publicity. Under W.W. Bullock's name at the close of the letter is the title "Chief Snower of the Week." "P.S. I will have to admit that you and Mr. Sharky have nothing in common." Two rare paper sleeves, each with different lead title, reflected in letter. 11 x 8 1/2 inches Letter 7 x 7 inches Single Sleeves. 11 x 8 1/2 inches Bullock Letter.

Both singles, "Don't Be Cruel," and " "Hound Dog," were both very popular songs and often fought for the number one slot. These singles sold so many units, Elvis was presented with five gold records at one time. Both singles reached number one on the "Billboard" chart for the week ending August 8, and stayed in the number one position on this chart for eleven weeks.

$1,500 - 2,000

A149 MAGAZINES OF LATE 1950S AND EARLY 1960 FEATURING ELVIS PRESLEY

"Official Elvis Presley Album"; red and yellow cover with Elvis is black and white; 50 pages; 1956 publication by Charlton Press, Inc. "Elvis Presley" four-color photo with yellow lettering; published by Bartholomew House, Inc., 64 pages. "Elvis Photo Album"; red, white, and blue cover; 1956 publication by The Girlfriend--Boyfriend Corporation, 66 pages. "Elvis Presley Speaks!"; white cover with color photo of Elvis and red lettering; published by Rave Publishing Company in 1956; 66 pages. "Rock 'n Roll Stars" cream-colored background, red and blue bars with white lettering; published by Fawcett Publications, Inc. in 1956; 64 pages. "Elvis Yearbook"; color photo of Elvis; headline reads "New Giant Elvis Picture"; published by Yearbooks in 1960; 98 pgs. Approx. 11 x 8 1/2".

Beginning in 1956, after Elvis' appearance on the Ed Sullivan show in September of that year, publications--from magazines to newspapers--gave fans much sought-after photographs and information about their idol, Elvis.

$500 - 700

A150 "LOVING YOU" CONTRACT ADDENDUM

One page typed on William Morris Agency letterhead, dated January 16, 1957. Signed in blue ink by Elvis Presley. Sent to Hal B. Wallis and Joseph Hazen at Paramount studios. Authorizes William Morris Agency to accept delivery of any payments from Paramount to Elvis. One page typed and dated January 17, 1957. Signed by Elvis Presley, Colonel Thomas Parker, Hal B. Wallis and Joseph H.

Hazen. Stipulates bonus payment of an additional $25,000 to Elvis during the filming of "Loving You." One page typed and dated March 8, 1957. Signed by Elvis Presley, Colonel Thomas Parker and Hal B. Wallis. Acknowledges payment of $25,000 bonus. Two-page letter dated August 7, 1957 on "Hal B. Wallis - Joseph H. Hazen" letterhead. The letter is from Hazen (with his signature) to Colonel Thomas A. Parker regarding misunderstandings they had

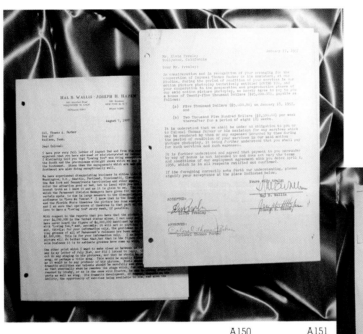

A150   A151

in previous correspondence in reference to "Loving You." In one comment, Hazen explains that he did not "intend to imply that Elvis should not do any singing in his pictures, nor should he be confined to one song, or perhaps a title song . . . Elvis should sing, but his dramatic abilities and talents should be carefully and steadily developed so . . . he can do strong dramatic parts as well as sing." Photographs included. 11 x 8 1/2 inches all documents.

Never content with a merely good deal, Colonel Parker was always working to make a contract better, and these addendum to Elvis' "Loving You" contract are a prime example. The bonus payment

of $25,000 made to Elvis from MGM is made "In consideration and in recognition of your arranging for the cooperation of Colonel Thomas Parker or his assistant, at our Studios, during the period of rendition of your services in our motion picture photoplay tentatively entitled LOVING YOU... ." Colonel Parker was listed as a "Technical Advisor" on the film. "Loving You" was Elvis' second feature film and included the screen debut of Elvis' band— Scotty Moore, Bill Black, D.J. Fontana and the Jordanaires. Elvis' parents, Vernon and Gladys Presley, can also be seen in the film.

$8,000 - 10,000

A151 PARAMOUNT PICTURES SETTLEMENT STATEMENT, AND ELVIS PRESLEY "TEEN -AGER" LIPSTICK AND CARD

One tube of "Tutti Frutti Red" lipstick in a gold tone case with the script "Elvis Presley" written on it. The end of the tube has a red and white circle sticker that reads "Teenager Lipstick Corp. Elvis Tutti Frutti Red Beverly Hills Calif."Original Paramount Pictures Corporation settlement statement dated January 16, 1957. Earnings include; music royalties, the Ed Sullivan Show, Radio Corporation of America, and Teen-ager Lipstick of America. Total earnings were $46,969.32. Attached are two adding machine tapes; one for a total of $5513.22, and the other $46969.32. Copy of Elvis Presley "Teen-Ager" lipstick ad. Photograph included. 11 x 8 1/2 inches settlement statement.

This is a typical weekly statement that Colonel Parker sent to Elvis. "Teenager" lipstick was sold in the 1950's and would come with a presentation card

$1,000 - 1,200

A152 "HEARTBREAK HOTEL" GOLD RECORD

Framed award. Gold, 45 rpm record of "Heartbreak Hotel" with black RCA label with RCA victrola and dog logo. Record on green velvet background and above a gold plaque reading, "To Col. T. Parker... million seller, 1956." Frame is silver painted wood. 16 x 14 inches framed award

"Heartbreak Hotel," backed with "I Was the One," was Elvis' first release of new material with RCA. Just 17 days after the recording session, "Heartbreak Hotel" was released on January 27, 1956. "Billboard" described it as "a strong blues item wrapped up in his usual powerful style and a great beat." "Heartbreak Hotel" spent seven weeks at number one on "Billboard's" Top 100 chart. By April it sold a million copies and "Billboard" listed it as the number one single of 1956. "Heartbreak Hotel" was the second record in history (the first being Carl Perkins' "Blue Suede Shoes") to reach all three "Billboard" charts. $30,000 - 40,000

A153 "JAILHOUSE ROCK" CORRESPONDENCE

Western Union telegram to Colonel from Ann Rosenthal regarding negotiations for an Elvis Presley film entitled "The Rock" (later to be named "Jailhouse Rock") to be produced by Loews. Terms include: 10 week film period starting May 1, 1957. Elvis' salary to be $250,000 plus 50% of net profit from the film after Loews nets $500,000. Loews to furnish first class accommodations: round trip transportation and living expenses for Elvis, Colonel, and two others, with a car and chauffeur. Also - Loews responsible for furnishing Colonel Parker with an office and secretary. Elvis Presley's publishing company to provide music for score of film (at a reasonable cost) and Elvis to retain rights for the same. Two six page, black, white and blue photo folios, with advertising for "Jailhouse Rock". 10 x 8 1/2" Telegram. 10 x 8" Photo folio (2).

Loews also agrees to give rights of the soundtrack to Elvis (at no cost) for use under his contract with his record company. Elvis to receive top billing "above title in 100% size of title". $200 - 300

A154 EXPENSES FOR ELVIS' THIRD "ED SULLIVAN SHOW" APPEARANCE

A memo to accountant Bill Fisher dated January 7, 1957 from Tom Diskin. Memo lists expenses incurred for Elvis during appearance on "The Ed Sullivan Show" on January 6, 1957. Expenses included tips, food, and cash advance. Total bill $68. Memo is signed in ink by Tom Diskin.

A155

A153

A152

A154

Photo included. Cover of EP "Peace in the Valley," blue background with black-and-white photo of Elvis on front; 4 songs: title song, "It Is No Secret," "I Believe," and "Take My Hand, Precious Lord." 7 1/4 x 8 1/2 inches memo. 7 x 7 inches EP.

On January 6, 1957, Elvis appeared for his last engagement on "The Ed Sullivan Show." Elvis wore a gold lame vest over a blue velvet shirt. With his band--Scotty, Bill, and D.J.--and the Jordanaires backing him on vocals, Elvis sang a medley of his popular recordings, including "Don't Be Cruel." He also sang "When My Blue Moon Turns to Gold Again," which had just been released as a single,

and "Peace in the Valley." At the end of the show, Ed shook his hand and told the audience "this is a real decent, fine boy. . . ." After this show, the Colonel raised Elvis' fee for TV appearances to $300,000, purposely making it impossible for him to appear on future TV shows. $600 - 700

A155 CECIL B. DEMILLE THANKS THE COLONEL

One page typed letter on Paramount Pictures Corporation letterhead and sent from director Cecil B. deMille to Colonel Parker. Dated March 15, 1957 and signed by deMille. Has a black and red insignia at the bottom left corner of a knight on a horse that reads "Office of Cecil B. deMille" and below that reads "Current Production 'The Ten Commandments.'" With black and white autographed photograph. Typed message on "Paramount Pictures Corporation" letterhead with bold signature and handwritten note from Cecil B. deMille to Col. Parker, April 3, 1957. 11 x 8 1/2"

Probably best known for his biblical epics, Cecil B. deMille was one of the most powerful and prolific producers and directors in film history. In this letter deMille writes: "George Chapman puts this line into the mouth of one of his characters, 'There is a deep nick in time's restless wheel for each man's good.' Time will record that a certain Colonel Thomas A. Parker is a deep nick in Elvis Presley's wheel—and certainly to his good." deMille concludes by thanking the Colonel for his "warm welcome home wire" and "the Tennessee sausage." $500 - 700

A156 LETTERS FROM JEAN ABERBACH REGARDING "PEACE IN THE VALLEY"

In a letter dated April 16, 1957, Jean Aberbach writes to Tom Parker--on "Elvis Presley Music, Inc." pink stationery--to suggest "Peace in the Valley" as a future motion picture title and film for Elvis. In another 3-page letter, dated the same day, Aberbach broaches several subjects, including expenses (Hill & Range vs. Presley Music), songs chosen for "Jailhouse Rock" film, comments on popularity of "Treat Me Nice," RCA issues, and some personal comments about illness, weddings, and Easter. 11 x 8 1/2 inches each.

Colonel Parker directed Hill & Range Music Company, founded by Jean and Julian Aberbach, to establish and administer Gladys Music and Elvis Presley Music. The Colonel and Elvis could then receive partial royalties from royalties the songwriters made off Elvis' recordings. Elvis sang "Peace in the Valley" during his appearance on the January 6, 1957 Ed Sullivan Show. The song, written by Thomas A. Dorsey, was his final offering to the audience and showed his love of religious music. He recorded the song on January 13, 1957, and was included on his Christmas album.

$1,500 - 2,000

A157 RCA EXTENDS ELVIS PRESLEY'S CONTRACT

Two contracts on RCA letterhead, both dated February 14, 1957, both signed in blue ink by Elvis Presley and Colonel Tom Parker. 8 1/2 x 11 inches.

Contracts stipulate that RCA is exercising its options for his services, granting to their Victor Record Division the continuation of Elvis' contract for 5 additional years from the original. The contract would go until October 15, 1966, with the same terms and conditions. $8,000 - 10,000

A158 EASTER TELEGRAM TO GLADYS PRESLEY

Western Union telegram from April 20, 1957. Sent to "Mrs. Gladys Presley and Family 1034 Audubon Drive" from "Mrs. and Col. Tom Parker" wishing the family a "very happy Easter."5 1/2 x 8 1/2 inches.

Elvis spent this Easter with Hollywood starlet Yvonne Lime, who appeared with him in "Loving

You," which had completed production the month before. Lime visited Elvis in Memphis where they attended a party at Sam Phillips' home the night before Easter and then attended church together on Easter day. $700 - 900

A159 "JAILHOUSE ROCK" PROMOTION CORRESPONDENCE

Original one page, signed letter dated May 1, 1957, from the Colonel to Mr. Pandro Berman of MGM. The correspondence requests that Mr. Pandro approve copy for a rubber stamp used in the Colonel's office to promote "Jailhouse Rock." Letter is written on Colonel Parkers letterhead at MGM. Also included is the rubber stamp. 8 1/2 x 6 1/4 inches Letter. 3 x 3 1/2 inches Stamp.

On the rubber part of the stamp are the words "at MGM Elvis Presley "Jailhouse Rock". On the wood portion of the stamp are the words "Now filming"; these words have been removed from the rubber portion so that the stamp could be used before and after the release of the film.

$500 - 700

A159 INVOICE FOR TWO MARBLE LIONS IN FRONT OF GRACELAND MANSION

Original invoice dated August 1, 1957, from T.J. Malone & Son to Vernon Presley for two imported marble lions. Total bill was $1,000. 6 3/4 x 8 1/2 inches.

The two marble lions that Elvis bought for Graceland were purchased from a home at 160 Cherry Road.

$2,000 - 2,500

A156

A159

A160 LETTERS REGARDING ELVIS' FIRST CHRISTMAS ALBUM

Letter dated June 28, 1957 to Tom Parker from Julian Aberbach, Elvis Presley Music, Inc., lists the titles chosen for Elvis' Christmas album, including "I'll Be Home for Christmas," "Blue Christmas," and "You Are All I Want for Christmas." Julian indicates that they had a tough time getting various publishers to agree on a deal but were finally successful. Not all songs mentioned in letter made it to the album. Original carbon of personal letter dated December 15, 1957 to Bing Crosby from Tom Parker. Tom sent Bing the Christmas album, a box of their Lipsticks for Mrs. Crosby as a wedding present, and a membership in his "Snowmen's League of America Ltd." Gatefold record album, "Elvis' Christmas Album"; red with 4 bound-in pages of photos. EP called "Elvis Sings Christmas Songs" 11 x 8 1/2 inches letter 11 x 8 inches carbon of letter. 12 1/2 x 12 1/4 inches album. 7 x 7 inches EP.

Most recording artists usually completed a Christmas album during their careers, and RCA was pushing the idea with Elvis. He was not in favor of the suggestion at first, but he finally agreed to record the album if the session was held in Los Angeles, not Nashville. He recorded 11 songs in early September 1957. Some of the songs mentioned in the letter of June 28 failed to make the final cuts for inclusion in Elvis' Christmas Album. Even some that were recorded in September weren't on the final album. A few of the chosen songs included "Blue Christmas," "Silent Night," and "Santa Bring My Baby Back." To produce the right frame of mind for the session, Steve Sholes decorated the studio with a Christmas tree as well as wrapped presents beneath it .

$2,000 - 3,000

A161 FINANCIAL CORRESPONDENCE BETWEEN BILL BLACK AND TOM DISKIN

Handwritten letter to Tom Diskin from Bill Black, dated July 25, 1957, in which Black inquires of "the money situation" which Diskin was supposed "to look into". Goes on to say that Diskin's silence "has me worried". Ends the letter by noting "This is in the strictest confidence". Tom Diskin's response dated July 29, 1957, informs Black that any information he had would have been passed on. Notes that he mentioned it "to the people out there" who said they would look into it. Advises Black that if he has not heard anything about the matter yet, payment is not likely. 7 1/2 x 8" Letter. 11 x 8 1/2"Letter.

A162   A160   A161

Bill Black and Scotty Moore had expected to share in Elvis' success, however, by July of 1957, they were still only making two hundred dollars a week. They were in debt, and they needed financial help. Shortly after their correspondence with Tom Diskin, both Bill and Scotty resigned.

$1,000 - 1,500

A162 "JAILHOUSE ROCK" SCRIPT AND CORRESPONDENCE

One complete "Jailhouse Rock" script. All 109 pages are contained within a yellow three holed folder with brass clasps. One page original letter, on Elvis Presley letterhead, dated March 23, 1957, from Col. Parker to Mr. Pandro Berman of MGM Studios. In letter Col. Parker gives Mr. Pandro many suggestions for the title of what is to become "Jailhouse Rock." 10 3/4 x 8 3/4 inches Letter. 11 x 8 1/2 inches Script.

Pandro Berman was the producer on "Jailhouse Rock", and before the title was selected, Colonel Parker sent Mr. Berman many suggestions for it including such titles as, "Trouble Is My Name", "Don't Push Me Too Far", "Never Give Up", "The Hard Climb" etc. The Elvis Presley letterhead used for the correspondence to Mr. Berman, is rare and very unique. Border exhibits various photographs of Elvis.

$2,000 - 3,000

A163 "JAILHOUSE ROCK" PREMIER PROGRAM AND MOVIE POSTER

Heavy paper program for premier of "Jailhouse Rock". There are two images of Elvis on the cover with guitar in hand. Opens to reveal information in the film such as cast, screen play writer, producer, director, and others involved in the production of the film. Screen Play: Guy Trosper. Story: Ned Young Producer: Pandro S. BERMAN DIRECTOR: Richard Thorpe Also included is a blue, red and white movie poster for "Jailhouse Rock" 11 x 8 1/2 inches Premier (folds out to 17 x 11 inches) 25 x 38 inches Movie Poster.

Unlike most movie posters, this poster was specially made by the request of Colonel Parker in very limited quantities.. The poster that is shown behind Elvis in the photograph to the right is believed to be the very poster in this lot. "Jailhouse Rock" was Elvis' third film and premiered in Memphis on October 17, 1957. It opened nationally on November 8, and reached #3 in "Variety's" weekly list of top grossing films. For the year 1957 "Jailhouse Rock" ranked #14 in top grossing films. $8,000 - 10,000

A164 LLOYD'S OF LONDON FLEET INSURANCE FOR ELVIS PRESLEY AND VERNON PRESLEY

Original documents of insurance through Lloyd's of London for Elvis and Vernon. Document dated November 2, 1957, to expire on November 2, 1958. Fleet includes a 1955 Dodge truck, 1957 Isette Coupe, 1957 Cadillac limo, 1956 Lincoln Mark II Tudor, 1955 Cadillac four door, 1954 Cadillac limo, 1957 Harley Davidson motorcycle, and a 1956 Cadillac Eldorado Convertible. Photograph included. 12 3/4 x 8 1/2 inches Fleet schedule. 12 3/4 x 8 1/2 inches Insurance terms. 14 x 8 1/2 inches insurance certificate.

Elvis' fondness of automobiles and motorcycles was why he maintained a large fleet throughout his life. $1,000 - 1,500

A165 LETTER TO ELVIS PRESLEY FROM COLONEL TOM PARKER AND PHOTO FOLIO

Letter dated August 6, 1957 to Elvis from the Colonel on official "Thomas A. Parker" letterhead. Contents include information relating to book makeup on "Jailhouse Rock" stills, recording session dates, and Christmas album possible success. Colonel also makes jovial references to Col. Burro and the Donkeys and snowjobs. Envelope has "official" return address as Snowmen's League, Igloo 417, Madison, Tenn. and is addressed to "Snow Chief High Potentate Snower Elvis Snowchief Wallaby the First." Cover of Photo Folio, which includes 3 black and white photos of Elvis and an ad on the back for "Jailhouse Rock." 11 x 8 1/2 inches letter. 4 1/4 x 9 1/2 inches envelope. 10 x 8 inches photo folio.

This is just one example of Colonel Parker keeping Elvis informed about upcoming events. The letter is dated about two months before "Jailhouse Rock" had its official release in Memphis (October 17). However, Elvis and his parents saw a special preview on October 2nd. Elvis recorded his Christmas album in Hollywood on September 5-7. Some of the featured songs included "White Christmas," "Blue Christmas," and "I'll Be Home for Christmas."

$2,000 - 3,000

A163

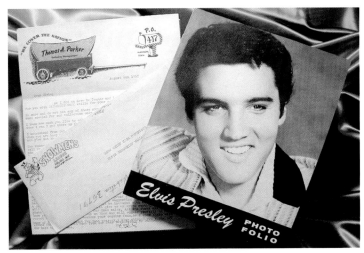

A165

A166 BEVERLY WILSHIRE HOTEL DAMAGE NOTICE AND CORRESPONDENCE

Letter from Beverly Wilshire Hotel dated November 4, 1957, to Colonel Parker regarding damage done to Suite 850 during Elvis' stay. Damage included broken sofa, broken dining room chair, 7 chipped and scratched dining room chairs, and a broken leg on a drum table. All above items needing repair or replacement. Peter Sharp, VP, writes to Colonel for input on how to handle the situation. Additional damage of three mirror panels being dislodged from the dining room table, it is noted, will be ignored. Total bill for damages: $695.00Dec. 23rd letter to Mr. W.E Fisher of James a Matthews and Co. in Memphis from Evelyn Sharp, president of the Wilshire, noting that the actual damage. 11 x 8 1/2 inches Letters. 7 x 6 inches Bill.

Damages to the hotel room were done during the filming of "Jailhouse Rock" when Elvis had may of his friends staying with him. The damage was paid for and Elvis continued to stay at the hotel.

$4,000 - 6,000

A167 TELEGRAM TO ELVIS PRESLEY FROM "THE ADMIRAL"

Western Union telegram dated December 22, 1956 from "Admiral" Parker to Elvis at his home on Audubon Drive. Message advises him to look out for a box being sent to him from Jean and Julian in New York, thanks him for the Christmas present, and hopes he received the ham and bacon. His final line wishes Elvis and his parents "the best of everything for Christmas and New Year." 5 3/4 x 8 1/2 inches.

The Colonel, always a jokester, occasionally called himself "Admiral." His wife, Marie, sometimes used that name with Elvis as well.

$450 - 500

A168 LEIBER AND STOLLER TELEGRAM

Western Union telegram dated November 3, 1957 to Col. Parker from song writing team Jerry Leiber and Mike Stoller in regard to Elvis' current movie project ("King Creole") and their desire to work on it with him. Two page, purple-tinted sheet music for the Leiber- and Stoller-penned "Hound Dog." Singles of "Too Much" and "Don't." 5 3/8 x 8 1/2 inches telegram. 12 x 9 inches sheet music.

Jerry Leiber and Mike Stoller are likely the greatest song writing and record producing team rock and roll has ever known. Starting in the early Fifties, when they were still teenagers, Leiber and Stoller wrote innumerable R&B classics, including Wilbert Harrison's "Kansas City," The Drifters' "There Goes My Baby" and Ben E. King's "Stand By Me." They perhaps reached their artistic peak, and certainly had their closest musical association, in the late Fifties and early Sixties with the R&B vocal group The Coasters. With The Coasters, Leiber and Stoller composed what they called "playlets," little narrative songs of sparkling wit, sublime humor and veiled social commentary, generally rooted in the vernacular world of urban black America. By the time Elvis performed their "Hound Dog" in 1956, Leiber and Stoller were already major figures in the R&B world, having written for giants like Ray Charles, Joe Turner and The Drifters. When the team (Leiber wrote the words, Stoller the music) was commissioned to write four songs for Elvis for the film "Jailhouse Rock," they were at first reluctant, having been unimpressed with Elvis' previous recordings of their songs, especially "Hound Dog" and "Love Me."

But when they actually met Elvis, their opinion of him was dramatically changed. Leiber and Stoller didn't think they'd meet another young white person as knowledgeable of and enthralled by "black music," but in Elvis they met their match, and their working relationship with the new king of rock and roll was smooth. The subtly satiric work they did for "Jailhouse Rock" (particularly the title song) was in the "playlet" mode they had perfected with The Coasters and was perfect for use in the film. Elvis recorded over 20 Leiber and Stoller songs, also including "(You're So Square) Baby I Don't Care," "Treat Me Nice," and three songs for the film "King Creole." $600 - 800

A169 REAL ESTATE PROPOSAL FROM GRACELAND REALTOR

Typed letter from Virginia Grant Realty to Col. Parker. Written on company stationery and signed in ink by Grant. Dated September 15, 1957. Letter is an inquiry about a 7,500 acre property in northern Mississippi that Grant wants to show the Presley's. Comes with Virginia Grant Realty Co. business card. Original copy of typed letter from Tom Diskin to Grant. Dated September 16, 1957. Diskin informs Grant that all personal property investments are handled directly by the Presley family. 11 x 8 1/2 inches letters. 2 x 3 1/2 inches card.

Virginia Grant was the realtor who sold Graceland to Elvis. This particular property was not purchased by the Presley's, but Elvis would buy a much smaller estate in Mississippi a decade later. $400 - 500

A170 GENERAL ELECTRIC PROMOTIONAL CORRESPONDENCE TO COLONEL PARKER

Typed original letter from Sally Chackow of General Electric Company dated August 26, 1957. Correspondence requests permission to use Elvis Presley's favorite recipe for an upcoming promotion. Copy of reply letter dated September 6, 1957, from Tom Diskin of Col. Parker's office. 11 x 8 1/2"

Request was tuned down; the Colonel thought they would be getting promotional material without having to pay for it.

$300 - 400

A171 INVOICE AND CORRESPONDENCE FROM MATSON NAVIGATION COMPANY

Original letter, and two copies of an invoice from Matson Navigation Company dated November 14, 1957. Correspondence is to Bill Fisher from Lloyd Pflueger requesting an additional $47.50 for charter service when Elvis and band were in Hawaii. Copies of invoice is included listing Elvis, band members, and each airfare. Photograph included. 11 x 8 1/2 inches Letter 7 x 8 1/2 inches invoice.

Elvis went to Hawaii in November of 1957 to do his Hawaiian concert. The letter lists who went, and the extra charges incurred. $500 - 600

A172 ELVIS PRESLEY CHARITY LETTERS AND CHECKS

Five letters sent to local charities--Le Bonheur Children's Hospital, Crippled Children's Hospital, Cerebral Palsy Council, National Foundation for Infantile Paralysis, and American Children's Hospital--from Elvis Presley on December 31, 1957. Elvis Presley checks to the five charities.17 1/2 x 10 inches letters.

These are just two of the many charities Elvis would contribute money to each year around the holidays.

$4,000 - 5,000

A173 ELVIS' DOCUMENTS AND MEMORABILIA, 1957

Paramount, and Hal Wallis release, January 1957 ; a 4-page document that gave biographical information about Elvis for the film "Loving You." Besides the usual birthplace and date, early life, and career history, the biography also discusses his eligibility ("a prize catch for any young lady"), car collection ("four Cadillacs . . . as well as a motorcycle"), hobbies ("music of all types and tinkering with machinery"), favorite colors ("pink and black"), and favorite foods ("porkchops, brown gravy, apple pie, and vegetable soup"). Three pages typed on "Howard Strickling M.G.M. Studios" letterhead. Titled "Final Who, What and Why of Jailhouse Rock." Lists the film's final cast and gives a synopsis of "highlights." Ten-page Elvis Presley photo folio, black and white with blue trim. Cover signed in black marker "Best Wishes, Elvis Presley." Back cover is an advertisement for "Jailhouse Rock." Two-page cream-colored card stock program from the premiere for "Jailhouse Rock," with black-and-white Elvis photo on cover, production credits on inside, and song credits on back. Seven-page typed Elvis Presley bio from 1957, first page on M.G.M. letterhead. Four-page sheet music for "Jailhouse Rock"; blue cover.Four-page bulletin dated October 1957 from Hill and Range Songs in New York; white with green lettering; highlighting "Jailhouse Rock" and "Loving You" on front sheet. DJs from radio stations around the country sent

Elvis (through Tom Diskin) reports showing their top tunes of the week so he could see where his records were listed. This folder from 1957 contains 54 reports from such stations as KTUL in Tulsa, KENT in Shreveport, KXL in Portland, KJR in Seattle, and KDAY in Los Angeles. Some have personal handwritten notes from the DJs. 13 x 8 1/2 inches "Loving You" bio. 13 x 8 1/2 inches cast list. 10 x 8 inches photo folio. 11 x 8 1/2 inches program. 11 x 8 1/2 inches 7-page bio.. 12 x 9 inches sheet music 12 3/8 x 8 1/2 inches bulletin. 11 x 8 1/2 inches most disc jockey reports.

"Loving You," Elvis' second film, began production at Paramount in January 1957 and premiered in Memphis at the Strand Theater on July 9. It was Elvis' first color film. He played the role of Deke Rivers, a guitar-playing truck driver. Elvis' costars were Elizabeth Scott and Wendell Corey. Hal Kanter, former screenwriter, debuted his directing career with this film. "Jailhouse Rock" had its official release in Memphis (October 17). "Highlights" section of "Who, What, and Why . . ." reads: "The new furor was occasioned by the disclosure that, in several scenes, Presley would appear for the first

time without his sideburns and mop of long, wavy hair. For the prison sequences, he would be given a crew cut. If further proof were needed as to either the ardor or the number of Presley fans, it was supplied by the storm of protest that quickly ensued." The disc jockey report is a typical example of the Colonel's thoroughness in keeping tabs on Elvis' popularity and the success of his records at radio stations. Each week, many of the radio stations around the country would send reports on top songs in their areas, and the Colonel or his assistant, Diskin, would file them neatly in a binder for easy reference.

$4,000 - 5,000

A174 RUBBER STAMPS FOR ELVIS PRESLEY AND VERNON PRESLEY

Rubber stamp with Elvis Presley, 3764 Highway 51 So., Memphis 10, Tenn., and rubber stamp with Vernon Presley, the same street address, and Memphis 16, Tennessee. Stamp pad from Vernon's office. 2 7/8 x 2 inches Vernon stamp. 2 1/2 x 2 3/8 inches Elvis stamp

Vernon and Elvis used these stamps before the highway became Elvis Presley Boulevard on January 19, 1972.

$3,000 - 4,000

A175 PIECE OF ORIGINAL GRACELAND FENCE WITH INVOICE

Piece of painted white wooden fence from Graceland. Orders billed to Vernon Presley, Highway 51S., on July 2, 1957 for contract angle board fence and on July 13, 1957 for contract Kentucky Style Fence. Total bill $6,286.56. "No charge on well house in appreciation of your past business." Signed D.T. Chaffin. Photograph included. 11 x 8 1/2 inches.

The fencing was purchased to enclose the pasture area at Graceland.

$1,000 - 1,200

A177 ELVIS PRESLEY'S PETS

Original statement for Hart's Bakery, Inc., and Youngtown for chimp clothes.

Two page original letter dated August 27, 1975, to Linda Thompson from New England Institute of Comparative Medicine regarding their dog "Getlow'. Statement from Raines Road Animal Clinic regarding treatments for "Getlow". Notebook pages summary of lab work done on dog. "Getlow's" dog collar included.

Typewritten letter on Thomas A. Parker letterhead, dated May 14, 1957, regarding a wallaby given to Elvis. Letter typed on MGM letterhead dated May 22, 1957, addressed to "Mr. Wallaby." One invoice from Herb B. Myer & Co. Inc., regarding delivery and pickup of wallaby. One mailing envelope from Blue Cross Veterinary Hospital regarding the board and care of the wallaby.

One "Yankee Revenge" registration papers with picture of ancestors; black stallion that was foaled on April 18, 1970 ("Yankee Revenge" was the father) was named "Mare Ingram" by Elvis. Typewritten page listing the horses on the ranch in 1967. Horses included: "Rising Sun," "Domino," Midnight," "Beauty," "Flaming Star," "Star Trek."

Receipt from London Towne Livery Service, Ltd., for driving Elvis and Lisa's dogs "Brutus" and "Snoopy" from the Monovale home to "As Directed." Photograph included. Sizes vary from 6 x 4 to 11 x 8 1/2"

Elvis loved animals and was given a wallaby by his fans from Australia, later donating it to the Memphis zoo. However, for a while Colonel parker would sardonically refer to Elvis as "Wallaby." The Colonel sent Elvis a second letter saying that , "It is impossible to housebreak a Wallaby since it does not have any natural sanitation instinct." $3,500 - 4,000

A178 ELVIS PRESLEY HERTZ CHARGE CARD

Original carbon receipt from The Hertz Corporation in Las Vegas, dated November 12, 1956 with original carbon signature of Elvis Presley. Receipt for rental of a Cadillac convertible. Gold-and-white Hertz Rent-a-Car International Charge Card with raised black letters, expires December 1962. Attached to Hertz company brochure. Envelope from Hertz included. Hertz Rent A Car International Charge Card for E.A. Presley, expiring December 1966. Photograph included. 2 1/8 x 3 1/2 inches receipt. 2 1/4 x 3 3/4 inches cards. 3 3/4 x 7 1/4 inches opening to 7 1/2 x 7 1/4 inches brochure. 4 x 7 1/2 inches envelope.

The receipt for the Cadillac rental dates from a vacation trip Elvis and his cousin Gene Smith took to Las Vegas in November 1956. During this trip Elvis met Liberace and also began dating Dottie Harmony, a Las Vegas singer and dancer who would later accompany him to his pre-induction Army physical on January 4, 1957.

$5,000 - 6,000

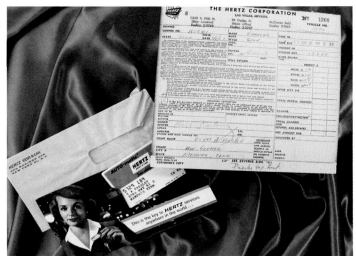

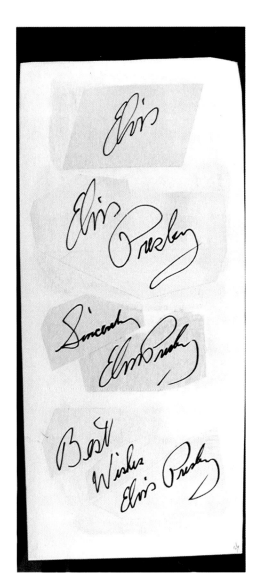

A176 ELVIS' SIGNATURE

Paste-ups of signatures "Elvis," "Elvis Presley," "Sincerely, Elvis Presley," and "Best Wishes, Elvis Presley." 17 1/4 x 8 3/4 inches.

These signatures were kept on hand for printing signatures on photographs, album covers, and other souvenir items.

$3,000 - 4,000

A179 ELVIS PRESLEY'S KEYS TO GRACELAND

Silver, round key chain with multiple keys attached; a spandex 1/6" silver chain is used to attach a silver charm to the key ring. The charm is shaped like a shield with a raised emblem of a race car on the front. Photograph included. 1 inch round Key Ring. 1 x 1 1/4 inches Charm. 2 x 1 inches Keys.

Back of charm has the name *Elvis Presley* engraved on it.

$8,000 - 10,000

A180 GRACELAND DECORATION INVOICES

Twenty pages of original carbons from Golden's of Memphis on North Cleveland in Memphis, TN. The invoices list purchases of furniture and home accessories for Graceland. Photograph included. 11 x 8 1/2 inches.

These are the bills for all the original furnishings at Graceland. Elvis liked the bold colors. George Golden was a former Lipton Tea salesman before he sold furniture. To advertise George would create three foot wide miniature rooms on top of flatbed trucks.

$4,000 - 5,000

A181 SETTLEMENT STATEMENT FROM JANUARY 31, 1957

One page original settlement statement, typed on Elvis Presley letterhead, dated January 31, 1957. Earnings include; a bonus payment, weekly pay from January 25, earnings from Elvis Presley Music, and traveling expenses for RCA recording session. Total amount of earnings are $5,513.22. 14 x 8 3/4 inches.

Settlement statement is typed on rare and unique stationery. On statement "Elvis" is spelled "Elbis".

$350 -450

A182 ELVIS PRESLEY-TWENTIETH CENTURY FOX CONTRACT—1958

Note to Ann Rosenthal from Colonel Tom Parker, on the Colonel's business letterhead, dated April 16, 1957, regarding Fox contract. Contract on 20th Century-Fox letterhead, dated December 22, 1958 and signed in blue ink by Elvis Presley. 11 x 8 1/2 "

Ann Rosenthal was the attorney for William Morris Agency that the Colonel would deal with on 20th Century Fox contracts. AC29The memo to Rosenthal was written prior to Elvis' being drafted into the Army, and lists contract stipulations for Elvis' future movie contracts. This MGM contract follows up on a contract signed right after Elvis left for his Army stint in Germany. It pertains to MGM securing the rights to Elvis' first post-Army film. The stipulations in the memo are hand-numbered in what seems to be the Colonel's order of importance. "Top billing in both pictures one hundred

percent" and "No TV trailers or personal appearances of any nature in connection with the pictures" seem to be most important. The list also includes "Can never cut his hair off without our permission." $6,000 - 8,000

A183 BING CROSBY LETTER TO COLONEL PARKER

Two page letter typed in blue ink on "Bing Crosby Hollywood" stationery. Dated May 13, 1957 and signed "Bing" in blue ink. Autographed photo. 10 1/2 x 7 1/4 inches.

In this wonderfully sardonic letter, Crosby praises Elvis and warns the Colonel about over-exposure. He then writes: "If what you say is true, that you are able to get all the money you need out of Hope, you indeed have a tremendous talent. I've never been able to get the right time off of him if he had wrist watches up to the elbow on both arms... "The only alarming factor you mention, is that Hope proposes to get what he's going to give you out of me. I've had a very bad season - what with storms, typhoons, tornadoes, fires, inclement weather, and picking up the rain checks...If you could let us have Elvis for a couple of weeks, I think we could get out of hock. "Enclosed is the picture you asked for, Tom. I hope it is of some value to you in elevating your prestige around MGM, but I doubt it very much. They're pretty snobbish over at that lot and prone to look down their noses somewhat at mere crooners - witness what happened to Sinatra, Vic Damone and myself. I hope Elvis is able in some way to put our profession on a higher plateau." $500 - 600

A184 ELVIS' RETURN TO TUPELO - TELEGRAM AND DOCUMENTATION

Western Union Telegram dated September 26, 1956 addressed to Tom Diskin or Oscar Davis from Colonel Tom Parker who sends his regards to all involved in the Tupelo show. Balance sheet for concession sales at the Elvis Presley Show in Tupelo, Mississippi on September 26, 1956. Information sheet regarding press, radio and movie interviews for the Tupelo show. One-page show line-up for the Tupelo show. 10 x 8 inches telegram 5 1/2 x 8 1/2 inches concessions balance sheet. 11 x 8 1/2 inches info sheet and line-up.

Tupelo, Mississippi, Elvis' birthplace, pulled out all the stops in welcoming Elvis home. On September 26, 1956, Elvis was back in Tupelo to perform two shows at the Tupelo Fairgrounds for the Mississippi-Alabama Fair and Dairy Show - the same place he nervously performed "Old Shep" as a child eleven years earlier. The day was declared "Elvis Presley Day" in Tupelo; a banner was strung across Main Street proclaiming, "Tupelo Welcomes Elvis Presley Home"; town shops had Elvis displays in their windows; and a parade in honor of Elvis marched down Main Street.

After several opening acts and an intermission, Elvis, wearing a velvet shirt given to him by Natalie Wood, entered the stage to face a sea of near hysterical fans. "'Elvis,' they shrieked," according to the "Journal," "tearing their hair and sobbing hysterically, 'Please, Elvis.'" Mississippi governor, J.P. Coleman was introduced on stage during Elvis' performance, at which time he proclaimed Elvis "America's number-one entertainer in the field of American popular music, [our] own native son." Elvis was then presented with a key to the city by Tupelo mayor, James Ballard. Forty policemen and 50 National Guardsmen were on hand to keep the peace and protect Elvis from the hysteria. Elvis had to stop the show to ask the crowd to settle down before someone was hurt, however, it did not take long before the pandemonium broke again. Although the auditorium seated 10,000, attendance for Elvis' performance far exceeded capacity, not to mention the mob of 50,000 who were unable to get in.

$10,000 - 15,000

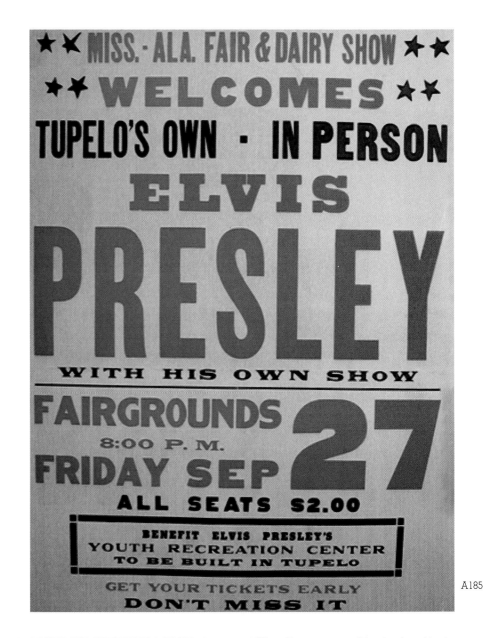

A185

A185 POSTER FOR ELVIS' TUPELO SHOW, 1957

Yellow poster with red and blue print, "Miss. - Ala. Fair & Dairy Show Welcomes Tupelo's own - In Person, Elvis Presley with His Own Show." Show was September 27, 1957 and benefited the Youth Recreation Center to be built in Tupelo. 27 x 22 inches

When Elvis, a native of Tupelo, played his hometown it was always an especially significant performance. This show was no exception. Over 12,000 fans crowded into a stadium that seated only 10,000, to catch a glimpse of their hometown hero shaking, wiggling and singing his heart out.

$6,000 - 8,000

A186 TOM DISKIN'S RECEIPTS FOR HANK SNOW SHOW

Forty five receipts from May 1-17, 1955. Received of Hank Snow Show and Tom Diskin, showing amount person received and signed by the recipient. Besides Elvis Presley, some of the signatures on the receipts include Slim Whitman, Maybelle Carter, June Carter, and Mae Axton. 3 x 5 5/8 inches.

In January 1955, Colonel Tom Parker became the manager of Hank Snow. He then placed his Jamboree Attractions under the umbrella of Hank Snow Enterprises. The Colonel booked all the acts for the Hank Snow Jamborees and made all the arrangements. Tom Diskin, his assistant, handled many of the financial obligations.

$6,000 - 7,000

A187 LETTER TO COLONEL PARKER FROM SAMMY DAVIS, JR.

Dated October 4, 1957, written on "Carlton House" letterhead in Pittsburgh, Pennsylvania, and signed by Davis: "Again allow me to thank you for being so nice, proving that the bigger they are, the nicer they are." Photograph included. 10 1/2 x 7 1/4"

In his note, Sammy Davis Jr. made reference to possibly seeing Elvis and the Colonel in October on the coast. Elvis was scheduled to begin the shooting for "King Creole" at that time, but production was moved into 1958.

$800 - 1,000

A188 SPECIAL PROMOTIONAL MOVIE POSTER FROM "JAILHOUSE ROCK"

Movie Poster from the film "Jailhouse Rock."

Covering the top three quarters of the poster is an artist rendering of a head shot of Elvis' left profile. Background is a dull green with blue overtones. Beneath the picture of Elvis is his name "Elvis

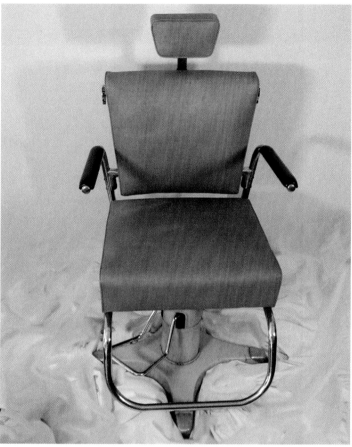

Presley" in yellow, and the words "At His Greatest" in white. Below these words is another artist rendition of a guitar, jailhouse bars, and Elvis twisting inside a doorway. Background behind Elvis is white; the remainder is bright red. 50 x 40 inches.

"Jailhouse Rock" opened nationally on November 8, 1957, and reached #13 on "Variety's" weekly top-grossing film list. Elvis was paid $250,000 and 50% of the films profits. During the filming, Elvis swallowed a tooth cap and had to be hospitalized at Cedars Lebanon Hospital. Crisp bacon, mashed potatoes, and dark brown gravy was added to the commissary menu during filming because Elvis loved that kind of food. "Jailhouse Rock" was rereleased on March 9, 1960, to coincide with Elvis' discharge from the Army.

$1,500 - 2,000

A189 ELVIS' BARBER CHAIR WITH RECEIPT FOR REPAIR

Barber chair, green vinyl upholstery, green and chrome four-footed base, chrome arms with black plastic armrests, metal plate "Modecraft, New York, NY, Muncy, PA" located at base of seat on back side. Yellow receipt from Beauty and Barber Mart dated November 25, 1969, for the repair of a barber chair, billed to Elvis Presley for $100.57. 47"x27" inches chair. 8 1/4 x 5 5/8 inches receipt.

This long term fixture in Elvis' personal quarters, at his bath house at Graceland, was his seat for regular sessions with his hair stylist, or—as Colonel Parker would say—"beautification expert."

A190 "JAILHOUSE ROCK" GOLD RECORD

Framed award. Gold, 45 rpm record of "Jailhouse Rock" with black RCA label with RCA victrola and dog logo. Record on green velvet background and above a gold plaque reading, "To Col. T. Parker... million seller, 1957." Frame is silver painted wood. Taken from Colonel Parker's personal collection.
16 x 14 inches framed award.

"Jailhouse Rock" was written by Jerry Leiber and Mike Stoller for Elvis' 1957 movie. After three weeks on "Billboard's" Top 100 chart, "Jailhouse Rock" had hit number one where it remained for seven weeks. Elvis sang this song in the movie "Jailhouse Rock" and in two TV specials, "Elvis" and "Elvis in Concert." This is one of three Elvis songs to reach the number one spot on all three "Billboard" charts.

$15,000 - 20,000

A191 "ALL SHOOK UP" GOLD RECORD

Framed award. Gold, 45 rpm record of "All Shook Up" with black RCA label with RCA victrola and dog logo. Record on green velvet background and above a gold plaque reading, "To Col. T. Parker... million seller, 1957." Frame is silver painted wood. Taken from Colonel Parker's personal collection. 16 x 14 inches framed award.

Otis Blackwell was at the Shalimar music office when Al Stanton, one of Shalimar's owners walked by shaking his Pepsi-Cola bottle. Stanton suggested to Blackwell the name for a new song, "All Shook Up." Blackwell took him up on his suggestion and wrote the song. Elvis recorded the song, the third person to do so, on January 12, 1957. After only three weeks on "Billboard's" Top 100 chart, it was at number one where it stayed for eight weeks. It remained on the chart for 30 weeks, longer than any other Presley single.

$15,000 - 20,000

A192 "TEDDY BEAR" GOLD RECORD

Framed award. Gold, 45 rpm record of "Teddy Bear" with black RCA label with RCA victrola and dog logo. Record on green velvet background and above a gold plaque reading, "To Col. T. Parker... million seller, 1958." Frame is silver painted wood. Taken from Colonel Parker's personal collection. 16 x 14 inches framed award.

Kal Mann and Bernie Lowe composed "Teddy Bear" especially for Elvis because of his affinity for teddy bears. Elvis recorded the song on January 24, 1957 and spent seven weeks at number one on "Billboard's" Top 100 chart. Elvis sang "Teddy Bear" in "Loving You" and during his 1977 TV special, "Elvis in Concert." This was one of three Elvis songs to top all three "Billboard" charts.

$15,000 - 20,000

A193 "LOVING YOU" (THE MOTION PICTURE) PRINT AND ACETATE CASE

One film case with 16mm of Loving You included. Red label with raised white letters reads: "Loving You" 1957, #2. Border label indicates film title, production company, director, and release date. One acetate case (no acetates at this time). Cases are brown with metal corners, a handle on one end, and a horizontal and vertical buckled strap. 15 1/4 x 15 3/4 inches film case.

Loving You was released by Paramount Studios in 1957. A Hal Wallis release, directed by Hal Kanter, the film premiered in Memphis at the Strand Theater. The film was Elvis' second acting debut; he starred as Deke Rivers, a gas station worker who becomes a country-western star. Gladys and Vernon Presley show up as extras in the audience at one of the concerts.

$2,000 - 3,000

A194 "KING CREOLE" MUSIC NOTES

Two pages typed with handwritten notes in blue ink, dated January 8, 1958. Internal memo sent from producer Hal Wallis to director "Mike" Curtis and six others. With three sets of two-page sheet music from the film: green-tinted "Dixieland Rock," red-tinted "Crawfish," and maroon-tinted "New Orleans." 11 x 8 1/2" notes. 12 x 9" sheet music.

This document gives instructions for placement of songs in the 1958 film "King Creole." Remarkably prolific director Michael Curtis, who also helmed classics like "Casablanca," Errol Flynn's "The Adventures of Robin Hood," and James Cagney's "Angels With Dirty Faces," was the only "A-list" director Elvis ever worked with.

$1, 500 - 1,700

A195 ELVIS' PERSONAL FILM AND ACETATES FOR "KING CREOLE"

Audio/visual Paramount film of "King Creole", and five acetates. Items are contained in square, brown film/acetate cases with metal corners, and a plastic handle on the side. There are two buckled straps, one horizontal and one vertical.Three acetates are contained in plain white sleeves with top opening. The remaining two are in plain white sleeves with top flaps. First record contains the song "King Creole" (RCA Victor). Second record contains the songs "Lover Doll," and "Dixieland Rock." (Presto). Third record contains the songs "King Creole," and "New Orleans." (Presto). Fourth record contains the song. "Dixieland Rock" (Associated Recording). Fifth record contains the song "Hard-Headed Woman." (Allegro). 15 1/4 x 15 3/4 inches Movie and case.10 1/4 x 10 1/4 inches Sleeves (2). 10 x 10 1/4 inches Sleeves (2). 12 1/4 x 12 inches Sleeves (1). 12 x 12 inches Acetate (1). 10 x 10 Acetates (4)

This is just one of many copies of Elvis' films that belonged to Colonel Parker. "King Creole" opened nationally on July 21, 1958. In order to be able to do this film, Elvis had to request a deferment from the local draft board. Michael Curtiz directed this film, and Elvis' portrayal of the character Danny Fisher was his most solid performance ever in a film.

3,000 - 4,000

A196 "KING CREOLE" CONTRACT AMENDMENT AND RELATED LETTERS

Three-page letter to Elvis Presley from Hal Wallis and Joseph Hazen dated October 18, 1957. Amends the original April 2, 1956 contract for "King Creole." Changed terms include such items as beginning date and reimbursement of expenses. Signed in blue ink by Elvis Presley and Hall Wallis, and in black ink by Joseph Hazen. Letter dated January

17, 1958 to William Morris Agency in Beverly Hills from Elvis and Colonel Parker regarding changes that affect their agency in the contract changes. Letter dated January 20, 1958 from the Lou Goldberg of the William Morris Agency to Colonel Parker regarding the expenses now being paid by

Wallis-Paramount-Hazen. All documents have three-hole punches in left margin. Photograph included. 11 x 8 1/2 inches each.

This letter is formal notification of Elvis' second Hal Wallis film, "King Creole." Although the agreement reads that the filming of "King Creole" would start November 6, 1957, it did not actually start until January 20, 1958. In order for Elvis to be available for filming, he had to request a deferment from his local draft board who granted him a 60 day deferment. "King Creole" was filmed on location in New Orleans. During the filming, Elvis stayed at the

Roosevelt Hotel. Michael Curtiz directed the film and said of Elvis, "Just like in his music, he really got involved in his acting, you'd look in his eyes and, boy, they were really going." Elvis' performance in "King Creole" is regarded by many, including Elvis himself, as one of his strongest performances.

$5,000 - 7,000

A197 "KING CREOLE" SHEET MUSIC, LAYOUT AND MEMO

In a memo dated May 26, 1958, Tom Diskin writes to Grelun Landon regarding "King Creole" songs. Tom suggests various changes for sheet music covers and attaches a "super rare" sketch of the layout changes. These include placing "Sung By" above Elvis' name, deleting mention of title from artwork, substituting "in" for "from" on line above "King Creole." Sheet music for "King Creole,"; 2 pages--green and white. Sleeve from EP of "King Creole" Vol. 2, blue background with color photo of Elvis on it; EP not included. 11 x 8 1/2 inches memo. 11 x 8 1/2 inches layout sketch. 12 x 9 1/8 inches sheet music. 7 x 7 EP sleeve.

The song "King Creole" was written by Jerry Leiber and Mike Stoller. It took several sessions to record the song, and finally on January 28, 1958, Elvis completed the version that would be published. In this final taping, they brought someone else in to assist D.J. on drums, Scotty and Bill were back after their rift over the Christmas album, and one of the Jordanaires had to assist Bill on some difficult parts on the electric bass. All this was accomplished to highlight the Jordanaires backup singing.

$4,000 - 5,000

A198 SQUARE GLASS BRICKS TAKEN FROM GRACELAND

Clear, white, and gold square glass bricks. The gold color is from fabric that was once attached to one side of the bricks. 6 x 6 inches

Glass bricks were used at the end of the living room, and the opening to the music room at Graceland. One side of the bricks was covered with a gold fabric, and the other side was plain glass. These bricks were used from 1957 until 1974 in the area that is now occupied by the glass peacock at Graceland.

$3,000 - 4,000

A199 TELEPHONE LAMP WITH SHADE

Gold phone with white phone cord and electrical cord. Tan burlap shade with dents and small tear. 20 1/4 inches high x 22 inches wide.

The Presley family used this item in their Audubon Drive home in the mid-Fifties. The Audubon house, in upscale East Memphis, was the first home that

Elvis bought after becoming a singer. In this context a novel item like this phone lamp could be seen as a Fifties-era symbol of the Presley's' newfound upward mobility.

$1,000 - 1,500

A200 GRACELAND SCREEN DOOR

One aluminum screen door, with solid aluminum bottom and aluminum strip across center of the door where handle rests. Decorative scrolls highlight the center portions of the screening. This screen door was once attached to the back door of Graceland. In 1967, the Presley's replaced the screen door and added an ironwork door. Visitors to Graceland today can see the ironwork door as they leave the Jungle Room and move toward the carport.

$1,500 - 2,000

A201 THE PRESLEY'S TELEPHONE TABLE

One wood telephone table painted white. This item is a combination seat and table where one side is a single seat with a green vinyl cushion; the other side has a one tiered flat shelve for a telephone. Seat is 18" from floor with the back of chair reaching another 10" for support. Top shelf is 27 3/4" from the floor. Table is 17 1/2" wide.

Table was used by the Presley's at their 1034 Audubon Drive home. It is a combination seat and telephone table which was used by Elvis and his family in their living room. $1,500 - 2,000

A202 ELVIS' NIGHTSTAND

Black and white wood nightstand. White top and two white drawers with gold metal handles. Black sides and legs. 24 inches high x 24 inches wide x 16 1/2 inches deep

This nightstand was used beside Elvis' bed at Graceland during the Fifties.

$14,000 - 16,000

A202

A203 CHRISTMAS CARD WITH SHIPPING INSTRUCTIONS

1958 Christmas card from Elvis and the Colonel with red background and green tree. Elvis--in black and white--is in his Army uniform waving to his fans and the Colonel, dressed as Santa--in black and white--is in an inset photo. Message reads "Holiday Greetings to You All from Elvis and the Colonel." Telegram included is dated December 9 to Colonel Parker from Bill Bullock (RCA executive) and reads "Rushing you list of distributor record managers. Ship each one 500 cards and send me bill. Thanks for other cards. Regards." 5 1/2 x 8 1/2 inches card. 3 3/4 x 8 1/2 inches telegram

The Colonel and Elvis sent Christmas cards every year. In 1958, Elvis posed in his uniform, indicating his tour of duty with the Army.

$500 - 600

A204 ELVIS PRESLEY'S LIFE INSURANCE POLICY

Eight page insurance policy from The Equitable Life Assurance Society of the United States insuring Elvis Presley. The policy for $37,500 is dated March 27, 1957 and had an annual premium of $606.38. The beneficiaries of the policy were Gladys and Vernon Presley. Two-page photocopy of doctor's bill for an insurance examination done on March 27, 1957. Elvis complained of, "Nervousness, insomnia. Just felt 'jittery' because of pressing professional obligations. No medication or treatment required. No other symptoms." His profession was listed as "Entertainer - 2 1/2 years." Elvis responded "No" to the question, "Do you contemplate... any change in occupation." Photocopy of Elvis' signature. Two light blue tri-fold booklets. One booklet gives the 20 Year Summer of Elvis' life insurance policy. The second booklet details another life policy for the face amount of $62,500, and with an annual premium of $1,010.62. 15 x 8 1/2 inches policy; 6 1/2 x 5 1/8 copy of doctor's bill; 13 3/4 x 8 3/4 inches blue booklets

Several days before this policy was purchased, on March 22, 1957, Elvis was accused of pulling a gun on a young Marine, Hershal Nixon, in downtown Memphis across from the Hotel Chisca. Nixon claimed that Elvis had insulted his wife. The incident was settled in a judge's chambers on March 25. That same day, Elvis sent Nixon a long telegram apologizing for the incident. He explained that the gun was a Hollywood prop gun. He was showing some people the gun when Nixon and some of his friends called Elvis over and accused him of bumping into Nixon's wife. Elvis explained that there are a few people in the world who mean to cause him harm and that he only meant to protect himself in the event that Nixon was one of those people. Elvis expressed his respect for the Marines and the other armed services, and wished Nixon the best.

$2,000 - 3,000

A205 CORRESPONDENCE TO COLONEL TOM PARKER FROM NICK ADAMS

Western Union Telegram to Colonel Parker from Nick Adams dated May 7, 1959 telling him about his show "The Rebel" and thanking him for his advice and friendship. Two-page personal letter dated February 12, 1959 to Colonel from Nick on Nick Adams stationery. Discusses snow jobs, offers thanks for the nice things he was saying about him, mentions a letter he got from Elvis. Signed "Nick" with a hand printed P.S. about someone he ran into who knew the Colonel. Letter dated November 4, 1959, from Nick Adams to Colonel Parker. Correspondence is regarding a recent phone call to the Colonel, and a mention of a recent episode on "The Rebel". Letter is typed on Paramount Pictures letterhead, and signed by Nick. Letter dated November 2, 1960 on Nick Adams letterhead that has a portrait of the battle of Gettysburg along the top margin. Letter regards his "commission in the Georgia Militia." Signed by Nick. Black cowboy boots that were given to Colonel Parker as a gift from Nick Adams. Brown leather patch on the shin of the boot with tooling reads, "Colonel Snow from The Rebel." 7 1/2 x 5 3/4 inches telegram. 10 1/2 x 7 1/4 inches 2-page letter. 11 x 8 1/2 inches 1-page letters.

Nick Adams was a long time friend of both Elvis and Colonel Parker. Elvis met Nick Adams during the filming of "Love Me Tender." They became fast friends and it was Nick that introduced Elvis to Natalie Wood. Nick often visited Elvis at Graceland and traveled with him on tour. Nick Adams was hungry for fame and success. He was known for his detailed logs of Hollywood society and for never forgetting to send a thank you note or congratulatory note to producers, directors, other Hollywood moguls and, of course, Colonel Parker.
$800 - 1,000

A206 WESTERN UNION TELEGRAM FROM COLONEL PARKER TO MILTON BERLE

Original Western Union telegram dated October 6, 1958, from Colonel Parker to Milton Berle wishing him the best of luck with his new show. Page from the "Daily Variety" with advertisement from Elvis' first appearance on the Milton Berle Show April 3, 1956. 5 1/2 x 8 1/2 inches Telegram. 18 1/3 x 12 1/4 inches "Daily Variety"

Western Union telegram was sent during the time Elvis was in Germany. The Milton Berle show was broadcast from the deck of the aircraft carrier, the U.S.S. Hancock, in San Diego. Elvis was paid $3000 for his appearance.
$400 - 600

A207 CORRESPONDENCE REGARDING POSSIBLE POST-ARMY "ED SULLIVAN SHOW" APPEARANCE

Original Western Union telegram dated June 17, 1958 from Harry Kalcheim of the William Morris Agency to Col. Tom Parker regarding an Elvis appearance after he is discharged from the army. An original signed letter from Ed Sullivan to Col. Parker. 4 3/4 x 8 1/2" Telegram. 7 1/4 5 1/4". Letter. Telegram is in regards to Ed Sullivan offering Elvis $100,000 for a personal appearance on his show when Elvis returns from the Army. The letter sent to the Colonel from Ed Sullivan is thanking him for his kind wishes.
$800 - 1,000

A208 TELEGRAM TO DEAN MARTIN

Western Union telegram sent to Dean Martin in Beverly Hills from "Your Pals, Elvis and The Colonel." Telegram reads: "CONGRATULATIONS AND GOOD ROCKING TONIGHT--WITH SO MANY FRIENDS LOVING YOU--AND FEELING LIKE A TEDDY BEAR--WE KNOW THAT YOU MUST BE ALL SHOOK UP--SO DON'T, I BEG OF YOU, DON'T BE CRUEL, I'M COUNTING ON YOU NOT TO GET ON JAILHOUSE ROCK, TREAT ME NICE OR YOU'RE NOTHING BUT A HOUND DOG." Framed photograph of Dean Martin included. 6 x 8 1/2 inches telegram.

Elvis and the Colonel frequently sent these whimsical telegrams that incorporated titles of Elvis songs into the message. Singer and actor Martin was one of Elvis' favorite performers in the early Fifties, and Elvis recorded Martin's "I Don't Care If the Sun Don't Shine" while he was at Sun.
$500 - 600

A209 LETTERS FROM DICK CLARK

Two typed letters on blue and orange "Dick Clark" letterhead with raised "dc" imprint. Both signed in green ink by Dick Clark. One dated March 5, 1959 sent to Col. Parker in Madison, Tennessee. One dated May 23, 1960 sent to Tom Diskin in Hollywood. 11 x 8 1/2 inches.

The Parker letter is in reference to the "birthday party" Clark threw for Elvis on "American Bandstand" earlier that year.
$1,000 - 1,500

A210 ROBERT TAYLOR'S CORRESPONDENCE TO COLONEL PARKER

Typed letter on beige-colored "Robert Taylor" stationery boldly signed "Bob" to Col. Parker, dated December 28, 1958. 6 5/8 x 8 5/8 inches.

Taylor was a prolific film actor who appeared in "Bataan" and "Camille" among countless others.
$175 - 250

A211 CORRESPONDENCE BETWEEN ELVIS PRESLEY, COLONEL PARKER, BOB HOPE, AND JIMMIE RODGERS

Original, typewritten letter dated April 23, 1959, to Elvis and the Colonel from Jimmie Rodgers. Letter is on Honeycomb Productions, Inc., letterhead, and signed by Jimmie Rodgers. In the letter Mr. Rodgers is thanking Elvis & the Colonel for sending their best wishes for his opening night. Copy of a typewritten letter from Bob Hope to Colonel Parker. Correspondence is dated May 5, 1959, and acknowledges an earlier wire sent by the Colonel regarding Mr. Hope's eye injury and health problems. 10 1/2 x 7 1/4 inches Rodgers Letter. 10 1/2 x 7 1/4 inches Hope Letter.

Jimmie Rodgers, not to be confused with country singer Jimmie Rodgers or Jimmie Rogers Snow, was a folk-rock singer who recorded such songs as "Honeycomb," "Kisses Sweeter Than Wine," and "Oh-Oh I'm Falling in Love Again." In 1966 Rodgers composed and recorded "It's Over", which Elvis sang in concert in the 1970's. Bob Hope was a fan of Elvis' and admired the Colonel.

$200 - 300

A212 LETTER TO COLONEL TOM PARKER FROM JEANETTE MACDONALD

Letter to Mr. Tom A. Parker from Jeanette MacDonald dated January 15, 1958. Letter on "Jeanette MacDonald" stationery, thanks Mr. Parker for the Presley Christmas records and photo. 8 1/2 x 5 1/2 inches.

Jeanette MacDonald was a well known singer and actress during the 1930's and 40's.

$300 - 400

A213 LETTER TO COLONEL PARKER FROM CORNEL WILDE

"Columbia Pictures Corporation" memo paper. Typed note from Cornel Wilde to Colonel Parker expressing appreciation and gratitude. Dated September 3, 1959. Cornel Wilde autographed photograph to Colonel Parker 5 7/8 x 7 5/8 inches memo. 10 x 8 inches photo.

Cornel Wilde played a leading man in many Hollywood films of the 1940s.

$200 - 300

A214 LETTER TO COLONEL PARKER FROM BING CROSBY

Dated December 16, 1959, on "Bing Crosby" stationery and signed by the singer: "Just got back from an extended vacation and hunting trip up in the Northwest to find the beautiful smoked sausage awaiting me . . . something that happens to be one of my very favorites." 10 1/2 x 7 1/4 inches.

One of singer Bing Crosby's greatest accomplishments was for recording the best selling record of all time, "White Christmas." He also acted in many films, including "Going My Way." Cosby remained friendly with the Colonel for two decades, always receiving gifts from him, such as the Colonel's famous Tennessee smoked sausages.

$250 - 350

A215 CORRESPONDENCE BETWEEN SAMMY DAVIS JR. AND COLONEL PARKER WITH AUTOGRAPHED PHOTO

Original typewritten letter to Col. Tom Parker from Sammy Davis, Jr., dated July 24, 1957. "You will find my picture enclosed. I would be pleased if Elvis would send me one in return." Carbon copy of reply letter dated July 31, 1957, from the Colonel thanking him for the picture and promising a nice picture of Elvis. One autographed photo of Sammy to the Colonel. 10 1/2 x 7 1/4 inches Original letter. 11 x 8 1/2 inches Reply letter.

Autographed photo to the Colonel reads, "To Col Tom - It is people like you that make this business exciting for people like me. Very good wish. Your boy, Sammy Jr. Both Elvis and the Colonel were friends of Sammy Davis Jr.

$600 - 800

A216 NOTE TO COLONEL PARKER FROM ED SULLIVAN

Dated June 24, 1959, note from Sullivan (on his stationery) thanks the Colonel for his thoughtful congratulatory wire. Note ends with "Give our best to Elvis." Signed "Ed." . 4 5/8 x 4 1/4 inches.

Elvis and the Colonel became friends with Ed Sullivan when Elvis made his 1956 and 1957 appearances on the Sullivan show. They maintained their friendship throughout the years, with the Colonel continuing to send holiday greetings and congratulatory notes and telegrams.

$300 - 400

A217 JAILHOUSE ROCK SOUNDTRACK CORRESPONDENCE, SHEET MUSIC, AND A COLOR PHOTO EP COVER

Letter on "Elvis Presley Music, Inc." letterhead dated March 30, 1957, from Jean Aberbach to the Colonel. Outlines songs to be performed for "Jailhouse Rock" soundtrack, and the song's composers. Includes: Tepper - Bennett: "Quarters, Nickles, and Dimes", "Young Hearts", "One More Day." Leiber and Stoller: "Jailhouse Rock", "Sands of Time", "Treat Me NIce", "I Want to Be Free", "Yeah, Yeah, Yeah". Bernie Weisman: "Lonesome Blue". Aaron Schroder and Josephine Peoples: "That Ain't Right'. Rosemarie McCoy and Kelly Owens: "Don't be Afraid". Also included is three pages of sheet music for "Jailhouse Rock", and a color photo EP cover. 11 x 8 1/2 inches Letter, 12 x 9 inches Sheet Music, 7 x 7" EP Cover.

The only songs actually recorded for "Jailhouse Rock" out of all the ones submitted were; "Jailhouse Rock", "I Want to be Free", and "Treat me nice".

$800 - 1,000

A218 ELVIS PRESLEY PERSONAL APPEARANCE CONTRACTS

Eight blank contracts with a large black and white photograph at the top of the contract. Contract begins: Personal Appearance Contracts, Elvis Presley, The Nation's Only Atomic Powered Singer."
Border of twenty-six black and white photographs. 38 x 8 1/2 inches

These contracts were frequently used by the Colonel in the early days of his management of Elvis. The top of Elvis at the tip of the contract is the same that was used on the cover of his RCA debut album ("Elvis Presley").

$4,000 - 5,000

A219 "LOVE ME TENDER" SINGLE SILVER RECORD

Mounted and framed award, connotating one million records sold. Plaque reads: "To Colonel Parker

in Appreciation of his Contribution Toward Making Love Me Tender a Million Dollar Seller 1958" From Colonel Parker's personal collection. 16 x 14 inches framed award.

The ballad "Love Me Tender" was released as a single in September 1956 and became one of Elvis' biggest hits and trademark songs, staying at #1 on the Billboard pop chart for a solid month. The song was recorded for Elvis' first film, tentatively called "The Reno Brothers," but the title of the film was changed to "Love Me Tender" in response to the tremendous success of the song. The song also made top five on both the country and rhythm and blues charts and was featured on all three of Elvis' appearances on "The Ed Sullivan Show."
$15,000 - 20,000

A220 "TOO MUCH" SINGLE SILVER RECORD

Mounted and framed award, connotating one million records sold. Plaque reads: "To Colonel Parker in Appreciation of his Contribution Toward Making Too Much a Million Dollar Seller 1957" From Colonel Parker's personal collection. 16 x 14 inches framed award.

"Too Much" was released as a single in January of 1957 and reached #2 on the Billboard chart. It also hit #3 on the country chart. Elvis performed the song during his third appearance on "The Ed Sullivan Show." $10,000 - 15,000

A221 CORRESPONDENCE REGARDING ELVIS' THIRD "ED SULLIVAN SHOW" APPEARANCE

Letter, on William Morris Agency letterhead, dated December 3, 1956, from Harry Kalcheim to Colonel Tom Parker. Message states that Elvis is to report to Paramount on Thursday, January 10 for pre-production and begin, on salary, on January 17, allowing Elvis to appear on Ed Sullivan on January 6. Kalcheim mentions that Paramount suggests staying at the Knickerbocker since it's closer to the studio. 11 x 8 1/2 inches.

The Ed Sullivan Show, still known to many as Toast of the Town, invited Elvis for his third and last appearance on January 6, 1957. Sullivan had high praise for the entertainer after he performed.
$750 - 1,000

A222 "HEARTBREAK HOTEL" TELEGRAM FROM MAE AXTON

Western Union telegram dated February 2, 1956, sent to Colonel Parker and Elvis Presley from "Heartbreak Hotel" co-writer Mae Axton. 10 x 8."

WAITED UNTIL NOW SO I COULD WIRE YOU MY ENTHUSIASTIC CONGRATULATIONS ON BOTH THE TELEVISION APPEARANCE AND THE HEART-BREAK HOTEL RECORD WHAT A WONDERFUL JOB YOU BOTH HAVE DONE AND ELVIS THE RECORD CAME TODAY AND IS SIMPLY TERRIFIC I AM SO THRILLED AND ALSO DELIGHTED WITH YOUR TELEVISION DEBUT HAD AN OPRY SHOW IN HERE LAST SATURDAY NIGHT SO I BORROWED A PORTABLE TELEVISION AND TOOK IT ALONG AND ALL THE DEE JAYS AND I GATHERED IN THE ARMORY OFFICE FROM 8 UNTIL 8:30 TO WATCH YOU WE WERE ALL OVERJOYED The co-author of "Heartbreak Hotel," Mae Axton once worked as a publicist for Colonel Parker client Hank Snow, and, at the time this telegram was written, worked for the Grand Ole Opry. The television appearance Axton refers to is Elvis' performance on "Stage Show" on January 28, 1956, his national television debut. "Heartbreak Hotel" had been released the day before. $1,000 - 1,500

A223 LETTER TO COLONEL TOM PARKER FROM MAE AXTON

Handwritten letter to Colonel Tom Parker from Mae Boren Axton. Letter is on notepaper that reads, "From The Desk Of Mae Boren Axton." Mae discusses the song "It Takes a Little Love" which she had sent to Elvis. She thought he would like it after the success with "Heartbreak Hotel." 8 3/8 x 5 1/2"

Elvis first met Mae Boren Axton in early 1955 when she served as a publicist for some of Elvis' engagements in Florida. Prior to one of his Florida performances, Mae tried to convince Elvis to give her the frilly pink shirt he was wearing. She told him, "Elvis, that's vulgar. And it would make me such a pretty blouse." Axton co-wrote "Heartbreak Hotel" with Tommy Durden. After "Heartbreak Hotel," Elvis did not record any more of Axton's songs.

$250 - 300

A224 PURCHASE PAPERS ON VERNON PRESLEY'S 1956 PLYMOUTH

Conditional sale of purchase contract for 1956 Plymouth; dated January 4, 1956 and purchased from John Wellford Co. Dodge & Plymouth. Price was

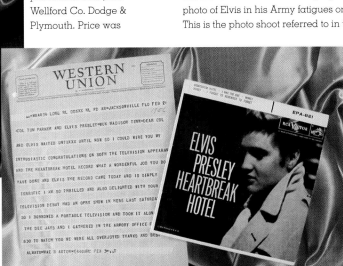

223

222

$3,469.50 less a $600 down payment, leaving 30 payments of $95.65 each. Signed in red ink by Vernon Presley. Blue envelope from John Wellford Co. and addressed to Vernon at his Getwell address. Four-page form from Commercial Credit Plan outlining specifics of payment. Receipt from Testing Station for inspection on the Plymouth; dated March 9, 1956. 11 x 8 1/2" contract. 4 1/8 x 9 1/8" envelope. 7 1/4 x 8 1/2" commercial credit . 2 3/4 x 5" testing station. Elvis purchased this Plymouth station wagon for his father.

$800 - 1,000

A225 ELVIS TELEGRAMS AND PHOTOPLAY MAGAZINES

Two Western Union telegrams dated January 30, 1959. One telegram sent to Vernon Presley at the Hilberts Park Hotel in Bad Nauheim, Germany, from Tom Diskin in Madison, Tennessee. Telegram concerns an award Elvis is to receive from Dick Clark's "American Bandstand" and the possibility of a phone interview. One telegram sent to Elvis at the Hotel Grunewald in Bad Nauheim from Photoplay magazine in New York. Telegram thanks Elvis for allowing one of their photographers to do a photo shoot on Elvis' Army life. Two copies of Photoplay magazine, one dated July 1957, one dated March 1960, both with Elvis on the cover. 6 x 8 1/4" telegram. 11 x 8 1/2" magazines.

The March 1960 issue of Photoplay features a color photo of Elvis in his Army fatigues on the cover. This is the photo shoot referred to in the telegram.

Dated the month Elvis was discharged, the magazine features a "Date with Elvis" contest and poses the question "Will you be the girl to welcome Elvis back?"

$1,500 - 2,000

A226 ELVIS PRESLEY SETTLEMENT STATEMENTS FOR 1956 AND TAX RETURN FOR 1955

Statement from the August Tour 1956 for All Star Shows #350, dated August 18, 1956, showing Elvis paid $14,307.16. Signed by Elvis Presley. Attached to this statement was the1955 Individual Income Tax Return (1040) for Elvis Presley at Audubon Drive; signed by Elvis and dated August 10, 1956. Adjusted Gross Income: $25,214.15. Tax: $7,112.65. Air Mail Special Delivery envelope included was sent to Vernon Presley from the Colonel.

Letter dated September 18, 1956 addressed to Mr. Presley and signed, "Col.." The Colonel states that he has enclosed Elvis' check for the Sullivan show. After tax and expenses, Elvis received $6,025.36. Included is original envelope addressed to Mr. and Mrs. Vernon Presley on Audubon Avenue, from Col. Tom Parker in Dressing Room 6 at the Twentieth-Century-Fox Film Corporation studios in Beverly Hill. 11 x 8 /2" documents. 4 1/4 x 9 3/4"envelopes

Found in Vernon Presley's office, these statements of income and the tax return were indicative of documents Colonel Tom Parker would send to Vernon for his records. The tax return shows Elvis earning just over $25,000 in 1955 (and counting his parents and grandmother as exemptions); however, from that year on his earnings increased, due to his film roles and his RCA contract, which he signed at the end of 1955. $1,000 - 1,500

A227 LETTER FROM STEPHEN SHOLES TO COLONEL PARKER

Two pages typed letter on RCA letterhead, dated December 22, 1958 and sent to Colonel Parker from RCA A&R Director Stephen H. Sholes. Concerns

A228

possible recordings for Elvis' next single. Sholes lists six titles in order of preference: "A Big Hunk O' Love," "A Fool Such As I," "I Need Your Love Tonight," "When it Rains it Really Pours," "My Wish Came True" and "Tell Me Why." With 45 RPM single of "I Need Your Love Tonight"/"A Fool Such As I," and acetates of "A Fool Such As I," "I Need Your Love Tonight" and "My Wish Came True." 11 x 8 1/2 inches letter. 7 inches diameter single.

Sholes suggests the first three titles and dubs the last three "all pretty weak." He says he's "particularly opposed" to "Tell Me Why" because of its similarity to the gospel hymn "Just a Closer Walk With Thee." Of the other two "weak" songs, Sholes writes "The other two are not only weak songs, but not very well performed by Elvis." This last sentence is circled in black ink and handwritten beneath is "Please return this letter to me—Col." with "Col." underlined four times. There is a small tear on the second page.This document reveals part of the struggle between RCA and Colonel Parker over the release of Elvis product while he served in the Army.

The handwritten note from the Colonel, who also had strong ideas about records, probably reveals no small measure of irritation over Sholes' dismissive remarks. The "I Need Your Love Tonight"/"A Fool Such As I" single was released in March, 1959. Elvis' next single followed three months later. It contained "A Big Hunk of Love," one of the tracks Sholes recommends here, and "My Wish Came True," which Sholes had determined to be "weak."

$800 - 1,000

A228 ELVIS PRESLEY AND COLONEL PARKER CHRISTMAS CARDS

Assorted package of 17 Christmas cards sent by the Presley family or Elvis and the Colonel. Very rare. Sizes ranging from 5 1/2 x 3 1/2 to 10 1/2 x 7 inches. One card, from 1956, depicts Santa Claus ringing a bell and two zoot-suited reindeer—both carrying horns and one with a goatee. Very rare card reads "Dig that crazy Swiss bell ringer." Inside of card reads in red "To wish you a Cool Yule and a Frantic First - Elvis Presley Colonel Parker."

$4,000 - 5,000

A229 NOTE FROM RED WEST TO COLONEL TOM PARKER.

Handwritten note to Tom regarding two songs Elvis was interested in: "Ain't Nobody Gonna Take My Place" written by Red, and "You'll Be Gone" by Elvis, Red, and Charlie Hodge. Photo 11 x 8 1/2"

One of Elvis' close friends and a member Memphis Mafia, Red West wrote songs for Elvis, Pat Boone, Ricky Nelson, and others. Elvis eventually recorded "You'll Be Gone," a song which he helped write. West also played minor roles in about 15 of Elvis' films. Today, West still lives in Memphis, where he runs a school for actor

$1,000 - 1,200

A230 ARMY TELEGRAM TO ELVIS PRESLEY FROM COLONEL PARKER; CLAIM FOR RENT & DAMAGES ON HOUSE IN GERMANY

Lot contains: a) Letter to Elvis, Family and friends in Germany. b) Telephone receipt from Germany. c) Western Union telegram dated October 7, 1958, sent to Elvis at First Medium Tank Battalion, 32nd Armored-Third Armored Division, Friedberg, Germany. d) letter dated February 27, 1960 from Ray Barracks in Friedberg, Germany concerning claim for rent and damages to 14 Goethe Strasse, Bad Nauheim, Germany. e) Letter from George Klein on WHEY Radio (Millington, Tn.) letterhead. addressed to "Dear Elvis, Mr. Presley, Mrs. Minnie, Red, and Lemoine." f) Telephone receipt dated August 6, 1959, for telephone service from May 29 to June 8, 1959. On front of bill is landlady Frau Pieper's name, and the address is listed as Goethe Strasse 14. Photograph included. Sizes vary from 4 x 6 and 11 x 8 1/2 inches.

Elvis arrived in Germany on October 1, 1958. Three days later Vernon Presley, Elvis' grandmother Minnie and Memphis friends Red West and Lamar Fike arrived. On October 6, the day before this telegram was sent, Elvis received permission to live off base with Vernon and Minnie. The damage and rent claim was signed and witnesses by three people that Sgt. Elvis Presley payed Mrs. Piever 6,000 deutsche marks for damage to her property, and for one month's rent. George Klein letter was later used by a member of the family, or possibly Elvis Presley. On the back are written directions to go with a loosely sketched map that features the Autobahn. Notes the house phone as 3201. Elvis, Vernon, and Minnie Mae lived at this address in Bad Nauheim, West Germany. The house was a five bedroom, white stucco home which Elvis rented for $800 a month. Marie Pieper lived in a room off the kitchen.
$6,000 - 8,000

ELVIS IN THE ARMY

A231 ELVIS ON LEAVE: WEEKEND PASS, HOTEL BILLS AND LETTER

Army weekend pass dated November 13, 1959. Issued to Elvis A. Presley for leave from November 13 - 15, 1959 with permission to visit "Western, Germany." Signed in blue ink "Elvis A. Presley" by Elvis and by Capt. Robert Childress. Photograph included. Original one page typewritten letter, dated July 7, 1959, from Tom Diskin to Elvis in Paris. Correspondence mentions record sales for "My wish Came True," and the continuous support Elvis is receiving from his fan clubs. Diskin also informs Elvis that they are looking after his dad and that he "sure looked fine". P.S. "Just read a fan magazine article that printed your connect (2714) phone number. You may have to have it changed." Also included is the original air mail envelope,

addressed to Private 4th Class Elvis Presley. The envelope is unique in that the back side is covered with promotional items. Light orange card with insignia title and location of Hotel Prince de Galles detailing charges in blue ink totaling $169.25 for both lunch and dinner served to Elvis' hotel room plus the appropriate 15% service charge for January 18, 1960. The front card includes a hotel stamp with date in black ink. The backside of this card details an $18 charge for telephone service. Photo incl. 8 x 5 1/4" pass. 6 3/4 x 8 1/4" hotel bills.

Leave pass is stamped "Hitchhiking is prohibited." The hotel bills date from a trip to Paris Elvis made in mid-January 1960, while on leave from his Army post in Germany. While in Paris, Elvis attended karate classes and American gospel group performances. $5,000 - 6,000

A232 "G.I. BLUES" CONTRACT

Contract agreement made on October 28, 1958, between Hal B. Wallis and Joseph H. Hazen (employers) and Elvis Presley (artist) for the film "G.I. Blues." Services were to begin as soon as Presley left the Armed Forces. The 61-page contract specifics include total salary of $125,000 plus $50,000 for expenses for first 8 weeks. If services go beyond 8 weeks, artist to be paid $21,875 per each additional week up to 10 weeks. Contract signed by Hal B. Wallis, Joseph H. Hazen, Elvis Presley, and Colonel Thomas Parker. 11 x 8 1/2 inches per page.

This agreement, made between the Colonel, Wallis, and Hazen, transpired while Elvis was in the Army. It updated and superseded the original contract from 1956, including the salary requirements, which were increased to $175,000 for "G.I. Blues," and options for three more pictures. "G.I. Blues" began production in May 1960, soon after Elvis returned from the Army. The Paramount film was Elvis' fifth picture, and the first of nine in which he would work under the direction of Norman Taurog. Elvis played the character Tulsa McLean, and Juliet Prowse costarred as Lili. The film opened nationally on November 23, 1960. $15,000 - 20,000

A233 SIGNED LEASE FOR ELVIS PRESLEY'S BEVERLY WILSHIRE APARTMENT

Letter dated September 8, 1959 to Colonel Tom Parker from Evelyn Sharp on Beverly Wilshire letterhead. Letter discusses arrangements for Elvis Presley to lease Apartments #615/621 and #1000 at the Beverly Wilshire at a rate of $2,000 a month for six months from April 15, 1960 through October 14, 1960. Copy of a letter dated September 21, 1959 to Evelyn Sharp from Tom Diskin. States that he has enclosed three signed leases and wishes to have two returned. Letter dated September 22, 1959 to Tom Diskin from Evelyn Sharp on Beverly Wilshire letterhead. States that she is enclosing two signed copies of Mr. Presley's lease. Two double-sided page contract dated September 8, 1959 between Mr. Elvis Presley and the Beverly Wilshire Hotel. States that Elvis agrees to pay $12,000 for the rental of apartment #615/21 and #1000 for six months in 1960. Signed in blue ink by Elvis Presley. 11 x 8 1/2 inches letters. 13 1/2 x 8 1/2 inches contract.

When Elvis first stayed in Los Angeles he stayed at the Knickerbocker, however, he came to prefer staying at the Beverly Wilshire because it was fancier. He even lived at the Beverly Wilshire during the filming of his fifth movie, "G.I. Blues."

$4,000 - 5,000

A234 "ELVIS SAILS" ACETATE

Acetate of an album RCA released of Elvis' press conference before leaving for his Army stint in Germany. With 45 rpm "Elvis Sails" EP and original cardboard sleeve. 10 inches diameter acetate. Label reads "RCA Victor Reference Recording."

Acetate label reads "RCA Victor Reference Recording." Single sleeve is a black and white newspaper mock-up with the headline "EXTRA ELVIS SAILS" and a photo of Elvis in his Army hat. Released in December 1958, two months after Elvis

A234

docked in Germany, "Elvis Sails" consists of three interviews Elvis gave before leaving. Elvis' ship set out for Germany on September 22, 1958, the date of the mock newspaper on the cover of "Elvis Sails." The cardboard sleeve has a small hole in the top center. It was manufactured like this so that fans could hang the sleeve on their walls. "Elvis Sails" peaked at #2 on the Billboard EP chart.

$4,000 - 6,000

A235 LETTERS TO ELVIS PRESLEY IN THE ARMY FROM COLONEL PARKER

Five typed letters, on "Thomas A. Parker" letterhead, sent from the Colonel to Elvis: Letter dated November 13, 1958 to Elvis and Vernon; contains two newspaper clippings about Presley from the New York Mirror. One discusses Elvis buying a castle in Germany. Letter dated December 30, 1958 to Vernon and Elvis. Letter dated April 15, 1959; 2 pages to Elvis and Vernon. Letter dated October 7, 1959; 2 pages to Elvis. Letter dated January 9, 1960; 2 pages to Elvis. Three special delivery, air mail, stamped envelopes addressed to Elvis and Vernon with "Thomas A. Parker" return address and one envelope (unstamped) to Elvis and Vernon Presley marked Personal. 11 x 8 1/2 inches letters. 4 1/8 x 9 inches envelopes.

The Colonel's letters elaborate on personal issues, including rumors that were spreading about an incident at a hotel, constant stories about different girlfriends, Mrs. Parker's illness, and Bobby Smith charging calls to Elvis' number. The Colonel relates how well some of Elvis' records and movies are doing, possible new releases, and royalties on special gimmicks. He constantly reassures Elvis about his successes, even though he is not visible in the marketplace at the time. In one letter he sends along contracts to sign; in another, the Colonel asks Elvis to sign his preference of how to work with Frank Sinatra Production Company when he leaves the Army.

$4,000 - 5,000

A236 ELVIS IN THE ARMY

Army press release; RCA radiogram to Elvis Presley from Colonel Tom Parker; invoice of shipment for Elvis Presley's belongings from Germany; Western Union Telegrams from Elvis Presley to his fan club in Ohio, and to Colonel Parker; letter to Elvis Presley from Tom Diskin; dental bill signed by Elvis Presley; German hotel receipts; letter from the U.S. Navy Recruiting Station to Elvis Presley, and one metal army trunk

Three page typewritten press release from Brooklyn Army Terminal, dated September 22, 1958. Release states that Elvis would depart from the Brooklyn Army Terminal aboard the U.S.S. Randall schedule to arrive in Bremerhaven, Germany, October 1.

Copy of RCA radiogram dated January 21, 1960, sent to Elvis in Bad Nauheim, Germany from Col. Parker. Radiogram is red and white with RCA letterhead.

Copy of shipping invoice from Universal Carloading & Distributing Co., for the shipment of Elvis' belongings from Germany. Shipping invoice lists items shipped from Bad Nauheim to SGT. Elvis Presley in Memphis. A copy of Elvis' signature is at the bottom of the invoice.

Original Western Union telegram dated March 20, 1958, from Elvis to Wanda L. Grubb of the Elvis Presley fan club in Bradford, Ohio. Original one page copy of a Western Union Telegram from Elvis Presley to Colonel Parker. Handwritten date indicates it was sent in February of 1960. Telegram is regarding Elvis' return to Memphis from the Army. A one page signed letter dated January 5 1960, to Elvis from Tom Diskin on Thomas A. Parker letterhead.

Dental bill on white paper, signed in pencil by Elvis Presley. Three restaurant receipts dated October 19, 1958, from Hilberts Parkhotel in Bad Nauheim, West Germany.

One hotel receipt dated October 6, 1958, from Hilberts Parkhotel in the name of Vernon Presley.

Typewritten letter to Pvt. Elvis Presley from Robert White of the U.S. Navy Recruiting Station dated March 27, 1958. Correspondence is typed on Navy stationery, and signed by Robert White.

One green army trunk 32" in width, 13.5" high with three handles; one on each side and one in center front, three latches across the front. Letters in white paint read, "SGT. Elvis A. Presley Us - 533 1 0761 3764 Highway 51, South Memphis, Tenn - USA."

Two page typewritten redeployment orders.

Typewritten letter to Elvis from Ira Jones dated July 15, 1959. Original envelope addressed to "Acting Sergeant Elvis Presley"; right side of envelope is torn. Photographs included. Sizes vary from 11 1/2 x 8 1/4 to 6 3/4 x 8 inches.

The press release was set up by Colonel Parker, and also outlines Elvis' career in the army thus far. Message on radiogram reads, "Dear Elvis: Congratulations on your promotion to sergeant which was in the paper today. Still trying to work out our RCA problems...Regards to all. The

Colonel."Western Union telegram to Colonel Parker from Elvis asking the Colonel to convey his thanks to the people who would throw him a special homecoming in Memphis. However, he declines because he wishes to return in the same manner as other servicemen who are returning home. Two hotel receipts are signed in blue by Vernon Presley, and one signed in blue by Elvis Presley. Letter from recruiting station was sent to congratulate Elvis on his induction in the Army, and to send him pamphlets on the "many opportunities" offered by the Navy if by chance he didn't like the Army.

$10,000 - 12,000

A236 ELVIS IN THE ARMY:
DOCUMENTS AND MEMORABILIA

Typed memo from Elvis in Bad Nauheim, West Germany to "Elvis Presley Fans" care of Col. Tom Parker. Two full color Elvis Presley Christmas post cards. Letter, on "James A. Matthews & Company" letterhead, dated November 21, 1958 sent to Vernon Presley at Gruenwald Hotel in Bad Nauheim, Germany. Letter concerns Elvis business dealing while in the service, including the production of Christmas cards. With original mailing envelope. Christmas card from 1958, showing Elvis in his uniform and the Colonel in Santa outfit; red and green background. Message: "Holiday Greeting to You All from Elvis and the Colonel." Pink ad mat used in the printing of the the card. Telegram dated September 1, 1959, sent to Colonel Parker from Elvis in care of RCA Victor Records in New York. He asks the Colonel while he is in New York if he can get RCA to get a message to the fans "to thank them not only for buying my records and for their loyalty to me but also for the help they have given me in deciding the kind of songs to sing, for in talking with them and reading their letters I was able to get some idea of what they liked. I'm deeply grateful to them and I want them to know it. When I'm out of the army and recording again I will always listen to their ideas just as I did before. I just wanted to let my fans know how I feel." 7 1/4 x 8 3/8" memo. 3 1/4 x 5 1/2" post cards. 11 x 8 1/2 inches letter. 4 1/4 x 9 1/2" envelope. 8 1/2 x 5 1/2 inches card. 9 34 x 6 5/8" print mat. 5 x 8 1/2" telegram.

The memo reads: "Dear Fans, Many of you asked for a new record. So that my career would not interfere with my Army duties I did not record in Germany. Will do my best to have a new record soon as I return. Thanks to all the disc jockeys, record dealers and distributors and RCA Victor for making this message possible." This message is reprinted on the back of the 1959 Christmas cards and labeled as "Copy Telegram From Elvis to the Colonel for his Fans." These cards were promotional items sent to radio disc jockey and others in the industry. The post card features two color photographs of Elvis in his Army suit and bears the message "Holiday Greetings to You All from Elvis and the Colonel."

$3,000 - 3,500

A237 DOCUMENTS RELATING TO ELVIS' TEXAS ARMY STATION

Western Union telegram sent to Private Elvis Presley on April 5, 1958, to Fort Hood, Texas, from Mrs. Parker and "The Admiral." They wish Elvis and the boys in his outfit a happy Easter, and regret that they cannot be there with him. Lease contract dated June 24, 1958, for Elvis and Vernon Presley to rent the home at 605 Oak Hill Drive in Killeen, Texas from July 1, 1958 to August 31, 1958 for a sum of $1500. Lease is signed by Vernon. Envelope included with Vernon Presley written on it. Return address from the law offices of Crawford & Harris in Killeen, Texas.   Manilla envelope postmarked June 27, 1958, sent from Col. Parker in Madison, Tn., to Vernon Presley in Killeen, Texas. Front has sticker with Col. Parker's covered wagon logo. Back has an extremely rear sticker for "King Creole" - a red drawing of Elvis wearing a crown that reads "Now Elvis Presley in King Creole, Hal Wallis production, directed by Michael Curtiz, a Paramount picture. Three checks dated June 25July 27, and September 6, 1958 written on The First National Bank of Killeen, Texas. Checks paid for

items bought at Piggly Wiggly, Mid-Texas Telephone, and Household Furniture Company. Mid-Texas telephone bill for Vernon Presley while in Killeen during the month of September, 1958. Typed bill is for long distance service and telegram. Total amount due is $267.03 with a handwritten note that says, "Paid Sept. 2" in the amount of $241.62. Original typewritten letter from Major General W. P. Johnson to Mr. & Mrs. Vernon E. Presley. Correspondence is dated April 10, 1958 announcing Elvis' safe arrival at Fort Hood, Texas. Photograph included. Sizes vary from 2 3/4 x 6 1/4 to 14 1/4 x 9 inches.

While Elvis served his country in the Army, the Colonel communicated with him daily by letter. He felt as if he constantly needed to reassure him that his career would not falter while he was in the service. The Colonel would re-release some of his records every six months to help keep his popularity alive. The Colonel often called himself "Admiral," but he occasionally called Marie by that nickname as well. On June 15, 1958 Elvis arranged to bring his mother and father to Killeen. An agreement was made to use a three bedroom trailer in exchange for a photograph of Elvis and his family in the unit. Gladys, Vernon, Vernon's mother Minnie, and Lamar Fike moved in on July 1, 1958. However, soon the five adults outgrew the trailer, and by July 1, they moved to 605 Oak Hill Drive. The monthly rent was $1500, and Gene & Junior Smith joined them. Shortly after this Gladys became ill, and in August moved back to Memphis where she passed away on August 14. It was common practice for the Army to notify the family regarding the safe arrival of each soldier.

$2,000 - 3,000

A238 ELVIS PRESLEY'S ARMY FATIGUES

Army Fatigues issued and worn by Elvis Presley while he served in the U.S. Army in. Olive Green shirt and pants. The shirt has a white patch with a black patch over the right breast pocket that reads "Presley." The black patch over the left breast pocket reads U.S. Army.

Elvis' serial number in the army was 53310761. It was during Elvis' 18 month assignment in West Germany when he met Priscilla Ann Beaulieu, who was the daughter of an American Air Force captain's daughter.

$60,000 - 80,000

☐ A240 LANSKY'S BULLETIN BOARD RECORDS

Two large black bulletin boards in the shape of records. One marked at center on faux label as "R.C.A., Hound Dog, Elvis Presley;" second marked at center on faux label as "R.C.A., Heartbreak Hotel, Elvis Presley."

The "Heartbreak Hotel" and "Hound Dog" records were made by Bernard Lansky for display in the Lansky clothing store in the 1950's. The records were used as bulletin boards to showcase the many hundreds of press releases and photographs of the Memphis boy who was very much a rising star. The Lansky brothers were very proud of their famous customer "Elvis", and they were just as proud of his accomplishments as Elvis Presley.

$2,000 - 4,000

A239 SNOWMEN'S LEAGUE LETTER TO ELVIS FROM COLONEL PARKER

Letter dated August 6, 1957 to Elvis from the Colonel on official "Thomas A. Parker" letterhead. Contents include information relating to book makeup on "Jailhouse Rock" stills, recording session dates, and Christmas album possible success. Colonel also makes jovial references to Col. Burro and the Donkeys and snowjobs. Envelope has "official" return address as Snowmen's League, Igloo 417, Madison, Tenn. and is addressed to "Snow Chief High Potentate Snower Elvis Snowchief Wallaby the First." Cover of Photo Folio, which includes 3 black and white photos of Elvis and an ad on the back for "Jailhouse Rock." 11 x 8 1/2 letter, 4 1/4 x 9 1/2" envelope, 10 x 8" photo folio.

This is just one example of Colonel Parker keeping Elvis informed about upcoming events. The letter is dated about two months before "Jailhouse Rock" had its official release in Memphis (October 17). However, Elvis and his parents saw a special preview on October 2nd.

Elvis recorded his Christmas album in Hollywood on September 5-7. Some of the featured songs included "White Christmas," "Blue Christmas," and "I'll Be Home for Christmas."

$1,500 - 2,000

THE SIXTIES

B1 "WELCOME HOME, ELVIS" DOCUMENTS AND RECEIPTS

Documents relating to Elvis' stay in Miami for the Frank Sinatra "Welcome Home, Elvis" television special, including: five hotel bills from the Fontainebleau Hotel in Miami, dating March 22-27, 1960. Two bills assigned to Elvis Presley and one each to Joe Esposito, Lamar Fike and Gene Smith. Handwritten receipts from Ace Formal Wear in Miami, both dated March 26, 1960, issued to Elvis Presley for tuxedo purchase and rental for the "Sinatra TV Show." One check to Ace Formal Wear, dated March 26, 1960 and signed "E.A. Presley" by Elvis in blue ink. Check made out to "Cash" in the amount $250.00, dated March 23, 1960 and signed "E.A. Presley" in blue ink. One handwritten room service bill in the amount of $7.50 for "Elvis Presley Rm 1562." One handwritten breakfast order for Elvis Presley at the Fountainebleu, contained "Eggs fried hard, yokes broken" and "bacon crisp." Statement on "Thomas A. Parker" letterhead from accountant Bill Fisher, dated March 30, 1960, concerning expenses for the Miami trip. Photograph included. 6 7/8 x 6 1/4 inches hotel bills. 6 3/8 x 4 1/4 inches tuxedo receipts. 3 1/8 x 8 1/4 inches checks. 5 x 4 inches room service bill. 5 1/4 x 4 inches breakfast order. 11 x 8 1/2 inches statement.

"Welcome Home, Elvis" was Elvis' first public appearance after being discharged from the Army on March 5, 1960. Hosted by Frank Sinatra, the special was taped at the Fontainebleau in Miami on March 26, 1960 and aired on ABC on May 12. Elvis was paid $125,000 for what amounted to a six-minute appearance. Elvis performed "Fame and Fortune" and "Stuck on You" and was then, in a meeting of two musical giants, joined by Sinatra for a duet of Sinatra's "Witchcraft" and Elvis' "Love Me Tender." Sinatra, who had once dubbed rock and roll music for "cretinous goons," was now sharing the stage in celebration of the once and future King of the music he had publicly scorned. As the title of his forth-coming album would assert, Elvis was back. This would be his last television appearance until 1968.

$10,000 - 12,000

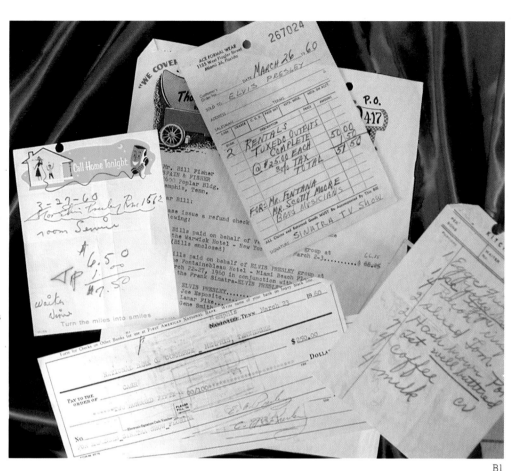

B1

B2 AMUSEMENT PARK BILLS

One bill typed on Memphis Park Commission letterhead and addressed to Mr. Elvis Presley at Graceland. Bill dated July 12, 1960 in the amount of $200 for the charter of amusement park rides on July 10, 1960. One bill from Spain & Fisher in the amount of $50 for the purchase of 250 "Cozy Dogs" by Elvis at the Fairgrounds on July 22, 1960. Photographs included. 11 x 8 1/2 inches park ride bill. 8 7/8 x 8 1/2 inches "Cozy Dogs" bill.

When Elvis rented the Mid-South Fairgrounds on this date for a private party, he began what would become a practice that continued throughout his life. Elvis' parties at the amusement park usually began after midnight and extended through the early morning hours, often with as many as 100

friends and acquaintances in attendance. These post-midnight soirees were the only way that Elvis could enjoy the park in relative peace. Elvis' favorite rides were the "Dodgem Cars" and the "Zippin Pippin", a rickety old wooden roller coaster that is the prime attraction at the park to this day. The last time Elvis rented out the fairgrounds was on August 8, 1977, just a week before his death, as a treat for his daughter Lisa Marie.

$500 - 700

B3 "WELCOME HOME ELVIS" SCRIPT

May 12, 1960 TV script from the Frank Sinatra Timex Show, "Welcome Home Elvis." Fifty-nine pages of dialogue, rehearsal schedule, stage directions, and index with changes marked in pencil. Photograph included. 11 x 8 1/2 inches

The Sinatra show was broadcast on the ABC network from 9:30 to 10:30 EST and attracted 41.5% of the viewing audience. Elvis took a train to Miami for this show, but returned on the bus at the insistence of Colonel Parker, who thought he should save money. The film is annotated by Colonel Parker.

$8,000 - 10,000

B4 LETTER AND STATEMENT FROM HARRY LEVITCH JEWELERS

Original typed letter, dated April 15, 1960, to Elvis from Harry Levitch. Levitch expresses his thanks for Elvis' patronage, and mentions repairs to a horseshoe ring. Attached statement lists the following items: two black suede straps for watches, man's diamond ring, a Longines watch, a 14K diamond pendant, and a charge for repairing a gold piece missing from the horseshoe ring. Total amount of bill $1423.65. 11 x 8 1/2 inches Letter. 8 1/2 x 5 1/2 inches statement

These pieces were purchased after Elvis had returned from the Army. $400 - 600

B5 BILLIARD SUPPLIES, INVOICE AND CHECK FOR GRACELAND POOL TABLE

Twenty-four pool balls; nine striped and ten solid. Five bumper pool balls; two white, two red and one yellow. Blue cue chalk. Invoice from the Rex Supply Company dated March 11, 1960, for a pool table and accessories for Graceland. Total bill $437.75. Original bill from "Bitsy" Mott Billiard Service for supplies and repairs. Total cost was $451.88. Check included for total amount of bill dated September 9, 1974, written on the Elvis

Presley Payroll & Expense Fund, and signed by Vernon Presley. Photograph included. 8 1/2 x 5 1/2 inches invoice. 7 1/2 x 5 1/2 inches bill. 3 x 8 1/4 inches check.

The pool table remains at Graceland today, in the basement pool room. "Bitsy" was Colonel Parker's brother-in-law. $3,500 - 4,000

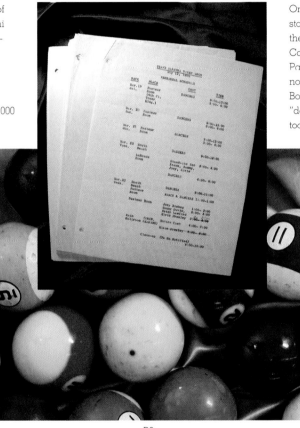

B3
B5

B6 COMPILATION OF SONGS FOR RECORDING SESSION

Original type and handwritten pages compiled in a folder, listing possible songs for future recording sessions. Dates vary from January 11, 1960 to August/ September of 1967. Songs are noted as to Elvis' top choices for material. Also included are lists of completed demos, and the dates they were

submitted to Charles Hodge. 11 x 8 1/2 inch pages. 11 3/4 x 9 1/4 inch Folder.

Charles Hodge worked closely with Elvis on selecting songs for each session. $1,750 - 2,000

B7 THANK YOU NOTES FROM BOBBY DARIN

One signed note from Bobby Darin on his personal stationery dated May 16, 1960 to Colonel Parker at the Beverly Wilshire Hotel in Beverly Hills, California. He thanks the Colonel, Elvis, and Mrs. Parker for his opening night wire. One copy of a note to Col. Parker and Elvis "From the Fingers of Bobby Darin," dated "Fri. 21 - 62." Darin expresses "deep appreciation of your gesture in the trades today. Long before this, and long after, I'm proud to be a friend to both of you. Love, Bobby." Photograph included. 10 1/2 x 7 1/4 inches May 16 note. 11 x 8 1/2 inches note.

Bobby Darin was a popular rock & roll singer during the 1950s and 1960s. Darin composed "I'll Be There" which Elvis recorded in 1969. Darin was one of Elvis' favorite singers and attended several of his performances.

$1,500 - 2,000

B8 LETTER FROM COLONEL PARKER TO ELVIS PRESLEY ABOUT TRAVEL TO HAWAII

Two pages typed on 20th Century Fox letterhead, dated November 21, 1960. Handwritten note in blue ink at bottom of second page: "Boat" and "Jet" are written with blanks next to each and there is a check in blue ink next to "Jet." Photograph included. 11 x 8 1/2 inches.

Letter regarding travel arrangements to Hawaii for Spring 1961 and whether or not to take a jet instead of a boat to extend Elvis' home vacation for an extra 10 days. They did indeed fly to Hawaii in March, where Elvis filmed "Blue Hawaii" and gave a benefit concert at Pearl Harbor.

$800 - 1,000

B9 ELVIS AND THE COLONEL—CHRISTMAS CARD

Proof and Photoproof of a Christmas card/advertisement featuring Elvis and the Colonel , dated December 16, 1960 and sent to "The New Musical Express" magazine in London. Photo of Elvis and the Colonel as Santa with the greeting "Everything good to all of you. Elvis and the Colonel." Original black and white photo of Elvis and the Colonel used for Christmas card and ad layout. 11 x 13 inches layout. 10 x 8 1/4 inches photo.

This photo of Elvis and the Colonel was taken on the set of Elvis' 1961 film "Wild in the Country."

$700 - 800

B10 PHOTOGRAPHS OF JOHN F. KENNEDY AND LYNDON B. JOHNSON AUTOGRAPHED TO COLONEL TOM PARKER

Black and white photograph of John F. Kennedy autographed to Colonel Tom Parker. Black and white photograph of Lyndon B. Johnson autographed to Colonel Tom Parker. 10 x 8"

Colonel Parker had friends in high places, not the least of which were the 35th and 36th presidents of the U. S. $3,500 - 4,000

B11 THE COLONEL AND THE CHAIRMAN

Typed note on "The Sinatras" stationery, dated December 18, 1963 and signed in blue ink "Tina, Frank Jr., Nancy Jr., Nancy & Frank." Typed letter on "Frank Sinatra" stationery, dated December 30, 1963. Signed in blue ink "Frank." Thank you note on white card dated February 3, 1971. Sent to "Colonel and Marie" and signed "Frank" in blue ink. Letter from Frank Sinatra to Col. Parker dated

August 26, 1960. The letter is on Beverly Hills Friars Club letterhead. Sinatra discusses an upcoming Charity Friar dinner, celebrating Gary Cooper, to be held November 27, 1960, at the Beverly Hilton. Signed in blue ink by Frank Sinatra. Western Union telegram, dated June 15, 1973, to Frank Sinatra from "Elvis & The Colonel," wishing Sinatra a happy Father's Day. Black and white photograph of Sinatra and the Colonel seated at a desk with a photo of Elvis on a table behind them. Color photograph of Sinatra and the Colonel embracing. 7 x 6 1/4" note. 10 1/2 x 7 1/4" letter. 7 3/4 x 5 3/4" thank you note. 11 x 8 1/2" letter. 4 7/8 x 8" telegram. 8 1/4 x 10" black and white photo. 13 1/4 x 10 3/4" photo.

photo .

B9   B10
B9   B13

These documents, which span a decade, illustrate both the personal and professional relationship the Colonel and Frank Sinatra shared. The black and white photo pictures Sinatra and the Colonel in Sinatra's Beverly Hills office discussing plans for the 1960 "Frank Sinatra's Welcome Home Party for Elvis Presley" TV special. In one of the notes, Sinatra writes "My thanks to you and Mrs. Parker for the electric foot massager. I am using it with pleasure." It was typical of Colonel Parker to send unusual gifts. $4,500 - 5,000

B12 "G.I. BLUES" PROMOTIONAL HAT AND CORRESPONDENCE

One brown paper "G.I. Blues" hat with red, white and blue logo on each side—one logo promoting the movie and the other promoting the soundtrack. One letter on 20th Century Fox letterhead, dated October 27, 1960 and sent to Tom Diskin. One two-sheet Western Union telegram sent to Colonel Parker at 20th Century Fox Studios in Los Angeles from Al Dvorin of Dvorin Enterprises. Photograph included. 5 1/2 x 11 1/4 inches hat. 11 x 8 1/2 inches letter. 5 3/4 x 8 inches telegrams.

Letter breaks down the distribution of 10,000 promotional hats: 4,000 to fan club presidents, 2,000 for "G.I. Blues" premiere, 1,000 for Paramount executives, 800 for a "G.I. Blues" showing in Westwood, 300 to Colonel Parker's office in Madison, TN, 100 for small promotional packages and 1,800 to have on hand. $1,400 - 1,600

B13 FRANK SINATRA'S SIGNATURE ON COLONEL PARKER'S LETTERHEAD

Typed note on Col. Tom Parker's letterhead with a penciled in date of March 28, 1960, in the upper right hand corner. Letterhead is a red wagon with Thomas A. Parker Exclusive Management in blue lettering, and "We Cover The Nation" in red print curved over the wagon cover. On the right upper corner is a red, white, and blue mailbox with the number 417 on the box, and the letters P.O. on top of the box. Photograph included. 5 1/2 x 8 1/2 inches.

Note reads, "Received one package and letter for Mr. Frank Sinatra." Below that is Sinatra's signature.

$800 - 1,000

B14 CONTRACT AMENDMENTS WITH TWENTIETH CENTURY FOX

Copy of a letter to Elvis Presley dated July 26, 1960, referring to employment agreement of October 29, 1958. Includes changing the starting date of employment to begin August 1, 1960, and specifies where to report for preproduction services for "Flaming Lance." Letter is signed in ink by Twentieth Century Fox and by Elvis Presley. Copy of a letter from Twentieth Century-Fox Film Corporation to Elvis Presley, dated September 27, 1960, regarding a change in the starting date of the film "Wild In The Country." Letter states that the film "is hereby accelerated from November 15, 1960 to November 9, 1960." Copy is signed and agreed to by Elvis Presley. Photograph included. 11 x 8 1/2 inches.

When a film was scheduled to begin production, cast members would receive instructions regarding specifics such as starting date and location for filming. "Flaming Lance," which was ultimately titled "Flaming Star," was directed by Don Siegel and was Elvis' sixth film. He played the dramatic role of Pacer and co-starred with Barbara Eden. Filming began August, 1960. Elvis co-starred with Hope Lange in "Wild in the Country," which began filming on November 11, 1960, at the Victorian Inn House in St. Helena, California. Exterior scenes were filmed in and around Napa Valley. While filming a scene for the movie Millie Perkins broke her wrist as she slapped Elvis. Filming was completed on January 18, 1961. Two endings were originally shot for this film: one in which Lange dies, and the other in which she lives. Sneak preview audiences, who voted on both endings, elected to see Lange live and thus, the film ended on an uplifting.

$7,000 - 8,000

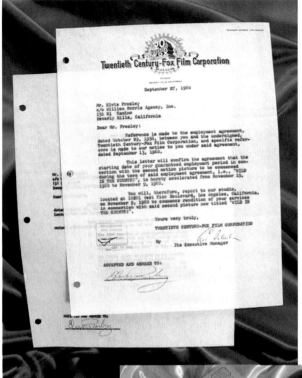

B14
B16

B15 ELVIS PRESLEY'S POWER OF ATTORNEY DOCUMENT

Two page power of attorney between Elvis (dba TCB Productions) and Vernon Presley. Typed on onion skin paper, and attached to a powder blue backing. The logo for the law offices of Montedonico, Heiskell , Davis, Glankler, Brown &

Gillilan is stamped on the back of the cover. It is signed by Elvis Presley. Original manila envelope with handwritten, "TCB Power of Attorney.' 13 3/4 x 8 1/2 inches Power of Attorney. 14 1/2 x 9 inches backing. 4 1/2 x 10 3/8 inches envelope.

As Elvis' business became increasingly complicated, it was necessary for Vernon to have Power of Attorney for TCB Productions. $3,000 - 4,000

B16 "IT'S NOW OR NEVER" TELEGRAM

Two sheet Western Union telegram sent to Elvis Presley from Paul Ackerman at *Billboard* magazine. Ackerman informs Elvis of the election of the single "It's Now or Never" as best single of 1960 by the nation's disc jockeys." With single of "It's Now or Never" b/w "A Mess of Blues," with original sleeve. 5 3/4 x 8 inches telegram. 7" diameter single.

"It's Now or Never," released in July 1960, was Elvis' best selling single, with world-wide sales exceeding 22 million. Paul Ackerman was the first person to write about Elvis in *Billboard*, noting the young performer when his first single, "That's All Right" was released. $750 - 850

B17 MIAMI TO MEMPHIS TRIP

Copy of the Itinerary for the Greyhound charter from Miami, FL to Memphis, dated March 25, 1960. Travel was from March 27 through the 28th. Included is a memo that contains brief notes regarding the chartered bus. 11 x 8 1/2" itinerary. 5 1/2 x 8 1/2" Memo.

Elvis chartered a bus for his return to Memphis from the filming of the Frank Sinatra television special. Though Elvis preferred to travel with his entourage by train, the Colonel advised Elvis to conserve his expenses by choosing less expensive transportation when possible, such as a chartered bus.

$1,000 - 1,250

B18 LETTER TO COLONEL THOMAS A. PARKER FROM THE ROY ROGERS FAMILY

Letter to Colonel Parker, dated January 6, 1960, 1960 on "Roy Rogers" stationery. Rogers thanks Colonel Parker for the sausage and the Elvis records that he sent the Rogers family as a Christmas gift. 8 1/4 x 7 1/4 inches.

As Elvis was in the Army during the Christmas of 1959, Colonel Parker was determined to maintain Elvis' status and his Hollywood contacts. Roy Rogers hosted "The Roy Rogers Show" during the 1950's.

$250 - 300

B19 CHRISTMAS CARDS AND ORDER FROM TOOF & COMPANY

Green and white Delivery Ticket dated 11-28-60 and pink invoice dated 12/21/60 from S.C. Toof & Company in Memphis for Christmas folders and embossed envelopes. 4,000 of each were ordered for a total of $445.99. Attached paper reads: "This was for the 4000 Christmas Cards and Envelopes--December 1960." Three green and beige Christmas cards with a message from "The Presleys" and five renderings of Graceland inside. 3 5/8 x 7 1/2 inches delivery ticket. 7 x 8 1/2 inches invoice. 5 3/4 x 8 1/2 inches attached sheet. 5 1/2 x 8 1/2 inches opening to 10 1/4 x 16 5/8 inches cards.

This was the first Christmas after Elvis' stint in the Army. The Toofs were the original owners of the land on which the Graceland mansion was built. Graceland was named in honor of Grace Toof, ancestor to the Moores who built the house in 1939.

$1,500 - 1,750

B20 ELVIS PRESLEY DISPLAY

Free-standing, cardboard, display with lights featuring a city landscape and changeable marquees. Marquee that appears is an advertisement for Elvis' "Indescribably Blue/Fools Fall in Love." 27 x 24 inches.

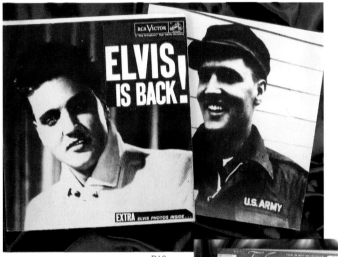

B19
B21

This display was originally created to advertise Elvis' 1960 movie, "G.I. Blues." Under the current advertisement is a transparent picture of the "G.I. Blues" album cover.

$2,000 - 2,500

B21 ARTWORK FOR "ELVIS IS BACK"

Artwork for the front and back of the "Elvis is Back" album. Both sides are black and white. Front features close-up photograph of Elvis in civilian clothes and the title, "Elvis is Back!" Back features photograph of Elvis in his army fatigues. Photographs are glued to a cardboard backing. 12 3/5 x 12 3/5"

On April 3, 1960, Elvis had an intense recording session at RCA's studios in Nashville, laying 12 tracks between 7:30 P.M. and 7:00 A.M.. Some of the songs included, "It's Now or Never," "Fever," and "Are You Lonesome Tonight" which was recorded at the request of Colonel Parker because it was his wife's favorite song. In their anxiousness to get the album released, RCA rushed the session tapes to the pressing plant and "Elvis is Back!" was shipped just four days after the recording session. No song titles were listed on the original album jacket as they were pre-printed. Instead, the titles were printed on stickers and affixed to the cover. Later pressings printed the titles directly on the album. "Elvis is Back!" had a 50-week stay on "Billboard's" Best-selling LP's chart.

$1,400 - 1,600

B22 ACETATE OF "RUBBER NECKIN'" AND "DON'T CRY DADDY"

Acetate of Elvis Presley's "Rubber Neckin'" and "Don't Cry Daddy." In original envelope from Tansco, "...a 'Sound' Investment." 10" diam. acetate. 10 1/8 x 10 1/8" envelope.

Both of these songs were recorded at American Sound Studios in Memphis in January, 1969. "Don't Cry Daddy" earned a certified Gold Record by the RIAA on January 21, 1970. $650 - 750

B23 "ARE YOU LONESOME TONIGHT" GOLD RECORD

Framed award. Gold, 45 rpm record of "Are You Lonesome Tonight" with black RCA label and RCA victrola and dog logo. Mounted on green velvet background with the gold plaque below reading: "To Col. T. Parker... million seller, 1960." Frame is silver painted wood. Taken from Colonel Parker's personal collection. 16 x 14 inches.

Although Colonel Parker exclusively dealt with handling Elvis' business relations, he did make one exception. It was the Colonel's suggestion that Elvis sing "Are You Lonesome Tonight" as it was his wife, Marie's, favorite song. Elvis gladly accepted the suggestion and recorded the song in April of 1960. By its third week on the chart, it was at number one on "Billboard's Top 100" chart where it remained for six weeks. On top of selling an estimated four million copies worldwide, "Are You Lonesome Tonight" also earned Elvis three Grammy nominations.

$14,000 - 16,000

B24 CONTRACT FOR LEASE OF APARTMENTS AT THE BEVERLY WILSHIRE HOTEL

Three-page lease for for rental of apartments in the Beverly Wilshire Hotel for the 6-month period of April 15-October 14, 1960. Total rent came to $12,000. Contract is signed by the President of the Beverly Wilshire and by Elvis Presley. 13 x 8 1/2 inches.

During this period, Elvis set up residence in Los Angeles while filming "G.I. Blues" and "Flaming Lance" (which was later named "Flaming Star"). He left Memphis by train with five friends, arriving at the Beverly Wilshire on April 20 to begin preproduction the next day.

$3,000 - 5,000

B25 ELVIS' PERSONAL FILM AND ACETATE OF "FLAMING STAR"

Audio/Visual film and acetate for Twentieth Century Fox movie "Flaming Star." Contained in square, brown film and acetate cases. 15 1/4 x 15 3/4" film and case. 15 x 15" acetate and case.

Barbara Eden and Steve Forrest co-starred with Elvis in this movie, which opened nationally December 21, 1960. Although a double was hired for the filming of the fight scenes, Elvis held his own during these scenes and the double was not

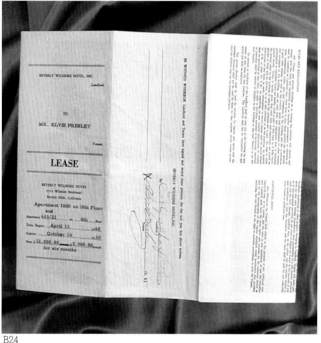

B24

needed. Elvis suffered a fall from a runaway horse, but was not injured. Acetate contains the "Flaming Star" vinyl album, manila envelope, and cardboard spacers.

$2,000 - 3,000

B26 AN ASSORTMENT OF CHRISTMAS CARDS TO ELVIS FROM VARIOUS CELEBRITIES

Christmas cards to Elvis from the following people: Liberace, Gracie and George Burns, Don Ho, Sonny and Cher, Jerry Lee Lewis and Kay Martin, D.J. Fontana, Edward Byrnes, Rick Nelson and family, Bob Hope and family, Lyndon and Lady Bird Johnson, Mae West, Jayne Mansfield, Jackie Gleason, Lawrence Welk, Connie Francis, Ina and Gene Autry, Larry Geller and Family, Charlie Rich, Hal and Martha Wallis, the Blackwood Brothers, Chet Atkins, Robert Mitchum and family, Red Skelton and family, the Kingston Trio, Dave Clark, Hedda Hopper, and Bobby Darin.

Many of these cards are personally signed by the senders and include photos.

$7,000 - 8,000

B27 CORRESPONDENCE TO ELVIS PRESLEY REGARDING CHARITY EVENTS

Original, typewritten letter with envelope, from Johnny Carson to Elvis dated April 7, 1970, sent as a reminder of Elvis' invitation to the 33rd Anniversary Benefit of the Wiltwyck School for Boys. Signed in brown by Johnny Carson. Original invitation included with return envelope and a list of suggested contribution amounts. One page letter, typed on "The Dick Cavett Show" stationery and dated March 25, 1971. Sent to Elvis Presley as an invitation to the Johnny Carson Tribute Dinner. Signed in brown marker by Cavett. Tribute dinner invitation with return envelope and enclosures. Letter on Jack Hylton letterhead addressed to Elvis dated February 26, 1960, inviting Elvis to perform for Queen Elizabeth and other Royal in a charity even. Letter dated October 26, 1967 to Elvis Presley from Robert O'Brien on MGM letterhead. The letter invites Elvis to join Variety Club International's Honorary Committee which was planning to honor Jack Valenti with a testimonial dinner on January 16, 1968. Signed in blue, "Bob." Two letters from Madame Tussaud's addressed to Elvis and the Colonel requesting Elvis to spare an hour of his time for their sculptor to "make the necessary observations for a portrait." Additional letters also included. 10 1/2 x 7 1/4" Carson Letter. 5 1/2 x 7 1/2" Envelope. 7 1/4 x 5 1/4" Invitation. 5 x 7" Return envelope. 6 1/2 x 4 3/4 " Contribution list. 9 1/2 x 7" journal order form. 10 1/2 x 7 1/4" Cavett letter. 7 5/8 x 5 1/4" invitation sent by Cavett. 9 5/8 x 8" Hylton letter. 11 x 8 1/2 O'Brien, Diskin, Tussaud's letters 10 1/4 x 7 1/4.

Elvis was known for his generosity and was frequently asked to donate money to charities. As with most such invitations to public events, Elvis did not attend.

$400 - 600

B28 RARE RECORD AND W.W. BULLOCK'S CORRESPONDENCE TO COLONEL PARKER INCLUDING RARE RECORD

Two typed letters on W.W. Bullock's personalized "Radio Corporation of America" stationery to Col. Parker in Beverly Hills, Ca. The first two page letter, dated July 27, 1960, addresses the idea of creating an Elvis Presley seven inch 33 1/3 rpm record.

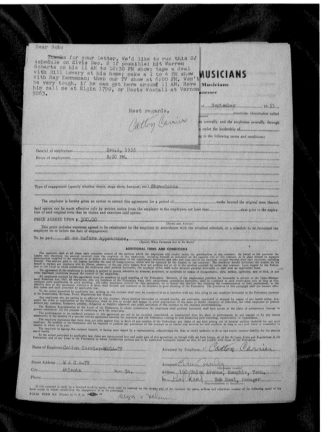

B29

The second one page letter, dated August 18, 1960, abandons the idea. One seven inch 33 1/3 rpm record. 10 1/2 x 7 inches.

These recordings are very rare, only a few of these seven inch 33 1/2 rpm records were ever made.

$8,000 - 10,000

B29 CONTRACT FOR FOUR MOVIES BETWEEN ELVIS PRESLEY AND MGM

Eighteen-page contract between Elvis Presley and Metro-Goldwyn-Mayer Inc..Contract dated March 10, 1961 on MGM letterhead. Signed in blue ink by Elvis Presley and Colonel Tom Parker. Photograph included. 11 x 8 1/2 inches.

From when he was a child, Elvis always dreamed of becoming a movie star like James Dean or Marlon Brando. This was a dream realized. He starred in 31 feature films between 1956 and 1969, sometimes making three movies in a single year. This contract was for four Elvis movies: "It Happened at the World's Fair," "Viva Las Vegas," "Kissin' Cousins," and "Girl Happy."

$8,000 - 10,000

B30 VISIT TO TENNESSEE GENERAL ASSEMBLY

Original letter dated February 23, 1961, from Senator Lewis Taliaferro of Tennessee regarding the passage of a Senate Joint Resolution, inviting Elvis to appear before a session of the Tennessee General Assembly as an honoree. Included is the original envelope, addressed to Elvis at Graceland on Highway 51. Typewritten letter from Governor George Wallis dated November 6, 1974, to Ed Bonja of Colonel Parker's office. Original white, one page typewritten resolution with a blue back cover. Photographs included. 11 x 8 1/2 inches Letters (2). 4 1/4 x 9 1/2 inches Envelope.. 14 1/4 x 9 inches Resolution. 10 1/2 x 7 1/4 inches Letter.

Elvis had returned from the army a year before he was presented this honor. He drove to Nashville in his Rolls Royce to appear before the Joint Session on March 8, 1961. Being honored for his service to his country as well as his charitable works. Elvis thanked the lawmakers saying it was the "finest honor he's ever received," and added that he would never abandon his Memphis home to move to Hollywood.

$1,250 - 1,500

B30A "BLUE HAWAII" PAYMENT

Two page statement from Colonel Parker on his own stationery regarding "Elvis Presley Earnings" for "Blue Hawaii", dated April 17, 1961. Statement outlines payments due, deductions, and reimbursable expenses. Attached are two check stubs for payment. Check stub # 18542, made payable to Elvis Presley, is for the net amount of $15,625.00 for salary of week 4/3 - 4/8/61. Check stub # 18544, also payable to Elvis Presley, is for the net amount of $6,250.00 for reimbursable expenses as pursuant to contract. An adding machine receipt of calculations is attached. Handwritten letter to Bill Fisher from Tom Diskin, dated April 14, 1961, explaining the payments referenced above. Deposit slip for checks from William Morris Agency and Paramount totalling $14,306.24, dated April 18, 1961. 11 x 8 1/2 inches Statement. 3 3/4 x 8 1/2 inches Check stubs. 3 1/2 x 7 3/4 inches Deposit slip. 11 x 8 1/2 inches Letter. 1 1/2 x 2 1/4 inches Scrap.

"Blue Hawaii" was released on November 22, 1961 and reached # 2 on "Variety's" weekly list of top-grossing films.

$1,250 - 1,500

B31 CHARITY SHOW CORRESPONDENCE, 1961

Original one page letter dated February 2, 1961 to Colonel Tom Parker from Henry Loeb and Bill Graham, who were both on the committee for Elvis' Charity Show. Letter confirms the February 25th show at the Ellis Auditorium in Memphis. Included is the original forty page *Music Reporter Magazine*. A pink typewritten copy of the tentative Show Line-up, and a typed letter from Johnson Flying Service dated February 13, 1961 regarding Airplane banner towing promotion is also included. 11 x 8 1/2". Letter and Airplane banner.

B31   B32

12 x 9" Music Reporter Magazine.
9 1/2" x 6". Show Line-Up.

RCA awarded Elvis a diamond studded watch at this Charity luncheon for record sales, over 75 million. Comedian George Jessel emceed the event, and a portion of the money went to Elvis' Youth Home in Mississippi. "Elvis Presley Day" was declared in Tennessee as Elvis performed in charity shows for the Benefit of 26 Memphis Charities and the Tupelo Youth Center, raising over $55,000.

$2,500 - 2,800

B32 U.S.S ARIZONA MEMORIAL FUND BENEFIT

One admission ticket reading: "The Pacific War Memorial Commission Proudly Presents In Person Elvis Presley with All-Star cast at Block Arena Saturday March 25 Pearl Harbor, 8:30 pm. Doors open 7:15". Ticket has small photo of Elvis. Admission for one for the "Main Floor 288, $100 section". Back of ticket notes: "For the 100% U.S.S. Arizona Memorial Fund Benefit." Also included is a gold, black and white poster for the benefit, and a white ribboned press pass with gold print that reads, "Press Presley U.S.S Arizona Benefit". 2 1/4 x 5 1/8 inches Ticket. 12 3/8 x 9 1/4 inches Poster. 4 1/4 x 2 Press Pass.

Elvis flew to Honolulu with comedian and show business veteran Minnie Pearl, who was booked to appear as well on the benefit show. The show raised over $62,000 toward building a memorial for the entombed sailors of the U.S.S Arizona.

$2,000 - 2,500

B33 ELVIS "DANCE PARTY" TELEGRAM

Western Union telegram dated December 8, 1961, sent to "Top Ten Dance Party, Television Channel Thirteen" in Memphis from Elvis wishing a "Merry Christmas and Happy New Year." 5 1/2 x 8"

"Dance Party" was a local Memphis show hosted by Wink Martindale. Elvis had appeared on the show on June 16, 1956 but didn't perform. At the time this telegram was sent Elvis was in Hollywood preparing to begin production on "Kid Galahad."

$200 - 250

B34 TICKET, HANDBILL AND PRESS PASS FOR U.S.S. ARIZONA MEMORIAL FUND BENEFIT

White cardboard ticket with blue and red print. Front specifies main floor seating in the $100 section for show at Bloch Arena on Pearl Harbor on Saturday, March 25. Ticket reads "The Pacific War Memorial Commission proudly presents in person Elvis Presley with all-star cast" and has photo of Elvis on left side of ticket. One page, double-sided handbill for the show, with gold and black print. Handbill lists Minnie Pearl as a "Special Guest." One white cloth ribbon with gold print "Press -- Presley U.S.S. Arizona Benefit." 2 1/4 x 4 1/8 inches ticket. 12 3/8 x 9 1/4 inches handbill. 4 x 2 inches press ribbon

This 1961 benefit show was Elvis' last live performance until 1968.

$2,000 - 2,500

B35 ELVIS' PERSONAL FILM AND ACETATE OF "G.I. BLUES"

Film case containing Elvis' personal 16 mm print of "G.I. Blues." Acetate case including two-sided acetate of the "G.I. Blues" soundtrack album and two song lists, one handwritten. Cases are brown with metal corners, a handle on one end and a horizontal and vertical buckled strap. 15 1/4 x 15 3/4 inches film case. 15 x 15 inches acetate case.

The 1960 Paramount production "G.I. Blues was Elvis' fifth film. His first film project after being released from the Army, "G.I. Blues" began production in May 1960, just two months after Elvis' return from the military. In a film obviously modeled to take advantage of his stint in the Army, Elvis portrays a guitar-playing soldier stationed in West Germany.

$3,000 - 4,000

B36 LETTER AND ALBUM COVER SKETCHES

Letter, on official RCA letterhead, dated November 14, 1961 from RCA division vice president Bill Bullock to Colonel Parker. Bullock suggests making a double feature LP to highlight "Follow That

B36

B34

Dream" and "Kid Galahad," which were both due for release within a few months of one another. He is seeking the Colonel's suggestions and sends along 2 hand-drawn sketches for album covers; his comments include, "You can tell right off that I am

not an art director!" EP Cover of "Elvis Presley in 'Kid Galahad'"; EP missing DJ promotional copy of "Kid Galahad" EP; white with black letters. 11 x 8 1/2 inches letter and sketches. 7 x 7 " cover and EP.

"Kid Galahad" EP was released in 1961; however, no LP ever made it to fans, except in bootleg copies. $2,000 - 2,500

B37 ELVIS CHARITY SHOW, 1961

Four gold, cardboard ticket stubs, numbered 1, 2, 155 and 156 from the Memphis Charity Show Luncheon held in the Hotel Claridge Balinese Room on Saturday, Feb. 25, 1961 at 12:30 p.m. Western Union telegram dated February 24, 1961 sent to Col. Parker from Minnie Pearl and her husband Henry. Pearl sends "best wishes for a wonderful show." Western Union telegram dated January 20, 1961 sent to Col. Parker concerning accommodations at the Claridge for Col. Parker and comedian George Jessel. Colonel Parker's personal "ticket commitments" list for the show, on white ruled paper. One original letter from Nat Lefkowitz, of the William Morris Agency, to Colonel Parker requesting twenty show tickets and ten luncheon tickets. One page original paper with tentative program for the luncheon. Photographs included. 2 x 2 inches ticket stubs. 3 1/4 x 7 3/4 inches telegram #1. 5 3/4 x 8 inches telegram #2. 9 1/2 x 6 inches ticket commitment sheet. 11 x 8 1/2 inches letter. 11 x 8 1/2 inches program.

February 25, 1961 was declared "Elvis Presley Day" by Tennessee Governor Buford Ellington and Memphis Mayor Henry Loeb. The luncheon was held in the afternoon before two later charity performances. At the luncheon, RCA presented Elvis with a diamond-studded watch to honor sales of over 75 million records. Jessel was brought in to emcee the charity shows that afternoon and evening.

$1,400 - 1,600

Blue Hawaii

B38 "CAN'T HELP FALLING IN LOVE" / "ROCK-A-HULA BABY" CONTRACT

One page typed on RCA Victor letterhead, dated November 28, 1961. Signed in blue ink by Elvis Presley, Colonel Thomas Parker and RCA Vice-President W.W. Bullock. Handwritten changes initialed in blue ink by Presley, Bullock and the Colonel. Stamped "Received Jan. 11, 1962 All Star Shows" at top right corner. With blue-tinted, two-page sheet music for "Can't Help Falling (In Love With You" and a mint-condition 45 rpm single of "Can't Help Falling In Love"/"Rock-A-Hula Baby." 10 3/4 x 8 1/2 inches contract. 12 x 9 inches sheet music. 7 x 7 inches record.

Contract amends earlier contract from October 18, 1956 with respect to royalties for "Can't Help Falling in Love"/"Rock-A-Hula Baby" single. Both songs were featured in the film "Blue Hawaii."

$7,000 - 8,000

B39 TELEGRAM TO TWENTIETH CENTURY-FOX AND "FLAMING STAR" ALBUM

Original 2-page tan Western Union telegram dated January 10, 1961 sent from Lew Dreyer of Gladys Music to Jerry Wald at Twentieth-Century Fox in Beverly Hills, California, regarding bootleg tape recordings of "Flaming Star" film sound track that were being played in various cities without permission. Telegram states that stations with the exclusive recordings feel they are at a disadvantage, and the sound is poor on the recorded ones, as well. The request: to contact reps in these cities and stop this unauthorized use. Copy of same Western Union telegram, marked Received Jan. 13, 1961, All

Star Shows. Album of "Elvis Sings 'Flaming Star" 5 3/4 x 8 inches original. 11 x 8 1/2 inches copy. 12 1/4 x 12 1/4 inches album.

Colonel Parker vetoed the original idea for the album for "Flaming Star" because there were not enough songs to make it worthwhile for the fans to buy. However, some radio stations were playing bootleg copies of the sound track for the fans in their cities. In February 1961, the Colonel compromised with Fox to release an EP for "Flaming Star," featuring the title song and "Summer Kisses, Winter Tears." It also included "It's Now or Never" and "Are You Lonesome Tonight?" In 1969, RCA, on its Camden label, released an album called "Elvis

Sings 'Flaming Star'," which was the only song from the movie. Other songs included "Yellow Rose of Texas" and "Wonderful World."

$800 - 1,000

B40 BLUE HAWAII EARNINGS

Typewritten Statements of Earnings for "Blue Hawaii" from Radio Corporation Of America with

payment stubs attached. Statement number 57, dated May 1, 1961, containing itemized earnings and deductions from "Blue Hawaii." Attached to statement is a mail deposit receipt with figures on the backside. Copy of Settlement Statement number 56 dated April 27, 1961 listing payments for section five of contract. Two green and one white check stub. One "Blue Hawaii" promo album poster included. 11 x 8 1/2 inches Letters. 8 1/2 x 4 inches Green Check Stubs. 8 1/2 x 3 1/2 inches White Check Stub.

Elvis was paid $9,301.55 salary for April 17 to April 21, 1961, with an additional $1,000 from the Radio Corporation of America. Production began of "Blue Hawaii" on March 17, 1961, in Hawaii. The film reached #2 on "Variety's" weekly list of top-grossing films. It ranked #18 for the year.

$2,500 - 3,000

B41 PARAMOUNT MUSIC MEETING MINUTES

Music meeting minutes dated March 20, 1961 on official Paramount Pictures Corporation letterhead. Meeting held at 10:30 a.m. in Hal Wallis' office; those present were Wallis, Paul Nathan, Charlie O'Curran, Elvis, Freddy Bienstock, and Tom Diskin. A schedule of songs for the movie "Blue Hawaii" was developed for the recording session the following Tuesday. Five pages of specific songs, instruments and singers needed, and other notes, including order of the numbers, were submitted by Joseph J. Lilley for discussion at the meeting. "Blue Hawaii" soundtrack album. 11 x 8 1/2 inches minutes and attachments.

As he had for "G.I. Blues," Joseph Lilley served as musical director for the film "Blue Hawaii." The actual recording sessions took place on March 21-23, 1961, at Radio Recorders Studio in Hollywood. Songs in "Blue Hawaii" included the title song as well as "Can't Help Falling in Love," "Hawaiian Sunset," and "Hawaiian Wedding Song," as well as 10 other numbers. "Can't Help Falling in Love" required 29 takes to create the classic that it would soon become.

$2,500 - 3,000

B42 PARAMOUNT BIOGRAPHY OF ELVIS PRESLEY AND MEDALLION PROMOTIONS

Five-page biographical sketch of Elvis released in March 1961 by Wallis-Paramount for "Blue Hawaii" promotion. In-depth discussion of his background--both personal and musical--and discussion of his movie career to date. The information ends with "The boy who ran all the way to his first audition is up there in orbit, for all to see. And, from the looks of things, he's just getting his second wind." 2 pencil sketches of medallions to promote "Blue Hawaii" and Elvis Mauve-colored lei with "Blue Hawaii" medallion attached. Photograph included. 13 x 8 1/2 " biography pages. 3 1/2 " and 4 " medallions.

Production for Paramount's "Blue Hawaii" began on March 27, 1961, two days after Elvis' concert to raise money for the U.S.S. Arizona. The movie opened nationally on November 22. In the Colonel's usual pattern of highly promoting each of Elvis' events, he produced medallions with the name of the film and "Elvis" printed on them; these were made for attachment to Hawaiian leis.

$2,500 - 3,000

B43 ELVIS' PERSONAL FILM AND ACETATES OF "BLUE HAWAII"

One film case with 16mm film of "Blue Hawaii;" from Colonel Parker's collection. Red and white label with raised letters reads: "Blue Hawaii" 1961, #8. Border label indicates name of film, production company, director, and release date. Cases are brown with metal corners, a handle on one end, and a horizontal and vertical buckled strap. 15 1/4 x 15 3/4" film case,

Blue Hawaii, a Hal Wallis production, was released from Paramount Studio in November 1961. Norman Taurog directed the film, which starred Elvis as a ex-GI who worked with a tourist agency. Filming took place in Hawaii and on the Paramount lot.

$4,000 - 6,000

B44 "BLUE HAWAII" CORRESPONDENCE

One page original letter from Hal Wallis to Colonel Tom Parker dated January 30, 1961, stressing the importance that Elvis maintain a tan and keep fit before the production of "Blue Hawaii". One copy of a letter from Tom Diskin to Elvis dated February 1, 1961 expressing his concern that Elvis keep fit and work on achieving a tan. In the letter, Diskin suggests that Elvis purchase an ultraviolet lamp. Diskin also reminds Elvis not to give any radio or television interviews . 11 x 8 1/2 inches.

B44
B42

Hal Wallis had some serious concerns about Elvis' appearance for the production of "Blue Hawaii"; he wanted Elvis to look as fit and healthy for the film as he did for "G.I. Blues" with an all over, even tan.

$750 - 1,000

B45 CONTRACT WITH HAL WALLIS FOR MULTI-FILM DEAL

Two nine page signed copies of contract with Hal Wallis for "Blue Hawaii", "Girls! Girls! Girls!", "Fun In Acapulco", "Roustabout", and "Paradise Hawaiian Style". Photograph included. 11 x 8 1/2"

This contract was renegotiated from an original contract of seven feature films. Elvis had only completed two films before the Army disrupted his movie career. Upon returning, on January 6, 1961, the contract was revised for five pictures. For the first three pictures Elvis was to get $175,000, and for the last two pictures he was to receive $200,000.

$4,000 - 5,000

B46 CHECK STUBS FOR CALIFORNIA EXPENSES

Green check book showing 151 check stubs from October 14, 1961 to March 9, 1962. Some items and amounts include: Bel-Air Patrol, $20.40; Sahara Hotel, $2,152.33; Victor Honig (haircut for Elvis), $30; Mr. George Barris (custom work on Cadillac Limo), dep. of $2,000; and Harry Levitch Jewelers (purchase of wrist watch), $89.60. Five light green checks signed in blue ink by Elvis Presley. 9 1/4 x 12 1/2 inches check book. 3 x 8 1/8 inches check.

These checks are for personal and household expenses. During this time, Elvis was filming "Kid Galahad." This was the only Christmas he spent away from Memphis, except while he was in the Army.

$8,000 - 10,000

B47 BUILDING PERMIT FOR SECURITY GUARD SHACKS AND SECURITY GUARD ITEMS

Receipt dated November 27, 1967 for permit to build 3 accessory prefab units at 3764 Hwy. 51 S. to be used as Security Guard Headquarters. Total value $15,000; total fee $32.70. Original envelope sent Special Delivery to Vernon Presley. Shelby County Sheriff's Department ID for Billy W. Smith, Special Deputy with laminated color photo. Gold star badge, reads, "Smith - Graceland Security Officer." Gold garland pin with "Chief Deputy" written across middle. Four original invoices, three dated February 26, and one dated March 1, 1971 for monitors, cameras, and installation of security equipment at Graceland. One invoice for ten badges. Invoices are from the Law Enforcement Equipment Company. Copy of a advertising commitment from Elvis and Vernon Presley to the Fraternal Order of

Police dated March 3, 1971. Six 1971 sponsor stickers. 8 x 5 inches receipt of permit. 4 x 9 1/2 inches envelope. 2 1/8 x 3 1/4 inches ID. 2 1/2 x 2 1/2 inches star. 3 x 2 inches garland pin. 7 x 8 1/2 inches invoices for monitors, etc. 8 1/2 x 5 1/2 inches invoice for badges. 4 1/4 x 5 1/4 inches Contract. 3 x 3 1/4 inches Stickers.

Elvis had a strong relationship with the Shelby County Sheriff's Department. Many members of his entourage, including Billy Smith, were officially

B46
B47

deputized by Sheriff Roy C. Nixon. Smith, cousin of Elvis and member of the famed "Memphis Mafia," worked various jobs for Elvis, including valet, traveling companion, and extras in some of his movies. Billy and his wife, Jo, played with racquetball with Elvis the day he died, August 16, 1977. Cameras were placed at the gates and in several rooms in Graceland. They were hooked up to monitors which Elvis sometimes watched instead of the tele-

vision. This security system is still operational today at Graceland. $3,000 - 3,500

B48 PARTY AT FAIRGROUNDS AMUSEMENT PARK

Invoices from Memphis Park Commission, and Fairgrounds Amusement Park for food and rental of amusement park. Two page typewritten bill, on Memphis Park Commission letterhead, dated July 3, 1961, for food and rental of the amusement park for June 30th and July 1st. The rental charge for the park was $150.00 per day, and food charges for cozy dogs and soft drinks totaled $173.50 for both days. One page typewritten invoice, on Fairgrounds Amusement Park letterhead, dated May 16, 1966, for food and drinks. Total bill is for $35.85. Photograph included. 11 x 8 1/2 inches.

Elvis loved to rent out the amusement park for his friends. He threw a party for his friend Red West, who was married on July 1, 1961. They celebrated at the amusement park on June 30, the day before his wedding, and on July 1, the day after the wedding.

$750 - 1,000

B49 ELVIS PRESLEY SONG LIST

One page typed, dated July 24, 1961. List of recorded Elvis Presley songs with date recorded and movie connection listed. With two-page, green-tinted sheet music for "Little Sister," one of the songs on the list. 11 x 8 1/2 inches song list. 12 x 9 inches sheet music.

This document was used in the office of RCA Vice-President W.W. Bullock.

$400 - 500

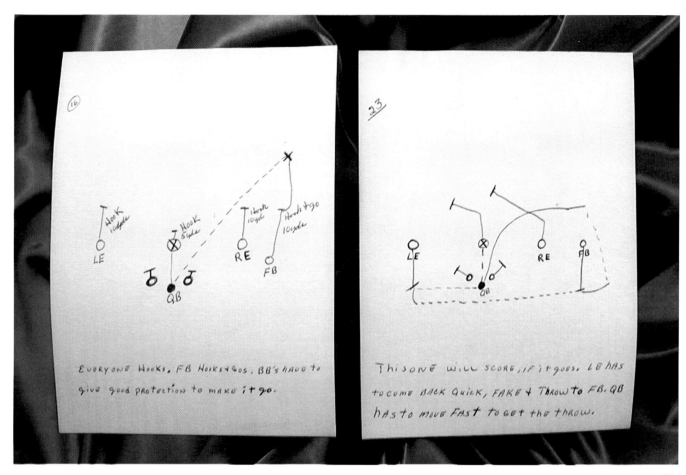

B50 RARE HANDWRITTEN FOOTBALL SKETCHES AND NOTES BY ELVIS PRESLEY

Three pages of football plays handwritten and sketched by Elvis. 5 3/4 x 7 3/4 inches.

Elvis loved football although he never played in school because Gladys was afraid he would injure himself. However, he did sponsor several teams over the years. On Saturdays and Sundays Elvis and his entourage of friends and neighbors would get together to play football; Elvis would take the quarterback position. During these games several fans would gather, and Elvis would give out autographs.

$15,000 - 20,000

B51 ELVIS' FAVORITE SPORT

One football helmet, white with blue stripe, used by Elvis and his friends on the Elvis Presley Enterprises football team. Handwritten invoice from York Arms Co., a Memphis sporting goods store, dated October 7, 1961 and in the amount of $60.27. Billed to Elvis Presley at 3764 Highway 61[sic] So. for one pair of tennis shoes, one football and 16 football jerseys. Printed invoice for same purchase. Copy of bill from Commercial Charter Coach for use by Elvis Presley and party from Graceland to the Memphis Memorial Stadium for a Memphis Grizzles football game. Bill is dated August 2, 1975, for $101.20. 5 5/8 x 8 5/8 inches invoice #1. 6 1/4 x 5 7/8 inches invoice. #2 11 x 8 1/2 inches charter bill.

Football was Elvis' favorite sport, and he organized touch football games wherever he lived—at Graceland among Memphis friends, in Germany with other American G.I.'s, and in California between Memphis Mafia friends and celebrities like Pat Boone and Ricky Nelson. For a while "Elvis Presley Enterprises" sponsored a touch football team, for which Elvis played, in a local Memphis league. This receipt is for the purchase of jerseys for that team. Elvis had season tickets for the Memphis Grizzlies of the short-lived World Football League, and he attended every home game.

$2,000 - 2,500

B52 ELVIS ' PALOMINO, "RISING SUN'

Two original Certificates of Registration for a Palomino named "Midget's Vandy" which Elvis nicknamed "Rising Sun." One certificate is from The American Quarter Horse Association dated November 22, 1961. The second certificate, which is fully matted, is from the National Palomino Breeders Association dated December 24, 1963. Brown and tan western saddle; pommel reads "Big (picture of Steer) Horn" - "Trademark Registered." Seat has decorative stitching, and each side has three double medallions. One wood block saddle stand; back reads "C.P. Rising Sun." Photograph included. 11 x 8 1/2 inches American Quarter Horse Association. 11 x 14 inches National Palomino Breeders.

"Rising Sun" was Elvis' favorite Palomino. The horse died in June of 1996.

$7,500 - 8,000

B52A INVOICES FOR REMODELING OF GRACELAND

Invoice of June 9, 1961 on official letterhead from Memphis Paneling Co.on South Cooper in Memphis for remodeling, including Vernon's bedroom, Elvis' dressing room, and installation of mirrors in basement stairwell. Total contract price was $3,742 less payments; balance was $2,233.31. Invoice dated January 2, 1963 from Soft-Lite Fiber Glass & Construction Co. in Memphis to Mr. Presley. Bill is for installation of indirect neon lighting in bedroom and nylon carpet over sponge pad in bedroom. Total price $987. Ink memo notes paid on 1/4/63, check # 335. Photograph of Graceland included. Pink invoice from Interiors by Grenadier in Memphis billed to Vernon Presley at Graceland Estates. Bill was for Fountain and Lighting, Construction, Landscaping, and Decorative Items. Total bill $20,912.26; showing a balance due of $10,148.83. Mark paid on January 4, 1966. Three page invoice from Interiors by Grenadier dated June 10, 1966 for addition of bathrooms and decorating. Total $6,643.92. Bill dated December 5, 1969 addressed to Vernon Presley from Robert McCall on Central Home Improvement Company letterhead. Details the cost to install built-in televisions in a basement room at Graceland. Along with the installation of trim and the painting of the recreation room and stairwell, the bill totals $1005.00. 11 x 8 1/2 inches others. 7 1/4 x 8 1/2 inches Soft-Lite. 7 x 8 1/2 inches pink invoice.

Elvis and Vernon continually made improvements at Graceland--including adding bathrooms, remodeling bedrooms, and adding a meditation garden. The Meditation Garden at Graceland was completed in December 1965. Elvis had visited the Self-Realization Garden in Pacific Palisades, California, and then made plans to build his own. For the installation of the three built-in TVs, Elvis got the idea from President Lyndon B. Johnson, who had three so he could watch all network newscasts simultaneously. Elvis, however, preferred to watch three sporting events simultaneously.

$2,000 - 2,500

B53 NICK ADAMS CORRESPONDENCE

Original typed and signed letter, on Paramount Pictures letterhead, from Nick Adams to Elvis, dated March 15, 1961, regarding a karate belt from Japan that he has enclosed. Handwritten letter dated October 28, 1958, on Beverly Wilshire letterhead, from Colonel Parker to Nick Adams congratulating him on the "FBI Story." Two page typewritten letter dated June 6, 1959, from Nick Adams to Colonel Parker. In the letter he talks about Red West, personal business, and writes his new phone number for the Colonel's use. Photograph included. 8 1/2 x 5 1/2 inches.

Nick Adams was a very good friend of Elvis and traveled with him extensively until Mr. Adams death in 1968. Natalie Wood was introduced to Elvis by Nick Adams. The Colonel was also very good friends with Adams.

$400 - 500

B54 PRESS RELEASE DRAFTS AND CHARTERED BUS INVOICE

Two typed drafts, with edits, of a press release about Elvis signing with The Mirisch Company to star in "Pioneer, Go Home!" (later renamed "Follow That Dream"), which was set in Florida. Drafts were typed by the Colonel or someone in his office. An invoice from Southeastern Greyhound Line dated July 7, 1961, for chartered service to Crystal River, Florida. Total cost: $779.59. EP cover of "Follow That Dream"; slightly damaged. Photograph included. 11 x 8 1/2 inches press releases. 7 x 8 1/2 inches invoice. 7 x 7 inches EP.

Following his usual grand fireworks show on July 4, 1961, Elvis and his entourage boarded a rented bus to head for Crystal River, Florida, where he would begin shooting "Follow That Dream," a United Artists, Mirisch Company production (Elvis' ninth film). Alan Fortas and Lamar Fike followed in the Cadillac limousine, towing Elvis' new 21-foot powerboat.

$800 - 1,500

B55 ELVIS PACIFIC WAR MEMORIAL BENEFIT TICKETS

Ten multi-colored tickets for Elvis' benefit performance at Bloch Arena at Pearl Harbor, Hawaii on March 25, 1961. One used $100 ticket, two unused $10 tickets, six unused $5 tickets and one unused $3.50 ticket. 2 5/8 x 5 inches.

This benefit performance was Elvis' last appearance before a live audience until the tapings for his "comeback" special in June 1968, and his last concert until his Las Vegas shows in 1969. This concert raised over $62,000 for a memorial to entombed soldiers on the U.S.S. Arizona.

$14,000 - 16,000

B56 U.S.S. ARIZONA MEMORIAL FUND BENEFIT

Original four page program from the U.S.S. Arizona Memorial Fund Benefit given March 25, 1961, at Bloch Arena, Pearl Harbor Hawaii. A single one hundred dollar ticket and envelope for the main floor section. White cloth "press" ribbon that says, "Press -- Presley U.S.S. Arizona Benefit". Black, white and gold, advertisement hand bill. 11 x 8 1/2 inches Program. 3 1/2 x 4 1/2 inches Ticket. 3 3/4 x 4 3/4 inches Envelope. 8 x 2 inches Press ribbon. 12 1/4 x 9 1/4 inches Advertisement hand bill.

When Elvis arrived in Honolulu on Saturday, March 25, he was mobbed at the airport. Minnie Pearl, who was on the same flight and scheduled to appear for the benefit, remarked: "Those women could kill you." Elvis' reply was: "They're not going to hurt me." Benefit raised over $62,000 toward building a memorial for the entombed sailors of the U.S.S. Arizona. Recordings of the show reveal a joyful, uninhibited Elvis.

$4,500 - 5,000

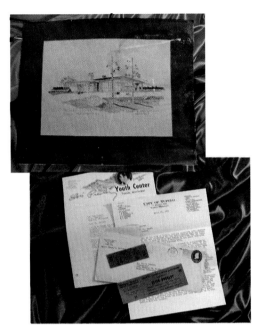

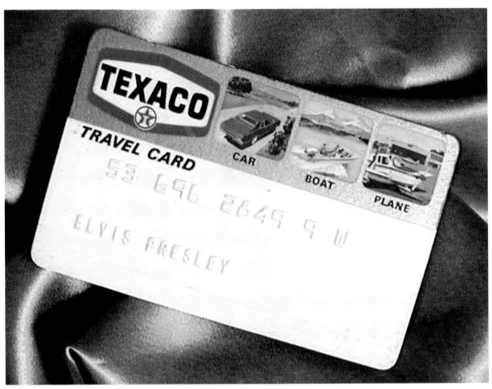

B57 CITY OF TUPELO CHARITY LETTER TO ELVIS PRESLEY

Two pages typed on "City of Tupelo" letterhead, dated March 28, 1961. Sent to Elvis Presley at Graceland from then Tupelo mayor James L. Ballard. Two page typed letter from James M. Savery of the Elvis Presley Youth Center to Tom Diskin. Correspondence discusses a $14,000 donation by Elvis, an outline of the money for the center, and an autograph picture of Elvis sent to Mr. Savery's daughter. One gold and black Memphis Charity Show Luncheon ticket. One brown and black Memphis Charity Show ticket. With pencil rendering of proposed Elvis Presley Youth Center. 11 x 8 1/2" letters. 4 1/8 x 9 1/2" envelope. 10 1/2 x 14 3/4" rendering. 2 x 6" Luncheon ticket. 1 1/4 x 3 1/4" Show ticket.

Letter informing Elvis of the status of the Elvis Presley Park and Youth Center in Tupelo, which was never fully completed. Ballard thanks Elvis for his donation of $3,792.70 raised at his Memphis Charity Show on February 25th, as well as an earlier donation of $14,005.78. Ballard also informs Elvis of $2,628.87 in donations received from Elvis Presley Fan Clubs. $6,000 - 7,000

B58 ELVIS PRESLEY'S SIGNED TEXACO CREDIT CARD

White and gold Texaco credit card issued to Elvis Presley with white raised lettering. Front of card pictures a car, boat, and plane at top. Back is signed by Elvis Presley in blue ink. 2 x 3 1/2 inches.

This card shows signs of use.

$8,000 - 10,000

B59 ORIGINAL ART WORK FOR "WOODEN HEART", AND BLACK & WHITE JACKET COVER FOR "PUPPET ON A STRING, " AND "WOODEN HEART"

Original art work for the Gold Standard Series of "Wooden Heart". Art work is divided in half: right side is a puppet in the image of Elvis holding a guitar in his left hand on a blue background. At the bottom of the page are the words "From The Album "Girl Happy." Left side is a drawing of snowman, bear, wooden soldier, and a hot air balloon on a green background. At the bottom of the page are the words "From The Album "G.I. Blues." Across the top of jacket are the words, "Gold Standard Series 45 RPM RCA Victor."

Art work is mounted on white card stock paper, and has the words "transpose panels" written in blue pen. This art work was never used. Original black and white single sleeve for "Wooden Heart," and "Puppet On A String." Front side has a shoulder shot of Elvis wearing a jacket over his shirt. Back side has two small photos of the album cover for "Girl Happy," and "G.I. Blues." 9 1/2 x 7 3/4 inches art work. 7 x 7 inches sleeve.

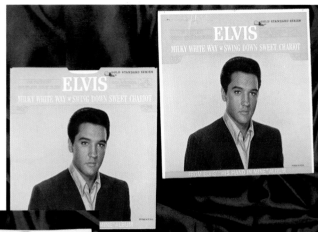

"Puppet On A String" was written by Tepper & Bennett for Elvis' 1965 film "Girl Happy." Elvis recorded the song at Radio Recorders June/July of 1964. The single reached #14 on "Billboards Hot 100" chart, remaining on the chart for ten weeks. "Wooden Heart" was recorded by Elvis for his 1960 Film "G.I. Blues" recorded at RCA's Hollywood studios on April 28, 1960. It wasn't until 1964 that RCA released a single of "Wooden Heart" in the United States. It reached #107 on the "Bubbling Under" list, and reissued the following year to reach #110 on the list.

$1,800 - 2,000

B60 FINISHED COPY AND SLICK OF THE JACKET FOR "MILKY WHITE WAY," AND "SWING DOWN SWEET CHARIOT"

Copy of finished sleeve for "Milky White Way," and "Swing Down Sweet Chariot." Front side is an upper body photo of Elvis wearing a peach shirt and a collarless dark blue jacket. Background is a lime green with a medium blue banner on top that lists the songs. Bottom of sleeve has a thin medium blue line with the words "From Elvis' "His Hand In Mine" Album."

Back side of sleeve has a small photo of the cover for Elvis' "His Hand In Mine" album listing the songs included in the LP. Slick copy is same as finished sleeve except that Elvis' flesh tones are less brassy and his jacket appears to be black and not dark blue. 7 x 7" sleeve cover. 7" x 7 1/2" slick.

"Swing Down Sweet Chariot" was recorded by Elvis on October 31, 1960, at RCA's Nashville studios. Vocal background was by the Jordanaires. "Milky White Way", which is a gospel standard, was recorded by Elvis on October 30,1960, at RCA's Nashville studios. $400 - 600

B61 LETTER TO COLONEL PARKER CONCERNING STORY IN VARIETY DAILY ABOUT ELVIS' GRAMMY NOMINATIONS

Letter to Col. Tom Parker from Herb Spencer of Daily Variety. Letter is on green Daily Variety letterhead and is dated March 30, 1961. 11 x 8 1/2"

Spencer asks for the Colonel's authorization and a copy to run in Daily Variety if Elvis should win any of the Grammy's for which he was nominated.

B59   B60

$300 - 325

B62 HAWAII HOUSE RESOLUTION NO.105

Letter dated April 8, 1961, to Vernon Presley from Herman Lum, Clerk of Hawaii House of Representatives. Letter explains attachment of House Resolution No. 105. The Resolution, with a peach-colored front and back cover, expresses "gratitude and appreciation to Elvis Presley and Colonel Tom Parker on behalf of all Hawaii for their services in helping to raise the funds needed for the U.S.S. Arizona Memorial." Ticket for show; pink and tan with stars and stripes and photo of Elvis. 11 x 8 1/2 inches letter. 14 x 9 inches peach covers. 13 x 8 1/2 inches actual resolution. 2 3/4 x 5 inches ticket.

The show to raise money for the U.S.S. Arizona took place on March 25, 1961, in front of a sold-out crowd at Bloch Arena, and raised more than $52,000 for the cause. The Resolution was adopted on March 30, 1961.

$4,000 - 4,500

B63 SINGLE AND ACETATE OF "I GOTTA KNOW,"
AND "ARE YOU LONESOME TONIGHT"

RCA Victor acetates of "I Gotta Know," and "Are
You Lonesome Tonight." Acetate is in a plain white
paper sleeve. Single is in a white cardboard
sleeve with a jacket that has an upper body photograph of Elvis in a lime green shirt. The background is green/blue with the name "Elvis" in yellow lettering, and "Presley" in white lettering. The
titles of the songs are done in yellow and white lettering. The RCA Victor logo is
located on the upper right corner on both sides. 10 x 10 inches
Acetate.

"I Gotta Know" was recorded by
Elvis on April 4, 1960, at RCA's
Nashville studios. The single
reached #20 on "Billboards" Hot
100 chart. Elvis recorded "Are
You Lonesome Tonight" on April
4, 1960, at RCA's Nashville studios. It is reported that this was
the only song Colonel Parker
ever urged Elvis to record. The
long spoken passage was loosely based on Jacques' speech in
Act II, Scene VII of
Shakespeare's "As You Like It."

$800 - 1,000

B64 ACETATE AND SINGLE OF "SURRENDER"
AND "LONELY MAN"

Acetate (Reference Recording) of "Surrender" bearing RCA Victor label and #L-0233-A, in brown
sleeve. Side B is "Lonely Man," #L2-PW-5381-2.
Single 45 rpm of "Surrender." Single 45 rpm of
"Surrender" / "Lonely Man" with sleeve; front and
back exactly the same: blue with red, blue, and
black lettering, photo of Elvis in brown shirt holding
his guitar. 10-inch acetate, 7-inch single

"Surrender" was recorded in Nashville on October
30, 1960. "Lonely Man," from the film "Wild in the
Country", was recorded on November 7, 1960 at
Radio Recorders studio in Hollywood.

$500 - 750

B65 COLONEL PARKER'S COMPLETE PHONE
LOG

Phone log typed on white paper, and bound with a
medium brown folder, from January 19, 1961,
through June 9, 1961. Contains a list of phone calls
received and made with brief notes about each
call, and a list of visitors for Col. Tom Parker, Tom
Diskin, and Jim O'Brien. Photograph included. 11
1/2 x 9 inches.

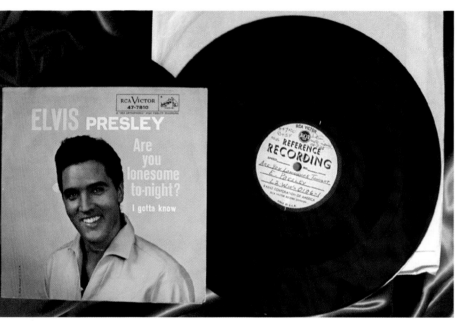

B63

The Colonel meticulously recorded his daily activities for future reference, including meetings, office
visits and telephone calls. Some visitors listed in
this record are: Elvis Presley, Nick Adams, Hal
Wallis, Joe Esposito, Rory Calhoun.

$1,000 - 1,200

B66 PRESS RELEASE, RADIO SPOT, AND
CORRESPONDENCE FOR THE 1968 ELVIS
SPECIAL

Press Release, dated January 17, 1968 on NBC letterhead, titled "Elvis Presley Signed By NBC For His

First TV Special To Be Presented on Network During
1968-69 Season." Announcement was made by
Thomas Sarnoff of NBC and Colonel Tom Parker.
Photograph included. Copy of 60-second promotional spot for radio stations. Produced by Ken
Clanton Advertising in Tampa, Florida, for All Star
Shows. Spot was to be run on Sunday, December 1,
1968 (two days before the special) and discusses
the upcoming special and Elvis' Christmas album.
Original telegram, dated December 3, 1968, to Elvis
and Col. Tom Parker from
Tom Sarnoff congratulat-
ing them on an outstand-
ing telecast. Telegram is
printed on plain white,
perforated paper.
Typewritten letter, dated
July 2, 1968, from Bob
Finkel to Colonel Tom
Parker expressing the
pleasure he received
working with Elvis on taping the Special, and his
developing friendship
with Mr. Parker. Letter is
on thick bond paper with
Robert S. Finkel letterhead
written in silver. 11 x 8 1/2
inches press release and
radio promo. 8 3/4 x 8 1/2
inches telegram. 8 1/2 x 6
3/4 inches letter.

The '68 Special was the first time Elvis performed in
front of a live audience since 1961 when he performed in Hawaii to raise money for the U.S.S.
Arizona. The Performance was seen by 42% of the
viewing audience, making it the number one show
for the season and giving NBC its biggest ratings
victory of the year. Tom Sarnoff was the head of
NBC. Robert S. Finkel, who was the Executive
Producer for the show, won a Peabody Award for
his work on the show. Ken Clanton worked with the
Colonel for many years to help with his advertising.

$3,500 - 4,000

B67 PEARL HARBOR SHOW—TRAVEL ARRANGEMENTS AND TELEGRAM TO VICE-PRESIDENT LYNDON B. JOHNSON

Two pages typed with flight information to Honolulu in the names of Tom Diskin and Hal Wallis. One Western Union telegram dated April 22, 1961 sent to Vice-President Lyndon B. Johnson from "Elvis & The Colonel." 11 x 8 1/2 inches travel arrangements. 9 3/4 x 8 1/4 inches telegram.

Telegram reads: DEAR MR. JOHNSON: WE HAVE JUST COMPLETED RAISING MORE THAN $62,000.00 FOR THE U.S.S. ARIZONA MEMORIAL FUND AT PEARL HARBOR. NOW MORE THAN EVER WE FEEL IT PROPER TO LET YOU KNOW THAT WE ARE WILLING, ABLE AND AVAILABLE TO SERVE IN ANY WAY WE CAN OUR COUNTRY AND OUR PRESIDENT IN ANY CAPACITY, WHETHER IT IS TO USE OUR TALENTS OR HELP LOAD THE TRUCKS. SINCERELY, YOUR FRIENDS. ELVIS & THE COLONEL

$400 - 600

B68 FINISHED COVER COPY AND SLICK FOR THE RECORD SLEEVE OF "JOSHUA FIT THE BATTLE," AND "KNOWN ONLY TO HIM"

Finished cover copy and slick for the record sleeve of "Joshua Fit The Battle," and "Known Only To Him." Front of cover copy is an upper body photo of Elvis wearing a blue/white stripped shirt, and a black jacket. Background is a medium green blended with a medium blue/gray with the song titles listed in white on the right and left side of Elvis' photo. Top has a grey/blue band with the words "Gold Standard Series Elvis". Bottom of cover is a small yellow band with the words "From Elvis' "His Hand In Mine" Album" in blue lettering. Back side is a small photo of Elvis' "His Hand In Mine" album, and a list of the songs included in the LP. Slick copy is same except that the lighting on

Elvis' face is brighter on this copy. 7 x 7 inches Cover Copy. 7 1/4 x 7 1/2 inches Slick Copy.

"Joshua Fit The Battle, " and "Known Only To HIm" was recorded by Elvis on October 31, 1960, at RCA's Nashville Studios.

$400 - 600

B71
B68

B69 COLONEL PARKER'S U.S.S. ARIZONA BENEFIT CERTIFICATE

One page "Certificate of Appreciation" from the Pacific War Memorial Commission to Col. Thomas Parker. Dated March 25, 1961. Photograph included. 8 1/2 x 11 inches.

This was given to the Colonel in appreciation of the benefit concert Elvis gave the same day at Pearl Harbor, which raised over $52,000 for the U.S.S. Arizona Memorial Fund.

$550 - 650

B70 RARE SKETCH AND NOTES OF A FOOTBALL PLAY BY ELVIS PRESLEY

Sketch and notes of a football play by Elvis on plain white paper in purple ink. 7 3/4 6 3/4 inches.

Note at bottom of play says "watch this one, especially, the ball will be thrown to the Right End, who will in turn, pitch back to Flecher. Watch him he is fast!!" Elvis loved football, and as an adult he would play often on weekends at nearby high school football fields.

$7,000 - 9,000

B71 THANK YOU CARD FROM PRESIDENT NIXON AND INAUGURATION INVITATION OF PRESIDENT KENNEDY

Photograph of Richard Nixon and family, with seal of Vice President of U.S. on note thanking people for support in his unsuccessful 1960 Presidential campaign, as well as the privilege of spending 14 years in the nation's capital. Includes envelope addressed to Elvis Presley; with return address from the Office of the Vice President; postmarked February 13, 1961.. Gold three-fold frame with black-and-white photos of John Kennedy and Lyndon Johnson, and Inauguration invitation for both; gold Presidential seal on invitation. 6 x 4 1/2 inches note with photo. 12 3/4 x 9 5/8 opening to 12 3/4 x 29 1/2.

Both the thank you note from Nixon, as he left office, and the Inaugural invitation for Kennedy were dated January 20, 1960.

$2,000 - 2,500

B72 ELVIS' PERSONAL FILM AND ACETATES OF "WILD IN THE COUNTRY"

One film case with 16mm film Wild in the Country. Red label with white raised letters. One acetate case containing 6 acetates, including "In My Way," "Lonely Man," "Forget Me Never," "Wild in the Country," "Presley and guitar," and "Presley with orchestra and vocal group." Most are two sided. Case also includes one manila folder, index card with list of songs, and piece of cardboard. Cases are brown with metal corners, a handle on one end, and a horizontal and vertical buckled strap. 15 1/4 x 15 3/4 inches film case. 15 x 15 inches acetate case.

Wild in the Country, a Twentieth Century Fox (A Company of Artists, Inc.) film produced by Jerry Wald and directed by Philip Dunne, opened in June 1961. Elvis starred as Glenn Tyler, an aspiring writer, and costarred with Tuesday Weld and Hope Lange. "Lonely Man" and "Forget Me Not" were both cut from the film. $2,000 - 3,000

B73 "SURRENDER" GOLD RECORD

Framed award. Gold, 45 rpm record of "Surrender" with black RCA label with RCA victrola and dog logo. Record on green velvet background and above a gold plaque reading, "To Col. T. Parker... million seller, 1961." Frame is silver painted wood. Taken from Colonel Parker's personal collection. 14 x 16 inches framed award

"Surrender" was the contemporary version of "Torna a Sorrento" ("Come Back to Sorrento"),an Italian ballad written by G.D. de Curtis and Ernesto de Curtis in 1911. In 1960 the song was given new English words and a new title by Doc Pomus and Mort Shuman. Elvis recorded "Surrender" on October 30, 1960. It had a two-week stay at number one on "Billboard's" Top 100 chart, and at only 51 seconds, was one of the shortest songs to ever hit number one. $15,000 - 20,000

B74 1962 CHARITY DONATIONS

Three page original typewritten list of Elvis"charity donations for 1962. List consists of 51 named chari-

ties with addresses and check amounts. 11 x 8 1/2 " This list details Elvis' annual Christmas gift to Memphis area charities for the Christmas of 1962, though Elvis regularly donated monies to various organizations throughout the year.

$1,000 - 1,250

B75 SONG LIST FOR THE LP "POTLUCK"

Original typewritten letter dated March 30, 1962, from Bill Bullock of RCA to the Colonel. Mr. Bullock requests a title for Elvis' new LP so that his office can finish printing the sleeve. Handwritten and typed copy of a song list for the LP album titled "Potluck" dated April 9, 1962. Photo of Album image. 11 x 8" Letter. 11 x 8 1/2 " Typewritten Song List. 3 1/2 x 3 1/2 " Handwritten song list. 10 x 3 1/2" Handwritten song list.

Rare song list is handwritten by Elvis - then typed by Colonel Parker's office. The songs listed are almost the exact songs he chose for his "Potluck" album except for a few changes.

$1,750 - 2,000

B76 ELVIS AND PRISCILLA'S TRIP TO LAS VEGAS

Five sheet packet of bills from the Sahara Hotel in Las Vegas. Bills dating from June 19 - July 2, 1962 in the name of Elvis Presley. Attached note, handwritten in blue ink, reads "Presley wants all copies mailed when filled." Also with carbon copy of American Airlines ticket receipt, dated December 17, 1962 and signed in blue ink by Elvis Presley. Receipt also lists "Mrs. V. Presley" and "Priscilla Fisher" as passengers. 7 x 6 1/4 inches hotel bills. 3 1/4 x 7 3/4 inches airline receipt.

This set of hotel bills documents a trip to Vegas taken by Elvis Presley and his future bride Priscilla Beaulieu. Elvis and Priscilla, the step-daughter of an Army Captain, had met in Germany while Elvis was in the Army. On June 17, 1962, when Priscilla arrived in Los Angeles for her first post-Army visit with Elvis, it was the first time they had seen each other in over two years. He was 27. She was 16. The visit itself was the result of months of intense negotiations between Elvis and Priscilla's parents, with the Beaulieus insisting on a complete itinerary, a chaperone at all times and, of course, that Priscilla not stay with Elvis. Elvis had asked George Barris, who customized cars for him, if his young visitor could live with Barris and his wife during her stay. Upon arrival Priscilla did indeed move in with the Barrises at their Griffith Park Home, an arrangement that lasted all of a day. Priscilla moved in with Elvis at his Bellagio Road home the next day and then on July 19 Elvis, Priscilla and the gang headed for Las Vegas for a two-week stay, where they checked into the Sahara hotel. Priscilla had written a series of postcards before leaving that were mailed to her family each day, containing that all important Los Angeles postmark. Priscilla flew back to Germany on July 2, but would return for a Christmas visit in Memphis, documented by this airline ticket where "Priscilla Fisher" is a thinly-veiled pseudonym for Priscilla Beaulieu. In March of 1963, Priscilla would move to Memphis to stay.

$1,300 - 1,400

B77 UNION 76 CARD

White, blue and orange plastic credit card with raised letters, "Mr. Elvis Presley." 1 3/4 x 3 1/2 inches

Card dated 1962.

$2,500 - 3,000

B78 PHILLIPS 66 CARD

White, brown and red plastic credit card. 2 1/8 x 3 3/8 inches.

With raised print, "Mr. Elvis A. Presley I."

$2,500 - 3,000

B79 UNION 76 GOLD CARD

White, blue and orange plastic credit card with raised letters, "Mr. Elvis Presley." 2 1/8 x 3 3/8 inches.

Card dated 1962.

$2,500 - 3,000

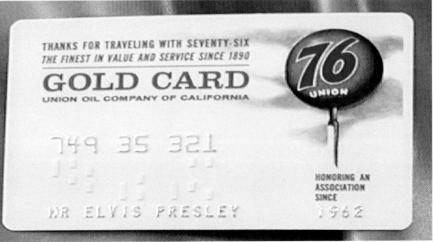

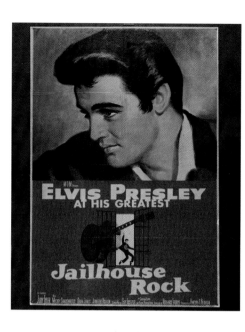

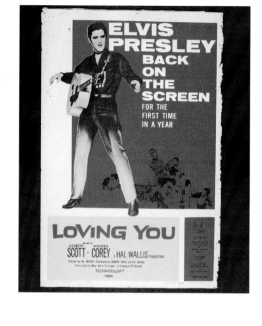

The six movie posters depicted on this and the following are part of lot B227.

B80 "FOLLOW THAT DREAM" TELEGRAMS AND PUBLICITY IMAGE

Western Union telegrams dated April 2, 1962. One sent to Mr. L.J. Finske, President of Florida State Theatres, Inc., the other sent to Joe Taylor of Tampa Theatre, both from "Elvis and The Colonel." Black and white head-shot of Elvis Presley with black and white drawing of body. 10 x 8 1/4 inches telegrams. 10 x 8 1/8 inches promotional image.

Telegrams are in regard to the premiere of "Follow That Dream," which was in Ocala, Florida on April 11, 1962. Promotional image is a prototype for the "Follow That Dream" poster.

$1,400 - 1,600

B81 ELVIS' PERSONAL FILM AND ACETATE OF "KISSIN' COUSINS"

Copy of the MGM film "Kissin' Cousins," and one acetate. Contained in square, brown film/acetate cases with metal corners, and a plastic handle on the side. There are two buckled straps, one horizontal and one vertical. 15 1/4 x 15 3/4 inches film

and case. 15 x 15 inches acetate and case.

This film belonged to Colonel Parker who had a large collection of Elvis' films. "Kissin' Cousins" opened nationally in April of 1964. It reached number 11 on "Variety's" weekly list of top-grossing films. Acetate contains "Catchin' On Fast," "Kissin' Cousins," "Once Is Enough," "One Boy, Two Little Girls," "Smokey Mountain Boy," and "There's Gold in The Mountains." The soundtrack LP to Kissin' Cousins was recorded in Nashville instead of Hollywood as to give the songs a country feel.

$3,000 - 4,000

B81A PROMOTIONAL DOCUMENTS FOR ELVIS PRESLEY MOVIES

Colonel Parker's promotion, publicity, exploitation, and activity reports for Elvis movies including "Kid Galahad," "Roustabout," "Spinout," "Follow That Dream," "Take Me to the Fair," "It Happened at the World's Fair," "Viva Las Vegas," "Girls! Girls! Girls!" "Girl Happy," and "Kissing Cousins." Promotional newspaper titled, "Fun Times." Four-page newspaper advertising "Fun in Acapulco" with such arti-

cles as "Two Beauties Vie for Elvis" (Ursula Andress and Elsa Cardenas). Paramount Booking Chart for block bookings of "Fun in Acapulco." Shows dates film was booked in certain cities around the country. Souvenir package envelope promoting Elvis' movie "Kissin' Cousins." Envelope is dark beige with black lettering, and the MGM lion emblem. 33rd Annual Audit of Personalities of Screen and Television for 1965 entitled, "Fame" with several pages dedicated to Elvis Presley. 11 x 8 1/2 inches reports. 11 1/2 x 7 5/8 inches "Fun Times." 22 1/8 x 17 inches booking chart. 13 1/2 x 13 1/4 inches souvenir envelope. 13 x 10 inches "Fame."

Most movies at this time opened in a few major cities and then spread out to smaller markets. The Colonel felt that block bookings worked better for Elvis movies. Movies would hit a number of markets from the very beginning where fans could see them immediately. Colonel Parker often got paid by the studios for his promotional work with Elvis' movies. The Colonel considered "exploitation" to be a positive term. To be able to properly exploit someone was a virtue and a skill. "Fame" named Elvis at the #6 top money-making stars of 1965.

$3,000 - 3,500

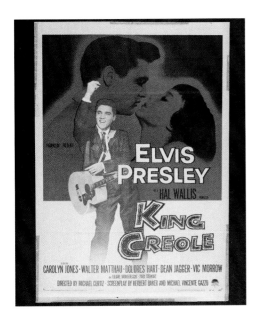

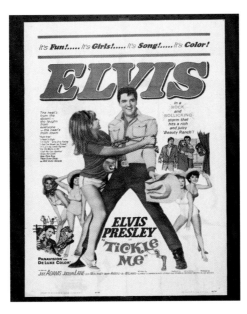

B82 ELVIS' PERSONAL FILM AND ACETATES OF "KID GALAHAD"

Case features a red and white label reading: "'Kid Galahad,' A Mirisch Company Production, Producer: Phil Karbon, Released: August 1962. Case is brown with metal corners, a handle on one end and a horizontal and vertical buckled strap. 15 1/4 x 15 3/4 inches film case. 15 x 15 inches acetate case.

"Kid Galahad" was Elvis' tenth feature film. The film, in which Elvis plays a boxer, was a remake of a 1937 film that starred Humphrey Bogart, Bette Davis and Edward G. Robinson.

$3,000 - 4,000

B83 ELVIS' PERSONAL FILM AND ACETATES OF "FOLLOW THAT DREAM"

Case containing Elvis' personal 16 mm print of "Follow That Dream." Case features red and white label reading: "'Follow That Dream,' A Mirisch Company Production, Producer: David Weisbart, Director: Gardon Douglas, Released April 1962."

Acetate case with three acetates from the film, including the songs "Whistling Tune," "Sound Advice" and "Follow That Dream." Also includes a song list and an envelope reading "'Pioneer Go Home' Acetates." Cases are brown with metal corners, a handle on one end and a horizontal and vertical buckled strap. 15 1/4 x 15 3/4 inches film case 15 x 15 inches acetate case.

The 1962 Mirisch Company production "Follow That Dream" was Elvis' ninth film. Originally titled "Pioneer, Go Home," "Follow That Dream" concerns a group of Florida homesteaders who get caught up in a political conflict.

$3,000 - 4,000

B84 ELVIS' PERSONAL FILM AND ACETATES OF "GIRLS! GIRLS! GIRLS!"

Audio/Visual MGM film of "Girls! Girls! Girls!" and five acetates. Items are contained in square, brown film/acetate cases with metal corners, and a plastic handle on the side. There are two buckled straps, one horizontal and one vertical. Four Acetates are contained in plain white sleeves with a top flaps; one is in a regular white sleeve

with an open top. First record is "Because Of Love" (Hill & Range) recorded at Associated Recording Studio. Also included are two copies of the sheet music on white xerox paper with brown lettering. Second record has the songs "Song Of The Shrimp," and "The Walls Have Ears" (Radio Recorders). Third record has the song "Girls" (Associated Recording Studios). Also included are two copies of the sheet music on faded white paper. Fourth record has the songs "Comin' In Loaded," and "I Don't Want To" (Radio Recorders). Fifth record has the songs "Earth Boy" (Picture Version), and "Earth Boy" (Alternate Version). 15 1/4 x 15 3/4 inches Film and case. 10 x 10 1/4 inches Sleeves (5). 13 1/4 x 9 inches Sheet Music ("Because Of Love") 11 x 8 1/2 inches Sheet Music ("Girls")

This film was found among Colonel Parker's collection of Elvis' films. Stella Stevens co-starred with Elvis in the movie "Girls, Girls, Girls." It opened nationally on November 21, 1962, and reached number 6 on "Variety's" list of top-grossing films. When Elvis arrived in Hawaii to begin filming, he was mobbed by several thousand fans, and was stripped of his diamond ring, tie clip, and watch.

$4,000 - 6,000

B85 FILMING "IT HAPPENED AT THE WORLD'S FAIR"

One page original typewritten letter from Joe Esposito to Bill Fisher. The correspondence is written on *MGM* letterhead and dated September 18, 1962. Letter is regarding the reimbursement of expenses for Elvis and his staff from September 1 through the 15th while shooting "It Happened At The World's Fair" in Seattle, WA. Original hotel bills from September 5th through the 14th from the Doric New Washington Hotel. Total bill $3,084.13. 11 x 8 1/2 inches letter. 8 3/4 x 6 1/2 inches hotel bill.

Elvis arrived in Seattle on September 4th to film "It Happened At The World's Fair" with his cousins, Billy and Gene Smith, Leo West, Richard Davis, Jimmy Kingsley, Allan Fortis, and Ray Sitton. About this time his entourage was dubbed "The Memphis Mafia." They stayed at the *Doric New Washington Hotel* on the fourteenth floor where they each had separate rooms, and an extra room for dining so they would not have to use the regular dining area. During the filming of "It Happened At The World's Fair," an unknown child actor (who was never mentioned in the credits), Kurt Russell, went up to Elvis and kicked him in the shins. Later Russell would go on to portray Elvis on film.

$2,500 - 3,000

B86 JOKE LETTER FROM THE COLONEL TO RCA

Letter dated June 29, 1962 to R.C.A. Victor, Records Division (Bill Bullock) from A Fan (none other than the Colonel). Message praises Elvis and how wonderful his new "Pot Luck" album is and how handsome the star is on the cover. "I think Elvis is the King--you should give him much more recognition then you have been giving him . . . I hope you will get my point." The letter ends with "You're lucky to have such a great, wonderful singer and person recording for you. Your for Elvis Always, A Fan." A copy is sent to Elvis Presley. 11 x 8 1/2 inches.

The Colonel had just negotiated with RCA on the "Pot Luck" album, which was songs from "Follow That Dream." There weren't enough songs from the

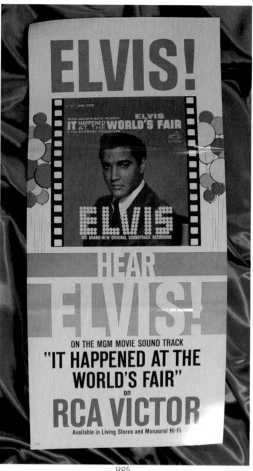

B85

movie for an album, so the Colonel found additional possibilities from recording sessions in 1961 and from a Nashville session in March 1962. This joke letter is letting RCA know what a great idea this was. Letter is from Colonel's personal typewriter, with his specific style of writing, such as placing asterisks before and after *Elvis*. $100 - 150

B87 MEMO REGARDING AND SHEET MUSIC FOR "SHE'S NOT YOU," AND "TELL HER JIM SAID HELLO"

Original memo signed by Joe Esposito to the Colonel advising him of Elvis' choice of his next single(s). "Tell Her Jim Said Hello" and "She's Not

You". Memo is written on Thomas A. Parker letterhead and dated May 21, 1962. Sheet music for above two singles included. Front cover of "She's Not You" has a photograph of Elvis sitting in a chair wearing a casual striped shirt. 5 1/2 x 8 1/2 inches memo. 12 x 9 inches sheet music.

Elvis recorded "She's Not You" on March 19, 1962 at RCA, Nashville The song had a ten week stay on Billboards "Hot 100" chart, and reached a #5 ranking on the "Hot 100". "Tell Her Jim Said Hello" was the B side of the single. $500 - 600

B88 CORRESPONDENCE BETWEEN ELVIS PRESLEY, COL. PARKER, AND THE DURANTES

Dark blue and silver Christmas card from Jimmy Durante with a handwritten personal note. Original envelope included. Christmas card with a fold out three dimensional nativity scene from the Durantes; CeCe, Margie, and Jimmy. Original note signed by Jimmy Durante, on plain white paper, dated December 31, 1963, to Elvis and the Colonel. Original envelope also included. Typewritten note circa 1965, on CeCe Durante letterhead, from CeCe Durante to "Uncle Elvis and Col. Parker." Four thank you letters from Jimmy Durante addressed to Colonel Parker. Letters dated December 15, 1963, October 7, 1964, December 1, 1964, and December 20, 1965. All four letters are signed by Jimmy in blue ink. Photo of Jimmy Durante in his famous "spotlight" pose. Autographed to Colonel Parker. 7 1/4 x 5 1/4 inches card. 8 x 3 1/2 inches card. 8 x 5 inches Jimmy Durante note. 3 3/4 x 8 1/4 inches envelope. 4 x 5 inches CeCe Durante note. 8 x 5 inches letter. 12/15/63 11 x 8 1/2 inches letter. 10/7/64 8 1/4 x 6 inches letter. 12/1/64 10 x 8 inches photo.

Note from Jimmy Durante expresses his thanks for Christmas gifts Elvis sent his daughter CeCe; "Gee, thanks a million for all those lovely presents you sent CeCe for Christmas." Typewritten note from CeCe, Jimmy's daughter, says, "Dear Uncle Elvis and Col. Parker, ...Thank you again -- you're so nice to me, and I loves ya!"

$800 - 1,000

B89 DELL COMICS LETTER

Letter dated March 21, 1962, to Colonel Parker from Stanley A. Weston of Weston Merchandising Corporation in New York. "They have recently expressed interest in doing a life-story comic on Elvis Presley. Their initial printing of this comic would be over 500,000 copies. . . we could hope to receive a minimum royalty from Dell of at least $1,600 for each tie-in comic that they would publish, which . . . we would share in equally with your company." 11 x 8 1/2 inches.

Charlton Comics received permission in 1956 to publish information about Elvis; however, the Colonel would not allow his future star to be trivialized by having a comic strip composed about him. A few years later, Stanley Weston was working with Dell Publishing to produce Dell

B90　　　B89

Comics on life stories of some celebrities and wanted to include some on Elvis. The Colonel refused to grant permission. This is just one example of an endless stream of proposals for merchandising Elvis.

$300 - 350

B90 CORRESPONDENCE REGARDING THE BOOK "ELVIS THE SWINGIN' KID"

One copy of book, and four memos from Tom Diskin regarding book. Original typewritten letter to Colonel Parker from Gordon Landsborough of May Fair Books, Ltd., dated January 21, 1963. Correspondence is in regards to the book, "Elvis The Swingin' Kid", by Charles Hamblett. Letter

details some disagreements between the two regarding the book, and a letter Mr. Parker sent to Landsborough on January 18th, 1963. Copy of Mr. Parker's letter is included. Two page typewritten letter from Charles Hamblett to Colonel Parker dated January 22, 1963 regarding the book. One page typewritten letter from Gordon Landsborough to the Colonel dated February 6, 1963. Copy of book. Four memos from Tom Diskin regarding changes on book. 10 x 8 1/4 inches Original letter. 11 x 8 1/2 inches Copy of the Colonel's letter. 10 x 8 inches Hamblett letter.

10 x 8 1/4 inches Landsborough letter. 7 x 4 1/2 inches Book (159 pages). 6 x 4 inches Memos.

Gordon Landsborough writes to the Colonel: ....."everything is okay and the deal is on. Good luck to you.....though you don't need it. You're quite a character, you know. Colonel Parker is an item of conversation I've heard crop up many times over the years. I don't know what you're really like but you come over as a very tough baby, a real shrewd man."

$1,000 - 1,250

B91 CONFIDENTIAL LETTER TO COLONEL PARKER FROM BILL BULLOCK

Two page typewritten confidential letter from Bill Bullock to the Colonel dated December 7, 1962. Correspondence discusses, in detail, prices on the photo album "It Happened At The World's Fair." Bullock proposes a deal contrary to what he and Colonel Parker had previously agreed upon. The Colonel responds at the bottom of the letter in a handwritten note informing his assistant that "If Bill Bullock calls - advise him we are not interested in his proposal." 10 1/2 x 8 inches.

This correspondence is typical of Colonel Parker's attempt to make "side deals" with RCA. Colonel Parker was always looking for ways to improve the contracts with RCA in order to make more money. In this letter the Colonel wants to make sure that the only photographs RCA receives are from him and are at a cost of twenty cents per photo. This arrangement was not the common practice of record companies. $400 - 500

B92 ELVIS CHRISTMAS SPECIAL ACETATE AND RECORD

Acetate and vinyl record of an Elvis Christmas radio program from 1966. 12 x 12 inches acetate and record.

To wish Elvis fans a merry Christmas, Elvis and the Colonel would do a Christmas radio show. It was one way they had of thanking the fans throughout the year. $800 - 1,000

B93 ELVIS PRESLEY MERCHANDISING CONTRACT

Two page typed contract on Thomas A. Parker wagon letterhead, dated June 25, 1965 and signed in blue ink by Elvis Presley, Col. Thomas A. Parker and Harry E. Jenkins of RCA Victor. Four postcards with gold borders and a picture of "Elvis' Gold Car On Tour." 11 x 8 1/2 inches contract. 3 1/2 x 5 1/2 postcards.

Colonel Parker frequently worked out side deal contracts. This contract concerns Elvis Presley merchandise, including color postcards, wallet size calendars and photo reproductions from "Harum Scarum." The contract called for a 50/50 split between Elvis and the Colonel.

$4,500 - 5,000

B94 WESTERN UNION TELEGRAMS FROM ELVIS AND COLONEL PARKER TO THE "RAT PACK"

Five Original Western Union telegrams from Colonel parker to the "Rat Pack." First telegram is dated February 2, 1962, to Frank Sinatra wishing him the best on his performance at the Riviera Hotel. Second telegram is to Dean Martin, dated June 7, 1962, wishing him a happy birthday, "Your picture is hanging in the conference room and we will give it a special greeting on your birthday." Third telegram is to Sammy Davis Jr., dated June 13, 1962, wishing him "luck and standing room only" for his engagement at the Harrah's Club. Fourth telegram is to Sammy Davis Jr., dated March 25, 1964, sending him best wishes for his opening night at the Sands Hotel. Fifth telegram is to Sammy Davis Jr., dated October 19, 1964, congratulating him on his latest film. 5 3/4 x 8 inches telegrams.

Sammy Davis Jr., Frank Sinatra, and Dean Martin were part of the "Rat Pack" clan. Davis appeared with Elvis on the 1960 "Frank Sinatra-Timex Special." Dean Martin was one of Elvis' singing idols in the early 1950's. It was on Sinatra's May 12, 1960 TV special that Elvis made his first TV appearance after his discharge from the Army.

$375 - 450

B95 THE COLONEL AND BOB HOPE

Original Western Union Telegram dated February 2, 1962, from Colonel Parker to Bob Hope. Telegram is to congratulate Mr. Hope on his "Big Performance" that night. Two typewritten and signed letters from Bob Hope to the Colonel. First letter is dated June 21, 1963, which thanks Colonel Parker for remembering his birthday. Second letter is dated August 13, 1964, regarding Jack Benny, "Viva Las Vegas," and a memorial for a relative. Signed photograph of Bob Hope to Thomas A Parker. 6 1/2 x 8 inches Telegram. 10 1/2 x 7 3/4 inches letter. 10 1/2 x 7 1/4 inches letter. 10 x 8 inches photo.

Bob Hope was fascinated by the Colonel and desired to make a movie of Colonel Parker's life. He called Colonel Parker the greatest con-man since Barnum.

$900 - 1,000

B96 ELVIS' THUNDERBIRD—NAMEPLATE, PATCH AND LETTER

One page typed letter on Ford Motor Company letterhead, dated February 16, 1962, congratulating Elvis on his purchase of a 1962 Thunderbird. Silver metal nameplate with a raised "T-Bird" logo and "Elvis Presley" engraving. Gold card reading "1962 Thunderbird Owner" with Elvis' name and address printed. 10 1/2 x 7 1/4 inches letter. 7/8 x 4 1/4 inches nameplate. 2 1/2 x 3 1/2 inches ownership card.

This letter, from Ford Vice-President L.A. Iacocca, suggests that Elvis carry his ownership card with him in order to get "preferred service" from Ford dealers. The nameplate was never actually placed on the car.

$2,500 - 3,500

B97 TELEGRAM FROM COLONEL TOM PARKER TO W.W. BULLOCK

Western Union telegram dated January 8, 1963 sent to W.W. Bullock at RCA Record Division from the Colonel. Message suggests abandoning project relating to album layout. He feels it is unfair to Elvis' fans to sell merchandise similar to another

project and at a higher price. "Am sure you and the entire company will agree that our past albums having exploited thirteen great songs, fourteen great songs, and now only ten songs that it would be taking unfair advantage of their loyalty, especially by charging more on top of this. Please return all photos." Photograph included. 10 x 8 1/2 inches.

The Colonel always had the fans in mind. From the beginning, he communicated with the fans, as did Elvis, and encouraged them to stay in touch with him. "It Happened at the World's Fair" album was planned to have only 10 songs and a higher price tag. The Colonel felt they were "ripping off" the public and that they would alienate them, so he nixed the project.

$600 - 850

B98 THE COLONEL'S JANUARY, 1963 JOURNAL

Original twenty-one page journal, bound within a gold colored folder, outlining the Colonel's activities for the month of January, 1963. In this journal, the Colonel lists his activities, and who he saw while on location at Paramount Studios in Hollywood, California. 11 x 8 1/2 inches pages. 11 3/4 x 9 inches folder.

Colonel Parker kept these records to document and detail all activities surrounding Elvis Presley. He prided himself on being a top promotions man, and always kept meticulous records.

$1,200 - 1,500

B99 ELVIS PRESLEY TELEPHONE CARDS AND BILLS

1963 and 1964 Bell System Credit Cards issued to Elvis Presley. 1963 card on white, yellow and brown card stock, 1964 card on white, green and blue card stock, both with original mailing envelopes. Four Southern Bell Telephone and Telegraph Co. bill stubs dated August 1 and August 17, 1963. 3 1/2 x 7 inches credit cards. 3 1/2 x 3 1/2 inches bill stub.

These items were sent to Elvis at Graceland.

$1,800 - 2,000

B100 ELVIS PRESLEY AUTOGRAPHED BASEBALL

Near-mint condition Wilson Official "Little League" baseball. Signed with the note: "Good Luck / Elvis Presley". Includes signatures of little league players.

Though Elvis was not known to play on organized sports teams, he enjoyed an occasional friendly game with the guys. As his fortune grew, he was a magnanimous patron of various teams of local and underprivileged children, often cheering them on from the stands in person. This baseball became a legend when Elvis brought it to a championship game featuring one of his sponsored teams. The team took the ball, signed by Elvis for "Good Luck," and the championship title. Out of respect for the King, they signed the baseball themselves and returned it.

$2,000 - 3,000

B100

B102

B101 ELVIS PRESLEY ENTERPRISES BASEBALL SPONSORSHIPS

One page typed letter, dated February 28, 1963, from the Whitehaven Junior Baseball Association in Memphis to Elvis Presley Enterprises. Letter thanks Elvis Presley Enterprises for sponsoring a team in their baseball league. Invoice from United Sporting Goods in Los Angeles dated March 18, 1963 for the purchase of $75.87 in softball equipment and receipt dated March 20, 1963 for $141.60 for a men's softball fee. Trophy won by the E.P.E. sponsored softball team. Gold and silver metallic trophy on wooden base, with stamp of the "Amateur Softball Association of America." 10 7/8 x 8 1/2 inches letter. 8 1/2 x 8 1/2 inches invoice. 2 7/8 x 5 1/2 inches receipt. 22 1/2 inches tall trophy.

The men's softball fee receipt is for a total of 18 games played.

$750 - 850

B102 ELVIS PRESLEY'S HAMILTON WRISTWATCH

Elvis had a penchant for exciting design. This was expressed in his clothing, automobiles, with objects in his home, and in this case, with his choice of wristwatch.

This Hamilton electric wristwatch reflects avant-garde thinking of the era. It was perhaps the most innovative watch of its day. Both its electric movement and dramatic design were years ahead of their time. To this day (and one suspects well into the future) this model wristwatch will be sought after by collectors. The fact that - in this case - this wristwatch belonged to Elvis, argues the point that it is *the ultimate collector's wristwatch.*

$4,000 - 6,000

B103

B103 ELVIS PRESLEY DRY CLEANING BILLS

Twenty-nine handwritten receipts from Malone Studio Service, Inc. Dry Cleaners in Hollywood, billed to Elvis Presley. Dry cleaning bill from Kraus Cleaners in Memphis, dated January 7, 1964 and billed to Elvis Presley. With a black wooden hanger used personally by Elvis. Photograph included. 8 1/2 x 5 1/2 inches Hollywood bills. 3 1/8 x 7 inches.

Memphis bill Hollywood receipts range from fall 1973 through spring 1974

$800 - 1,000

B104 KEY, BILL AND RECEIPT FOR ELVIS PRESLEY'S SAFE DEPOSIT BOX

Original bill and receipt dated October 21, 1963, from the National Bank of Commerce for a safe deposit box. Total charge was $16.50 for rental and U.S. Tax due. Original envelope included. One gold key with red ribbon. 6 1/4 x 5 1/2 inches Receipt. 3 1/2 x 7 3/4 inches Bill. 4 1/4 x 9 1/2 inches Envelope

Elvis rented this particular safe deposit box for the period of October 19, 1963, through October 19, 1964. $800 - 900

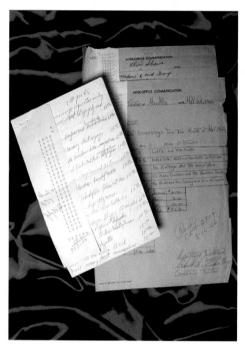

B105

B105 ELVIS' PRIVATE SCREENINGS

List of movies Elvis viewed with his friends at the Memphian Theatre; handwritten in pencil on stationery printed with , "Memo from - - Paul Shafer." The cost was $2.50 per hour and ranged from $10 - $15 for each movie. Between May 13 and June 23, there were 25 screenings. Attached is adding machine tape totaling the cost of the screenings which is $342.50. A handwritten note on the adding machine tape indicates the bill was paid on July 25, 1963. Memo from Paul Shafer at the Memphian Theatre with bill for movies rented from September 23 to October 1, 1963. Movies included "Hootenanny Hoot" "Horror Hotel," "Beach Party," "All the Way Home," and "Snake Woman." Total bill: $75. Elvis rented out the Memphian Theatre for private movie showings. From April 28, 1966 through June 23, 1966, Elvis' bill was $971. Eight

itemized Inter-Office Communications (on pink paper) explain name of movie, date, times and fees for projectionist, manager, and doorman. One sheet from the Crosstown Theatre shows his private screenings for the month of May 1966 for a total of $156.50. Movies include "Dr. Zhivago," "Three on a Couch," "The Chase," and "Battle of the Bulge." Adding machine tapes are attached to the bills. Photograph included. Four handwritten pages of expenses from December 2, 1966 through January 18, 1967, for private movie screening at the Memphian Theatre for Elvis and friends. Itemized costs include, film rental, operator, manager, doorman, concessions, for a total of $796. Attached is an adding machine tape that shows the bill paid April 14 with check number 3090. 8 1/2 x 2 1/4 inches list from 1963. 7 3/4 x 5 1/2 inches adding machine receipt for 1963. 8 1/2 x 5 1/2 inches Shafer memo. 11 x 8 1/2 inches itemized bills May 1966. 8 3/4 x 2 3/4 inches and 6 1/4 x 2 3/4 inches adding machine tapes May 1966. 11 x 8 1/2 inches list December 1966. 13 3/4 x 2 1/4 inches machine tape December 1966.

Elvis was a movie fan from the time he was a youngster. His excitement for viewing films didn't lessen as he grew older and became famous. When he was in Memphis, he would rent out the Memphian and Crosstown Theatres to have private showings of films for his friends.

$2,000 - 2,500

B106 ELVIS PRESLEY BOOK WITH RECEIPT

Receipt from Whitehaven Readin' & Ritin' Shop in Memphis, dated June 4, 1963 and billed to Elvis Presley. Handwritten in blue ink on Readin' and Ritin' Shop letterhead. For purchase of "Stranger Than Science" in the amount of $5.10. Elvis' personal copy of the hardbound book. 11 x 8 1/2 inches receipt. 8 1/8 x 5 1/2 inches book.

Receipt reads that the book was purchased by "Joe" (Esposito) and picked up by Elvis' cousin, Billy Smith. The well-worn book's cover describes it as "A fantastic yet factual collection of fascinating stories taken from life."

$700 - 800

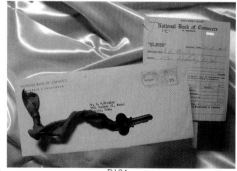

B104

B107

B107 SIGNED CHECKS AND BILL FOR HANDWRITING ANALYSIS

Invoice from Earl E. Davenport, Certified Grapho Analyst, dated August 17, 1963. Davenport analyzed Elvis' signatures on 60 checks July 31, 1963 for a fee of $50. Several checks with Elvis' signature.9 1/8 x 6 inches.

There was some fear that someone was forging Elvis' signatures, so Vernon hired an expert handwriting analyst to look at 60 checks. No problems were found during the analysis. (The three checks in this lot carry Elvis' signature; however, they were not ones that were analyzed.)

$4,000 - 6,000

B108

B108 CONTRACT BETWEEN COLONEL PARKER, ELVIS PRESLEY, AND RCA, REGARDING VOLUME THREE GOLDEN LP; AND BETWEEN ELVIS PRESLEY AND COLONEL PARKER REGARDING MERCHANDISING, PLUS PICTURE FOLIO AND ALBUM

Contract from W.W. Bullock of RCA Victor to Elvis and All Star Shows. The letter is on Radio Corporation of America letterhead and is dated May 21, 1963. The letter confirms the arrangements for the release of "Volume Three Golden LP." The letter has "CONFIDENTIAL" stamped on it in purple, and is signed by W.W. Bullock and Thomas Parker in blue ink under the words, "Accepted and Agreed To," and signed by Elvis Presley in blue ink under the word, "Approved."

Also included is a letter from Elvis Presley and Col. Parker on Tom Parker's wagon letterhead regarding "Merchandising - Special Souvenir Folios and Pictures." The letter is dated May 25, 1963 and discusses merchandising arrangements. Signed in blue in by Elvis Presley and Col. Tom Parker.

Six page picture folio with a special giant size pin-up picture of Elvis. Cover has a dark blue 2 3/4" strip across the top with "Elvis" printed in bold letters of Yellow and orange. A picture of Elvis is on the front cover with him sitting and holding a guitar. Background is medium blue. Back cover is a photo of Elvis from his shoulders up; he is wearing a white shirt with blue pinstripes, Medium blue jacket, and black tie. Copy of "Elvis' Gold Records Vol. 3". 11 x 8 1/2 inches Contracts. 11 x 8 1/2 inches Folio. 12 x 12 inches Album.

This represents another one of Colonel Parker's special "side deals". $8,000 - 9,000

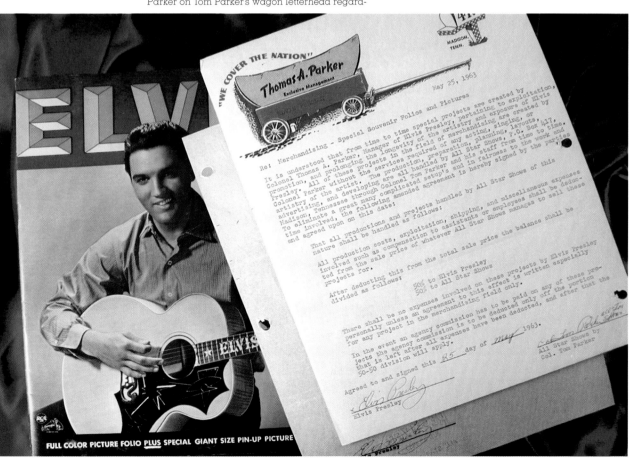

B109 ELVIS' HUMIDOR, CIGARS AND CIGAR COMPANY BILL

Elvis' personal humidor, several of Elvis' choice cigars, and invoice dated 5/14/63 and Statement dated 6/1/63 from Bianchi Cigar Company on Vance Avenue in Memphis. Humidor of dark well-worn wood, with gold metal plate on the lid and the engraving: "TO ELVIS, THANKS FOR A GROOVY SHOW, RONNIE, LARRY, JERRY, JAMES AND JOHN, INTERNATIONAL AUG. '69." Humidor contains ten unopened packages of "Tipalet" cigars and a tag with a "Dunhill" logo. Invoice includes breakdown of order, including humidor, gum, and cool smokes. Total: $48.69. Statement is sent to Spain & Fisher for Elvis Presley Account and indicates Paid, ck #845, 6/4/63. Photograph included. Several of Elvis' cigars 10 1/2 x 8 1/2 invoice. 8 1/2 x 5 1/2 statement.

Elvis was home at this time for Priscilla's graduation. He spent the month of June in Memphis before returning to the West Coast. While at home, Elvis and his dad would smoke cigars together and discuss the state of the world.

$10,000 - 15,000

B110 COLONEL TOM PARKER'S HUMIDOR

Humidor in light wood, two drawers with dividers
behind two doors. 17 inches tall x 13 inches wide x
9 inches deep.

Colonel Parker had an ever-present side-kick - his
cigar. This humidor was where he kept his cigars
before indulging.

$5,000 - 10,000

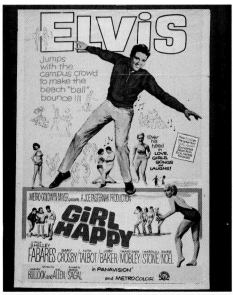

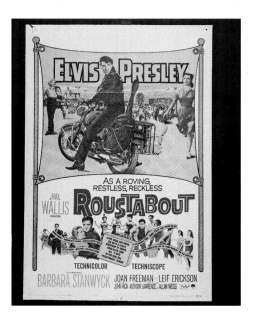

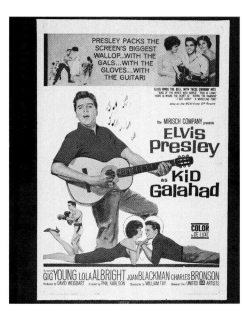

The six movie posters depicted on this and the following are part of lot B227.

B111 ITEMS FROM "IT HAPPENED AT THE WORLD'S FAIR"

Brown bag with black lettering to advertise "It Happened at the World's Fair." Bag says "Souvenir Package Compliments of ELVIS and the Colonel" and shows the MGM logo with the lion in center. Two Psycho-sticks; wooden with black top; made by the Junior Achievement Co.; included in souvenir bags. "Take Me to the Fair" sheet music Acetate of "It Happened at the World's Fair" "It Happened at the World's Fair" record. 13 3/8 x 13 1/2 inches bag. 10-inch stick with 2 1/4 inch top.

The Colonel was given an office at each of the film companies when Elvis was shooting a picture. He produced promotional packets for each of the films, so fans could have some souvenirs. $2,500 - 3,000

B112 "ROUSTABOUT" PROMOTIONAL PACKET

Production information and synopsis, eleven typed pages with red Paramount Pictures logo on first page. Promotional booklet sent to theaters, eleven pages with publicity images and copy. "Roustabout" soundtrack album. 13 x 8 1/2 inches information packet. 15 x 12 inches publicity packet.

The 1964 Paramount film "Roustabout" was Elvis' 16th film. He starred opposite screen legend Barbara Stanwyck, probably the most accomplished and celebrated of all of his co-stars. A young Racquel Welch also made her screen debut in "Roustabout," in a very minor role. $400 - 500

B112A LETTER FROM COLONEL PARKER TO ELVIS PRESLEY REGARDING A 16 MM PRINT OF "FUN IN ACAPULCO," AND A CONTRACT/LETTER FROM ELVIS PRESLEY TO HAL WALLIS

Typewritten letter, on Paramount Pictures Corporation, dated December 12, 1963, to Elvis from the Colonel. Correspondence is regarding the shipping, and agreement regarding the 16 mm film. Original typed letter/contract, dated December 13, 1963, and signed by Elvis. Letter was sent to Hal Wallis Productions regarding a 16 mm print of "Fun In Acapulco" that was given to Elvis as a personal gift. Elvis writes; "I hereby agree that the film will be for my personal use only at my home and I will not use it any way commercially or for profit."

Elvis always received a 16 millimeter copy of his films. The "boys" (his entourage) claimed that Elvis would never watch "Loving You" because his mother appeared as part of the audience in that film.

$4,500 - 5,000

B113 LETTER FROM COLONEL PARKER TO ELVIS PRESLEY REGARDING A 16 MM PRINT OF "FUN IN ACAPULCO," AND A CONTRACT/LETTER FROM ELVIS PRESLEY TO HAL WALLIS

Typewritten letter, on Paramount Pictures Corporation, dated December 12, 1963, to Elvis from the Colonel. Correspondence is regarding the shipping, and agreement regarding the 16 mm film. Original typed letter/contract, dated December 13, 1963, and signed by Elvis. Letter was sent to Hal Wallis Productions regarding a 16 millimeter print of "Fun In Acapulco" that was given to Elvis as a personal gift. Elvis writes; "I hereby agree that the film will be for my personal use only at my home and I will not use it any way commercially or for profit." 11 x 8 1/2 inches.

Elvis always received a 16 millimeter copy of his films. The "boys" (the band) claimed that Elvis would never watch "Loving You" because his mother appeared as part of the audience in that film.

$4,500 - 5,000

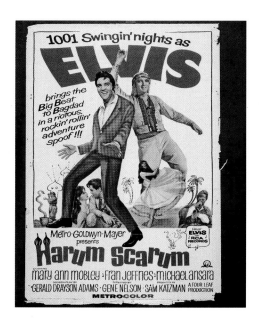

B114 ARTWORK FOR KISSIN' COUSINS

Black-and-white artwork with red border at top highlighting Elvis' New Hit Album "Kissin' Cousins." Yellow border at bottom also highlights the album. Center section promotes 19 other RCA albums completed by Elvis. Stamp on back reads Received, April 29, 1964, All Star Shows. 14 x 12 1/4 inches.

The majority of the soundtrack recordings for "Kissin' Cousins" took place on September 29-30, 1963 in Nashville for budget reasons and to give a country flavor to the music. The remaining songs were recorded on October 10 at MGM studios in Culver City. The album was released in March 1964, with all nine songs from the movie included, as well as three bonus songs.

$1,300 - 1,500

B115 ELVIS' PERSONAL FILM AND ACETATES OF "FUN IN ACAPULCO"

One original movie case containing the 16 millimeter film of "Fun in Acapulco." Label on case is white with a red border and reads, "Fun in Acapulco, A Hall Wallis Production, Paramount

Studio Release, Director: Richard Thorpe, Released November 1963." Red label with raised white letters "Fun in Acapulco - 1963." One original acetate box containing 32 "Fun in Acapulco" acetates including: "Allegro," "The Bull Fighter Was a Lady," "Malaguena," "Fun in Acapulco," "I Think I'm Going to Like It Here," "Bossa Nova Baby," "Vino, Dinero Y Amor," "Guadalajara," "El Toro," "Mexico," and "You Can't Say No in Acapulco." Sheet music to some songs is also included. Orange label with raised letters reads, "Fun in Acapulco - 1963." Cases are brown with metal corners, a handle on one end, and a horizontal and a vertical buckled strap. 15 1/4 x 15 3/4 inches film case. 15 x 15 inches acetate case.

Elvis played s a lifeguard and singer at an Acapulco resort in the film "Fun in Acapulco." During the filming, the closest he actually came to Acapulco was on the Paramount lot in Hollywood. The film was released in November 1963 and co-starred Ursula Andress, the Swiss-born actress.

$3,000 - 4,000

B116 ELVIS' PERSONAL FILM AND ACETATES OF "IT HAPPENED AT THE WORLD'S FAIR"

Copy of the MGM film "It Happened At The World's Fair", and four acetates. White cardboard inside one acetate box has a handwritten note that says "To Col. Thomas A. Parker(& Staff) From Ron Jacobs 'It Happened At The Worlds Fair' MGM Radio Spots 33 1/3 RPM Souvenir Record - 98 cents Thanks. Ron." Items are contained in square, brown film/acetate cases with metal corners, and a plastic handle on the side. There are two buckled straps, one horizontal and one vertical. 15 1/4 x 15 3/4 inches Movie and case 15 x 15 inches Acetate.

This film belonged to Colonel Parker's personal collection of Elvis Presley movies. "It Happened At The World's Fair" opened nationally on April 10, 1963. MGM had to hire a hundred special policemen to protect Elvis from the Fair crowds while filming. Six Pinkerton plainclothes detectives were at his side every second he wasn't in front of the camera. Acetates contain "Broken Heart For Sale," "Remind Me Of You," "Take Me To The Fair," "The Bright New World of Tomorrow," "Beyond the Bend," "I'm Falling in Love Tonight," "A world of Our," "Cotton Candy Man," etc.

$3,000 - 4,000

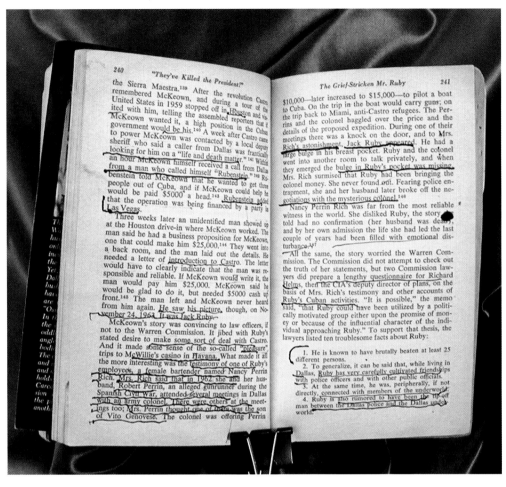

Letter dated December 23, 1963, on Music, Inc., stationery from Bobby Darin (with signature) to the
Colonel and Mrs. Parker: "Thank you very much for
the foot massager. I now need one for my brain
and I will be replete . . . Please say "hello" to the
King for me and may you all have happy holidays." 11 x 8 1/2 inches   Bobby Darin,
famous rock and roll singer of the 50s and 60s, was
one of Elvis' favorite entertainers. He even introduced Bobby at one of his Las Vegas concerts.
Darin composed "I'll Be There," a number that Elvis
recorded in 1969.

$400 - 500

B119 PEPSI-COLA RECEIPT AND CHECK

Pepsi-Cola receipt dated April 1963, and addressed
to Elvis Presley on South Bellevue in Memphis,
Tennessee. A handwritten note indicates the bill
was paid on May 6, 1963. Receipt has red and blue
Pepsi-Cola logo and has a square of discoloration
on the top half. Green Elvis Presley Payroll &
Expense fund check written for the amount of
$29.50, and signed by Vernon Presley. Photograph
included. 6 1/4 x 8 1/2 inches Receipt. 3 x 8 1/4
inches Check.

Elvis loved Pepsi and had it delivered weekly to his
house.

$500 - 600

B117 ELVIS PRESLEY'S COPY OF "THEY'VE KILLED THE PRESIDENT"

was interested in the study of history. He was
known to memorize speeches made by Martin
Luther King. $8,000 - 10,000

Elvis' personal copy of "They've Killed the
President!", a 414-page paperback book written by
Robert Sam Anson. A number of passages and
words in the book have been underlined by Elvis.
A small article from the Commercial Appeal newspaper inside book relates a case of charges being
dropped against a local Memphis service station
owner. 7 x 4 1/4 inches.

Elvis was fascinated by Kennedy's assassination
and the mystery that surrounded it, as evidenced
by the large number of passages that are marked
throughout this book. Beyond just Kennedy, Elvis

B120 ELVIS PRESLEY TV ANTENNAS AND RECEIPT

Receipt and invoice from McDonald Brothers Co. in
Memphis, dated April 18 and April 30, 1963, respectively. For purchase by Elvis Presley of one RCA
television in the amount of $204.68. With rooftop
VHF and UHF antennas. 8 1/2 x 8 1/2 inches
invoice. 8 1/2 x 5 1/2 inches receipt.

Elvis loved to watch television. Graceland had
fourteen televisions, five in Elvis' bedroom alone,
including two in the ceiling over his bed.

$650 - 750

B121

B123

B121 ESSO GASOLINE CARD

White and red plastic credit card with raised blue letters, expiration February 1963. Envelope with Elvis Presley return address imprinted and "Credit Cards" written on front. 2 1/8 x 3 3/8 inches card. 5 1/2 x 7 1/2 inches envelope. The card reads "Elvis A. Presley," but is unsigned. $3,000 - 3,500

B122 AMERICAN OIL CARD

White, red and blue plastic credit card with raised letters, "Elvis Presley." 2 1/8 x 3 3/8 inches.

With expiration date October 1964.

          $2,500 - 3,000

B123 ELVIS PRESLEY CAR AND MOTORCYCLE LICENSE PLATES

Two green metal motorcycle tags from 1973. Larger tag has raised imprint "Cycle ZM-8446 Tenn. 73." Smaller tag has raised imprint "1973 Motorcycle 1467 Memphis." 1971 Tennessee white metal license plate #1-S0366, for Elvis' Bronco. Black metal license plate dated 1963 with raised yellow imprint "California VE 9203." 1966 Tennessee white metal license plate with raised imprint "ON-4739." 4 1/2 x 7 3/4 inches motorcycle tag. 2 1/4 x 3 inches motorcycle tag. 6 x 12 inches all license plates.

These motorcycle tags may have been used for a custom made Harley-Davidson motorcycle Elvis

bought in 1971. The California plate comes in an original mailing envelope with a "Ronald Reagan, Governor of California."

$10,000 - 12,000

B124 TEXACO CARD

White, red and green plastic credit card with raised letters, "Elvis Presley." 2 1/8 x 3 3/8 inches.

Card lists "Graceland" as address.

$2,500 - 3,000

B125 ELVIS PRESLEY'S HEALTH INSURANCE CARD

Elvis Presley's health insurance card from Blue Cross. Card dated July 1, 1964. 4 x 3 3/8.

Card was issued to Elvis Presley and dated July 1, 1964.

$1,800 - 2,000

B126 LOWENSTEIN'S CREDIT CARD AND STATEMENTS

Statement from Lowenstein's for Elvis Presley. Amount remitted is $23.44. Attached is a pay statement dated July 22, 1963 indication that a payment of $23.44 had been received and the balance was $00. "Paid" is handwritten in blue ink. Also included is an unsent envelope with Lowenstein's mailing address typed in the center and Vernon Presley's mailing address stamped in the upper left corner. Account Receipt for a $13.05 bill at Lowenstein's department store in Memphis. Account is in the name of Miss Priscilla Beaulieu and billed to Vernon Presley at his Dolan Road address. Receipt is marked Paid--April 10, 1967. Lowenstein's credit card; white with gold letters. VIP card with Mr. Elvis Presley and account # 187-199-61 imprinted. Card is in folder. 3 1/4 x 6 1/2 inches statements. 4 1/8 x 6 1/2 inches pay statement. 4 1/8 x 9 1/2 inches envelope. 1 3/4 x 3 1/2 inches credit card. 3 1/2 x 6 78 inches opening to 7 x 6 7/8 inches folder.

Besides Lansky Brothers, Lowenstein's was one of the other apparel shops in Memphis that Elvis Presley frequented. While yet unmarried to Elvis, Priscilla continued' to have her bills sent to Vernon's Dolan Road address.

$3,500 - 4,000

B127 GROCERY LIST AND RECEIPTS

December, 1965, handwritten grocery list, and receipts from Krogers, Wahlgreen's, Day & Night

Food Mart, and McLemore Grocery. 8 x 5 inches The above businesses were located in Memphis. The handwritten list includes: Pet milk, turnip greens, collard greens, ground beef, bacon, wieners, steak, cabbage, onions, bell pepper, carrots, lettuce, fruit, apple jelly, t.v. guide, milk, and potatoes.

$450 - 500

B125

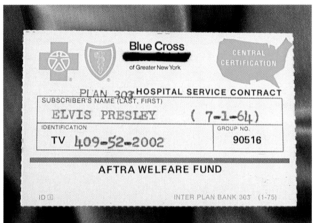

B128 SCREEN ACTORS GUILD CARD, RECEIPT, AND ENVELOPE

Elvis Presley's 1964 Screen Actors Guild Card-- number 42838, receipt of payment of $125, and envelope with Screen Actors Guild return address Hollywood Glamour Shot photograph included. 2 1/2 x 3 1/2 inches card. 3 3/8 x 6 1/8 inches receipt. 3 1/2 x 6 1/4 inches envelope.

Elvis appeared in 31 feature films; therefore, he was required to be a member of the Screen Actors Guild.

$3,000 - 3,500

B129 ELVIS PRESLEY'S NET WORTH STATEMENTS FROM SPAIN AND FISHER

Two six page statements, typed on white paper and bound by dark beige folders, documenting Elvis Presley's assets, income, and net worth.

Documents were prepared by Spain and Fisher; certified public accountants, Memphis, TN. 11 1/2 x 9 inches.

First document is for December '63 through December '64 with a gross income of $2,068,596.62; the second document is for December '64 through December '65 with a gross income of $3,207,307.36.

$4,250 - 5,000

B130 ELVIS PRESLEY'S NET WORTH STATEMENTS FROM SPAIN AND FISHER

Copy of Elvis Presley's 1962 and 1966 Net Worth Statements which detail his income, expenses, and net worth. All pages are typed on Spain and Fisher letterhead, and bound in a dark beige folder. 11 x 8 1/2 inches Pages. 11 1/2 x 9 inches Folder.
The five page 1962 document lists Elvis' gross income as $1,681,126.55 and the portion of the Sun Record Contract price at $9,285.09. Net Worth statement for 1965 is seven pages long and lists Elvis' gross income at $3,276,120.28

$4,000 - 5,000

B131 ELVIS PRESLEY'S FINANCIAL STATEMENTS FOR 1963 AND 1967

Elvis Presley's financial statements for 1963 and 1967, prepared by Spain and Fisher. Statements, in beige spiral-bound books, show Balance sheet, Statement of Income and Net Worth, and Statement of Changes in Net Cash Position. 1963 statement signed by William Fisher; 1967 statement signed by H.M. Spain. 11 1/2 x 9 1/8 inches.

Statements extensively detail Elvis' financial situation. Elvis' total taxable income was $1,825,303.69 in 1963, and $3,593,323.52 in 1967. In 1963, Elvis spent almost $10,000 on hair and scalp care.

$4,000 - 5,000

B132 HARD-BOUND RCA "ELECTRONIC AGE," WINTER 1964/1965

Red, cloth covered, hard bound edition of RCA's publication, "Electronic Age," for the winter of 1964/1965. Front cover of book is silkscreened in gold lettering "COMPLIMENTS, ELVIS AND THE COLONEL". An article regarding Elvis Presley is in this edition.13 1/8 x 10 3/8 inches.

Five page Article on Elvis is written by Robert Kotlowitz. The article details his rise to fame to 1965 when Elvis marked his 30th birthday and his 10th year at RCA Victor. There are six pictures of his albums; "Elvis Roustabout Elvis,", "Elvis is back," "Elvis Kissin' Cousins," "His Hand in Mine," "Elvis Girls, Girls, Girls," and "Elvis Gold Records Volume 2. Other photographs include Elvis on stage in action, Elvis waiting to go onstage in the early days of his career, Presley with friends during the Army stint, a typical crowd that welcomed him, and Elvis with the Jordanaires.

$800 - 1,000

B133 LITERARY AGENTS MISCELLANEOUS CORRESPONDENCE, 1956 - 1965

Letters bound in folder entitled, "Literary Agents Miscellaneous Correspondence 1956 - 1965." Letters include proposals for, and rejections of, books and screenplays related to Elvis Presley and Colonel Thomas Parker.. 11 1/2 X 9 1/8.

With Elvis' growing popularity and success, many fans and business persons alike devised proposals for Elvis' sponsorship, endorsement, and partnership in a wide variety of business schemes and plans, hoping that Elvis' involvement would mean success. $500 - 750

B134 ELVIS PRESLEY ACCOUNTING LEDGER

Empty accounting ledger. Cover is green with a black sticker in the bottom right corner which reads, "Elvis Presley." Black piece of vinyl with gold printing stating, "'Girls! Girls! Girls!' 1962 Elvis Presley." 9 x 11 3/4 inches ledger. 7 1/4 x 27 inches vinyl.

When this ledger was found in Vernon Presley's office, the "Girls, Girls, Girls" promotional item was stuck inside. $1,200 - 1,400

B135 BULLOCK'S CREDIT CARD ISSUED TO ELVIS PRESLEY

Beige and brown Bullock's credit card issued to Mr. Elvis A. Presley. Original cream colored two page card holder included. On the front cover of the holder is the Bullock's coat of arms; instructions on inside page opposite a drawing of a light brown purse; back page lists: "The Bullock Ideal" creed. 1 3/4 x 3 1/2 inches Card. 7 x 5 inches Brochure.

Bullock's is an upscale California clothing store.

$3,000 - 3,500

B136 ELVIS PRESLEY'S WATCH AND JEWELRY BILLS

Two page receipt from Harry Levitch Jewelers in Memphis, dated December 27, 1965 and made out to Elvis Presley. Bill totaling $3,235.39 marked as "Christmas Gifts."Bill includes a $1,355 diamond ring, three men's gold wristwatches, two gold bracelets , a gold butterfly pin, and a knife among other items. Bill totals $3235.39. Hamilton watch has black face in the shape of a sideways pyramid and is surrounded by 14k white gold. Band is stainless steel. 7 x 8 1/2 inches.

Harry Levitch came to Elvis' attention through an association with Red West dating back to high school. Two of the three watches Elvis purchased were engraved, one with "GK" for George Klein and the other with "EP" for Elvis Presley.

$3,500 - 4,000

B137 MGM CONTRACTS—JAILHOUSE ROCK REISSUE AND OTHER MOVIE MUSIC

Four pages typed on Metro-Goldwyn-Mayer letterhead, dated December 22, 1964. Signed twice in blue ink by Elvis Presley and Col. Tom Parker. Photograph included. 11 x 8 1/2 inches.

This contract reaffirms the initial agreement concerning music for "Jailhouse Rock," in regard to the re-release of the film in 1964. $7,000 - 8,000

B138 NOTES ON RECORDING SESSION FOR "KISSIN' COUSINS"

Colonel Parker's notes, dated September 29 and 30, 1963, and written on back of four time cards, highlight recording session for "Kissin' Cousins," including meeting time, musicians, singers, and songs. Two different colors of ink used."Kissin' Cousins" LP; Elvis in red jacket and white shirt on front, scenes from film on back. 7 1/4 x 4 3/8 inches notes. 12 1/4 x 12 1/4 inches LP.

The recording session for "Kissin' Cousins" took place in Nashville. Elvis had a cold, so he appeared at the session but didn't actually do the vocals until later. They laid down the background music at this time.

$600 - 800

B139 "FUN IN ACAPULCO" FIRST PROOFS

Two first proofs for "Fun In Acapulco". First proof is stamped October 4, 1963, and has five photographs of Elvis (various head shots), on both sides of the cover; two photographs of Elvis on the bottom and one on the top. In the middle are the words: "Paramount Pictures presents Elvis in "Fun In Acapulco" a Hall Wallis production." Background is yellow with pictures done in black, white and red. Middle is multi-colored. Second proof has a green background with a photo of Elvis in a red shirt with a multi-colored mexican rug hanging behind him. On top of proof, written in blue ink

B140   B137

B139   B139

are the words: "Col. Tom Think "Fun In Acapulco" must be much lighter - do you agree? Bob" 20 x 14 1/4 inches Posters.

Production of "Fun In Acapulco" began on January 28, 1963. Ursula Andress co-starred with Elvis. The film reached #5 on "Variety's" weekly top-grossing films. For the year 1963, it ranked #33. The Beatles went to see this film at a drive-in theater in Miami on February 18, 1964, during their first American tour.

$2,000 - 2,500

B140 TWO FIRST PROOF POSTERS FOR THE FILM "KISSIN' COUSINS

Two first proof posters for the film "Kissin' Cousins." First proof has two photos on each side of the poster of Elvis with the hound dog Hezekiah. There are four photographs that line the bottom of the poster; two of Elvis as his character Jody, and two as his character Josh in "Kissin' Cousins." On the far right upper corner, and the far left upper corner are drawings of the RCA phonograph and dog: "His Master's Voice". Side one of the "Kissin' Cousins" album is listed on the upper left, and side two in the upper right. In the middle of the poster on a background of bright red are the words "Metro-Goldwyn-Mayer presents Elvis in "Kissin' Cousins", then goes on to list his costars and other film credits.

Second proof is divided in two with the left side a photo of Elvis from the waist up wearing a white shirt and a red jacket; background is light red and green. On the right side are the words "RCA Victor presents Elvis in an original soundtrack album from the Metro-Goldwyn-Mayer picture "Kissin' Cousins" a Sam Katzman four Leaf Production." Drawing of a log cabin with a wood fence in the foreground. 20 x 14 1/4 inches Posters.

Kissin' Cousins was filmed in October 1963; the exteriors were shot at Big Bear Lake, California, and all interiors were filmed at MGM's Culver City studios. The sixteen day shoot was budgeted at $800,000; and Sam Katzman was known as Hollywoods "King of the Quickies."The film reached #11 on "Variety's weekly list of top-grossing films, and was ranked #26 for the year 1964.

$1,000 - 1,200

B141 ELVIS' LEADING LADIES

Black and white photograph of Anne Helm autographed to "Colonel Parker and his Mrs." Cast list typewritten on white paper for "What A Wonderful Life", which later was renamed "Follow That Dream." Original Western Union telegram to Ann Margret from Elvis & The Colonel, dated July 10, 1967. Invoice from Sada's Flowers sold to Elvis Presley for the leading ladies on "The Trouble With Girls." Original letter to Colonel Parker from Mary Ann Mobley dated June 30, 1964, on white paper with the monogram of MMM in gold on top. Original letter to Colonel Parker from Barbara Stanwyck sent on her stationery, dated April 22, 1964. Postcard from Ursula Andress to the Elvis Presley Family dated June 16, 1964. Front of card is a photograph of The Red Kanyon in the Southern Negev. Signed photograph of Lizabeth Scott to Mrs. Parker and the Colonel. Original handwritten note to Colonel Parker on Ms. Scott's stationery. Invoice from Sada's Flowers for Nancy Sinatra, Marianne Ashman. Cream colored thank you card from Juliet Prowse on her stationery. Christmas card with Mary and Jesus riding a horse, and Joseph standing next to them sent to Elvis from Mary Ann Mobley. Christmas card to Elvis & Priscilla from Joan Blondell. Card is a red felt with a white outline of santa. Card reads, "dear Elvis & Priscilla..a happy Christmas..a gentle New Year." Original envelope included. One "Roustabout" banner. Banner is square, light green with yellow fringe on three sides except top that has a wood stake stapled to the banner; a yellow chord is attached to the stake for hanging purposes. In black letters are the words, "Now Barbara Now Stanwyck and Elvis in "Roustabout" A Hal Wallis Production Paramount Picture Release." Sizes vary from 11 x 8 1/2 inches to 4 3/4 x 8 inches. 14 x 12 inches banner. 2 inches fringe.

These women were leading ladies in Elvis' films: Anne Helm co-starred with Elvis in "Follow That Dream", and they dated during the filming. Elvis sent Ann Margret flowers every time she performed until his death. Elvis sent Marilyn Mason, Nicole Jaffe, and Sheree North flowers with the note "Good luck on the picture. Love Elvis." Mary Ann Mobley co-starred with Elvis in "Harum Scarum", and "Girl Happy." Barbara Stanwyck co-starred

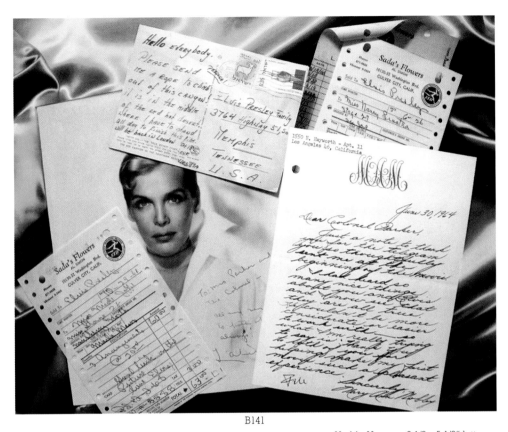

B141

with Elvis in "Roustabout." Ursula Andress co-starred with Elvis in "Fun In Acapulco." Elzabeth Scott co-starred with Elvis in "Loving You." Nancy Sinatra and Marianne Ashman co-starred with Elvis in the film "Speedway", which was called "Pot Luck" before the final title change. Juliet Prowse played "Lili" in "G.I. Blues." $3,000 - 3,500

B142 PHOTOGRAPH AND CORRESPONDENCE FROM HEDDA HOPPER TO COLONEL PARKER

Two original, signed and typewritten letters, dated January 20, and June 4, 1964, to Colonel Parker from Hedda Hopper. January letter is regarding a contribution to the "Nursery for Visually Handicapped Children." In the June 4th letter Hedda sends the Colonel love on behalf of Suzie Traynor, Patsy Gaile, Treva McClure, and herself. Photograph of the Colonel Parker, wearing an overcoat with "Girls, Girls, Girls" printed on the outside, with

Hedda Hopper. 8 1/2 x 5 1/2" letters. 8 x 10" photo.

Hedda Hopper was a famous gossip columnist in Hollywood at this time. She regularly made her comments publicly known regarding the lives of the many celebrities in the entertainment industry. $1,000 - 1,200

B143 LETTER FROM EDDIE FISHER

Letter dated February 4, 1964, to Elvis and the Colonel at Paramount Studios from Eddie Fisher. He thanks them for their Christmas card and apologizes for the delay in his replying. 11 x 8 1/2 inches.

In 1951, singer Eddie Fisher recorded "I'll Hold You in My Heart" (written and originally recorded by Eddy Arnold in 1947); Elvis cut his version of the song in 1969, playing the piano on the recording. $200 - 250

B144 CORRESPONDENCE WITH LYNDON AND LADY BIRD JOHNSON

Cream-colored invitation to Lyndon Baines Johnson's Presidential Inauguration on January 20, 1965. Black calligraphy print with an embossed gold presidential seal. Card addressed to the Presley's at Graceland with an illustration of the White House on the front. Inside is a gold eagle seal over a printed note thanking them for their holiday greetings with printed signatures of Lyndon B. Johnson and Lady Bird Johnson. The back side of the envelope has notes and doodles in red ink by Elvis Presley. Western Union telegram dated January 23, 1973 addressed to Mrs. Lyndon B. Johnson from Elvis and the Colonel. Expresses their condolences stating, "...our sincere thoughts are with you." Photograph of Lyndon B. Johnson autographed to Colonel Parker. 11 x 8 1/2 inches Inaugural Invitation, 10 7/8 x 7 1/4 inches card (open.) 5 3/4 x 7 3/8 inches envelope. 4 1/2 x 6 5/8 inches telegram. 10 x 8 inches photograph.

Lyndon B. Johnson, the 36th president of the United States, visited Elvis in 1966 on the set of the movie, "Spinout." Elvis' doodles on the envelope are related to music and his spiritual endeavors and are a rare written record of his thoughts.

$6,000 - 7,000

B145 TELEGRAM TO ELVIS PRESLEY FROM MARIE PARKER

Western Union Telegram, with envelope, sent December 24, 1964, to Elvis in Memphis from Marie Parker (signed "The Admiral in Charge of the Colonel") from Hollywood. Message wishes him a Merry Christmas and happy new year-- and thanks him for the fine gift. Acetate holiday envelope goes with the telegram. 5 1/2 x 8 1/2 inches telegram. 3 5/8 x 6 1/2 inches envelope. 3 1/2 x 6 inches acetate envelope.

Elvis frequently sent the Parkers lavish gifts as expressions of his gratitude. In 1964, the gift was a piano.

$350 - 400

B146 ELVIS' RECORDING OF BING CROSBY'S "WHITE CHRISTMAS"

Letter to Colonel Parker dated June 19, 1965, from Bing Crosby (with signature). The letter thanks the Colonel for his letter and for the new Elvis single. "Sounds quite beautiful, and I'm sure is a possible hit."

B147   B148

Crosby also discusses his son, Gary; Cremo cigars; fish from Mexico; and the Colonel's proposal to buy 100,000 copies of Elvis' autographed pictures. He included a signed photo of himself: "To my good friend Col. Tom--wishing you success and happiness. Bing Crosby." "White Christmas" sheet music by Elvis. Elvis' 45 rpm of Bing Crosby's "White Christmas." 10 1/4 x 7 1/4 inches letter. 10 x 8 inches photo.

Bing Crosby recorded one of the best selling records of all time, "White Christmas." Elvis sang his version of the popular holiday song for his Christmas album in 1957.

$600 - 700

B147 WEDDING ANNOUNCEMENT FROM BETTE DAVIS TO ELVIS PRESLEY, AND A WESTERN UNION TELEGRAM FROM COLONEL PARKER TO MISS DAVIS

Wedding announcement dated January 6, 1964, from Bette Davis to Elvis announcing the wedding of her daughter, Barbara. Announcement is cream in color with light pink lettering. On bottom of page Ms. Davis drew her trademark "Bette Davis eyes," wrote in a new address, and signed her name. Original, cream envelope included. Western Union telegram dated April 3, 1964, to Miss Davis from the Colonel expressing a birthday wish. 6 1/2 x 4 1/2 inches Announcement. 4 3/4 x 6 3/4 inches Envelope. 5 3/4 x 8 inches Telegram

The telegram to Ms. Davis from the Colonel reads: "On behalf of Mrs. Parker, Elvis, and myself a happy birthday and our best wishes to your family."

$1,250 - 1,500

B148 LETTER AND CHRISTMAS CARD FROM HEDDA HOPPER TO ELVIS PRESLEY

Original, signed and typewritten letter to Elvis from Hedda Hopper circa 1965. Correspondence is thanking Elvis for his donations to the Nursery School, and the John Tracy Clinic......"I wish other actors were as generous." Original, white envelope included. White Christmas card with no lettering on the outside; on the inside in red letters are the words, "Happy Holiday and Healthy 1965 Hedda Hopper," and a black penciled sketch of Hedda in a suite wearing a broad hat. 10 1/2 x 7 1/4 inches Letter. 4 x 7 1/2 inches Envelope. 8 x 5 1/2 inches Card.

Elvis, always generous; anonymously donated $50,000 to the charity for which Hedda Hopper canvassed.

$600 - 700

B149 ELVIS PRESLEY'S BASKETBALL

Official Voit Basketball.

Elvis was a fan of all sports, from football to karate to racquetball to basketball. He tried almost every sport at one time or another, although his first loves were football and karate. He frequently played basketball at his Palm Springs home from which this ball came.

$1,500 - 2,000

B150 ELVIS PRESLEY SLOT CARS AND RECEIPTS

Handwritten receipts for slot car materials. Two receipts from Brown Hobby Distributors in Memphis and three from Robert E. Lee Raceway in Memphis. Receipts total over $5,800. Blue slot car with #1 and red slot car with #2 from Elvis' collection. Portion of original track with remote control. 11 x 8 1/2 inches.

At Christmas 1965 Priscilla gave Elvis a small slot car racing set. He loved it so much he went out and got a huge one. When he found he had no room for the set, he built a room on the patio between the house and the pool to set up the tracks. He and his friends all had cars which they raced against each other. The slot cars and tracks were later removed when Elvis and Priscilla had their Memphis wedding reception in this room. It is now the trophy room.

$2,000 - 2,500

B151 HARLEY DAVIDSON GOLF CART AND INVOICE

Receipt from Taylor Harley Davidson dated May 18, 1967, for a Harley Davidson golf cart for Elvis. Also included is an original sales receipt, paid receipt, and a copy of the invoice for $1,055.38. Two seater white Harley Davidson golf card with silver handles and black trim. Photographs included. 8 1/2 x 5 1/2 inches Sales receipt. 7 x 5 1/2 inches Invoice copy. 3 1/2 x 5 1/2 inches Paid receipt .

Elvis purchased multiple golf carts for his Graceland home to employ as a quick and fun ride around his property.

$10,000 - 12,000

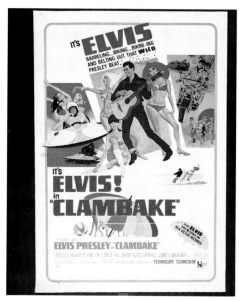

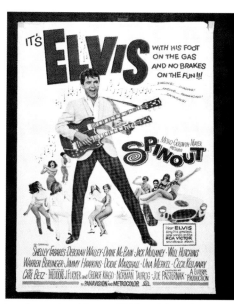

The six movie posters depicted on this and the following are part of lot B227.

B152 "FRANKIE AND JOHNNY" CONTRACTS

Sixty-eight pages typed, dated May 19, 1964. Contract with Admiral Pictures, Inc. Signed twice in blue ink by Elvis Presley. Photograph included. 11 x 8 1/2 inches.

Released in 1966, "Frankie and Johnny" was Elvis' 20th feature film. This contract stipulates total compensation for Elvis in the amount of $525,000.

$8,000 - 10,000

B153 SCRIPT AND INVITATION TO PREVIEW OF "GIRL HAPPY" STARRING ELVIS PRESLEY

Orange, peach, black and white invitation flyer to a preview of Elvis Presley in the movie, "Girl Happy." The preview was to take place January 13, 1964, at 8:30 at the Paramount Theatre Hollywood. One hundred and two page movie script of "Girl Happy, " typed on white and green paper with light orange covers bound by two brass clasps. 10 3/8 x 7 3/4 inches Invitation. 11 x 8 1/2 inches Script.

Elvis costarred with Shelley Fabares in "Girl Happy" which began filming on June 22, 1964 and completed filming on July 31. Ms. Fabares also

costarred with Elvis in "Spinout" and "Clambake; Elvis once said that Shelley Fabares was his favorite costar. Some location shots were done in Fort Lauderdale, Florida; interiors were shot at MGM's Culver City studios. "Girl Happy" was ranked #25 in "Variety's" list of top-grossing films for the year 1965. $1,000 - 1,200

B154 COLONEL PARKER'S REPORT OF PUBLICITY ACTIVITIES FOR ELVIS PRESLEY MOTION PICTURES

Colonel Parker's "Report of Publicity Activities in Conjuction with Motion Pictures." Documents in binder, related to the publicity activities done by Colonel Parker for three Elvis Presley movies: "It Happened at the World's Fair," "Fun in Acapulco," and "Viva Las Vegas." 11 1/2 x 9 x 2 inches.

Colonel Parker took movie promotions very seriously, as both he and Elvis received a cut of the profits. He was meticulous in recording his promotional activities. $3,500 - 4,000

B155 "GIRL HAPPY" SETTLEMENT STATEMENT AND PREMIERE PROGRAM

Two pages typed on "Thomas A. Parker Exclusive Management" letterhead, dated August 31, 1964. Statement breaks down Elvis Presley earnings for

two days salary (August 17-18) and three days expenses (August 16-18) from the MGM film "Girl Happy." With an 8-page blue-tinted "Souvenir Program of the Premiere Showing of 'Girl Happy.'" 11 x 8 1/2" statement. 11 x 8 1/2" program

According to this statement, Elvis earned $8,243.64 out of $20,000 total salary and expenses, minus deductions. "Girl Happy" opened in April, 1955.

$650 - 750

B156 ELVIS' PERSONAL FILM AND ACETATES OF "VIVA LAS VEGAS"

One 16 millimeter film of "Viva Las Vegas" in original case. Labeled, "Viva Las Vegas, Metro-Goldwyn-Mayer Production, Producer: Jack Cummings, Director: George Sidney, Release June 1964." One acetate case containing 15 acetates of the songs for "Viva Las Vegas" including: "Today, Tomorrow & Forever," "What I'd Say," "If Your Think I Don't Need You," "I Need Somebody to Lean On," "Climb," "Santa Lucia," and "Viva Las Vegas." Includes original manila envelope with a Colonel Parker sticker reading, "To: 'Viva Las Vegas' Acetates, Elvis Presley - 1963." Stamped three times in blue ink on envelope reads, "Elvis in 'Viva Las Vegas", Metro-Goldwyn-Mayer, Produced by Jack Cummings, Directed by George Sidney." Cases are brown with metal corners, a handle on one

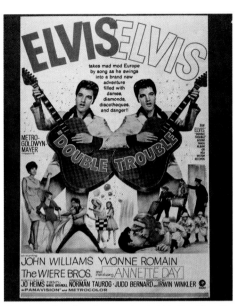

end, and a horizontal and a vertical buckled strap. 15 1/4 x 15 3/4 inches film case. 15 x 15 inches acetate case.

"Viva Las Vegas", Elvis' fifteenth film, was film released by MGM in 1964. He played a race car driver. Elvis and his co-star Ann-Margret had chemistry both on-screen and off.

$5,000 - 7,000

B157 ELVIS' PERSONAL FILM AND ACETATES OF "ROUSTABOUT"

One film case with 16 mm film Roustabout. Red label with raised white label reads "Roustabout" 1964, #16. Border label indicated film title, producer, director, and release date. One case for acetates: 17 (33 1/3 rpm) acetates, including "Roustabout," "One Track Heart," "Big Love, Big Heartache," "There's a Brand New Day on the Horizon," "Wheels on my Heels," "Poison Ivy League," "Little Egypt," "It's Carnival Time," "It's a Wonderful World," "Carny Town," "Shout It Out," and "Hard Knocks." Many have music and lyric sheet with them. Box also includes production information and synopsis, handwritten Roustabout sheet with list of songs, and presentation envelope containing vinyl 45 rpm and sleeve of "Roustabout"/ "One Track Heart." Cases are brown with metal corners, a handle on one end, and buckled straps.

Roustabout, a Hal Wallis production by Paramount, was directed by John Rich and released in November 1964. In his sixteenth film, Elvis plays Charlie Rogers, a singer who joins the carnival. Elvis stars with Barbara Stanwyck and Joan Freeman. Shooting for the film took place on the Paramount lots, as well as a location near Thousand Oaks, California, where the producer had a traveling carnival set up its tents and equipment.

$3,000 - 4,000

B158 ELVIS' PERSONAL FILM AND ACETATES OF "LIVE A LITTLE, LOVE A LITTLE"

One copy of the MGM film "Live A Little, Love A Little," and three acetates. Items are contained in square, brown film/acetate cases with metal corners, and a plastic handle on the side. There are two buckled straps, one horizontal and one vertical. 15 1/4 x 15 3/4 inches Film and case. 15 x 15 inches Acetate and case.

"Live a Little, Love a Little," opened nationally on October 23, 1968. Michele Carey co-starred with Elvis in this film. The two-hundred pound Great Dane, Albert, was actually played by Brutus, Elvis' real-life dog. Vernon Presley had a role in this film as an extra sitting at a table. Rudy Vallee played Louis Penlow in the film, and while filming in

downtown Los Angeles, a pair of old ladies literally knocked Elvis to the pavement in their haste to get Rudy Vallee's autograph. Acetate contains "Almost In Love," "Edge Of Reality," "Wonderful World," and "A Little Less Conversation."

$2,000 - 3,000

B159 ELVIS' PERSONAL FILM AND ACETATES OF "SPEEDWAY"

One original movie case containing the 16 millimeter film of "Speedway." White label with red border reads, "Speedway, Metro-Goldwyn Mayer, Producer: Winkler - Lawrence, Director: Norman Taurog, 1968." Red label with raised white letters reads, "Speedway - 1968." One original acetate case containing one two-sided "Speedway" acetate and typed listing of songs. Cases are brown with metal corners, a handle on one end, and a horizontal and a vertical buckled strap. 15 1/4 x 15 3/4 inches film case. 15 x 15 inches acetate case.

In "Speedway," Elvis' twenty-seventh film, Elvis played a race car driver opposite Nancy Sinatra, daughter of Ole Blue Eyes himself. "Speedway" premiered in Charlotte, North Carolina on June 12, 1968 and grossed $3 million during 1968.

$2,000 - 3,000

B160   B162

B160 RCA CONTRACT—CRYING IN THE CHAPEL

Two-page typed contract dated January 14, 1965 on
Thomas A. Parker wagon letterhead. Letter is
regarding merchandising and promotion for
"Crying in the Chapel" and "His Hand in Mine."
Signed in blue ink by Elvis Presley, Col. Tom Parker
and RCA Victor Vice President Harry E. Jenkins.
"Crying in the Chapel" single. "His Hand in Mine
by Elvis" LP. 11 x 8 1/2 inches.

"His Hand in Mine," Elvis' first gospel album,
achieved sales of over $1 million and received a
RIAA Gold Record. "Crying in the Chapel" was
recorded in 1960, however, it was not issued until
May 1965. It spent seven weeks as #1 on
"Billboard's" Hot 100.

$8,000 - 10,000

B161 FOUR-TRACK TAPE RECORDING OF ELVIS PRESLEY'S "SOMETHING FOR EVERYBODY", PLUS ARTWORK FOR COVER

Four-track tape recording of "Something For
Everybody." Tape is housed in a sturdy cardboard
case. Front cover is a photo of Elvis from the shoulders up wearing a blue shirt with a background
done in medium red. Back cover lists songs and
sequence. Artwork for cover of four-track; two identical photos of Elvis, one from the shoulders up and
the other from the waist up, attached to a white art
board. 7 1/2 x 7 1/2 inches Recording. 10 x 9 inches
photograph. 11 x 9 1/2 inches photograph. 11 1/2 x
14 inches art board.

All songs except "I Slipped, I Stumbled, I Fell" were
recorded at RCA's Nashville Studios on March 12
and 13, 1961. "Something for Everybody" reached
number one "Billboard's" top LP's for three weeks.
"I Slipped, I Stumbled, I Fell" was recorded on
November 8, 1960, at Radio Recorders. Two versions were recorded: the first was released on
record and is in a higher key than the second.

$2,000 - 2,500

B162 PROTOTYPE COPY OF THE SLEEVE FOR "THE FAIR IS MOVING ON," AND "CLEAN UP YOUR OWN BACK YARD"

Prototype of the record sleeve for Elvis' recordings
of "The Fair Is Moving On," and "Clean Up Your
Own Back Yard." Front and back sides of sleeve
are divided in two: the left side has a yellow background with an upper body photo of Elvis wearing
a dark green shirt unbuttoned half way down the
front, and a black scarf with red polka-dots around
his neck. Right side of cover has a purple background with a black and white photo of Elvis' RCA
"Elvis In Memphis" album on the bottom. In white
are the words "Elvis Sings," and in yellow the song
title "The Fair Is Moving On."

Flip side of cover is exactly the same except on the
right side the title song is "Clean Up Your Own
Back Yard," and below the title are the words,
"from the MGM picture "The Trouble with Girls,"
and the name of the producer and director. 7 x 7"

Elvis recorded "The Fair Is Moving On" on
February 21, 1969, at American Sound Studios.
"Clean Up Your Own Back Yard" was recorded by
Elvis on August 23, 1968, at United Recorders in Los
Angeles. It was sung in the 1969 movie "The
Trouble With Girls," and reached #35 on the Hot 100
chart for eight weeks.

$2,000 - 2,500

B163 COMPILATION OF ELVIS" RECORDINGS

Compilation of Elvis Presley's recordings from the
1950's, 1960's, and 1970's. Book is divided into the
categories of; Sessions, Motion Pictures, Song List
and How Used, Singles, Extended Play Albums,
Long Play Albums, and Compact 33 double. Pages
are kept in clear plastic page covers. Book is a
black, hard back, three ring binder. 11 x 8 1/2"

This mammoth book found in Colonel Parker's
office is a testament to the mammoth musical
career of Elvis Presley. Without a doubt, Elvis
changed the face of music forever, earning his title,
"The King of Rock and Roll."

$4,500 - 5,000

B163 ELEVEN REEL-TO-REEL TAPES OF ELVIS' MUSIC

Ten 71/2 inch per second 4-Track Heads: "Pot Luck With Elvis," "Blue Hawaii," "Elvis' Golden Records, Volume 3," "Roustabout," "Fun in Acapulco," "Elvis Is Back," "Girls, Girls, Girls," "Harum Scarum," "Frankie and Johnny," and "It Happened at the World's Fair." One 3 3/4 inch per second 4-Track stereo tapes of "Spinout" and "Double Trouble." All eleven reel-to-reel tapes are boxed and shrink-wrapped. 7-inch diameter tapes. 7 1/4 x 7 1/4 inch boxes.

Eight of the tapes are sound tracks from Elvis' movies. The others included a Volume 3 of some of his Gold Records, a combination of songs produced when he returned from the Army, and "Pot Luck," a collection of a dozen hits.

$4,500 - 5,000

B164 "CRYING IN THE CHAPEL" GOLD RECORD

Framed award. Gold, 45 rpm record of "Crying in the Chapel" with black RCA label with RCA victrola and dog logo. Record on green velvet background and above a gold plaque reading, "To Col. T. Parker... million seller, 1965." Frame is silver painted wood. Taken from Colonel Parker's personal collection. 17 x 14 inches framed award

Although Elvis recorded "Crying in the Chapel" in October, 1960, it was not issued for five years. When the single was finally released in 1965, it had a 14 week stay on "Billboard's" Top 100 chart, peaking at number 3. "Crying in the Chapel" had a two-week stay at number one in England. This was his first number one in England since the Beatles' rise to fame.

$8,000 -12,000

B165 ELVIS PRESLEY GOSPEL SONG BOOK AND RECORDS

"We Call on Him: A Collection of Gospel Songs as Recorded by Elvis Presley"—32 pages of sheet music published by Gladys Music in 1968 with a

cover price of $1.50. Cover features purple and pink print and a black and white photo of Elvis in a suit and tie. Two 45 rpm gospel singles, with color sleeves: "Milky White Way"/"Swing Down Sweet Chariot" and "Joshua Fit the Battle"/"Known Only to Him." Also includes acetate of "Joshua Fit the Battle." 12 x 9 inches sheet music. 7 x 7 inches singles.

Gladys Music, named, of course, after Elvis' mother, was the first of three publishing companies owned by Elvis, and was a subsidiary of Hill and Range. Gospel music was at the absolute foundation of Elvis' musical heritage and influences. He claimed to know almost every gospel song ever written and record a significant amount of gospel music. Elvis won each of his three Grammy awards for gospel performances.

B163
B165

$800 - 1,000

B166 WROUGHT IRON PATIO FURNITURE FROM
ELVIS PRESLEY'S PALM SPRINGS HOME.

Four cream colored wrought iron patio chairs, one
serving cart on wheels, one lounge chair, one
round table, one square table, and one recliner
used in Elvis Presley's Palm Springs home located
on Chino Canyon Drive.

These chairs once graced Elvis' patio at the Chino
Canyon home. The songs "I Miss You," and "Are
You Sincere" were recorded here.

$8,000 - 12,000

B167 VELVET BEAN BAG

One crushed velvet blue bean bag.

Bean bags were all the rage in the 1970's, and Elvis
was not one to be left behind on a trend. He, however, took the bean bag craze one step farther by
having this one done in crushed blue velvet.

$4,000 - 6,000

B168 TWO FOOT STOOLS AND ONE DANISH
CHAIR FROM ELVIS PRESLEY'S PALM SPRINGS
HOME

Two square, red vinyl foot stools (the seat and back
tie together) with wooden legs. Top cushion on one
of the stools is missing.   One square, red vinyl
Danish chair with dark wooden legs. Back of chair
consists of seven vertical wooden posts, but no
cushion. Arms of chair are also made of wood. 16
inches height x 23 inches wide Foot Stool
28 inches height x 23 inches wide Danish Chair

Foot stools and chair were used at Elvis' Palm
Springs home on Chino Canyon Drive. Elvis
bought this home in 1965 and sold it in 1970 to
Frankie Valli.

$3,000 - 5,000

B169 ELVIS PRESLEY'S TELEVISION

Packard Bell 23" screen free-standing television. 33
1/2 inches tall x 19 inches wide

This television was used by Elvis at his Chino
Canyon Road home in Palm Springs in the late
Sixties. Elvis kept televisions in almost every room
where-ever he lived. He would turn on the television whenever he entered a room. Elvis liked the
din created by a turned on television because it
made it seem like people were around even when
he was alone. Elvis had 14 televisions at
Graceland.

$4,000 - 6,000

B170 ELVIS PRESLEY'S DESK AND CHAIR

Kidney shaped offices desk with burl wood trim.
Drawers have brass handles and each on has a
separate lock. One green vinyl desk chair with
rollers. 75 x 33 inches desk.

Elvis' home office was where he reviewed concert
arrangements. Elvis also read books at his desk as
he was an avid reader. This furniture was in Elvis'
home office in his Palm Springs home.

$40,000 - 50,000

B171 FAKE FUR BEAN BAG CHAIR AND PILLOWS

Gray leopard-looking fur bean bag chair with a
large and a small pillow covered in the same covering. 30 inches high x 46 inches wide bean bag.
31 x 22 inches large pillow. 17 x 18 inches small pillow.

From the Chino Canyon, Palm Springs' home, this
combination of items probably found plenty of use
for relaxing with friends or watching TV. Television
viewing ranked as one of Elvis' favorite pastimes,
as indicated by the 14 sets found around
Graceland at the time of his death.

$4,000 - 6,000

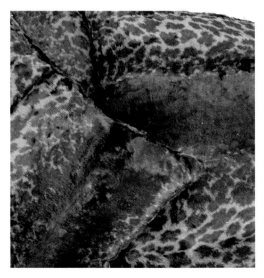

B172 AMPEX MUSIC CENTER

Silver and black Ampex music center with sliding doors; a reel-to-reel machine on one side, and a am/fm radio on the other. On top are two stickers that read, "C688969 Allied 26" and "C688969 Allied 27." Cabinet is a medium brown wood grain. 16 inches in height x 33 inches wide

The Ampex music center was used by Elvis at his Palm Springs home on Chino Canyon Drive to listen to tape demos from his recording sessions.

$8,000 - 10,000

B173 TWO OF ELVIS PRESLEY'S DINING ROOM CHAIRS

One pair of high back dining room chairs. Green suede with wood trim. 55" tall back chairs. 18" high seat. 25" wide, 19" deep.

This chair graced the dining room in Elvis' Chino Canyon home. Dinner at Elvis' was served late, around 9:00 or 10:00. It was a formal affair served in the dining room and everyone dressed for the occasion. Dinners usually consisted of southern

This lot actually contains two chairs.

fare. Some of Elvis' favorite meals included pork chops, crisp bacon, meatloaf, and the infamous fried peanut butter and banana sandwich.

$6,000 - 8,000

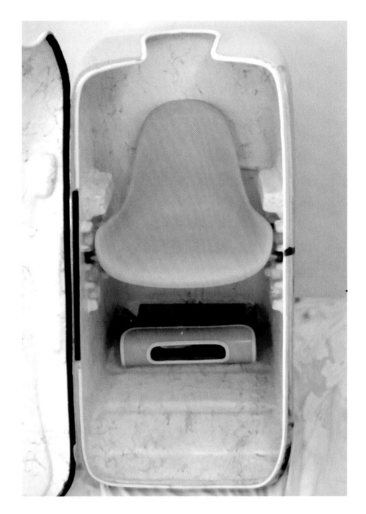

B174 PORTABLE SAUNA

Light blue Nordic Spa; plastic, portable, electric, with two back wheels. Sauna manufactured by Scandinavian Products Inc. (serial # 1189). 45 inches high x 33 inches wide.

Elvis showed much concern about his personal health and well-being, as indicated by his level of contact sports activity. He loved to participate in football, racquetball, and karate. He constantly tried to stay healthy and young by keeping fit. Elvis used this spa in his Chino Canyon, Palm Springs home as part of this health regimen.

$8,000 - 10,000

B175 ELVIS PRESLEY'S LOVESEAT

One loveseat. Diamond and striped pattern in orange and green.

This loveseat was in the TV room at Graceland prior to the 1974 redecoration. Elvis and his friends would gather in the TV room to watch movies while helping themselves to refreshments from the wet bar and soda fountain.

$2,500 - 3,000

B176 ELVIS' ROCKING CHAIR

Dark wood rocking chair with maroon vinyl upholstery on the seat and on the back of the chair. 60 x
20 z 24 inches.

During the 1960's this chair, originally placed in the
Jungle Room, was a favorite place for Elvis to relax
in his spare moments at Graceland.

$20,000 - 30,000

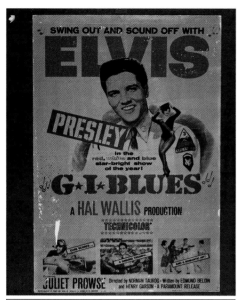

The six movie posters depicted on this and the following are part of lot B227.

B177 "TICKLE ME" SALARY SETTLEMENT AND PROMOTIONAL MATERIALS

Two-page letter, on Thomas A. Parker stationery, dated November 30, 1964, enumerates Elvis Presley earnings from Allied Artists Pictures Corporation "Tickle Me" for the week ending November 20, 1964. Checks and vouchers were sent to Bill Fisher, accountant, and copy sent to Vernon Presley for his records. Four-page color brochure advertising "Tickle Me" film and RCA records. About 2 dozen colorful feathers Sixteen-page Elvis Presley collectible booklet ; pink, with articles and black-and-white photos "Tickle Me" Campaign 3-ring folder, with newspaper clippings, photos etc. 11 x 8 1/2 inches letter and brochure. 11 x 8 1/4 inches Elvis collectible. 11 1/2 x 9 inches campaign booklet.

The one-week statement for "Tickle Me" payments shows Elvis' salary ($60,000) less deductions, payments to Wm. Morris Agency and All Star Shows, and then amounts payable directly to Elvis ($34,051.80).

$1,000 - 1,200

B178 HAL WALLIS - ELVIS PRESLEY CONTRACT 1966

Hal Wallis- Elvis Presley contract from 1966 bound in blue folder. Includes a music agreement and a copy of a 16-page letter dated September 23, 1965 offering a 1966 contract between Elvis Presley and Paramount Studios for a yet-to-be titled film (later "Paradise, Hawaiian Style"). Salary stated as $500,000. Contract signed by Elvis Presley, Hal Wallis, and Joseph Hazen. Photograph included. 11 x 8 1/2 inches.

This contract took over six months to negotiate. Every time that Wallis and the Colonel came to an agreement, the Colonel wanted to make changes. Hal Willis produced nine Elvis movies; the last, "Easy Come, Easy Go," in 1967.

$7,000 - 8,000

B179 ELVIS' PERSONAL FILM AND ACETATES OF "GIRL HAPPY"

Audio/visual film of "Girl Happy," and acetates. Acetate box contains a special Preview invitation with a pink envelope, a pink program book, a blue program book, exhibitors/campaign book, manila envelope, cardboard, and a handwritten song list. Film and acetate are contained in square, brown cases with metal corners, and a plastic handle on the side. There are two buckled straps, one horizontal and one vertical. 15 1/4 x 15 3/4 inches Film and case. 15 x 15 Inches Acetate and case

This film was taken from Colonel Parker's private collection of the films Elvis made. Shelley Fabares co-starred in this film which open nationally on April 14, 1965. "Girl Happy was ranked number 25 in "Variety's" list of top-grossing films for 1965. Acetate contains "Do Not Disturb," "Startin' Tonight," "Do The Clam," "Girl Happy," "I Gotta Find My Baby," "Spring Fever," "Cross My Heart," "Wolf Call," and many more with a total of twenty-five singles.

$3,000 - 4,000

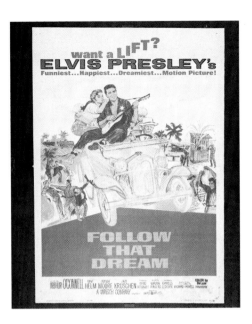

B180 ELVIS' PERSONAL FILM AND ACETATES OF "HARUM SCARUM"

Case containing Elvis' personal 16 mm print of "Harum Scarum." Acetate case with 19 acetates from the film, including the songs "Harum Scarum," "My Desert Serenade," "Go East, Young Man," "Wisdom of the Ages," "Golden Coins," "So Close and Yet So Far," "Hey Little Girl," "Shake That Tambourine," "Kismet," "Harem Holiday," "Mirage" and "Animal Instinct." Also includes a nine song 33 1/3 rpm vinyl soundtrack album titled "Harem Holiday." Cases are brown with metal corners, a handle on one end and a horizontal and vertical buckled strap. 15 1/4 x 15 3/4 inches film case 15 x 15 inches acetate case

The 1965 M-G-M production "Harum Scarum" was Elvis' 19th film. Elvis plays a singer kidnapped and taken to an Arabian palace. The film went through many title changes, with "Harem Holiday" being an early title for the film.

$3,000 - 4,000

B181 ELVIS' PERSONAL FILM AND ACETATES OF "PARADISE HAWAIIAN STYLE"

Audio/Visual film of "Paradise Hawaiian Style," and acetates. A copy of the lyrics and music sheet for "A Dog's Life" is included with the acetates.

Film and acetate are contained in square, brown film/acetate cases with metal corners, and a plastic handle on one side. There are two buckled straps, one horizontal and one vertical. 15 1/4 x 15 3/4 inches Film with case.

This movie belong to Colonel Parkers Collection of Elvis' films. "Paradise Hawaiian Style" opened nationally on July 6, 1966. Movie was filmed on location in Honolulu, Kauai, Maui, and the Kona Coast. For the "Drums of the Islands" production number, a war canoe was needed and the only one available was Samoan. "Drums of the Islands" was based on a Tongan chant, therefore, Tongan rowers were used for the scene. The Somoans took offense and several fights erupted between the two factions. Acetate contains twenty-two songs, "Scratch My Back," "A Dog's Life," "Drums Of The Islands," Datin'," Stop Where You Are," "Hawaiian Paradise," " This Is My Heaven," "Queenie Wahine's Papaya," "Sand Castles," "Hawaii USA," "House Of Sand," etc.

$2,000 - 3,000

B182 ELVIS' PERSONAL FILM AND ACETATES OF "TICKLE ME"

Two original movie cases containing the 16 millimeter films of "Tickle Me." One case has a white label with red border reading, "'Tickle Me,' Allied Artists Corporation, Producers: Ben Schwalb, Director: Norman Taurog, Release 1965 #18." Red label with raised white lettering reads, "'Tickle Me' - 1965 `8." One case has "2600 Feet 3Reel" in black ink, and an orange label with raised white lettering reading, "'Tickle Me - Film No. 2." One original acetate box containing a song list, music and lyrics for several songs, a "Tickle Me" promotion kit with feathers, one mono album with nine songs from the film, a souvenir envelope, the "Tickle Me" soundtrack, and ten acetates. Cases are brown with metal corners, a handle on one end, and a horizontal and a vertical buckled strap. 15 1/4 x 15 3/4 inches film case. 15 x 15 inches acetate case.

In "Tickle Me," Elvis played a rodeo cowboy and singer who was right at home working at an all-girl dude ranch. "Tickle Me" opened in May, 1965. Acetates include, "I Feel I've Known You Forever," "Fountain of Love," "Love Me Tonight," "Easy Question," "Night Rider," , "Something Blue", etc..

$3,000 - 4,000

B183 "COMING HOME ELVIS." A PREVIOUSLY UNDISCOVERED PORTRAIT BY RALPH WOLFE COWAN, THE ARTIST COMMISSIONED BY ELVIS TO PRODUCE THE PORTRAIT THAT HANGS IN GRACELAND

Oil on canvas, 37" x 48". Signed and dated in lower right Ralph Wolfe Cowan, 1969; copyright appears on canvas as follows: VAU - 986 - 553, Library of Congress

After seeing an album cover titled "Heavenly" created by Ralph Wolfe Cowan for Johnny Mathis, Elvis decided to commission the renowned artist to paint his portrait in 1968. Elvis sat for a full length portrait at the artist's studio in Caesar's Palace in Las Vegas. This painting now hangs in Graceland and was discussed in the movie "Graceland" in which the artist and Priscilla Presley referred to it as the "Heavenly Elvis." The artist created a second circular portrait that become known as the "Loving Elvis," which now hangs in the most prestigious venue a portrait can appear in - The National Portrait Gallery in Washington, DC. In fact, on the cover of the June 13, 1999 issue of the Sunday Washington Post Magazine, the National Portrait Gallery's painting appears adjacent to portraits of George Washington, Frederick Douglas, and Pocahontas for a feature article on the National Portrait Gallery.

It has been recently revealed that the Mr. Cowan painted a third oil-painted portrait of Elvis titled "Coming Home Elvis." Created in 1969, the artist made revisions to the work in the late 1980's before selling it to its current owner. This painting reflects a confident, healthy, intelligent and young looking Elvis. Elvis is clothed in a pair of leather trousers and an off-white Scottish knit sweater. Over his right shoulder, Elvis is holding a dark jacket. Elvis was actually taller in person then commonly thought and the painter tried to depict his stature correctly. The painting is complimented by a muted gold, antique wooden frame. The "Coming Home Elvis" has never been seen by the general public until now. Ralph Wolfe Gowan has been the only artist commissioned to paint a portrait of Elvis during his lifetime, making this painting ever more extraordinary and significant.

PLEASE NOTE: As indicated, this painting is copyrighted. The copyright is owned by the current owner of the painting who acquired the copyright from the artist. Should the successful buyer of this painting at the auction wish to purchase the copyright to the work as well, the copyright will be made available for an additional amount equal to one half the purchase price. If you have any questions regarding this matter, please contact Guernsey's.

ESTIMATE ON REQUEST

B184 LAYERED PUBLICITY PHOTOGRAPH OF ELVIS PRESLEY

Publicity photograph of Elvis Presley on a red background wearing a light blue jacket over a black collared shirt. Photograph has four cellophane overlays, each with a different color tint - black, blue, red, and yellow. 13 3/4 x 10 3/4 inches.

This is the color-separated artwork to be used for an Elvis Christmas card.

$2,000 - 2,500

B185 VERNON PRESLEY'S ADDRESS BOOK

Vernon Presley's address book from the 1970's. Cover is a olive green with a gold colored border. Cover is well worn and taped together. Photograph included. 8 x 5 1/4 inches   While Colonel Parker managed the business affairs of Elvis, Vernon Presley managed Elvis' personal affairs, from paying the bills, to taking care of Graceland. Vernon's address book includes contact information on friends and family such as Priscilla's phone number in California, Dee Presley's, Joe Esposito, Vester Presley, and Col. Tomas A. Parker among others. The book also lists contact information for employees and local businesses. Listed on the back, inside cover is Elvis', Vernon's, Minnie Presley's, and Jesse Dee Presley's social security numbers.

$4,500 - 5,000

B186 LARRY GELLER BARBER BILLS

Handwritten on three sheets of white note paper in red, blue and black marker. Bill for "barber and scalp treatments" received by Elvis Presley from Larry Geller during a period from October 17 to

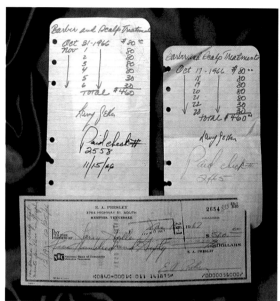

November 13, 1966. Bill for a total of $1,260 dated November 15, 1966, signed in blue and black marker by Larry Geller. 6 3/4 x 3 3/4 inches.

Larry Gellar began cutting and styling Elvis' hair in April, 1964. Gellar was a more than Elvis' personal stylist, however, he became a close friend and introduced Elvis to a world of spiritual exploration. They would talk for hours about religion, philosophy, mysticism, and all sorts of spiritual matters. The Colonel and many of Elvis' other close friends did not like Gellar's influence on, or relationship with Elvis and sought to break up their relationship. Eventually, they did. Gellar has written several books about Elvis. These receipts were during the time Elvis was filming "Easy Come, Easy Go."

$3,000 - 3,500

B187 GREYHOUND CHARTER TO NASHVILLE AND ACETATE

Invoice from Southern Greyhound Lines in Memphis, made out to "Elvis Presley Group" and dated July 12, 1966. Bill for chartered service to Nashville in the amount of $318.30. With carbon copy. Invoice dated June 10, 1966 on green paper

gives itinerary of trip. With EP containing "Indescribably Blue," "I'll Remember You," and "If Everyday Was Like Christmas." Also with acetate of "If Everyday Was Like Christmas." 7 x 8 1/2 inches invoice #1. 11 x 8 1/2 inches invoice #2. 7 inches diameter record and acetate.

This Nashville trip was for recording sessions at RCA Studio B on June 10-12, 1966, when Elvis recorded "Indescribably Blue," "I'll Remember You" and "If Everyday Was Like Christmas." The band recorded backing tracks and guide vocals and Elvis, who was suffering from a throat infection, overdubbed his vocals on June 12. Because of Elvis' condition, Red West did guide vocals for the first two sessions, including on "If Every Day Was Like Christmas," which he wrote. Elvis recorded his vocal tracks for the three songs in seven takes and only 30 minutes. He was so happy with the recordings that he later wrote a thank you letter to producer Felton Jarvis.

$2,000 - 2,500

B188 "ELVIS" PAINTING PRINT WITH CONTRACT

One color print of an Elvis painting by artist June Kelly. With one-page contract on Rinaldi Printing Company letterhead, dated February 14, 1966 an signed by June Kelly. 20 x 16 inches print. 11 x 8 1/2 inches contract.

Contract stipulates payment of $600 to Kelly for the original copy of the painting along with all publishing and distribution rights. This print was sold at Elvis Presley concerts.

$450 - 550

B189 LETTERS TO COLONEL TOM PARKER REGARDING PROMOTIONS FOR "CLAMBAKE" AND THE ELVIS PRESLEY CHRISTMAS ALBUM

Two-page letter addressed to Colonel T.A. Parker from Harry Jenkins at RCA regarding the "Clambake" sound track and the Elvis Presley Christmas Album. The letter is dated August 7, 1967 and is on RCA Victor Record Division letterhead. Signed in blue ink by Col. T.A. Parker and Harry E. Jenkins. Two-page letter addressed to Colonel Tom Parker from Clyde Rinaldi of the Rinaldi Printing Company in Tampa, Florida. The letter, dated July 12, 1967 on RCA letterhead, discusses the proposal for the Christmas card project, Clambake project, and the 1968 Wallet Calendar project. Bill totals $13,875. Wedding photograph of Elvis and Priscilla. Season's Greetings postcard with picture of Elvis. Elvis 1968 wallet calendar. 11 x 8 1/2 inches letters. 11 x 11 inches photograph. 5 1/2 x 3 1/2 inches postcard. 3 7/8 x 2 1/4 inches calendar.

The photograph of Elvis and Priscilla on their wedding day was used as an insert in the first 300,000 "Clambake" albums sold.

$3,000 - 3,500

B190 ELVIS PRESLEY-PRISCILLA BEAULIEU WEDDING RECEPTION RECEIPTS

One page typed receipt on Monte's Catering Service letterhead, dated June 5, 1967. Billed to Elvis Presley for total of $828.41 for a wedding cake and other items for his May 29 wedding. One page typed receipt on Tony Barrasso Entertainment Agency letterhead, dated June 1, 1967. Billed to Elvis Presley for total of $90.00 for "professional entertainment." Original light green check from Elvis Presley's account made out to Monte's for $828.41. Signed by Vernon Presley. Picture included. 11 x 8 1/2 inches catering letter. 8 x 8 1/2 inches entertainment letter. 3 x 8 1/8 inches check. On May 29, 1967 Elvis and Priscilla had a wedding

reception for their Memphis family and friends. They held it in the room that formerly housed Elvis' slot car track. They wore the same attire they had worn the day of the wedding. It was a intimate event with a lavish buffet, an accordion player, and white carnations decorating the head table.

$1,400 - 1,600

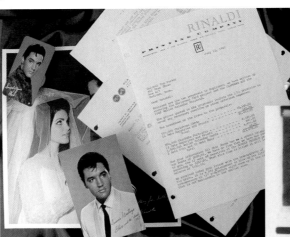

B189

B191 ELVIS PRESLEY RECEIPTS FOR WEDDING BAND AND OTHER JEWELRY

One typed invoice and three handwritten receipts from Harry Levitch Jewelers in Memphis. Receipts dated June 2 and 3, 1967. Invoice for total of $1,911 for purchases ranging from May 17-June 3, 1967. Wedding print of Elvis and Presley which shows their horseshoe rings and Elvis' wedding band. 7 x 8 1/2 inches invoice. 6 x 4 3/8 inches receipts. 11 x 11 inches print.

Invoice includes a "hand made special wedding band for Elvis with 1.57 cts. dia. special cut out let-

ters in center" which cost $1292.50. The wedding band was purchased one month after Elvis and Priscilla's wedding. Elvis lost his original wedding band while at the Circle G Ranch on their honeymoon. Other items on the receipt include a ruby and diamond engraved charm, a 14K "Mouse Trap of Love Charm," and a ruby and sapphire "Special Happy Birthday Charm" for Priscilla's 22nd birthday.

$700 - 800

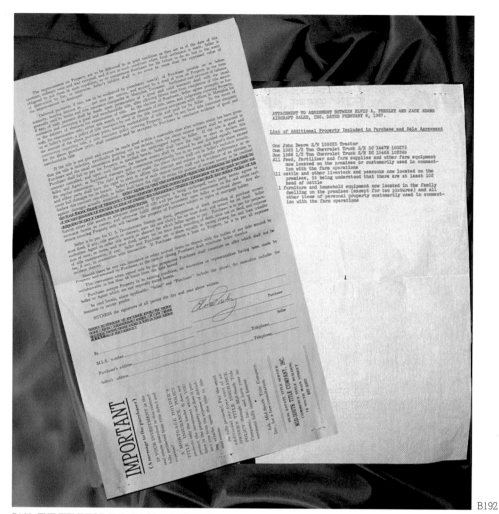

B192

B193 BILL FOR ELVIS AND PRISCILLA'S HORSESHOE RINGS

Bill dated March 20, 1967, from Harry Levitch Jewelers in the Hotel Sheraton Peabody to Elvis Presley. Order is for two handmade horseshoe rings. "Lady's white gold horseshoe ring with 10 brilliant diamonds weighting a total of 1.09 carats; mans white gold horseshoe ring with 10 brilliant diamonds weighing a total of 2 carats. Both rings with Circle G duplicated for authenticity." Bill totaled $1,659. Check number 3032, from "Elvis Presley Payroll & Expense Fund," made out to Harry Levitch Jewelers for $1,659; signed by Vernon Presley. Photograph of rings included. 7 x 8 1/2 inches 3 x 8 1/4 inches.

Elvis bought his Circle G ranch in Mississippi in early 1967. He and Priscilla loved horses and riding and spent as much time there as possible. To symbolize their love of the ranch, Elvis bought rings for both of them, which they are shown wearing in their wedding photos. $700 - 800

B194 DESOTO REDI-MIX CORPORATION INVOICE TO ELVIS' CIRCLE G RANCH IN MISSISSIPPI

Original invoice, and pink customer copy, from Desoto Redi-Mix Corporation to the Circle G Ranch dated April 18, 1967. Order is for red dye concrete for Elvis' trailer at his ranch in Horn Lake, MI 7 x 8 1/2" Invoice. 8 1/2" x 5 1/2" Customer copy.

Circle G Ranch was purchased by Elvis in 1967. Elvis extensively renovated the property to suit his needs; he often accommodated a number of friends for extended stays as guests at the ranch.

$600 - 700

B195 ELVIS PRESLEY ANIMAL HOSPITAL BILL

Bill from Whitehaven Animal Hospital in Memphis, dated May 1, 1967 and made out to Elvis Presley. Bill for cattle treatments in the total of $177.00. 6 3/4 x 5 1/2 inches.

Elvis and Priscilla were married on May 1, 1967. Elvis and Priscilla spent some of the honeymoon on the Circle G Ranch. $300 - 350

B192 THE TITLE FOR THE CIRCLE G RANCH

Two-page title from Mid-South Title Company in Memphis, dated February 8, 1967 for the Circle G Ranch. Signed in blue ink by Elvis Presley. Photograph included. 14 x 8 1/2 inches.

Elvis was returning home from a horse-buying excursion in Mississippi when he first saw the ranch. It was a 160-acre property in Desoto County, Mississippi, approximately 10 miles south of Graceland. The ranch was marked by 65-foot-high white cross overlooking a man-made lake. After inquiring about the ranch with the owner, Elvis and his friends brought their horses down to the ranch and spent the night to give it a test drive. The fol-

lowing morning, Elvis knew he had to buy it. Without even negotiating the price, Elvis put down an initial payment of $5,000 against the total price of $437,000. It was originally named Twinkletown Farm, but Elvis renamed it Circle G, with the "G" standing for Graceland. Elvis had eight trailers moved onto the property and spent almost $100,000 on automobiles to stock the ranch. Elvis loved spending time at the ranch. He and Priscilla even spent some of their honeymoon at the Circle G. The cost of maintaining the ranch, however, became too much of a financial burden. On May 20, 1969 Elvis sold the ranch for $440,000.

$13,000 - 15,000

B196 REPORT OF EXPENSES FOR CIRCLE G RANCH

Four-page report entitled "Bills Paid for February - 1967." Lists bills related to the Circle G Ranch. Adding machine tape calculates expenses totaling $99,709.30. 11 x 8 1/2 inches report. 22 1/4 x 2 1/4 adding tape.

The cost of maintaining the Circle G Ranch was extremely high. The expenses for February 1967 alone total $99,709.30.

$800 - 1,000

B197 ELVIS PRESLEY'S HORSE "BEAR"

Original typed statement from Southern Leather Company, and written receipt for supplies bought to show Bear in a horse show. The statement and receipt are dated April 19, 1967, with a total amount of $4.65 due. Photograph included. 8 1/2 x 5 1/2 inches statement. 10 x 8 1/2 inches receipt.

Elvis' interest in horses lead to his purchase of the Circle G Ranch. Elvis' interest began after he bought Priscilla a horse; then other horses were bought until there was no more room at Graceland. His horse "Bear" was a Tennessee Walker.

B197 $350 - 400

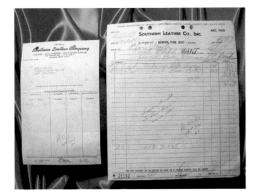

B198 BILLS FOR HORSE FOOD AND A TRAILER CIRCLE G RANCH

Statement from Ralston Purina Company dated March 17, 1967 noting an account balance of $460.14. Envelope included. Blue order form for horse chow dated March 3. Two invoices from Ralston Purina dated March 6, 1966. Both are for horse chow. They total $445.62 and $14.52. A hand-written note in blue ink on the statement and one invoice indicates the bills were paid on April 6, 1967. Westinghouse Retail Installment Contract dated February 20, 1967, for Elvis Presley, Circle G Ranch in Walls, Mississippi. Contract is for 2-bedroom mobile home with stack washer/dryer and 3-ton central air conditioner. Total contract with interest is $10,998.12, to be paid over 84 months for monthly installments of $79.68. Contract through Poole Trailer Sales in West Memphis, Arkansas. Bill of sale on items from Poole Trailer Sales and Filing receipt from state of Mississippi on contract dated February 27, 1967: $4 fee. 6 1/2 x 5 3/4 invoice statement. 3 1/2 x 6 inches envelope. 11 x 8 1/2 inches invoices. 6 1/2 x 8 1/2 inches blue order form. 10 1/2 x 8 1/2 inches contract. 5 1/2 x 8 1/2 inches bill of sale. 7 3/8 x 5 1/8 inches filing receipt.

Domino, Elvis' first horse, was bought for Priscilla, and it remained at Graceland. After he purchased the Circle G Ranch in Mississippi, he kept many horses there. The bill from Poole Trailers is for one of the many trailers purchased. $300 - 400

B199 LETTER AND CERTIFICATE FOR BRUCELLOSIS FREE CATTLE AT THE CIRCLE G

Original one page typewritten letter and certificate from the United States Department of Agriculture to Elvis, documenting his cattle to be Brucellosis free. One thirty-six page booklet on the eradication of Brucellosis. Original envelope from the Department Of Agriculture address to Mr. Elvis Presley. 11 x 8 1/2 inches letter. 8 3/4 x 8 3/4 inches certificate. 7 3/4 x 5 inches booklet. 9 1/2 x 12 inches envelope.

This certificate states that the cattle residing at Elvis' Circle G Ranch have been examined and found healthy and free of disease.

$600 - 700

As most Elvis fans know, Elvis starred in thirty three movies. Thirty one of these were feature films while two were documentaries. Obviously, the two documentaries did not have scripts. The scripts for the thirty one feature films that Elvis was in are being offered below. It is believed that with the exception of one of these scripts which was Colonel Parker's copy, all were the actual scripts used by Elvis.

The scripts are being sold in the following manner: Each script will be offered one at a time. The top bid on each script will be recorded. When the bidding is complete on all the scripts, the total bids on the thirty one lots will be tabulated. The auctioneer will ask the audience if anyone would like to place a bid on the entire collection of thirty one lots which will require a bid of 10% more than the total of the individual lots. If such a bid is tendered, the bids on the individual scripts will be erased and bidding will begin with that first bid for the collection. If no bid is made for the collection in its entirety, the successful bids for the individual scripts will stand.

1. Love Me Tender
Red binder with gold print
"Elvis Presley" printed on the cover
Outer cover sheet made of red cardstock reads "The Reno Brothers" (original title of film--many of the scripts have titles that are different from the release title) August 20, 1956. Also has a 20th Century Fox logo and "Elvis Presley" handwritten in black ink at the top of the page.
Inside paper cover sheet lists Robert Buckner as writer and says "Revised Final Script."
42 typed pages

2. Loving You
Plain white binder
Cover sheet reads "Wallis-Paramount-Hazen" and "Revised Final." Title is listed as "Stranger in Town" which is crossed out with "Loving You written over it in blue ink. Hal Kantor is listed as writer and is dated January 15, 1957.
115 typed pages

3. Jailhouse Rock
Grey binder with gold print
The title is written on the cover and spine.
Cover sheet lists writer as Guy Trosper and is dated 3-15-57.
Contains two inter-office memos regarding name changes for characters, including the change of Elvis' character from "Vince Edwards" to "Vince Everett."
102 typed pages

4. King Creole
Grey binder with gold print
Title printed on cover and spine
130 typed pages

5. G.I. Blues
136 typed pages

6. Flaming Star
Grey binder with gold print
Title on cover and spine
Cover sheet lists title as "Flaming Lance" and is dated July 20, 1960. Has 20th Century Fox logo and is labeled "Revised Shooting Final." Writers are listed as Nunnally Johnson and Clair Huffaker.
108 typed pages

7. Wild in the Country
Plain white binder
Blue cardboard binder inside has black print reading "Wild in the Country October 19, 1960" with "Final" at top of the page and a 20th Century Fox logo. There is a blue stamp reading "Exclusive Management Thomas A. Parker Box 417 Madison, Tennessee." Writer is listed as Clifford Odets. (The guy "Barton Fink" is based on!)
117 typed pages

8. Blue Hawaii
Plain grey binder
Cover sheet reads "Wallis-Paramount-Hazen" and "Revised Final White" Hal Kanter is listed as writer and is dated March 17, 1961
121 typed pages

9. Follow That Dream
Plain grey binder
Cover sheet lists title as "Pioneer Go Home" with a "Follow That Dream" sticker over it. Reads "Final Script" and is dated May 29, 1961 with Charles Lederer as writer.
120 typed pages

10. Kid Galahad
Red binder with gold print
"Elvis Presley" printed on the cover
Cover sheet is dated September 18, 1961 and lists William Fay as writer
148 pages

11. Girls! Girls! Girls!
Grey binder with gold print
Title printed on cover and spine
Cover sheet reads "Wallis-Paramount-Hazen" and "Final White Script" Dated March 15, 1962 and with Edward Anhalt listed as writer.
117 typed pages

12. It Happened at the World's Fair
Grey binder with gold print
Title printed on cover and spine
Cover sheet lists title as "Take Me to the Fair" and has an M.G.M. logo. Reads "Final" and lists Si Rose, Seaman Jacobs and John T. Kelly as writers. Dated Sept. 4, 1962
125 typed pages

13. Fun in Acapulco
Grey binder with gold print
Title printed on cover and spine
Cover sheet reads "Wallis-Paramount-Hazen" and "Final White Script." Has a sticker reading "Colonel Parker's Final Copy of the Script." Dated November

28, 1962 with Allan Weiss listed as writer.
124 typed p[ages

14. Kissin' Cousins
Brown binder with gold print
"Kissin Cousins MGM 1964" printed on spine
Cover sheet has "M.G.M." logo and lists writers as
Gerald Drayson Adams and Gene Nelson. Dated
September 18, 1963.
"Tom Diskin" is written at the bottom of the cover
sheet in red pencil and there are red pencil mark-
ings within the script noting the placement of
songs.
109 typed pages.

15. Viva Las Vegas
Green binder with gold print
"Viva Las Vegas MGM 1964" printed on spine
Cover sheet has "M.G.M." logo and a label reading
"Colonel Parker's Copy."
Dated July 3, 1963 with Sally Benson listed as writer.
Over 100 typed pages (page numbering is off)

16. Roustabout
Grey binder with gold print
Title printed on cover and spine
Cover sheet reads "Wallis-Paramount-Hazen" and
"Final White" Dated February 7, 1964 and Allan
Weiss listed as writer.
114 typed pages

17. Girl Happy
Brown binder with gold print
"Elvis Presley" printed on cover and "MGM's Girl
Happy 1964" on spine
Cover sheet has "M.G.M." logo and lists R.S. Allen
and Harvey Bullock as writers. Dated March 31,
1964.
102 typed pages

18. Tickle Me
No binder yet
Cover sheet reads "Allied Artists" and "First
Rough Draft," lists writers as Elwood Ullman and
Edward Bernds
101 typed pages

19. Harum Scarum
Brown binder with gold print
"Elvis Presley" on cover and "Harem Holiday MGM

1965" on spine
Cover sheet has "M.G.M." logo and lists title as "In
My Harem." Dated January 15, 1965 and lists
Gerald Drayson Adams as writer.
129 typed pages.

20. Frankie and Johnny
Cover sheet reads "Admiral Pictures. Inc." and lists
Alex Gottlieb as writer
226 typed pages

21. Paradise Hawaiian Style
Cover sheet reads "Wallis-Paramount-Hazen" and
"Final White Script." Lists title as "Hawaiian
Paradise." Allan Weiss and Anthony Lawrence list-
ed as writers, dated June 8, 1965.
108 typed pages.

22. Spinout
Green binder with gold print
"Elvis Presley" on cover and "MGM's SPinout 1966"
on spine
Cover sheet has "M.G.M." logo and lists George
Kirgo and Theodore J. Flicker as writers. Dated
January 11, 1966.
Has cast info and shooting schedule at beginning
of script
110 typed pages

23. Easy Come, Easy Go
Black binder with red print
Spine reads "Scripts Paramount Studios, 1966 Easy
Come, Easy Go, 1966"
Cover sheet reads "Wallis-Paramount-Hazen" and
"Final White" Allan Weiss and Anthony Lawrence
are listed as writers, is dated Sept. 8, 1966]
120 typed pages

24. Double Trouble
Green binder with gold print
"Elvis Presley" on cover, "MGM's Double Trouble
1967" on spine
cover sheet has "M.G.M." logo and lists writer as Jo
Heims. Dated May 23, 1966
128 typed pages

25. Clambake
Red binder with gold print
"Elvis Presley" printed on cover, "Clambake Untied
Artists 1967" on spine

Cover sheet is dated December 14, 1966 and lists
Arthur Browne, Jr. as the writer
126 typed pages.

26. Stay Away Joe
Black binder with gold print has title on spine

27. Speedway
Brown binder with gold print
"ELvis Presley" on cover and "MGM's SPeedway
1968" on spine
Cover sheet has "M.G.M>" logo and lists title as "Pot
Luck." Dated April 7, 1967 with Phillip Shuken as
writer.
126 typed pages

28. Live a Little, Love a Little
Brown binder with gold print
"Elvis Presley" on cover with "MGM's Live a Little,
Love a Little 1968" on spine
Cover sheet as "M.G.M." logo and lists title as "Kiss
My Firm But Pliant Lips."
Dated February 23, 1968 and lists writer as Michael
A. Hoey.
114 typed pages.

29. Charro
Dated 7/8/68
109 typed pages.

30. The Trouble With Girls
White binder with gold print
"Elvis Presley" on cover and "MGM's The Trouble
With Girls and How to Get Into It, 1969" on spine
COver sheet as "M.G.M>" logo and lists title as "The
Chautauqua." Dated September 9, 1968 with
Arnold and Lois Peyser as writers.
132 typed pages.

31. Change of Habit
Blue cover sheet reads "Property of Universal
Studios"
118 typed pages.

B201 COLONEL PARKER DESK SET

Metal desk with brown surface, three drawers on right, cabinet on left. Black vinyl chair, gold "RCA" logo on back, gold RCA dog logo on seat. Metal base with rollers. Plaque on back of seat reads: "To Colonel Tom Parker Commemorating 20 Years Association With RCA-Victor" with list of fifteen names including RCA executives Steve Sholes, Bill Bullock and Harry Jenkins. 29 x 31 x 59 inches desk. 46 inch tall chair.

Two gray metal file cabinets, each with four drawers. One cabinet marked with gold tape with raised letters, reads: "File No. 10". Second cabinet has orange tape with raised letters. reads: "File no. 2" Each drawer on this cabinet is labeled, reads: "Financial Reports Elvis Tours," each drawer allotted for a year(s): 1969/1970, 1971/1972, 1973, 1974. 52 x 28 1/2 x 15 inches.

Four mounted and framed award, connotating one million records sold. Plaque reads: "To Colonel Parker in Appreciation of His Contribution Toward Making (Record) a Million Dollar Seller (Year)." First: "Elvis Presley" RCA Debut LP, 1966; second: "Elvis Gold Records Vol. III" 1966; third: "How Great Thou Art," 1968; fourth: "Elvis Christmas Album," 1964. 22 x 19 inches.

Four framed, autographed photos: Fabian, Nick Adams, Bob Hope, Harry Carey. Approx. 16 x 13 inches.

Three framed photos: Andy Griffith (three panels from Elvis' performance on Andy Griffith Show), Faron Young (two panels, autographed), Elvis Presley (three panels). Approx. 16 x 35 inches.

One desk "name plate" that reads "Donations Accepted." Wood with the lettering on a gold plate. 2 x 10 1/2 inches. One silver desk name plate reading "Col. Tom Parker."

Two individual hand stamps, one reading "Now Elvis Now, Las Vegas Hilton" and the other for "Double, Trouble." Five large "RCA Victor" hand stamps.

Pipe engraved "Snow Chief's Pipe."

Silver "RCA Victor" ashtray.

White T-shirt with black print reading "Elvis Sings 'In the Ghetto'"

Wooden cane with rounded handle and black rubber tip. 37 inches.

Package of multi-colored Elvis banners; each 28 x 11 inches

Stationery pad reading "From the Desk of-" and with a black and white photo imprint of the Colonel's head on each page.

$30,000 - 40,000

B202 ARTWORK FOR "FRANKIE AND JOHNNY"

Cardboard black and white mock-up of the "Frankie and Johnny" album cover. Corresponding tracing paper with colored images. Mock-up of album sleeve. One side shows a portrait of Elvis painted by June Kelly. Other side features movie advertisement. 12 1/4 x 12 1/4 inches cover mock-up. 14 1/2 x 12 1/4 inches tracing paper. 11 3/4 x 11 3/4 inches sleeve mock-up.

"Frankie and Johnny," released in 1966, is set on a riverboat with Elvis playing a singer with an affinity for gambling. The 12 songs from the movie all appeared on the album. Album includes the songs, "Down by the Riverside" and "When the Saints Go Marching In."

$4,000 - 4,500

B203 ARTWORK FOR THE ALBUM COVER OF THE "ROUSTABOUT" MOVIE SOUNDTRACK.

Artwork for the front and back album cover of the "Roustabout" movie soundtrack. Front cover is done in black and white except for a white 2" banner near the top which has the words "Elvis" in red, and "Roustabout" in blue. In the foreground there is an upper body photo of Elvis wearing a long sleeved shirt. Background contains a drawing of people at a carnival with Elvis on stage with is guitar. Back cover is done in black and white with five photographs of Elvis. Photos consist of two upper body shots and two shots with Elvis standing and playing a guitar. Fifth photo is an upper body shot and located in the middle of the cover. On the top are the words "Elvis Roustabout Elvis", and below the photo of Elvis is a list of his co-stars, director, producer, and who wrote the screenplay. Artwork for front and back is done on thick cardboard. 12 x 12 inches.

Elvis recorded "Roustabout" , the title song to his 1964 movie of the same name, in March of 1964 at Radio Recorders. Athought the Jordanaires are credited with singing backup, it was actually the Mello Men who did the singing. They gave up their claim for credit on the album, and were paid by the hour for their services.

$4,000 - 4,500

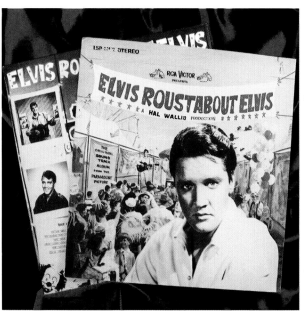

B203
B202

B204 SYNOPSIS AND PRESS RELEASE ON "DOUBLE TROUBLE" PLUS MEMORABILIA

Five typed pages of information regarding "Double Trouble" starring Elvis Presley and presented by Metro-Goldwyn-Mayer. Pages include cast of char-

acters, credits, and highlights from the move. Also included is a two page typed synopsis of "Double Trouble." Yellow prop poster of Elvis as his character Guy in the movie "Double Trouble" 11 x 8 1/2"

The 1967 film "Double Trouble" featured Elvis as Guy Lambert, a singer traveling around Europe. Norman Taurog directed this film, Elvis' 24th, which costarred John Williams and Yvonne Romain.

$6,500 - 7,500

B205 RCA PRESS RELEASE FOR "SPINOUT" ALBUM

November 1966 press release by RCA Victor regarding the album "Spinout." Release talks about Elvis Presley's role in the movie "Spinout" and highlights the nine songs from the film that are featured on their album, including "Stop, Look, and Listen" and "Beach Shack." The release wraps up with "DJs and fans will give 'Spinout' lots of spins. It's Elvis at the top of his form." Sheet attached to the press release lists order of songs on each side of the album. Two-sided black-and-white advertisement about "Spinout," with one side promoting the album and single and the other side promoting the film. Orange, green, gold, and yellow checkered flags tied together as a promotional banner: white lettering reads "Elvis in 'Spinout'" 11 x 8 1/2" release and ad. 95" banner; each flag 11 x 17".

MGM produced "Spinout," a Joe Pasternak production, in 1966. It was Elvis' 22nd film. Since this was his 10th year in films, MGM ran an enormous publicity campaign. RCA produced a single of the title song and "All That I Am." The RCA album featured the nine songs from the film--including "Adam and Eve," "Beach Shack," and "I'll Be Back"--and three other bonus songs that were not part of the film: "Tomorrow Is a Long Time" (a Bob Dylan song), "Down in the Alley," and "I'll Remember You."

$1,000 - 1,250

B206 "FRANKIE AND JOHNNY" LETTER

One page typed, dated April 20, 1966 addressed to United Artist Corporation in Hollywood, California. Holes punched on right margin. Letter is signed in blue ink by Elvis Presley. Record sleeve included. 11 x 8 1/2 inches.

Letter to United Artists Corporation acknowledges the receipt of a 16 mm print of "Frankie and Johnny" and agreeing to its private-only use. "Frankie and Johnny" was Elvis' 20th film. He starred opposite Donna Douglas. Elvis did not date Douglas during the filming, but did take an intellectual interest in her. Like Elvis, she was a member of the Self-Realization Fellowship. During the filming, they spent their time together discussing ideas, books, and spiritual matters; exchanging books; and meditating.

$3,000 - 3,500

B206

B207 MGM PRESS RELEASE FOR "HARUM SCARUM"

One-page press release on MGM's "Harum Scarum." Release states that the film "set an all-time MGM print order record by having over 550 play dates during the Thanksgiving holiday . . . racking up sensational grosses in all situations." "Baghdad Observer" 4-page newspaper promoting "Harum Scarum," with black-and-white photos from the movie. Black-and-white photograph of Elvis from the film; printed on heavy stock, but taped around the edges. 11 x 8 1/2 inches press release and newspaper. 14 x 11 inches photograph.

The Colonel was upset with "Harum Scarum" upon its release. He wrote to the movie company suggesting the only thing that would save it might be to have a "talking camel" help promote it.

$300 - 350

B208 MGM PRESS RELEASE AND PREMIER PROGRAMS FOR "SPINOUT"

Two-page copy of a wire featuring an MGM press release, stamped Fri. Dec. 2, 1966, highlights "Spinout" as "one of the most successful Elvis Presley films in the company's history." Record totals were registered in Chicago, Atlanta, Washington, St. Louis, and Baltimore. Chicago grossed $197,402 in the first week. Release also discusses Elvis' previous motion pictures and co-stars in "Spinout." Two orange and white programs for movie premier of "Spinout." Artist's black rendering of Elvis holding driving helmet on front; cast and credits listed inside. 11 x 8 1/2 inches release. 10 x 8 inches programs.

"Spinout," an MGM Joe Pasternak production, became Elvis' 22nd film and opened nationally in November 1966. Norman Taurog directed the picture. Elvis costarred with Shelley Fabares. He played a race car driver, Mike McCoy, who loved the women but also loved the single life.

$350 - 400

B209 ELVIS PERSONAL FILM, BOOK AND ALBUM OF "STAY AWAY JOE"

One original movie case containing the 16 millimeter film of "Stay Away Joe." One original acetate case containing an "Exhibitor's Campaign Book," labels, and one vinyl album, "Special Location Radio Program." Cases are brown with metal corners, a handle on one end, and a horizontal and a vertical buckled strap. 15 1/4 x 15 3/4 inches film case. 15 x 15 inches acetate case.

In his twenty-sixth film "Stay Away Joe," Elvis plays Joe Lightcloud, a Native American bull-rider. In this movie, "Elvis goes West... and the West goes wild!" $2,000 - 3,000

B210 ELVIS' PERSONAL FILM AND ACETATE OF "FRANKIE AND JOHNNY"

One 16mm film of Frankie and Johnny in film box. Red and white label reads "Frankie & Johnny" 1966, #20. Border label indicates name of film, production company, producer, director, and release date. One acetate box containing 23 acetates (mostly 33 1/3 rpms), including "Chesay," "Shout It Out," "What Every Woman Knows," "When the Saints . . .," "Frankie and Johnny," "Hard Luck," "Petunia," "Everybody Come," "Look Out, Broadway," "Beginner's Luck," "Everybody Come Aboard," "Please Don't Stop Loving Me," "Shout It Out," "Come Along," "What Every Woman Lives For," and some untitled selections under "Elvis Presley." Other items in acetate box: 2 cardboard pieces for spacing, a 2-page report of recording session, a pressbook, and a manila envelope for "Frankie and Johnny." Cases are brown with metal corners, a handle on one end, and a horizontal and vertical buckled strap. 15 1/4 x 15 3/4" film case. 15 x 15" acetate case.

Frankie and Johnny was produced by Admiral Pictures (United Artists) by Edward Small. The film was directed by Fred de Cordova. Release took place in April 1966. This film, Elvis' twelfth, premiered in Baton Rouge, Louisiana.

$3,000 - 4,000

B211 "GIRL HAPPY" ALBUM COVER ARTWORK

Original front and back cover art mock-ups for the 1965 soundtrack to "Girl Happy." Attached one page typed letter from RCA Art Director R.M. Jones to Tom Diskin, dated February 16, 1965 on RCA letterhead. With original shrink-wrapped copy of the "Girl Happy" album. 13 3/8 x 13 3/8 inches mock-up. 11 x 8 1/2 inches letter. 12 x 12 inches album.

Mock-up has corrections handwritten in red crayon, detailed in the letter.

$3,000 -3,500

B212 "GIRL HAPPY" JACKET

Off-white, belted lab style jacket. Printed all over the jacket are "Girl Happy," Elvis' name, and the names of Elvis' co-stars in the movie. Two pockets have the Paramount logo on them.

Colonel Parker never wasted an opportunity to promote Elvis or his movies. When he wore this jacket there would be no question as to Elvis' current project.

B211

$1,000 - 1,5000

B213 ELVIS' PERSONAL FILM AND ACETATE OF "SPINOUT"

One MGM audio/video for the film "Spinout," and one acetate for same. Items are contained in square, brown flim/acetate boxes with metal corners, and a plastic handle on the side. There are two buckled straps, one horizontal and one vertical. 15 1/4 x 15 3/4 inches film and case. 15 x 15 inches acetate and case.

This film was taken from Colonel Parkers collection of Elvis' films. "Spinout" opened nationally on November 23, 1966, making this Elvis' tenth year in films. Shelley Fabares co-starred with Elvis in this movie, and Deborah Walley, whom he dated during the filming. Acetate contains "All That I am, ", and "Spinout," on side one; and an untitled song on the second side.

$3,000 - 4,000

B214 DOUBLE TROUBLE ACETATES AND RECORDING SESSION ITINERARY

Copy of two-page typed itinerary for "Double Trouble" June 28-30, 1966 recording session. Letter on MGM letterhead and dated June 27, 1966. One page typed inter-office memo on MGM letterhead, sent to Tom Diskin and dated June 22, 1966 regarding songs for the film.

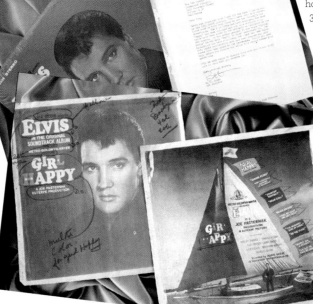

Five of Elvis' acetates for "Double Trouble" in original envelope which reads "Final Elvis Versions on 'Double Trouble.'" 11 x 8 1/2 inches.

The 1967 feature "Double Trouble" was Elvis' 24th film and all eight songs from the movie were featured on the album. The "Double Troube" soundtrack spent 20 weeks on "Billboard's" Top LP's, peaking at #47.

$800 - 1,000

B215 ELVIS' PERSONAL FILM AND ACETATES OF "DOUBLE TROUBLE"

Case containing Elvis' personal 16 mm print of "Double Trouble." Case features a red and white label reading: "'Double Trouble,' Metro-Goldwyn-Mayer Production, Producer Irwin Winkler & Jud Bernard , Director Norman Taurog, Released June 1967 #23. Acetate case with one acetate of the film's soundtrack. Also includes various promotion and production documents, including a "Special Preview" invitation, a song list, a press book, a program and a recording schedule. Cases are brown with metal corners, a handle on one end and a horizontal and vertical buckled strap. 15 1/4 x 15 3/4 inches film case. 15 x 15 inches acetate case.

"Double Trouble" was Elvis' 24th film. The film, about a singer in Europe torn between two women, was set in Great Britain and Belgium but was filmed at the M-G-M lot in Culver City, California.

$2,000 - 3,000

B216 ELVIS PERSONAL FILM AND ACETATES OF "EASY COME, EASY GO"

Case containing Elvis' personal 16 mm print of "Easy Come, Easy Go." Case features a red and white label reading: "'Easy Come, Easy Go,' Paramount Productions, Producer Hal Wallis, Director John Rich, Released March 1967." Acetate case with seven acetates from the film, including the songs "Yoga is as Yoga Does," "Easy Come, Easy Go," "You Gotta Stop," "The Love Machine" and "I'll Take Love." Also includes a merchandising manuel for the film and a recording schedule.
Cases are brown with metal corners, a handle on one end and a horizontal and vertical buckled strap. 15 1/4 x 15 3/4 inches film case 15 x 15 inches acetate case

"Easy Come, Easy Go" was Elvis' 23rd film. Elvis plays a frogman diving for treasure.

$3,000 - 4,000

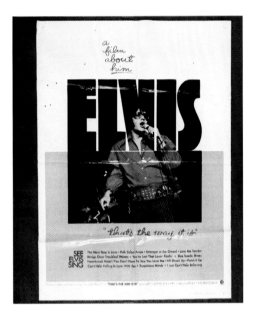

The six movie posters depicted on this and the following are part of lot B227.

B217 "HARUM SCARUM" PHOTOSTATS AND RELATED DOCUMENTS

Typed letter dated August 10, 1965 on MGM letterhead to "Tom" from Howard Strickling. Inter-office communication dated August 10, 1965 on MGM letterhead to Howard Strickland from Jim Raker regarding "Harum Scarum." Typed letter dated August 10, 1965 on plain paper addressed to the Colonel with no signature. Three black and white photostats for the layouts for "Harum Scarum" ads. 8 1/2 x 5 1/2 inches letter to "Tom." 5 1/2 x 8 1/2 inches inter-office communication. 11 x 8 1/2 inches letter to the Colonel. 13 x 7 1/2; 14 1/2 x 9 1/2; 13 x 9 inches photostats.

Harum Scarum," was Elvis' 19th movie. The advtisement did not, to the Colonel Parker's chagrin, announce, "a harum of hip honeys."

$650 - 750

B218 ELVIS PERSONAL FILM AND ACETATES OF "CLAMBAKE"

Case containing Elvis' personal 16 mm print of "Clambake." Case contains a red and white label that reads: "Clambake, LEVY-GARDER-LAVEN PRODUCTION, United Artists release, Director: Arthur Nadel, Released November-1967." Acetate case with eight acetates from the film, including the songs "Hey, Hey, Hey," "Who Needs Mary," "Clambake" and "Confidence." Also includes a "Clambake" press book, and a two-page recording schedule. Cases are brown with metal corners, a handle on one end and a horizontal and vertical buckled strap. 15 1/4 x 15 3/4 inches film case 15 x 15 inches acetate case

"Clambake" was Elvis' 25th film. Elvis plays a millionaire who switches places with a water ski instructor. The TV dolphin "Flipper" makes a cameo. $4,000 - 6,000

B219 ELVIS' PERSONAL "CHANGE OF HABIT" FILM

Case containing Elvis' personal 16 mm print of "Change of Habit." Case is brown with metal corners, a handle on one end and a horizontal and vertical buckled strap. 15 1/4 x 15 3/4 inches film case.

The 1969 Universal production "Change of Habit" was Elvis' 31st and final feature film. Elvis portrays Dr. John Carpenter, a name he would frequently use as an alias, and works in an urban ghetto with a nun played by Mary Tyler Moore.

$2,000 - 3,000

B220 "CHANGE OF HABIT"

One page typed on Universal Pictures letterhead, dated January 31, 1969. Press release titled "Elvis Presley to star in 'Change of Habit.'" Handwritten note in blue ink on MCA Records International note paper, written to Col. Parker from Richard L. Brodwick. Note says "Didn't think we would get together again this quickly. Welcome to the wonderful world of MCA." One invitation to a preview screening of "Change of Habit," on white card stock with peach and blue print. 11 x 8 1/2 inches press release. 5 1/2 x 4 1/4 inches note. 8 x 8 1/2 inches invitation.

"Change of Habit," in which Elvis co-starred with Mary Tyler Moore, was Elvis' last feature film.

$1,200 - 1,400

The six movie posters depicted on this and the following are part of lot B227.

B221 "CHANGE OF HABIT" SYNOPSIS AND NEWS

Memo dated September 19, 1969, on "Sales Promotion News" letterhead with Universal City Studios logo. Sent to Branch Managers from Jerry Evans, announcing Elvis Presley's film "Change of Habit." Four-page synopsis of film dated September 30, 1969, on "Murray Weissman" letterhead with Universal City Studios logo. Photograph included. 11 x 8 1/2 inches all sheets.

"Change of Habit," a Universal Pictures film, was Elvis' last film. It was part of a deal the colonel signed that included the '68 TV Special.

$650 - 750

B222 RCA PRESS RELEASE FOR "SPINOUT" ALBUM

November 1966 press release by RCA Victor regarding the album "Spinout." Release talks about Elvis Presley's role in the movie "Spinout" and highlights the nine songs from the film that are featured on their album, including "Stop, Look, and Listen" and "Beach Shack." The release wraps up

with "DJs and fans will give "Spinout" lots of spins. It's Elvis at the top of his form." Sheet attached to the press release lists order of songs on each side of the album. Two-sided black-and-white advertisement about "Spinout," with one side promoting the album and single and the other side promoting the film. Orange, green, gold, and yellow checkered flags tied together as a promotional banner: white lettering reads "Elvis in 'Spinout'" 11 x 8 1/2 inches release and ad. 95 inches banner; each flag 11 x 17 inches

MGM produced "Spinout," a Joe Pasternak production, in 1966. It was Elvis' 22nd film. Since this was his 10th year in films, MGM ran an enormous publicity campaign. RCA produced a single of the title song and "All That I Am." The RCA album featured the nine songs from the film--including "Adam and Eve," "Beach Shack," and "I'll Be Back"--and three other bonus songs that were not part of the film: "Tomorrow Is a Long Time" (a Bob Dylan song), "Down in the Alley," and "I'll Remember You."

$1,000 - 1,250

B223 PRESS KIT FOR ELVIS PRESLEY'S "CHARRO!"

Color photograph of Elvis with list of RCA records on the back. 32-page color brochure entitled "Elvis' RCA Records." 12-page newspaper, "The Superior Sun" dated August 1, 1968. Front page headline read, "Elvis Presley and crew are right next door." Black and white poster advertising "Charro!" with a picture of Elvis. Poster thanks the businesses of Apache Junction, including the Superstition Inn, for their cooperation during filming. Original "Charro!" envelope included. 10 x 8" photograph. 7 1/4 x 3 1/2" brochure. 17 1/4 x 11 1/2" newspaper. 17 1/2 x 22 1/2" poster. 8 3/4 x 11 1/2" envelope.

"Charro!" was filmed near Apache Junction, Arizona, in and around the Superstition Mountains. During the filming, Elvis stayed at the Superstition Inn. The town of Apache Junction embraced not only the excitement that Elvis' movie brought to their town, but also Elvis. According to the newspaper article, "Residents are enjoying Presley, Colonel Parker and their group not only because they are celebrities, but also because they are nice people." Three states, Oklahoma, Texas, and Louisiana declared "Charro!" Day upon the movie's release.

$800 - 1,000

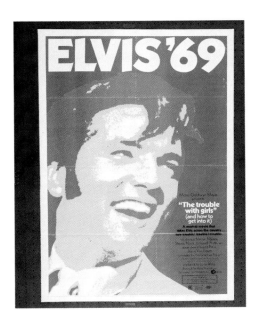

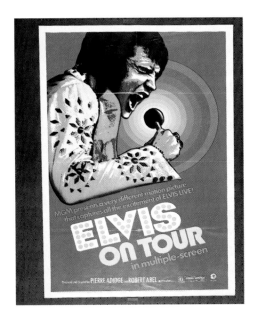

B224 SETTLEMENT STATEMENT FOR "ROUSTABOUT"

Two page typewritten settlement statement for the movie "Roustabout", dated May 12, 1964. Statement includes salary, deductions, and reimbursements. Elvis costarred with Barbara Stanwyck in "Roustabout" which began filming on March 9, 1964, and was completed April 20.

Racquel Welch made her film debut in this movie as a college girl. "Roustabout" was Elvis' sixteenth film and ranked #28 on "Variety's" list of top-grossing films for the year of 1965.

$2,000 - 2,500

B225 ELVIS' PERSONAL FILM OF "THE TROUBLE WITH GIRLS"

One original movie case with the 16 mm film of "The Trouble with Girls." Label with red border reads, "'The Trouble with Girls,' Metro-Goldwyn-Mayer Studio, Producer: Lester Welch, Director: Peter Tewksbury, Released May 1969 #30." Red label with raised white lettering reads, "The Trouble with Girls - 1969 - 30." Case is brown with metal corners, a handle on one end, and a horizontal and a vertical buckled strap. 15 1/4 x 15 3/4 in. i

"The Trouble with Girls", subtitled "And How to Get into It," was Elvis' thirtieth film. The movie opened nationally on September 3, 1969.

$2,000 - 3,000

B226 ELVIS PERSONAL FILM, ACETATES, AND PRESS BOOK FOR "CHARRO"

One original movie case containing the 16 millimeter film of "Charro." White label with red border reads "'Charro, National-General-Productions, Producer: Harry Caplan, Director: Charles M. Warren, Released: March 1969, #29." Red label with with white lettering reads, "Charro - 1969 29." One original acetate box containing two "Charro" acetates including the songs: "Memories," "Charro," and "Forget About the Stars." Also included is a "Charro" press book, labels, and \ sealed manila envelop reading, "GNC - National General Productions, Inc. Presents Elvis now in Production in Arizona." Cases are brown with metal corners, a handle on one end, and a horizontal and a vertical buckled strap. 15 1/4 x 15 3/4 inches film case. 15 x 15 inches acetate case.

"Charro," Elvis' twenty-ninth film, was the closest Elvis came to playing a purely dramatic role. Only

one song was featured in the movie and it played as the credits roll. Elvis sported a beard for this role as a cowpoke taking on a band of outlaws.

$3,000 - 4,000

B227 ELVIS MOVIE POSTERS

Thirty Three posters, one from each of Elvis Presley's films. All posters are paper, with the exception of the following, constructed of heavy cardboard: "Double Trouble," "Easy Come, Easy Go," "Paradise Hawaiian Style," "Tickle Me," "G.I. Blues", "Jailhouse Rock" and "Follow that Dream." Each poster measures approximately 40 X 27 inches. *The 33 posters in this lot have been pictured throughout the 1960's section of this catalogue.*

These poster come directly from the personal collection of Colonel Parker and were hung at various times during the Colonel's career as Elvis' manager. Each of these posters is an original promotional poster, each dating to the film's release date.

$20,000 - 30,000

B228 BRIAN EPSTEIN AND COLONEL'S LETTERS

Letter dated September 4, 1965 (letterhead Hille House, 9 Stafford Street, London W1) to Colonel Parker from Brian Epstein, manager of the Beatles, (with Epstein's signature). Letter thanks the Colonel for "the trouble and consideration you took towards making the meeting of the boys and myself with Mr. Presley such a wonderfully relaxing and happy evening." He also thanks him for the gift and the box of records and hopes to see him when "next on the West Coast." Copy of a reply letter (unsigned) from the Colonel dated September 10, 1965, with a humorous request for "a couple of midget ponies . . . so we can carry them in our trunk and perhaps to Las Vegas to play roulette to keep the dealer   B228

looking at the ponies while we pick up the chips." Photograph incl. 11 x 8 1/2 both letters.

The Beatles and Brian Epstein, their manager, visited Elvis on August 27, 1965 at his home on Perugia Way in California. Elvis basically ignored his guests, picking up a guitar and playing along with a tune on the jukebox. George discussed spiritual matters with Larry Geller, the Colonel and Epstein gambled at a coffee table, Ringo played pool with some of Elvis' entourage, and later John and Paul grabbed guitars and jammed a little with Elvis before the evening ended. $2,000 - 2,500

B229 - No Lot

182

B230 GUITAR PICK AND STATEMENT FOR GUITAR PURCHASE.

Statement from Amro Music Store on Highway 51S, dated March 16, 1967. Statement is billed to Elvis Presley. Order was made on January 25, 1967 for a Gibson S.G.Jr. Guitar with Case, used pacemaker, guitar chords, chord book, and chart. Total bill $243.83. Order picked up by Bob "Red" West. Vernon okayed payment of the bill. Photograph included. Gold guitar pick engraved with "Elvis Presley" and a musical note 8 1/2 x 5 1/2 inches invoice. 1 1/2 inches pick.

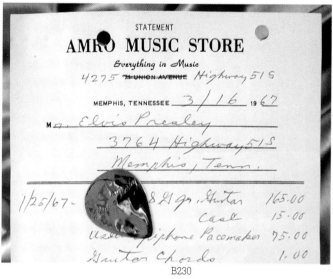

B230

Elvis owned many guitars throughout his career, but according to most sources he received his first six-string guitar on his 11th birthday, January 8, 1946.

$8,000 - 10,000

B231 SUGGESTED AD FOR "BILLBOARD" FROM ELVIS PRESLEY TO THE M.O.A.'S

Suggested "Billboard" ad from Elvis thanking the M.O.A.'s. Top of ad has a black and white photograph of Elvis dressed in a suite and tie, shot from the shoulders up. In bold green letters below the

photo is his name. On the left beside of his face are the words "My thanks to .. (and continuing on the right side of his face) .. the M.O.A." Bottom of ad has three round, black disks (representing albums) vertically arranged. Top disk reads 'Current single...#9 on Hot 100! (You're The) "Devil In Disguise" #8188.' Remaining two disks have the word "album" penciled in the middle on a square cardboard piece. Listed on the left side of the ad are the words: 'Current Movie "Fun In Acapulco" Title song by Elvis.' Listed on the right side are the words: 'Movie in Production: "Viva Las Vegas" Title song by Elvis.' Right below this, on the left side are the words "Recording RCA Victor" followed on the right side by "Personal Mgt." 15 1/4 x 11 1/4 inches.

Fun in Acapulco opened nationally on November 27, 1963. Although several locations were photographed in Acapulco, all of Elvis' shots were shot on the Paramount lot in Hollywood. Production began on January 28, 1963, and lasted until mid-March. It was costar Ursula Andress's first American film. "Fun In Acapulco" reached number five on "Variety's" weekly top-grossing films.

$800 - 1,000

B232 ELVIS PRESLEY'S SHOOTING TARGET

Police Silhouette Target. White paper with black and white figure, with bullet holes in it.

One of Elvis' many hobbies was guns. He and his friends practiced shooting behind Graceland. They hung the target in the smoke house and shot at it through the doorway while standing in Graceland's backyard. You can still see bullet marks around the door frame of the smokehouse from where they didn't quite hit the target.

$800 - 1,000

B233 ELVIS' 1967 CHRISTMAS SPECIAL ITEMS

Box of promotional materials for "Elvis Presley Special Christmas Program" which includes a reel to reel tape and a script for the special. Box is enclosed in original shrink wrap. In original envelope with letter to "Programmer" on RCA letterhead. Includes single of "If Every Day Was Like Christmas." Blue folder with Elvis Presley Christmas 1967 and 1968 items enclosed including brochures, brochure mock-ups and newspaper clippings. 7 1/4 x 7 1/4 inches Christmas Special box. 9 x 9 inches envelope. 7 x 7 inches single. 11 1/2 x 9 inches folder.

The "Elvis Presley Special Christmas Program" box was sent to radio stations to be played early in the month of December. The program included Elvis singing Christmas songs such as, "Here Comes Santa Claus," "Blue Christmas," and "I'll Be Home for Christmas."

$2,500 - 3000

B235
B233

B234 RECEIPT FOR ELVIS PRESLEY'S BIRTHDAY CAKE

Receipt for an 8" x 8" coconut birthday cake for Elvis Presley from Vernon and boys. 5 x 3 1/4 "

Cake was given to Elvis from Vernon and the "Memphis Mafia."

$200 - 250

B235 ELVIS PRESLEY CHRISTMAS CARDS INCLUDING LETTER AND INVOICE FROM SOUTHERN GREETING COMPANY

Four versions of gold accented Christmas cards offered by Southern Greeting Card Company. Two are printed, "Elvis Presley and Family," another is printed, "Elvis and Priscilla, and the third one is printed, "Elvis, Priscilla, and Lisa." One green Christmas card from "The Presley's" that folds out to display drawings of Graceland. Thank you letter on Southern Greeting Card Company letterhead addressed to Vernon Presley for order of 5,000 cards. Attached to memo of delivery to "Mr. Vernon Presley" on 51 South. Includes final proof of gold card. Typed invoice with carbon copy for 5,000 cards from Southern Greeting Card Company with handwritten thank you from president of company. Invoice totals $589.68, includes return envelope. Original check from the account of Elvis Presley included. Approximately 4 3/8 x 8 1/4 inches cards. 11 x 8 1/2 inches letter. 5 1/2 x 8 inches memo of delivery. 5 3/8 x 7 inches final proof of card. 6 3/4 x 6 1/4 inches invoice. 4 1/8 x 9 1/2 inches envelope.

Christmas was a cherished time of year for Elvis. He liked to send Christmas wishes to his family, friends, and fans.

$1,800 - 2,000

B236 GRACELAND TELEPHONE AND ELVIS PRESLEY PHONE BILL

Southern Bell phone bill in amount of $38.76, dated June 1, 1967 and billed in Elvis Presley. Turquoise blue telephone. 3 5/8 x 9 5/8 inches bill.

Telephone is original telephone that Elvis used in Graceland.

$300 - 350

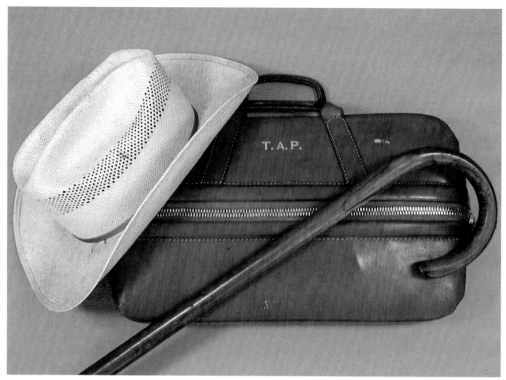

Yellow receipts from Burke's Florist. Three receipts are dated May 4, 1966 and are for $15 flower arrangements sent to Mrs. Tom Parker, Mrs. J.P. Beaulieu, and Mrs. Minnie Presley with notes wishing them happy Mother's Day from Elvis and Priscilla. A receipt dated May 14 is for a $7.50 basket arrangement his mother at the Forest Hill cemetery. A May 18, 1966 receipt is for a $20 arrangement for Mrs. Tom Parker for her birthday from Elvis and Priscilla. Elvis also purchases one dozen red roses on May 24, 1966 fro $10 for Priscilla's birthday. Photograph included. Statement for Burke's Florist in Memphis for Elvis Presley for April 29, 1967, to May 27, 1967. Fourteen attached receipts show flowers being sent to Elvis' mother's grave, Priscilla, Mrs. Beaulieu, Mrs. Parker, and Minnie Presley, among others. Copy of invoice and bill from Palm Springs Florists to Elvis, dated May 16, 1970. Flowers were sent to Marie, Colonel Parker's wife, for her birthday. Card reads, "Happy Birthday. Love Elvis, Priscilla & Lisa Marie." Bill is on white photocopy paper with blue lines, and blue print letterhead. Invoice is dark cream in color with brown lettering. Order for flowers, and instructions for card, are handwritten. Check from Elvis Presley Payroll & Expense Fund for $26.25 made out to Palm Springs Florist. 6 1/2 x 4 1/4 Burke's invoice receipts. 8 x 5 1/2 and 4 1/4 x 5 1/2 inches Burke's statement. 8 1/2 x 5 1/2" Palm Springs bill. 7 x 4 1/4" Palm Springs invoice. 3 1/8 x 8 1/4" check.

The Presleys always sent flowers to friends, relatives, and Gladys Presley's gravesite. From the time of Gladys' death, Elvis had a standing order for a weekly delivery of flowers to the cemetery.

$800 - 1,000

B239 ROY ORBISON TELEGRAM

Western Union telegram from Elvis and The Colonel to Roy Orbison congratulating him on the start of a film with Sam Katzman. 5 5/8 x 8 inches.

Roy Orbison recorded at Sun after Elvis. Sam Katzman made the first rock-n-roll movie, "Rock Around the Clock" in 1956 and also produced several Elvis movies, including "Kissin Cousins."

$450 - 500

B237 COLONEL PARKER'S HAT, CANE AND BAG

One straw Panama hat from "Knox" with brown ribbon. One wood cane with rounded handle and rubber tip. One brown leather personal accessory bag with the initials "T.A.P." engraved. Bag zips up and has two leather handles. 7 1/8 inches hat size. 38 1/2 OR 28 1/2 inches cane. 16 inches long x 10 inches wide x 4 inches deep bag.

These personal items belonged to Colonel Tom Parker.
$7,000 - 9,000

B238 BOUND VOLUMES OF CATALOGS OF MUSIC

Two Elvis Presley Music, Inc. catalogs with Table of Contents and 356 pages of Elvis sheet music from the 50's and 60's bound in black binder with Gladys Music, Inc. catalog with Table of Contents and 380 pages of Elvis sheet music. Bound together in black notebook. 11 3/4 x 10 x 3 inches binder.

Gladys Music and Elvis Presley Music Inc. were both subsidiaries of Hill and Range. They were set up under the direction of Colonel Parker in order for Elvis to receive partial royalties from the composers of Elvis' songs who wrote for Hill and Range. Gladys Music was named for Elvis beloved mother, Gladys Presley.

$650 - 750

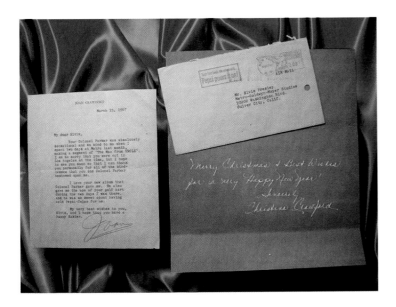

B241

B240 PULSAR WATCH AND CONGRATULATORY TELEGRAM TO COL. PARKER FROM ELVIS

One gold spandex watch with a square gold/maroon face. On back of watch is an inscription that says, "To Col. from Elvis 1956 - 1980." Watch comes with a black leather "Swarovski" pouch. Two page original Western Union Telegram dated January 23, 1967, from RCA to Elvis and the Colonel. The telegram is congratulating both Elvis and the Colonel for renewal of their contract with RCA through 1980. 5 1/2 x 8 inches.

This was the first contract that actually spelled out all monies that would be due the Colonel. The watch from Elvis to the Colonel lists on the back the dates of the longstanding contract with RCA - from 1956 until 1980. The telegram was sent to the Colonel's home in Palm Springs, which had been bought by the William Morris Agency for Mr. Parker. $4,500 - 5,000

B241 LETTER TO ELVIS PRESLEY FROM JOAN CRAWFORD, AND CHRISTMAS CARD FROM CHRISTINA CRAWFORD

Original typewritten and signed letter from Joan Crawford to Elvis, dated March 15, 1967. Original envelope included. Christmas card sent to Elvis at his Bel Air, California address from Christina

Crawford in December of 1964. Greeting is an all-in-one card and envelope. Front of card is two-toned with a holiday green on the right, and a copper color on the left with a green star. Written in white is Elvis' name and address. On back of the card is a golden broken seal. and at the top is Crawford's name and address. Inside written in white is "Merry Christmas & Best wishes for a very Happy New Year! Sincerely Christina Crawford." "How Great Thou Art" reissue album. 7 x 6 1/4 inches Letter. 3 3/4 x 6 1/2 inches Envelope. 4 1/4 x 8 1/4 inches Card. 12 x 12 inches Album.

Letter thanks Colonel Parker for Elvis' new album, and the use of Elvis' golf cart. "I am so sorry that you were not in Los Angeles at the time, but I hope to see you soon so that I can thank you personally for all the kindnesses that you and Colonel Parker bestowed upon me." $800 - 1,000

B242 TELEGRAM TO RINGO STARR FROM ELVIS PRESLEY AND COLONEL TOM PARKER

Beige Western Union Telegram dated September 14, 1965. Addressed to Ringo Starr in London from Elvis and The Colonel. Telegram congratulates Starr on the birth of his child and asks him to send a tape with a voice track if "Colonel Epstein is not interested in signing this new artist." 5 1/2 x 7 3/4"

Colonel Parker was always on the lookout for a new business opportunity. Elvis first met the Beatles on August 27, 1965, when the Colonel arranged for them to visit Elvis at his Perugia Way home in Bel Air. During their visit, Ringo played pool with Billy Smith and Richard Davis, members of the Memphis Mafia. $300 - 400

B243 CHRISTMAS AD AND LETTERS

"Fabulous--Las Vegas" magazine (December 24, 1966) back cover Christmas ad--photo of Elvis with "Seasons Greetings, Elvis and the Colonel, 1966." Letter to Colonel Parker from Jack Cortez indicates that a "last-minute cancellation opened the door for a prime location for your Christmas ad this year." Included is an invoice to Colonel Parker for $150 for the ad. Letter dated December 12, 1966, on Metro-Goldwyn-Mayer, Inc. stationary from Tom Diskin, asking for tear sheets on the ad be sent to Colonel Parker in Culver City, California. 9 1/4 x 6 1/4 inches magazine tear sheet. 7 x 5 inches Cortez note. 11 x 8 1/2 inches invoice and Diskin letter.

This ad ran even before Elvis appeared in Las Vegas, but the Colonel had many acquaintances in the city, and both he and Elvis loved to visit there "to play." $300 - 350

B244 ROAD TRIP MUSIC

Copy of a two page typewritten letter from George Barris of Barris Kustom City to Abe Lastfogel of the William Morris Agency. Letter is dated June 24, 1966, and discusses the arrangements surrounding the installation of a stereo system for Elvis Presley's bus. Photograph included. 11 x 8 1/2 inches.

Elvis bought this bus after he had purchased a house car. The bus was a Greyhound bought used in February of 1966, customized by George Barris, and driven home in April of 1966. Elvis liked to caravan to and from Los Angeles with the bus leading the way down Highway 40. To sound-proof the bus, heavy lead was attached. However, the extra weight caused the engine of the bus to breakdown. Elvis had to fly to Los Angeles on June 26, when the engine broke down.

$1,500 - 2,000

B245 BANK LOAN BOOK AND KEY FOR ELVIS PRESLEY'S CADILLAC

National Bank of Commerce payment book, circa 1967, for Elvis Presley's Cadillac. Book shows payments of $142.39 a month, and on May 23rd he paid off the balance of $1628.47. Original envelope is included with payment book. Silver GM key for Elvis' Cadillac, and one gold and silver key chain with an engraving of St. Christopher in the middle of a silver circle; inscription on metal says, "St. Christopher Protect us." 3 1/4 x 7 1/2" Payment book. 4 1/2 x 10" Envelope. 2 x 3/4" Keys.

This was Elvis' Cadillac sport model purchased on May 11, 1967.

$3,000 - 3,500

B246 PROPOSED GRACELAND SCREENING ROOM BLUEPRINTS AND FILM

Two page blueprint dated May 30, 1967 from National Theatre Supply in Memphis. For a proposed screening room at Graceland that was never built. Elvis' copy of "A Shot in the Dark." 18 x 24".

B245

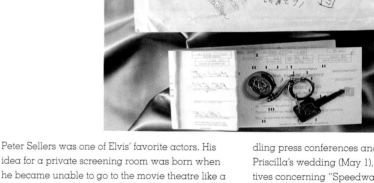

Peter Sellers was one of Elvis' favorite actors. His idea for a private screening room was born when he became unable to go to the movie theatre like a normal citizen. When he went to the theatre, he had to rent out the entire place, often in the middle of the night, to avoid a fan frenzy. Although a great idea, this screening room was never built.

$7,000 - 8,000

B247 ALL STAR SHOWS MONTHLY BUSINESS ACTIVITIES AND PERTINENT MEMORABILIA

Twenty-two page gold-metallic 3-ring folder showing 1967 monthly business activities for Colonel Parker while on location in Los Angeles Program for "Double Trouble"; 2-page blue with black-and-white photos, lists cast and crew. Exhibitor's Campaign Book from MGM for "Stay Away Joe"; 10-page black-and -white booklet with articles about the movie and possible ads the movie houses could use. Three-fold pamphlet advertising "Stay Away Joe" United Artists Pressbook for "Clambake"; 8-page black-and-white booklet showing possible ads for the movie. 11 x 8 1/2 inches folder and program. 17 x 12 1/2 inches ad booklet for "Stay Away Joe". 8 x 3 1/4 opening to 8 x 11 inches pamphlet. 17 x 11 inches pressbook for "Clambake".

General document showing how much work the Colonel encountered while taking care of Elvis' business. For example, May 1967 activities included handling press conferences and publicity on Elvis' and Priscilla's wedding (May 1), met with MGM executives concerning "Speedway" and "Double Trouble," sent out publicity on release of "Double Trouble" sound track, set up Mother's Day radio program, and met with William Morris agency about contracts. "Double Trouble" and "Clambake" were released in 1967; "Stay Away Joe" was filmed in the fall of 1967 and released in March 1968.

$2,500 - 3,000

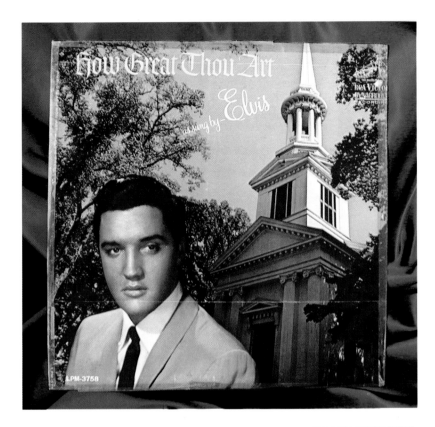

B248 ARTWORK FOR "HOW GREAT THOU ART"

Artwork for the album "How Great Thou Art." Front cover has a photo of Elvis in the lower left corner wearing a blue jacket with a white shirt and black tie. In the back ground is a white country church with steeple, and a blue cloudless sky with trees on both sides. Back cover has a full length picture of Elvis in the lower left corner; he is dressed in a white vested suite with a medium blue shirt, white collar, and black shoes. Background is a medium blue with "Elvis Sings" in white, and "How Great Thou Art" in pink. A list of songs on side one and two are listed on the right side. 12 1/2 x 12 1/2"

Elvis was awarded the first Grammy of his career for this album in the category of Best Sacred Performance. "How Great Thou Art" was released on March 8, 1967, and exceeded one million in sales. It was certified as a Gold Record by the RIAA on February 16, 1968.

$1,800 - 2,000

B249 RARE HANDWRITTEN RECORDING SESSION SONG LISTS OF "SPEEDWAY" AND "POT LUCK"

Two page schedule of the recording session for "Speedway" at MGM studios June 20 and 21, 1967. Lists the musicians and the songs recorded. On a page of "The Colonel" notepaper is a list of songs handwritten by Elvis in blue ink. Another page, entitled "Pot Luck" and dated April 12, 1967, lists "Order of Appearance in Script," "Page Location in Script," and "Song and Performers" in three columns. There are a number of notes handwritten in blue ink. "Speedway" soundtrack album. 11 x 8 1/2 inches schedule. 8 x 5 inches note paper.

Recording session for "Speedway" was held at MGM Studios in Culver City. Six songs by Elvis made it into the film: "Speedway," "Let Yourself Go," "Your Time Hasn't Come Yet, Baby," "He's Your Uncle, Not Your Dad," "Who Are You," and "There Ain't Nothing Like a Song." Nancy Sinatra had a solo called "Your Groovy Self."

$6,000 - 7,000

B250 "SINGER PRESENTS ELVIS" SCRAPBOOK

Oversized scrapbook which includes advertisements, posters, albums, newspaper clippings, T.V. Guide listings, and other promotional materials related to the '68 Special. The show was televised on NBC on December 3, 1968. 25 x 19 1/2 inches.

This scrapbook, compiled by Colonel Parker, documents a television special that stands as one of the signal moments of Elvis' career. Announced in January 1968 and mostly taped that summer, the "'68 Special," as it came to be called, reintroduced Elvis to a post-Beatles musical climate after nearly a decade in Hollywood. At the center of the show was an informal live performance, taped over the course of two nights in late June of that year, that was Elvis first concert performance since 1961. This "sit-down" segment, where a black leather clad Elvis was reunited with Fifties-era guitarist Scotty Moore and drummer D.J. Fontana, is undoubtedly what the program is remembered for today and the intense performance Elvis gives of several rhythm and blues classics is considered by many to be, after the Sun sessions, the finest music of his life.

$10,000 - 12,000

B251 LITERARY AGENTS MISCELLANEOUS CORRESPONDENCE, 1966 - 1970

Letters bound in folder entitled, "Miscellaneous Correspondence Propositions & Literary Agents 1966 - 1970." Letters include proposals for, and rejections of, books, screenplays, business ventures, and various propositions related to Elvis Presley and Colonel Thomas Parker. 11 1/2 x 9 1/8.

To say that Elvis was barraged with offers, requests, and opportunities is an understatement. One of the gems of an offer that Elvis and the Colonel passed on was a movie called "'Paco the Lawyer.'" It is about a Spanish lawyer who defends only young beautiful women and gets them off scott free regardless of what crime they have committed."

$1,400 - 1,600

B252 '68 SPECIAL PROMOTIONAL ITEMS

Full color Elvis Presley promotional pamphlet from 1968. One page copy of mock-ups of advertisements on the inside cover and back cover of the pamphlet. Original drawing/mock-up of ad on back cover of the pamphlet, on heavy cardboard. One page black and white advertisement for the 1968 "Elvis" television special, from the December 4, 1968 issue of Variety. Two copies of a two page typed song list for the show, one with corrections and additions handwritten in blue ink. 9 x 4 inches pamphlet. 11 x 8 1/2 inches mock-up copy. 9 1/2 x 7 1/4 inches cardboard mock-up. 12 x 9 1/4 inches Variety ad. 11 x 8 1/2 inches song list.

Advertisement on inside cover of the pamphlet is for the album of the 1968 television special. Advertisement on the back cover of the pamphlet and the cardboard mock-up is a Christmas greeting from Elvis and the Colonel, with the Colonel dressed as Santa Claus. These pamphlets were distributed through Singer stores, the company that sponsored Elvis' 1968 television special. The song list is an outline dated June 3, 1968—about two weeks before director Steve Binder came up with the idea of having Elvis perform the live sit-down performance that is now the hallmark of the show, and about three weeks before that segment was taped.

$3,000 - 3,500

B253 ELVIS' GOLD CAR TOUR PROMOTIONAL ITEMS

Three page typed "Fact Sheet on Elvis Presley's

Custom Built Cadillac" encased in a gold metallic binder. Eight page card stock "Elvis Presley's Gold Car" promotional folder. Contains a reprinted "fact sheet" as well as advertisements for an assortment of Elvis films. Four "Elvis' Gold Car on Tour" postcards. 11 1/2 x 9 1/4 inches binder. 11 1/2 x 9 1/2 inches folder. 3 1/2 x 5 1/2 inches postcards.

This gold-plated 1960 Cadillac was customized for Elvis by George Barris. It was taken this fan's tour in 1966. The fact sheet reveals that gold lame drapes were used to cover the back windows and to separate the front and back seats. The car also had a "ten record automatic changer RCA record player."

$600- 800

B252   B253

B254 WESTERN UNION TELEGRAM FROM ELVIS PRESLEY TO COLONEL PARKER, AND A VICTROLA

Western Union Telegram from Elvis to Col. Parker, dated June 4, 1967, congratulating him on his 25th anniversary with RCA. "It's been a happy association for me too - with you and with RCA. Look forward to the many more wonderful years ahead."

One RCA Victrola mounted on a wood base awarded to Colonel Parker from RCA Records. Wood base is 7 1/2" high with a 11" bottom width. Middle of base is inset by 2 1/2 inches, and top side measures 12" in width. There is a ten inch green turntable. Six inches above the turntable is a golden horn that measures twenty-two inches long with a 13 3/4" mouth. Horn is connected to the wood base with a 10" long by 1 1/2" wide handle that is black with a scroll design painted in gold. On the right side of the box is a crank-handle measuring 6 1/2" long with a wood knob at the end. On front of the wood case is a square metal RCA Victor logo with a black background, a gold picture of dog, and gold lettering. On the very bottom of the wood case is a rectangular gold metal plate with the words "To The Colonel From All Your Friends At RCA Records. August 10, 1984." 5 1/2 x 8" telegram.

The Colonel's connection to RCA had been well established by 1967, due to his professional representation of both Eddy Arnold and Hank Snow who preceded Elvis.

$3,000 - 4,000

B255 ELVIS PRESLEY EIGHT-TRACKS WITH RCA CONTRACT

Two page typed contract, dated August 18, 1969 and signed in blue ink by Elvis Presley and in black marker by Col. Tom Parker and RCA Vice-President Harry E. Jenkins. With copy. Twelve shrink wrapped, mint condition Elvis Presley 8-track cassettes. 11 x 8 1/2 inches contract.

Eight-track cassettes of "Elvis is Back!," "Having Fun With Elvis on Stage," "From Elvis in Memphis," "How Great Thou Art," "His Hand in Mine," "Pot Luck," "Roustabout," "Fun in Acapulco," "Girl Happy," "Blue Hawaii," "Kissin' Cousins," and "Speedway." These 8-tracks are in mint condition and in their original shrink wrap.

$4,000 - 5,000

B256 RECEIPT FOR RED WEST FROM ROY HARTE'S DRUM CITY

Yellow receipt from Roy Harte's Drum City in Hollywood, California dated March 19, 1966. The drums were purchased by Bobby West and "Red West" is written at the top of the page. Six items were purchased for a total of $289.15. A handwritten note in black ink indicates the bill was paid with check #2053 on March 20, 1966. Photograph included. 8 1/2 x 5 5/8 inches.

At this time Elvis was moving away from his spiritual exploration period--akin to his friendship with Larry Geller--and rekindling his interest in music. Drums were bought for his house in California so he and his friends could practice more.

$300 - 350

B257 ELVIS PRESLEY CLOTHING INVOICE, RECEIPTS AND HANDKERCHIEFS

Invoice from Snyder and Son Clothiers and Importers in Los Angeles, dated May 28. For the purchase of $1048.43 billed to Elvis Presley. Three handwritten receipts

B259

B255

from Snyders and Son for the same purchase. Includes a box of handkerchiefs purchased at this time. Three white handkerchiefs embroidered with an "E" in silver, brown and blue, respectively. 7 1/8 x 7 1/4 inches invoice. 7 x 3 3/4 inches receipts.

These purchases were made while Elvis' was preparing for his 1968 television special.

$400 - 500

B258 RECEIPT AND INVOICE FOR FIREWORKS AND CATERING ON NEW YEAR'S EVE, 1965

One page typed receipt dated January 4, 1966 on Monte's Catering Service letterhead addressed to Elvis Presley at Graceland. The bill is for catering at the Manhattan Club on New Year's Eve and totals $455.00. Invoice dated December 31, 1965 from Atomic Fireworks, Inc. addressed to Vernon

Presley. Attached is a one page order form with carbon copy. 143 dozen fireworks were ordered totaling $363.00. 11 x 8 1/2 inches letter. 11 8 1/2 inches invoice. 16 3/4 x 10 3/4 invoice order form.

Elvis celebrated New Year's Eve 1965 at the Manhattan Club with over 100 of his friends. It was catered by Monte's who catered many of Elvis' events. Willie Mitchell was the band leader and other entertainers included the Guillotines and Vaneese Starks who sang "Hound Dog."

$750 - 850

B259 ELVIS PRESLEY-MGM ANNIVERSARY BIO

A 21 page typed promotional document commemorating Elvis' 10th anniversary with MGM, titled "'Jailhouse to Spinout' - The MGM Anniversary Story of Elvis Presley." With note handwritten in black ink on the front page stating that this is a copy of the original and is still awaiting corrections. Two Elvis Presley Photo Folios, two pages and ten pages. Pictures are black and white. Back cover advertises "Jailhouse Rock." 11 x 8 1/2 inches.

This press release traces the story of Elvis Presley's musical and film career. Most likely written by the Colonel, it includes a fabricated biography of him. Page one reads, "Webster's Unabridged Dictionary defines 'phenomenon' as '...a rare fact or event, or one of especial or unique significance... an extraordinary or remarkable person.' Show business can define 'phenomenon' as: Elvis Presley."

$450 - 500

left: B269   above: B261

B260 ELVIS PRESLEY'S BLACK JACKET WITH RED LEATHER POCKET FLAPS

Black, long sleeved jacket with a pointed collar. There are two inside pockets with a yellow, brown, and white geometric designed lining. The front has two pocket flaps that are red with leather material. Each flap has a fabric covered black button. There are six buttons on each sleeve. On the back is a "kick" panel with a red leather piece, and two fabric covered black buttons.

This jacket belonged to Elvis' casual wardrobe. Elvis loved to dress differently than his peers, and would often start trends of his own. He loved flashy, flamboyant clothing that would set him apart for others.

$8,000 - 10,000

B261 ELVIS PRESLEY'S GREEN SHIRT

Green button-down shirt with long, full sleeves. Cuff is elastic with ruffle.

In the late 1960's and early 1970s, Elvis wore this shirt while lounging around. This style shirt was a staple of Elvis' wardrobe, so much so, that he would order several at a time in an array of colors.

$2,000 - 3,000

B262 ELVIS PRESLEY'S BLUE SHIRT

One "electric" blue long-sleeved moderate-weight polyester casual shirt with elastic cuffs and long pointed collar. Four buttons with raised squares in center of each one. Lapel stitching down front of each front panel. Tag reads "I C Costume Co., Hollywood, California."

One of the casual shirts with puffy sleeves that Elvis wore in the late 1960s or early 1970s. Bill Belew designed the costumes for Elvis' '68 Special. After that, Elvis hired him to design most of his personal clothing.

$2,000 - 3,000

B263 BROWN JACKET AND PANTS

Brown wool blend jacket and pants with tags from "I.C. Costume Co. Hollywood, California." Lined with brown satin and each with a brown and turquoise flower design. Jacket has pointed collar.

This suit was part of Elvis' late Sixties casual wardrobe.

$5,000 - 7,000

B264 ELVIS PRESLEY'S PILLOW CASE, AND PAJAMA SET

One red satin pillow case with the initials E P embroidered in white. One pair of Elvis' black satin-like PJ's with red trim around neck, arms and leg openings. Top is long sleeved, and the bottom is ankle length. Pocket on left breast side. 38 x 21 inches This was during the time Linda Thompson and Elvis were living together.

$14,000 - 16,000

B265 ELVIS' BLACK SHIRT

One long sleeve black button-up shirt. With ruffles and a pointed color. This style of shirt was a common part of Elvis' late Sixties casual wardrobe. He liked them so much that he would order them in large quantities of different colored shirts.

$2,000 - 3,000

B264
B266

B266 ELVIS PRESLEY'S RED COAT WITH BLACK FUR CAPE

One heavy-weight wool-blend red coat, fully lined with red satin. Made by International. Detachable black fur cape attaches at the high collar. Black fur also trims the collar, 3 buttons, 2 fake pockets, and cuffs. Length is just below the knee.

The design of Elvis' casual clothing imitated the style of his performance clothing--leaning toward a sense of flamboyancy and even many caped items. Elvis wore this coat for casual occasions during 1974-75.

$10,000 - 12,000

B267 ELVIS' CREAM-COLORED SHIRT

One long sleeve button-up cream-colored shirt. Tag reading "I.C. Costume Co. Hollywood, Calif." Ruffled shirt with a pointed collar.

This style of shirt was a common part of Elvis' late Sixties casual wardrobe. He liked them so much that he would order them in large quantities of different colored shirts.

$2,000 - 3,000

B268 ARTWORK FOR COVER OF "CLEAN UP YOUR OWN BACK YARD"

Two color proofs of photograph of Elvis for cover of single. Handwritten notes comment on the portions of photograph to be fixed by color separator; for example, "show highlights in eyes," "flesh too dark see Ekta," "shirt color too dark." 19 x 9 1/2 inches.

In August 1968, Elvis recorded "Clean Up Your Own Back Yard" for the movie "The Trouble with Girls." Billy Young and Mac Davis wrote the song. The single was released in June 1969.

$500 - 750

B269 IN THE GHETTO SHEET MUSIC AND SINGLE

Dated April 21, 1969, on "RCA News" letterhead/stationery announcing the release of a new single by Elvis Presley--"In the Ghetto" and "Any Day Now" Blue and white 6-page sheet music for "In the Ghetto" Single of "In the Ghetto" / "Any Day Now." 11 x 8 1/2 inches letter. 12 x 9 inches sheet music.

Elvis decided to do some recording in Memphis rather than Nashville. After making arrangements with RCA, they set up sessions at Chips Moman's American Studio on Thomas Street. While at the studio, he recorded about 20 songs, including "In the Ghetto" and "Mama Liked the Roses."

$600 - 700

B270 SLICK FOR "IF I CAN DREAM"

Black-and-white slick for single of "If I Can Dream" on one side and "Edge of Reality" on the other. 17 1/8 x 11 1/8 inches.

Elvis recorded "If I Can Dream" in Burbank on June 23, 1968 and "Edge of Reality" (from the film Live a Little, Love a Little) on March 7, 1968. A single of the two songs was released in November 1968.

$600 - 800

B268   B270

B271 RCA NEWS RELEASE ANNOUNCING ELVIS PRESLEY'S GOLD RECORD AWARD FOR "HOW GREAT THOU ART" AND ONE ACETATE OF "HOW GREAT THOU ART"

Original RCA news release, typed on RCA News letterhead, dated March 19, 1968. Release begins, "ELVIS PRESLEY AWARDED GOLD RECORD FOR "HOW GREAT THOU ART". Acetate of "How Great

Thou Art." Recording is in a plain white sleeve. 11 x 8 1/2 inches Press Release.

Elvis recorded "How Great Thou Art" on May 25, 1966, at RCA's Nashville studio. A live version from the 1974 album "Elvis Recorded Live on Stage in Memphis" won him his third and final Grammy Award for Best Inspirational Performance.

$450 - 500

B272 SONGS HELD IN FILE

Memo dated 12/13/68, signed by Charlie Hodge, lists "Songs Held in File as Per Elvis' Request." Songs included Eddie Rabbitt's "Inherit the Wind," Otis Blackwell's "You've Got Everything," and "Going Back to Memphis." Photograph included. 11 x 8 1/2 inches.

Hill and Range sent large amounts of songs to Elvis to consider singing and recording. These were just a few of the considerations that he kept for reference.

$600 - 750

B273 BLACK AND WHITE PROOFS FOR ELVIS ALBUM COVERS

Original black and white proofs for four Elvis albums including: "His Hand in Mine," "Milky White Way/Swing Down Sweet Chariot," "Joshua Fit the Battle/Known Only to Him," and "Frankie and Johnny." 10 x 8. "

Elvis always loved gospel music, and "His Hand in Mine" was his first gospel album. It earned a RIAA Gold Record on April 9, 1969 and had a 20-week stay on "Billboard's" Top LP's. "Frankie and Johnny," the soundtrack to Elvis' 1966 movie, had a 19-week stay on "Billboard's" Top LP's.

$1,400 - 1,600

B274 "IN THE GHETTO" MUSICAL ARRANGE-MENT

Original instrument charts and sheet music for "In the Ghetto," encased in large black folder. Typed receipt dated August 18, 1969. For payment of $725 from Elvis Presley to Glen Spreen in Memphis for arrangements of "Gentle on My Mind," "Only the Strong Survive," "Suspicious Minds," "In the Ghetto," "Movin' On," and "Any Day Now." Statement handwritten in blue ink from Bobby Shew of Bobby Morris Orchestra to Tom Diskin in care of Elvis Presley, dated August 3, 1969 for payment of $104.65 for transposing parts from "In the Ghetto" for use in concert. 14 x 12 inches "In the Ghetto" folder. 8 1/2 x 5 1/2 inches Spreen receipt. 8 x 5 inches Morris receipt.

Elvis first recorded the Mac Davis-penned "In the Ghetto" during January of 1969, during an extremely fruitful series of recording sessions at American Studios in Memphis. Released as a single in April, 1969, the song peaked at #3 on the billboard pop chart. Glen Spreen was a saxophone player and one time member of the Memphis Horns. He played on Elvis' 1969 sessions at American, and all of the songs he is being paid for arrangements of were recorded during those sessions. Bobby Morris was Elvis' musical conductor for his International Hotel shows and subsequent concert tours.

$2,500 - 3,000

B275 PLAY DATES FOR "LIVE A LITTLE, LOVE A LITTLE"

A one-sheet listing, dated 10/14/68, of Cities, Theatres, and Dates that "Live a Little, Love a Little" was scheduled to play during the months of September, October, and November of 1968. Photograph included. Eight-page black-and-white MGM Pressbook for "Live a Little, Love a Little." 11 3/4 x 8 1/2 inches listing. 17 x 12 1/4 inches pressbook.

The Colonel incorporated block bookings into the process when Elvis' movies were released. Rather than open in large markets and then move to smaller ones, they would hit quite a few markets from the very beginning where fans could see them immediately.

$200 - 250

B276 ACETATE OF "HEY JUDE" AND "SOMETHING"

Acetate of Elvis Presley singing, "Hey Jude," recorded in February 1969 in Memphis, and "Something," recorded in August, 1970 in Las Vegas. In original envelope from Tansco, "...a 'Sound' Investment." 12 inch diameter acetate. 12 1/8 x 12 1/8 inches envelope.

"Hey Jude" and "Something" were both Beatles songs. "Hey Jude" was one of the Beatles' biggest hits. Elvis sometimes sang these songs during his concerts. He sang "Something" during his TV special, "Aloha from Hawaii."

$650 - 750

B277 "STAY AWAY JOE" ACETATE

Summary of Elvis Presley Recording Session for January 15-16, 1968, to record songs for "Stay Away Joe." Schedule lists musicians, singers, others present, songs recorded, and cost apportions to RCA and MGM. "Stay Away Joe" premier program, compliments of Elvis and the Colonel. Gray and red two-page program lists cast and credits for the MGM film. Black-and-white photos of Elvis and other cast members. 33 /13 rpm vinyl of radio program promotional for "Stay Away Joe" 45 rpm acetate of "Stay Away Joe." 11 x 8 1/2 inches schedule. 11 1/4 x 7 inches program.

Elvis recorded new tracks for "Stay Away Joe" in Nashville on January 15-16; this included 30 takes of "Goin' Home." He also did some other recording for RCA, including Jerry Reed's "U.S. Male." This took place two weeks before Lisa Marie was born on February 1, 1968.

$2,000 - 2,500

B278 No Lot

B279 RCA PRESS RELEASE REGARDING THE RELEASE OF ELVIS PRESLEY'S "SUSPICIOUS MINDS" AND SINGLE

Two-page RCA press release dated August 25, 1969 on "RCA News" letterhead. Announces the release of Elvis Presley's "Suspicious Minds." Discusses the success of Elvis's recent engagement at the International Hotel Las Vegas. Press release also mentions the success of Elvis' records, the "Elvis TV Special," and his films. "Suspicious Minds" single included. "Suspicious Minds" single included in original sleeve. Other side is "You'll Think of Me." 11 x 8 1/2 inches press release, 7 x 7 inches single

The press release quotes Robert Hilburn of the "Los Angeles Times" who described Elvis as, "the man who more than any other has reshaped pop music and influenced a generation of musicians in the process." "Suspicious Minds" was Elvis last song to reach number one on "Billboard's" Top 100.

$550 - 650

B280 ELVIS AND THE COLONEL CHRISTMAS CARD ARTWORK

Mock-up of Elvis and the Colonel Christmas Card—photo of the Colonel dressed as Santa Claus, standing with Elvis 17 x 14 inches.

This photo was taken on the set of Elvis' 1961 film "Wild in the Country."

$2,500 - 3,000

B281 BIRTHDAY TELEGRAM FROM COLONEL PARKER TO ELVIS PRESLEY

Western Union telegram dated January 8, 1963. The Colonel wishes Elvis a happy birthday. 5 x 7 7/8 inches.

This telegram is from Elvis' 28th birthday. The Colonel writes "script on way...be on lookout" in reference to the film "Fun in Acapulco."

$400 - 500

B282 INVOICE FOR ELVIS PRESLEY EASTER POSTCARDS AND MISPRINTED SAMPLES

Invoice dated April 5, 1967, from All Star Shows to Harry Jenkins, RCA Victor Record Division. "As per letter of agreement dated November 2, 1966, first payment . . . for the half-million 1967 Easter cards and 300,000 . . . four-color photos for "Double Trouble." Amount: $50,000. Included with the invoice are two postcards--one with the photo overprinted and the other with the greeting on the reverse side misprinted. 11 x 8 1/2 inches invoice. 5 1/2 x 3 1/2 inches postcards.

"Double Trouble" opened nationally on April 5, the same day as this invoice.

$750 - 850

B283 ELVIS EASTER SPECIAL ACETATE

Acetate of an Elvis Easter radio program from 1962. 12 x 12 inches.

The label on this acetate is for station "KPOI" in Honolulu.

$400 - 500

B280

B284 ELVIS PRESLEY'S 1967 CHRISTMAS RADIO PROGRAM BINDER

Cream leather binder with gold engraving, "Record Album." Inside album are 38 acetate pages, eight scrapbook pages, and a pouch containing various ads, artwork, mock-ups and memorabilia related to Elvis Presley's 1967 Christmas radio program. Items include: artwork mock-up for "Special Radio Program," several final prints of ads to appear in magazines and newspapers, newspaper clippings of ad, Elvis postcard, Elvis 1968 wallet calendar, one color and one black and white single record jacket for "Season's Greetings from Elvis," one-page yellow fan bulletin from E.P.F.C.S.C, two green Christmas flyers, one red Christmas flyer, six page fan newsletter from the "Hound Dogs" EPFC in Portland, Oregon, copy of a schedule of airing radio programs in Tennessee, "Elvis Presley Christmas Special" brochure, Luce Press Clipping booklet, color "Give Elvis for Christmas" poster, newspaper article clippings, and articles from "Billboard," "Broadcasting," and "Cash Box." Pouch contains one original and one copy of a seven-page, typewritten "Elvis Presley Program of Sacred Songs" to be aired October 15, 1967. Has handwritten notes and corrections. Also in pouch is envelope with red and green printing, "ELVIS This is Your Complete Christmas Program for 1967." Envelope is still sealed and contains the 1967 Christmas Program items that were sent to radio stations. 15 x 12 3/4 inches Record Album. 11 x 8 1/2 inches "...Sacred Songs" 9 x 9 inches envelope

This Christmas program was a Christmas present of sorts to Elvis fans everywhere from Elvis and the Colonel. It was broadcast across the country on December 3 and 10, 1967. About 3,000 radio stations broadcast the program and were paid anywhere between $25 and $500 for a 30-minute segment. True to Elvis' generous nature, a one-minute spot was left at the end of the program for a public service announcement "for the charity of their choice."

$3,000 - 5,000

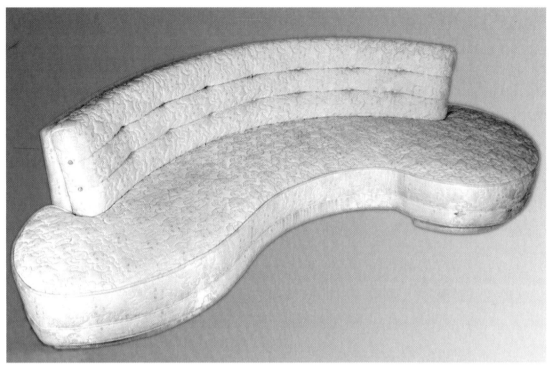

jumpsuits of the seventies, Elvis always forged his own distinctive and flashy fashion. This armoire was in his bedroom from 1974 until the time of his death.

$7,000 - 9,000

B289 JOHN F. KENNEDY BUST

Bronze bust of President John F. Kennedy on black base. 4 inches high x 5 1/4 inches wide x 5 1/2 deep base. 13 inches high x 11 inches deep x 7 1/2 inches wide bust

This bust was given as a gift to Colonel Parker, a man known for his connections in high places.

$2,000 - 3,000

B290 GRACELAND BAR WITH STOOLS

Wood bar with white sliding shelf panels. With three accompanying stools.

This bar was kept at Graceland. Elvis didn't drink but kept liquor in the house to entertain guests. Elvis preferred Mountain Valley Mineral Water and Pepsi.

$8,000 - 10,000

B285 LOVE SEAT

One armless sectional love seat with a gold and white geometric pattern. 16" high seat X 29" high back x 108" long.

This item was used in Elvis' Chino Canyon Road home in Palm Springs in the late Sixties.

$4,000 - 6,000

B286 KING AND QUEEN STATUES

Two black fiberglass and plastic sculptures of "King and Queen" chess pieces. 68 x36 inches "king" statue 61 x 31 inches "queen" statue.

These pieces were used as planters in the back yard at Graceland, and were bought by Elvis' girl-friend Linda Thompson at Haas Furniture in Memphis on July 25, 1974.

$1,000 - 1,500

B287 EXERCISE BIKE

One gold stationary bicycle.

This bike was used at Graceland. After having medical problems in the mid-Seventies, Elvis' personal physician Dr. Dean Nichopoulos introduced Elvis to racquetball and Elvis had a court built at Graceland. The racquetball building housed other exercise equipment as well, and this stationary bike may have been kept there. Certainly it is a remnant of Elvis' mid-Seventies exercise kick that also coincided with his most intense interest in karate.

$4,000 - 6,000

B288 ELVIS PRESLEY'S ARMOIRE WARDROBE

Indisputably, Elvis was known for his clothes. From the black pants with a pink stripe down the side in the fifties, to the black leather suit from the "68 Special," to the studded and caped

B285
B286

196

B291 LETTER REGARDING LOST GULF OIL CARD

Dated March 25, 1969, on "Gulf Oil Company" letterhead to Elvis Presley. Envelope included. 11 x 8 1/2 inches letter 4 1/4 x 9 1/2 inches envelope.

This letter regards the loss of Elvis' card and a new one being issued.

$350 - 400

B292 GULF TRAVEL CARD

White, red and blue plastic credit card with illustration of a car, boat and plane, with raised lettering "Elvis Presley." 2 1/8 x 3 3/8 inches.

With original mailing envelope postmarked March 28, 1969.

$3,000 - 3,500

B293 UNION 76 GOLD CARD

White, orange and blue plastic credit card with raised lettering "Mr. Elvis Presley." 2 1/8 x 3 3/8"

Card dated 1962.　　$3,000 - 3,500

B294 SHELL OIL CARD

White, gold and turquoise plastic credit card with raised lettering "Elvis Presley." 2 1/8 x 3 3/8 inches.

With original mailing envelope postmarked April 2, 1969.

$3,000 - 3,500

B295 ELVIS PRESLEY'S VEHICLE AND MOTORCYCLE INSURANCE POLICY WITH INVOICE, AND CHECK

Ten page insurance policy, on "Crump London Underwriters Inc" certificate-style letterhead, naming Elvis Presley and Vernon Presley as policy

holders for 18 vehicles. Invoice stapled to front of policy including handwritten notes documenting payment of $2805.00 paid annually, dated December 22, 1969. Original green check written on

B296 Elvis' Jetstar is similar to the one pictured.

Elvis Presley Payroll & Expense Fund for the amount of $21,103.32 paid to E. H. Crump Co., Insurance. 3 7/8 x 7 3/8 inches Invoice. 14 x 8 1/2 inches Policy. 3 x 8 1/4 inches check.

Elvis was charges $150 per vehicle and motorcycle, and $50 for one dressing room trailer.

$1,800 - 2,000

B296 TWO JETSTAR SNOWMOBILES, JETSTAR OWNER'S MANUAL, JETSTAR OPERATIONAL MATERIALS, AND JETSTAR PATCHES

Jetstar owner's manuel in an orange binder; Jetstar price list, June 1, 1969; Jetstar promotional and inventory materials, Champion (2) spark plugs snowmobile tips brochures, (2) orange trapezoid-shaped patches with white border and black/white embroidered logo. Two red Jetstar Snowmobiles which converts from skis to wheels. 2 5/8 x 3 inches Patches. 8 1/2 x 5 1/2 inches Snowmobile tips. 11 1/2 x 9 1/8 inches Promo/Inv. Price. 11 1/2 x 9 1/8inches Binder.

Elvis loved snowmobiles, and since Memphis rarely had snow he had wheels put on so they could be driven on the grass at Graceland.

$14,000 - 16,000

B297 ELVIS PRESLEY'S PHILLIPS 66 CREDIT CARD

Letter dated March 21, 1969 to Mr. Elvis A. Presley from Phillips Petroleum Company. White and Gold plastic card with raised gold lettering in paper card holder. 11 x 7 1/4 inches letter. 2 1/4 x 3 1/2 inches card. 8 1/2 x 3 1/2 inches card holder. 4 x 7 3/4 inches envelope.

The letter from Phillips Petroleum states that they have enclosed a new credit card to replace the one Elvis had reported as lost.

$2,500 - 3,000

B298 CHECKS SIGNED BY ELVIS PRESLEY FOR ASPEN TRIP

Three checks written on E.A. Presley account to Tom's Market ($46.89) on Jan. 31, 1969; Sunland Sports Lodge ($633.17) on Jan. 24, 1969; and Aspen TV and Appl ($177.48) on Jan. 25, 1969; all signed by E. A. Presley. Two checks written on National Bank of Commerce (NBC) in Memphis account to Aspen TV and Appl. ($52) on Jan. 31, 1969 and Alpine Triumph ($1,082.53) on Feb. 1, 1969; both signed by E. A. Presley. 3 1/8 x 8 1/4 inches E.A. Presley checks. 2 1/2 x 6 1/4 inches NBC checks.

On January 24, 1969, Elvis took Priscilla, Lisa Marie, and some of the entourage to Aspen, Colorado, for a ski vacation. The celebration of Lisa Marie's first birthday took place there on February 1. The vacation lasted until mid-February.

$6,000 - 8,000

B299 ELVIS PRESLEY DAILY TRAVEL EXPENSE

Reports—May 1968 Five Daily Travel Expense Account Forms with attached receipts for May 1, 4-5, 16-17, 18-19 and 20-21. Photograph included. 11 x 8 1/2 inches account forms.

May 1 was Elvis and Priscilla's first wedding anniversary and the "May 4-5" expense reports lists an "anniversary cake for Elvis and Priscilla." On May 18, Elvis and Priscilla flew to Hawaii and the expense report for this day lists baby food for daughter Lisa Marie, who was three months old at the time.

$3,000 - 3,500

B300 CHECK FOR RANCH DOWN PAYMENT AND LISTING OF RANCH HORSES AND EQUIPMENT

Green check dated Feb. 9, 1967 from the account E.A. Presley. Made out to Jack Adams for $5,000 and signed by E. A. Presley. Endorsed on back by Jack Adams. Vernon's three-page typed list of fees for horses, equipment, feed, and western clothes for the Circle G Ranch in Mississippi. Attached adding machine receipt totals $25,202.99. 3 x 8 1/8 inches

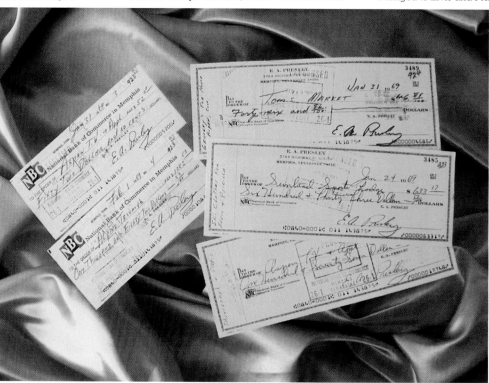

B298

check. 11 x 8 1/2 inches listing.

The check Elvis wrote to Adams was "earnest money towards purchase of Twinkletown Farms (all cattle, equipment as stated in contract)." Elvis changed the name of the ranch to the Circle G.

$3,000 - 3,500

B301 INSURANCE POLICY ON OFFICE AREA OF GRACELAND

United States Fidelity and Guaranty Company insurance policy dated 5/6//68 for Vernon Elvis Presley and Elvis Aron Presley. $8,000 insurance on office area of home at 3760 Highway 51S, for structure and contents; premium $280. Change endorsement on 6/30/68 included, with name of insureds changed to Elvis and Priscilla Presley. Signed by Jack Parker of the E. H. Crump & Company. Check # 4907 to "E.H. Crump & Co." for $280; signed by Vernon Presley. 10 3/4 x 8 1/2 inches policy. 3 1/8 x 8 1/4 inches check.

The policy carried a three-year premium for the period 6/12/68 to 6/12/71.

$1,600 - 1,800

B302 BOOK JACKET FROM "THE ELVIS PRESLEY STORY"

Book jacket from "The Elvis Presley Story," written by James Gregory with an introduction by Dick Clark. Back cover features a picture of Elvis in a red shirt on a red background and is signed by James Gregory, the book's editor, to Col. Tom Parker. The cost of the book was 35 cents. 6 1/2 x 9 inches.

Elvis Presley is one of the most written about people in popular music, however, few books were actually written during his lifetime. This is a color proof of a book jacket for one of the earlier Elvis books.

$1,200 - 1,400

B303 CIRCLE G "FOR SALE" SIGN AND AMENDMENT TO CONTRACT FOR SALE OF LAND

Contract amendment dated April 18, 1969, between Elvis Presley and North Mississippi Gun Club. Original agreement made March 21, 1969, for a total price of $440,100 for a 163-acre tract of land. Amendment added two paragraphs: One change states: "North Mississippi Gun Club, Inc., shall not publicly exploit the fact that it has a contract for the purchase of land owned by Elvis A. Presley, but it shall have the right to exploit the fact that it has a contract for . . . Circle G. Ranch." The other paragraph states the deadline for closing this agreement as May 5, 1969; otherwise the gun club would be in default. Contract amendment signed by Vernon E. Presley (power of attorney) and Lou McClellan (president of the gun club). Envelope included (not addressed but with a 6-cent stamp). Metal sign: white with red and black lettering on black metal frame. "For Sale. 163 Acre Ranch. Charles H. Davis. Memphis JA5-1325. Shown by Appointment." 14 x 8 1/2 inches contract. 4 x 9 1/2 inches envelope. 45 x 31 inches sign.

Elvis decided to sell the Circle G Ranch after it became a drain on him financially. This contract with the Mississippi Gun Club did not transpire.

$2,000 - 2,500

B304 ELVIS AT THE RODEO

Press Release on Elvis Presley's appearances at Houston Livestock Show and Rodeo. October 23, 1969, press release from the Public Relations Department of Lloyd Gregory & Associates in Houston. The 2-page release announces the appearances of Elvis at the 38th Annual "America's Wildest Rodeo" on February 27, 28, and March 1, 1970. Photograph included. Gold badge for Colonel Tom Parker for the 1970 Houston Livestock Show and Rodeo. "H" in Houston is wearing a cowboy hat and boots.

B305   B304

Check on E.A. Presley account to Astroworld Hotel, dated Feb. 2, 1970 in the amount of $2,042.53. 11 x 8 1/2" press release. 1 1/4 x 1/3/4" badge. 3 1/8 x 8 1/4" check.

The Houston show took place in the Astrodome. Acts appearing at the Houston Livestock Show and Rodeo after Elvis included Charley Pride and Bobby Goldsboro.

$2,000 - 2,500

B305 IMPERIALS CONTRACT FOR HOUSTON ASTRODOME

American Guild of Variety Artists contract, dated November 24, 1969. Contract between Elvis Presley and the vocal quartet the Imperials for a one-week engagement at the Houston Livestock & Rodeo at the Houston Astrodome. Contract runs from February 24 - March 1, 1970 and stipulates a flat fee of $3,750. Signed in blue ink by Elvis Presley and Joe Moscheo II of the Imperials. Photograph included. 14 x 8 1/2 inches.

The Imperials were a gospel quartet who backed Elvis in concert from 1969 to 1971. At one time Jake Hess was a member of the Imperials. Hess had been in the Statesmen, Elvis' favorite singing group as a teenager, and is said to have been a primary influence on Elvis' singing style. The Houston Livestock Show was Elvis' first post-Vegas performance, and the first time he had performed in front of a live audience outside of Las Vegas or a television studio in almost a decade.

$5,500 - 6,500

B306 CHECK FOR COMMISSIONED PORTRAIT OF ELVIS PRESLEY

Light green check from the account of E. A. Presley dated March 2, 1969 made out to Ralph Wolfe Cowan for $4,000. Signed by Elvis Presley. Photograph included. 3 x 8 1/4 inches.

There have been thousands of artist renderings of Elvis Presley, however, Ralph Cowan's is the only commissioned portrait of Elvis. Elvis never posed for Cowan, although they did meet on several occasions. The result is a striking life-size portrait of a slender Elvis wearing white and standing among billowing clouds. When Elvis went to pick up the portrait it was still wet. Although Cowan still needed to make some finishing touches, Elvis loved it exactly as it was and did not want any changes made. The portrait is housed in the trophy room at Graceland.

$3,000 - 3,500

B307 FOLDER WITH CONTRACT AND LETTERS BETWEEN QUASAR AND ALL STAR SHOWS

Seventeen-page folder containing copy of contract dated November 28, 1972, between All Star Shows and Quasar Industries in Hackensack, New Jersey. Provisions included two Sales Promotional Androids, one Support Robot, and two Robot Masters. Used in Las Vegas and in Hawaii shows. Copies of correspondence between Quasar and the Colonel. Quasar 20-page sales promotional booklet, with photos of robots, also included. Photograph included. 11 1/2 x 9 inches folder. 8 5/8 x 11 1/4 inches Quasar promo booklet.

The robots were just another gimmick that the Colonel used for the Las Vegas and Hawaii shows to promote Elvis.

$1,000 - 1,300

B308 NEWSPAPERS FROM ELVIS' CALIFORNIA HOME

Six copies of the Santa Monica, California, newspaper World Tribune, from May 6, 1973; June 3, June 21, June 24, June 28, and July 1, 1974. Newspapers are addressed to Elvis A. Presley, 144 Monovale Dr., Beverly Hills, CA 90210.

Highlights of the newspapers concentrate on President Ikeda of Japan on his General Meeting speech at the San Diego/Mexico Convention.

$600 - 800

B308

B309 ELVIS PRESLEY TELEPHONE CARDS AND BILLS

1963 and 1964 Bell System Credit Cards issued to

Elvis Presley. 1963 card on white, yellow and brown card stock, 1964 card on white, green and blue card stock, both with original mailing envelopes. Four Southern Bell Telephone and Telegraph Co. bill stubs dated August 1 and August 17, 1963. 3 1/2 x 7 inches credit cards. 3 1/2 x 3 1/2 inches bill stub.

These items were sent to Elvis at Graceland.

$1,800 - 2,000

B310 ELVIS PRESLEY'S SCREEN ACTOR'S GUILD EARNINGS, CLASSIFICATIONS, AND RECEIPTS FROM AMERICAN GUILD OF VARIETY ARTISTS AND SCREEN ACTORS GUILD

Elvis Presley's Screen Actor's Guild Earnings and Classifications by year from the years 1969, 1970, and 1971; printed with Elvis Presley's name c/o Goldberg-Morris in Beverly Hills. Original envelope is included. Receipt from the Screen Actors Guild, Inc., dated June 4, 1978, for dues from May 1 through November 1, 1970. Total amount due is $125.00. Bill from the American Guild of Variety Artists, paid on February 8, 1976, for dues through August 1, 1977. Total amount due is $240.00 Original envelope is included. Photograph included. 3 1/2 x 6 1/4 inches SAG Card. 3 3/4 x 6 3/4 inches Envelope. 3 1/2 x 6 inches Screen Actors. 3 1/2 x 7 inches American Guild. 4 x 7 1/2 inches Envelope.

Elvis' last feature film was "Change of Habit" in 1969. The documentary, "Elvis -That's The Way It Is" was released in 1970. Elvis had no releases during 1971, making it the first year in a decade in which Elvis did not release any films. In 1969 and 1970 Elvis was listed as a Class 2 by the Screen Actor's Guild, meaning he made between $50,000 and $100,000. In 1971 he dropped to Class 9, meaning he made less than $2,500.

$700 - 900

B311 INVOICE FOR GRAND PIANO

Invoice dated December 20, 1967, from Jack Marshall Music Co. in Memphis for 1 Kimball Grand Piano. Invoice is billed to Elvis Presley, to Vernon's attention, for $4,264. Photograph included. 7 1/4 x 8 1/2 inches.

Elvis loved to play piano and was gifted in that he could play by ear. After Elvis purchased this piano, Priscilla had it gold-leafed as a gift for him; however, he disliked the sound after that so he gave it to his aunt, who was a minister, for her church. The church, though, was in a trailer, so the piano wouldn't fit. She traded it in at a local mall for one that would. A gentleman purchased the piano and contacted Graceland in 1982, where it was on display until the early 90s. The piano now graces the Country Music Hall of Fame in Nashville.

$800 - 1,000

B312 ELVIS PRESLEY MUSIC RECEIPT

Receipt from Jack Marshall Music Co. in Memphis, dated June 7, 1967 and made out to Elvis Presley. Bill totaling $967.75 with note hand-written in black ink thanking Elvis for his business. Original check included signed by Vernon Presley. 6 5/8 x 5 7/8 inches receipt. 3 x 8 1/4 inches check .

This receipt is for a piano for Elvis' house at the Circle G Ranch.

$150 - 200

B313 CATERING BILL

Invoice dated 8/27/68 from Michelson's Catering Service, Inc. in Sun Valley, California. Billed to Elvis at Goldwyn Studios. Order is for 125 assorted hors d'oeuvres and seafood bar buffet services for a total bill of $577.50. Photograph included. 8 1/2 x 8 1/2 inches.

Whenever a film finished its shooting schedule, it was common to host a Wrap Party. This one was likely for the wrap-up of "Charro." Elvis had already returned home on August 25.

$500 - 550

B311

B315
B312

B314 ELVIS PRESLEY'S FIREWORKS INVOICE FOR NEW YEAR'S EVE 1969

Invoice to Elvis Presley at 3764 Highway 51 South from Atomic Fireworks of West Memphis, Arkansas. Invoice dated January 13, 1970 is for a delivery on December 30, 1969 and totals $612.41. Yellow itemized carbon copy invoice to Elvis Presley dated December 31, 1969 from Atomic Fireworks, Inc. Invoice totals $348 minus a 50% and a 10% discount leaving a total of $256.60. Signed by Marvin Gambill. White copy of an Atomic Fireworks Price List and Order Blank addressed to Elvis Presley. List is dated December 30, 1969 and totals $1012.92 minus a 50% and a 10% discount leaving a total of $455.81. Also signed by Marvin Gambill. 11 x 8 1/2 inches invoice. 10 1/4 x 8 1/2 inches yellow carbon invoice. 18 1/8 x 11 price list.

Elvis has a New Year's Eve party at T.J.'s. The entertainment included Ronnie Milsapp, Flash and the Board of Directors, and songwriter Mark James singing his song "Suspicious Minds."

$400 - 500

B315 ELVIS PRESLEY'S NOTICE OF RIGHT OF RESCISSION

Carbon copy of a Notice of Right of Rescission dated July 8, 1972 addressed to Elvis Presley at 1174 Hillcrest, Beverly Hills.

Rescission from Broadway Home Improvement Center informed Elvis that his transaction of a wrought iron fence "may result in a lien, mortgage, or other security interest" on his home. Original signature in blue ink by Elvis Presley and Priscilla Presley. Photograph included. 11 x 8 1/2 inches.

It is common to draw up a document like this when having construction work done, however, neither the customer nor the fence in this case were common. With fans that gathered outside of his homes on a regular basis, a fence was not a luxury, but a necessity. For privacy and for safety, Elvis had fences around all his homes.

$4,000 - 5,000

B316 INVOICE FROM THE MEMPHIS POLICE DEPARTMENT

Invoice for services rendered. Typewritten invoice from the Memphis Police Department to Elvis, dated January 2, 1969. Invoice is for services of four police officers for protection during the December 31st, New Year's Eve party at the Thunderbird Lounge. Photograph included. 11 x 8 1/2 inches.

Elvis paid three thousand dollars to rent the Thunderbird Lounge, which was located in the lobby of th Shelbourne Towers Apartments, for a New Year's Eve party. He bought his own security, and hired his own entertainment, which for that night was the Short Cuts, Billy Lee Riley, Flash and the Board of Directors, and B.J. Thomas. The party was by invitation only and was the talk of the town. However, the event was short since Elvis arrived late and left early: When he left everyone else followed.

$400 - 600

B317 MOUNTAIN VALLEY MINERAL WATER WITH STATEMENT

One case and three individual bottles of Mountain Valley Mineral Water. Statement dated February 1968 addressed to Mr. Elvis Presley at 1174 North Hillcrest Road, Beverly Hills, California. The statement is from Mountain Valley Mineral Water in Chicago, Illinois for a purchase in the amount of $78.75. 7 x 5 7/8 inches statement .

Mountain Valley was Elvis' preferred brand of mineral water. He often carried a bottle with him on stage for his live performances.

$1,400 - 1,600

B318 RECEIPTS FROM BAHAMA TRIP

Original invoice, typewritten from Bahamas Tourist Company Ltd., dated October 31, 1969, for Mr. &

Mrs. Elvis Presley and Party of eight. Bill is for two air conditioned Cadillacs and one Volkswagon Bus for round-trip transportation from airport to hotel on October 22, 1969, and one overseas call. Total bill is $90.00. A copy of the hotel bill from Paradise Island Hotel & Villas for $1717.66, signed by Elvis. Original green check written on the Elvis Presley Payroll & Expense Fund dated November 10, 1969, and signed by Vernon Presley. Amount of check is for $2,863.50, and paid to the order of Paradise Island

Hotel & Villas. Photograph included. 11 x 8 1/2 inches Invoice. 8 1/2 x 7 1/2 inches Hotel bill. 3 x 8 1/4 inches Check .

After Elvis' first Las Vegas engagement, the International Hotel gave him a trip to Hawaii for eight people. He had just finished "Change of Habit", and had no pending movies. Elvis wanted to go to Europe, and had obtained passports to do so. However, Colonel Parker had vetoed the plans and they went to the Bahamas instead. Elvis and

his guests stayed on Paradise Island, but remained in doors most of the time due to the presence of a hurricane during their trip. $450 - 600

B319 INVOICE FOR ELVIS PRESLEY WARDROBE FROM BILL BELEW

Handwritten invoice for "Designer's fee for wardrobe for Elvis nite club act International Hotel." Large blue Bill Belew logo with address handwritten below. Invoice totals $500. Original light green check from the payroll of Elvis Presley made out to Bill Belew for $500. Dated September 23, 1969 and signed by Vernon Presley. Photograph included. 4 1/2 x 5 7/8 inches invoice. 3 1/8 x 8 1/4 inches check.

In Las Vegas, September 1969, Elvis returned to the stage after a seven year absence. Bill Belew, with Elvis' direction, designed a modified gi for his stage wardrobe. The result was, as James Kingsley of the "Commercial Appeal" called it, the "karate tuxedo." On opening night, Elvis wore a gi with a black sash and low-cup Italian boots. $1,800 - 2,000

B320 ELVIS PRESLEY'S PERSONAL RECORDS AND POPLAR TUNES RECEIPTS

Three receipts from Poplar Tunes Record Shop in Memphis, made out to Elvis Presley and dated May 31, 1967. Receipt for the purchase of four 45 rpm records for a total of $3.91. Includes four records from Elvis' personal collection: Sam & Dave's "Soul Man," Stevie Wonder's "I Was Made to Love Her," Jackie Wilson's "Baby Workout," and Peter, Paul and Mary's "For Lovin' Me." Original check included made out to Poplar Tunes for $3.91. Signed by Vernon Presley. 8 x 5 1/2 inches receipt #1. 6 x 4 inches receipts #2-3. 3 x 8 1/4 inches check.

Elvis frequented Poplar Tunes, buying new music and checking on the sales of his own. Documentation attests that Elvis shopped there before, and long after he hit it big.

$800 - 1,000

B321 SIGNED RECEIPT FROM SEARS, ROEBUCK & COMPANY AND GRACELAND SKILLET

One receipt dated April 11, 1967 from Sears, Roebuck & Company. Purchases included kitchen wares, which were to be delivered to Graceland. The receipt was for $111.05 and signed by Mrs. Presley. Black iron skillet. 9 x 5 1/2 inches.

The remodeling of Circle G Ranch entailed the purchase of kitchen items from Sears. The skillet is from the kitchen of Graceland. $600 - 800

B322 MOUNTAIN VALLEY WATER

Two-page letter dated October 5, 1966 to John Dillon from the Colonel (unsigned); letter regarding bottles missing the gel band collars. One-page letter, dated October 7, 1966, on "Mountain Valley Water" letterhead to Parker from the water company: he explains the plant manager made that decision to leave off collars, but problem would be rectified. Statement dated May 1, 1967 and addressed to Elvis Presley at 10550 Rocco Place in Bel Air, California. The statement includes four invoices from March 1, 1967 through April 25, 1967 and totals 187.20. Handwritten not in blue ink indicates $140.40 was paid with check #3300 on June 7, 1967. One case and 3 single (28-ounce) bottles of Mountain Valley Mineral Water. Brown cardboard box with blue and red writing and design. Side reads "Mountain Valley Water from Hot Springs, Ark." Sealed box contains 12 (28-ounce) bottles. 11 x 8 1/2 " letters . 7 x 5 7/8 " statement.

Even before it was "cool" to use bottled water, Elvis was drinking it. $1,300 - 1,500

B323 GROCERY RECEIPTS

Three grocery receipts. Two receipts from Big Star are dated May 3, 1967 and May 20. They total $314.95 and $39.68. On the back of these two receipts are handwritten notes which state, "Daisy Mae Williams Groc. for Graceland." The third receipt totals $354.63. Original check from the account of Elvis Presley. 10 feet 3 1/2 x 1 1/4 20 3/8 x 1 1/4 3 3/4 x 2 1/4

Daisy May was a cook at Graceland. On May 3, Elvis, Priscilla and their entourage returned to

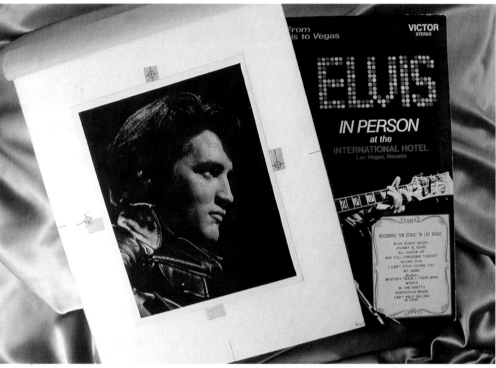

B326

Graceland after Elvis and Priscilla's California wedding. $650 - 750

B324 IBM INVOICE AND STATEMENT

IBM 3-copy invoice dated March 29, 1967, for office supplies. Total amount of $19.50 billed to Elvis Presley on a March 31, 1967 statement. 8 1/2 x 8 7/8 inches invoice. 7 3/8 x 6 3/8 inches statement.

With all Vernon's record-keeping on Elvis' business affairs, office supplies became a Graceland staple. $250 - 300

B325 ELVIS' BEATLE ALBUM AND INVOICE FROM POPLAR TUNES

Copy of an invoice from Poplar Tunes to Elvis, dated March 30,1967, for four 45's and one LP. Invoice is yellow in color with dark blue letters with a total due of $7.23. Written in pen, near left bottom, is the date invoice was paid and check number. Elvis' personal copy of the Beatles "Rubber Soul" album. 6 x 4 inches Invoice. 12 x 12 inches album.

Poplar tunes record store, which Elvis frequented to peruse the latest music selections (including his own), was and still is at 308 Poplar Avenue, Memphis, Tennessee.

$1,200 - 1,500

B326 THE 1968 SPECIAL

Black and white photo of Elvis taken from the 1968 Special. One can visually see traces of sweat from his forehead to his eyes and down his cheek. Photo is attached to a layout and covered with a heavy red cardboard. Two record set of "Elvis In Person at the International Hotel." 14 x 11 inches Layout. 9 x 7 inches Photo. 12 1/2 x 12 1/2 inches Album.

Album was recorded live at the International Hotel in Las Vegas. This two record set contains such songs as: "Blue Suede Shoes," "Johnny B. Good," "All Shook Up," "Are You Lonesome Tonight," "Hound Dog," "I Can't stop Loving You," "In The Ghetto," "Suspicious Minds," "Can't Help Falling In Love," "Words," "Mystery Train," "Tiger Man," "My Babe," and many others. $1,200 - 1,600

B327 '68 SPECIAL PROMOTIONAL CONTRACTS

One page typed contract on "Thomas A. Parker Exclusive Management" letterhead, dated August 15, 1968 and signed in blue ink by Elvis Presley and in black ink by Col. Tom Parker. Contract concerns expenses for promotional campaign for the 1968 television special. Merchandising and promotion agreement between Col. Tom Parker and Alfred DiScipio of The Singer Company related to the 1968 Elvis Presley Television Special. The agreement dated August 13, 1968 is signed by Colonel Tom Parker and DiScipio. With three 26-page "'68 Special" promotional pamphlets. Photographs included. 11 x 8 1/2 inches contracts. 9 x 4 inches pamphlets.

The sewing machine manufacturer Singer was the sole sponsor of Elvis' '68 Special. The contract between Parker and Singer is yet another example of The Colonel squeezing as much out of any deal as he can. In this case, the Colonel is supplying promotional items to Singer, for a cost of $50,000.

$4,000 - 5,000

B328 "'68 SPECIAL" FOREIGN DISTRIBUTION CONTRACT

Four page typed contract, dated March 20, 1969 and signed in blue ink by Elvis Presley. With a letter from Tom Diskin that accompanied this contract when it was sent to Colonel Parker's office. 11 x 8 .5

This contract stipulates that NBC will get 35% of gross receipts from the special and that Elvis will be paid a $25,000 advance against his share.

$6,000 - 7,000

B329 MEMO FROM STEVE BINDER TO COL. TOM PARKER REGARDING "'68 SPECIAL"

One page typed on Steve Binder stationery, dated June 11, 1968. Signed in blue marker by Steve Binder. Letter to the Colonel about audience selection for the two live tapings on June 29 for the 1968 television special. With ticket for 8 p.m. show. Photo included. 10 1/2 x 7" memo. 1 1/2 x 5 1/2" ticket. This letter, addressed to the Colonel at "Elvis

Exploitations" from director Binder, concerns audience arrangements for the live portion of Elvis' "'68 Special." Binder specifies the need for 328 "young people" for each of two live tapings on June 29 (though one of the live segments was actually taped on June 27), and conveys that all tickets will be delivered to the Colonel for distribution. These

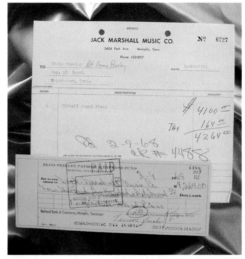

B328
B327

pair of performances marked the first time Elvis had appeared before a live audience since his 1961 Pearl Harbor benefit show. $5,500 - 6,500

B330 THE '68 SPECIAL—PAYMENTS AND PROMOTION

Two page typed contract on "RCA Victor Record Division" letterhead, dated August 20, 1968 and signed in blue ink by Elvis Presley, Colonel Parker, and RCA Vice President Harry Jenkins. Contract concerning a promotional album to be released prior to Elvis' Singer sponsored "'68 Special." With a copy of the album: "Singer Presents Elvis Singing Flaming Star and Others." Special Delivery letter on NBC letterhead, dated April 3, 1968, sent from J. L. Kubin to Colonel Thomas Parker. Enclosed is NBC check #83975 payable to Mr. Elvis Presley in the amount of $25,000. Attached is a copy of the check. 11 x 8 1/2 inches contract, letter and check copy. 12 inches diameter record.

The "Flaming Star" album was released in October 1968, two months prior to the television special. This contract stipulates a 90 day exclusive for Singer to distribute the record through their stores before rights on the album are turned over to RCA subsidiary Camden. The check from NBC was an advance payment against Elvis' share of profits and for distribution for the '68 Special.

$8,000 - 8,500

B331 INVOICES FROM INTERNATIONAL COSTUME CO

Three copies of invoices from the International Costume Company to Elvis from July and August of 1969. Invoices are typewritten on gold colored paper. Charges from July 22 are for a black mohair suit, black and brown twill suits, black gaberdine suit, black shirt and pants, black two piece outfit, black/red outfit, three pairs of zipper boots, and t-shirts. Total bill is for $4114.00. Charges from August 15 are for a black suit with woven satin belt, black mohair suit, blue mohair suit, black slacks with red insert, and black slacks with turquoise insert. Total bill is $1,625.00. Charges for August 21 are for two Cossack style suits with woven satin belts, black and red woven satin belts, and silk turquoise scarves. Total bill is for $895.00. Photograph included. 11 x 8 1/2 inches.

When Elvis made his live comeback in Las Vegas in 1969, Bill Belew, the same man who designed the leather suit for the '68 Special, designed his stage costumes. Elvis wore many karate inspired costumes. They costumes had brightly colored belts of which Belew said, "We taught him how to tie the belts so the cords would hang out and they would whip around." Elvis and Belew alike understood the value of a good stage costume. $1,400 - 1,600

B332 BARBRA STREISAND AT THE INTERNATIONAL HOTEL—INVITATION FLAG

Yellow, orange and purple satin flag with Las Vegas International Hotel logo and a yellow felt patch reading "Barbra July 2, 1969." Flag acted as an invitation to the Barbra Streisand concert that opened the hotel, with invitation inscription below the hotel logo. 16 1/4 x 23 1/2 inches.

Elvis signed a contract in February 1969 to play the showroom of the recently built International Hotel. It would be his first concert appearance in nearly a decade and the Colonel didn't want anything to detract from the King's return, so he declined to opportunity to open the new showroom for fear of technical "bugs" that may not have been ironed out. Instead the job went to Barbara Streisand , who opened the International on July 2, with Elvis in attendance. This flag was Elvis' personal invitation to the show. Elvis' engagement at the International commenced on in July 31, 1969.
$600 - 800

B333 MENUS FROM ELVIS PRESLEY'S 1969 INTERNATIONAL HOTEL SHOW

Four menus from Elvis Presley's 1969 International Hotel Show. Front of menu has a photo of Elvis dressed casually, and sitting in a chair. Back of menu is a photo of Elvis dressed in a formal white jacket with a white carnation. 11 x 8

On March 15, Elvis signed the official contract for his appearance at the Las Vegas International

Hotel; the contract included a clause permitting filming of a concert documentary. The engagement, which was scheduled to begin on August 31 with one show, was an invitation only show that attracted celebrities like Cary Grant, Carol Channing, Pat Boone, and FatS Domino. The performance was a great success; in fact Elvis enjoyed near-universal acclaim
$1,000 - 1,500

B331

B334   B332

B334 A.J. SHOOFEY'S CORRESPONDENCE TO ELVIS PRESLEY

Brief typed welcome message to Elvis Presley at the International Hotel from A.J. Shoofey, executive vice president of the International Hotel in Las Vegas. Dated July 24, 1969 on embossed International Hotel letterhead with blue and purple logo and blue, purple, and pink vertical borders, with original envelope. Included are cards and

envelopes addressed to "Mr. Elvis Presley" which were included in a basket sent by A.J. Shoofey. Oversized souvenir menu from Elvis' 1969 International Hotel engagement. Black cover with gold International Hotel emblem and round cutout showing a picture of Elvis. Inside displays the menu selection. Original light green check from the account of E.A. Presley made out to International Hotel for $1,000. Payment for "personal" expenses. Signed by Elvis Presley. 11 x 8 1/2 letter. 2 1/8 x 3 3/8" card. 2 1/4 x 3 1/2" envelope. 17 x 8 1/2" menu. 3 x 8 1/4" check.

Shoofey sent Elvis good luck fruit and liquor baskets prior to Elvis' Las Vegas comeback performance. To nobody's surprise, Elvis proved to be one of the best, and most lucrative, performers to hit Las Vegas. During this four-week engagement, Elvis set a Las Vegas record of 101,509 paying audience members producing a gross take of $1.5 million.
$2,500 - 3,000

B335 SCHEDULE OF PAYMENTS TO BAND AND SINGERS FOR ENGAGEMENT AT INTERNATIONAL HOTEL IN LAS VEGAS

Two page copy of a schedule of payments, typed on William Morris letterhead, dated September 4, 1969. Schedule lists the dates and salaries for the musicians and singers for the show at the International Hotel in Las Vegas. Three "Elvis On tour" badges; one badge done in blue lettering, the second in green, and the third in brown. Photograph included. 11 x 8 1/2 inches Schedule of Payments. 2 1/4 x 3 1/2 inches badges.

This was Elvis' first Las Vegas show beginning August 31, 1969, for fifty-seven shows. It cost him $98,000 to put on the show, and Elvis was paid $100,000 a week for four weeks.
$1,800 - 2,000

B336 RARE HANDWRITTEN NOTES AND PRESS RELEASE

July 1969, 9-page press release announcing his "first appearance in more than a decade . . . at the new International Hotel in Las Vegas." Release also discusses his career. Handwritten notes from Elvis relating to show on front and back of release, such as: "Bigger Intro, 'I--Can't--Stop Loving You' " and "Chord at the end of 'Runaway'<sic>" and "Record Player for Dressing Room." 11 x 8 1/2 inches.

"Amazing" document with Elvis' handwritten notes that show how he is thinking and how he liked his arrangements and helped orchestrate his appearances.

$18,000 - 20,000

B337 ITEMS RELATED TO THE INTERNATIONAL HOTEL CONTRACT

Western Union Telegram dated December 19, 1968, to Col. Thomas Parker in Palm Springs, California: "International Hotel accepts the offer transmitted by you as manager for Elvis Presley letter follows with details." Sent by Alex J. Shoofey, Exec. Vice President. Letter from Alex Shoofer to Colonel Parker dated January 17, 1969: "International Hotel hereby elects to take the services of Mr. Presley for a . . . 29-day period . . . a starting date . . . of September 11, 1969. AGVA contract from the William Morris Agency in regards to their financial arrangement with Elvis for this engagement. Contract states what they will pay and deduct from his gross compensation and then "after deducting

the foregoing shall be subject to ten percent commission, which shall be paid to us in the usual manner." Signed by Elvis Presley and Roger Davis

B336

B337

of the William Morris Agency. 5 3/4 x 8 inches telegram. 11 x 8 1/2" letter and contract.

After the "'68 Special", which was an enormous success, Elvis decided that he wanted to start doing live shows again. Almost immediately, the Colonel began setting up shows for him in Las Vegas.

$18,000 - 20,000

B338 THE '68 SPECIAL — SHOW ROUTINE AND SONG PARODY

Two page typed parody of "It Hurts Me", written by Earl Brown and Allan Blye. One page typed show routine for the 1968 Elvis Presley Television Special. With a mint condition copy of the "Elvis—TV Special" soundtrack LP. Photograph included. 11 x 8 1/2 inches show routine and song parody.   12 inches diameter album.

This show routine is from Colonel Parker's office, dated September 20, 1968.Brown and Blye were the writers for Elvis' '68 special, and they wrote this parody of a song Elvis first recorded in 1964 as a humorous commentary on the backstage tensions the show was generating. Elvis sang the song on the set of the show to Colonel Parker for his birthday. In the parody, director Steve Binder's name becomes "Bindle" and producer Bob Finkel becomes "Binkel," a play on the Colonel's penchant for purposefully mispronouncing names. "It hurts me/To see the budget climb up to the sky" goes the first line. The song also contains a wonderfully humorous and pointed commentary on the Colonel's biggest point of contention—the inclusion of Christmas songs. "They promised me sure/if I would give in/That I would-that I would/Never go wrong..." the song goes, and you can almost hear the mock anguish Elvis must have delivered the song with, "But tell me the truth/Is it too much to ask/for one lousy, tired ol' Christmas song...?"

$700 - 900

VEGAS

B339 LAS VEGAS SHOW AGREEMENT

Thirteen typed pages encased in blue folder titled "Agreement Between Elvis Presley and Las Vegas International." Includes four page contract dated April 15, 1969 and signed in blue ink by Elvis Presley, for a 29 day engagement at the International Hotel in Las Vegas; a copy of the same document; a one page letter dated April 15, 1969 from Col. Parker to the William Morris Agency and a copy of a two page contract between Elvis Presley and the William Morris Agency in regard to the Vegas shows. Photograph included. 11 1/2 x 9 1/8 inches folder.

This contract is for the first of Elvis' 15 Las Vegas engagements. It was his first concert appearance since 1961 and set a Las Vegas record for both attendance and ticket grosses. After an opening night performance, Elvis performed two shows a day for the remainder of the engagement, and this contract stipulates payment of $100,000 a week.

$18,000 - 20,000

B340 LETTER FROM COLONEL PARKER TO ELVIS PRESLEY REGARDING VEGAS SHOWS

One page typed on Las Vegas International Hotel stationary, dated August 22, 1969. With envelope. One menu from the International Hotel engagement. 11 x 8 1/2 inches letter. 4 1/8 x 9 1/2 inches envelope. 17 x 8 1/2 inches menu.

Colonel Parker writes: "Before I left I talked to Joe [Esposito] as the pressure is getting a little heavy regarding the off-color material. I am of course speaking mostly in regard to the dinner show when there are a great many children. I can only relay this to you. You are the only one that can change it." This is a rare example of the Colonel's written criticism to Elvis.

$1,400 - 1,600

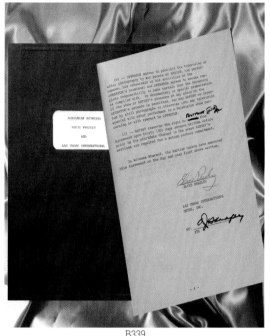

B339

B341 ARTWORK FOR BILLBOARD FOR ELVIS PRESLEY'S APPEARANCE AT THE LAS VEGAS HILTON

Original artwork from Clanton-Ross Inc. in Tampa, Florida, showing rendering of the billboard for Elvis' appearance at the Las Vegas Hilton. Black and white with black, gold, and blue strip across center over Elvis' picture. Blue and gold strips attached to show actual colors. Typed sheet included says: "Elvis, Elvis, Now, Las Vegas Hilton. Elvis, Elvis." 9 1/4 x 15 1/2 inches Rendering. 11 x 8 1/2 inches 48 x 150 inches billboard.

The typed sheet carries a RARE official embossed stamp of a snowman, surrounded by the words, "Snowmen's League of America, Chief Potentate, Col. Tom Parker"

$9,000 - 10,000

B342 CHARLES A. MANLEY'S CORRESPONDENCE TO COLONEL PARKER AND SINGER PROMOTIONAL MATERIALS OF ELVIS PRESLEY

One page "Singer" letterhead dated June 27, 1969 from Charles A. Manley, manager of Singer advertising to Colonel Parker at MGM, Inc. at Culver City, California, regarding Singer's promotional materials of upcoming NBC-TV "Singer Presents Elvis" special. Stapled to letter are 3 photostatic copies of newspaper ads and 3 pages of advertisement graphic layouts. One full page proof of advertisement graphic layout. Also included is 2-page text for a Singer advertisement of Elvis' February 23, 1970 performance at the International Hotel in Las Vegas. 11 x 8 1/2 inches letter and newspaper ads. 11 1/2 x 8 inches. 11 1/2 x 7 1/8 inches. 9 3/4 x 7 inches. and 22 3/4 x 18 inches graphic layouts for promotional materials.

Singer Sewing Machine Company sponsored the original '68 Special on December 3 on NBC. They also footed the bill for the rebroadcast in August 1969. The original airing helped restore Elvis' career as a singer, after many years in the film industry.

$2,000 - 2,500

B343 COLONEL PARKER'S PHONE LIST

Two pages typed on "Thomas A. Parker Exclusive Management" stationery, with handwritten additions and corrections. In clear plastic sleeve. 11 7/8 x 9 1/8 inches.

This is a personal phone list from the Colonel's Madison, Tennessee office, and can be dated from the 1960s. Among the names and numbers on the list are: Milton Berle, Joseph Hazen, Hal Wallis and Eddy Arnold. This document gives an excellent view of the Colonel's business universe.

$1,400 - 1,600

This classic 1967 Ford 5L500 Ranchero was purchased on February 15, 1967. The serial number is
7K48C168901. The original owners manual scrib-
bled with various names inside is also included.
The car's exterior has been restored utilizing correct
candy-apple red which was indeed its original
color. The interior of the car consists of reuphol-
stered` seats, as well as Elvis' initials on the inside
of the driver's door.

Elvis bought this automobile from the Oakley Motor
Company in Memphis. On Februaury 8, 1967 Elvis
put down a deposit on a 160 acre cattle ranch
called Twinkletown Farm which was located outside of Walls, Mississippi in a town called Horn
Lake. Elvis purchased the property from Jack
Adams in order to house the numerous horses he
recently acquired. Apparently, Graceland was
becoming too small to hold all of his horses. Within
one week after the purchase of the ranch which
Elvis called the "Circle G Ranch", Elvis bought this
Ford Ranchero to use for everyday tasks around
the property.

ESTIMATE UPON REQUEST

B345 ELVIS PRESLEY JOKE FINANCIAL REPORT

Six pages encased in blue folder with typed title "Annual Report for Mr. Elvis Presley." Includes four gold seals for Colonel's Parker's "Snowman's League of America," each with an imprint of a snowman and reading "Chief Potentate Col. Tom Parker." Two black and white photos, one under the heading "President and Vice President" is of Elvis and the Colonel; the other is of the Colonel in a Santa Claus suit. 11 1/2 x 9 ".

This document, prepared by Colonel Parker, is a prime example of the Colonel's lighter side. The "report" also lists "Mr. Presley's Active Staff" and gives them joke titles, such as calling Elvis' barber Larry Geller a "Beautification Expert."
$450 - 500

B346 PROMOTIONAL MATERIALS FOR "FOLLOW THAT DREAM"

Six piece promotional mat and proofs for the "Follow That Dream" EP. Included is the "Follow That Dream" EP

In 1961, Elvis Presley's starred in his ninth film, "Follow That Dream," a United Artists, Mirisch Company production, showcasing the song of same title.
$600 - 800

B347 METAL PLATES FOR ELVIS TV SPECIAL SOUNDTRACK

Two piece metal plates for "Elvis" TV Special soundtrack. Included is a record of same title.

The sewing machine manufacturer Singer was the sole sponsor of Elvis' '68 Special. Announced in January 1968 and mostly taped that summer, the '68 Special, as it came to be called, reintroduced Elvis to a post-Beatles musical climate after nearly a decade in Hollywood. Undoubtedly what the program is remembered for today is the intense perfor-

mance Elvis gives of several rhythm and blues classics, considered by many to be, after the Sun sessions, the finest music of his life. $400 - 600

B348 "G.I. BLUES" SOUNDTRACK LP SILVER RECORD

Mounted and framed award, connotating one million records sold. Plaque reads: "To Colonel Parker in Appreciation of his Contribution Toward Making G.I. Blues a Million Dollar Seller 1961" From Colonel Parker's personal collection. 22 x 19 inches framed award.

The soundtrack to the 1960 film, "G.I. Blues" was one of Elvis' most successful albums, having a longer stay on the Billboard album chart, 111 weeks, than any other Elvis album. It spent 10 weeks at #1. $8,000 - 12,000

B349 "GIRLS! GIRLS! GIRLS!" SOUNDTRACK LP SILVER RECORD

Mounted and framed award, connotating one million records sold. Plaque reads: "To Colonel Parker in Appreciation of his Contribution Toward Making Girls! Girls! Girls! a Million Dollar Seller 1962" From Colonel Parker's personal collection. 22 x 19 inches framed award.

The soundtrack to the 1962 film, "Girls! Girls! Girls!" spent 32 weeks on the Billboard album chart, peaking at #3.
$6,000 - 8,000

B350 "BLUE HAWAII" SOUNDTRACK LP SILVER RECORD

Mounted and framed award, connotating one million records sold. Plaque reads: "To Colonel Parker in Appreciation of his Contribution Toward Making Blue Hawaii a Million Dollar Seller 1961" From Colonel Parker's personal collection. 19 X 25 inches framed award.

The soundtrack to the 1961 film, "Blue Hawaii" hit #1 on the Billboard album chart and stayed there for 20 consecutive weeks, a record until Fleetwood Mac's "Rumours" topped it in 1977.
$7,000 - 9,000

B351 ELVIS PRESLEY AUTOGRAPHED PHOTO

Black and white photograph of Elvis Presley signed by Elvis to Colonel Parker, written in black marker ink. 44 x 34 inches.

This photograph of Elvis, which hung on the wall of the Colonel's office, reads: "To the 'Admiral' You know how I I feel so there's no need for a snow job. E.P."
$2,000 - 3,000

THE SEVENTIES

C1 ELVIS PRESLEY PERSONALIZED MATCHBOX COVER

Pink leather matchbox cover personalized with the name "Elvis Presley" in white letters.

This matchbox cover sat atop Elvis' desk at his Chino Canyon home in Palm Springs, California.

$600 - 800

C2 ELVIS PRESLEY'S CUFFLINKS

One pair of gold cufflinks with tiger's eye stones in a brown padded case with a tag marked "Cussens."

These cufflinks were kept in the home office of Elvis' Chino Canyon Road residency in Palm Springs, California.

$2,000 - 3,000

C3 ELVIS PRESLEY'S GLASSES

Ray-Ban glasses with rectangular-shaped prescription lenses in black plastic frames with a black vinyl protective case.

These glasses were stored in Elvis' desk in the office of his Palm Springs home on Chino Canyon Road.

$2,000 - 3,000

C4 ELVIS' POLICE BADGE PAPERWEIGHT

Beverly Hills Police Department Badge, "TCB" inscription, encased in a clear lucite disc. 1 x 3 3/4 inches.

This police badge paperweight, personalized for Elvis Presley, is exemplary of his fondness for police badges of which he had collected many from police departments around the country. This particular paperweight was a decoration which sat atop the desk in Elvis' home office in his Palm Springs home.

$1,500 - 2,000

C1
C2

C3
C4

C5 ELVIS PRESLEY'S TRAVEL JEWELRY BOX

Wooden jewelry box with black leather trim and two leather compartments, attached to the wood. Included in compartments are: one clock, shell necklace with faux diamond pin, square, silver necklace with large faux diamond, silver necklace with green stone, Star of David pendant and chain, rawhide necklace with shells decorations, Tie tack with three white stone accents, tie tack with single stone accent, and silver ring with red and orange enamel bull's eye design. 2 x 9 x 5 inches Box.

This jewelry box, which contains Elvis' personal effects, were housed in Elvis' home office at his Chino Canyon Road residency located in Palm Springs, California. $4,000 - 6,000

C6 ELVIS' RCA VICTOR TELEVISION REMOTE

Non-battery "clicker" style television remote with switches for channel, on-off/volume, color and tint. 4 1/4 x 3 x 1 1/2 inches.

This television remote, a style since replaced with a battery powered model, was kept in a handy spot on Elvis Presley's desk in his home on Chino Canyon Road to operate the television set also located in his office.

$300 - 400

C7 ELVIS' PRESLEY'S BLACK LEATHER WRISTBANDS

Two black leather wristbands: the first is designed with an embossed TCB lightening bolt, accented with silver studs and gold chain, the second features a gold tiger design and gold studs. 10x 2 1/2 inches.

These leather wristbands, belonging to Elvis, were discovered in Elvis' personal office at his Chino Canyon home.

$1,500 - 2,000

C8 ELVIS' ASHTRAY AND LIGHTER

Clear glass circular ashtray and silver accented desk lighter with square base. 2 x 8 inches Ashtray, 3 x 2 3/4 inches Lighter.

This set of an ashtray and lighter adorned the desk of Elvis Presley at his Chino Canyon home in Palm Springs, California.

$1,000 - 1,500

C9 ELVIS' SILVER CUFF BRACELET

Large silver cuff-style bracelet with a rectangular insert of mother-of-pearl adorning the surface.

This bracelet, belonging to Elvis, was discovered in Elvis' personal office at his Chino Canyon home.

$2,000 - 3,000

C10 ELVIS PRESLEY'S BRONZE STATUE

Bronze statue on base. 11 inches tall Statue, 4 x 4 inch Base.

This bronze statue of a faun, a mythological Greek figure of a man with a tail, sat atop the personal desk of Elvis Presley in his personal office at his home in Palm Springs, California.

$1,000 - 1,500

C11 ELVIS' PRESLEY'S METAL AND WOOD CASE

Wooden case bound with metal, interior lift-out shelf, with lid and latch. 6 x 11 x 7 inches.

This metal and wood case was discovered in the home office of Elvis at his Palm Springs residency.

$600 - 800

C12 ELVIS' PRESENTATION ENCASED CLOCK

A red presentation box contains wooden case and encased gold plated clock. 7 inches tall, 7 1/2 inch square base.

This red presentation box, with its interior gold plated box and clock were among the decor of Elvis Presley's personal office in his Palm Springs home.

$2,000 - 3,000

C13 ELVIS' INCENSE AND CANDLE HOLDER

Wooden incense and candle holder of ornate design. 9 inches tall x 8 1/2 diameter.

This large and unusual incense and candle holder was kept as a decoration in the personal office of Elvis at his residency in Palm Springs, California.

$1000 - 1,500

C14 RCA DRINKING GLASSES

Thirty-one clear drinking glasses with red RCA logo. Twenty regular glasses and eleven goblets. 5 x 2 1/2 inch Glasses, 4 1/2 x 2 1/2 inches Goblets. These glasses were a gift to Colonel Parker from RCA-Victor, Elvis' record label and the label of earlier Parker clients Eddy Arnold and Hank Snow. These glasses were used in the Colonel's home in Madison, Tennessee.

$2,000 - 3,000

C15 ELVIS PRESLEY SUMMER FESTIVAL SIGN

Large sign in white, orange, red, black and blue. Reads "Now Summer Festival, Elvis, Las Vegas Hilton" next to the Hilton logo. 118 x 255 inches.

Never one to understate things, the Colonel lined a corridor in the Las Vegas Hilton with this enormous sign during one of Elvis' engagements.

$3,000 - 4,000

C16 ONE 45 RPM ACETATE WITH "WAY DOWN" ON SIDE ONE, AND "PLEDGING MY LOVE" ON SIDE TWO.

One 45 RPM, stereo acetate with "Way Down" on side one and "Pledging My Love" on side two. Yellow "Masterfonics, Inc." label. In plain brown jacket. 10 x 10 inches.

In later years, Elvis became increasingly adverse to going into the recording studio, despite the recording obligations in his RCA contract. An alternative was to bring the studio to him. In February of 1976, RCA did this by setting up a recording session at Graceland. The red RCA recording van backed up to the jungle room. The ceiling was already carpeted which helped the acoustics, but to further help them, the walls were covered with moving blankets. The speakers that were brought to be used proved to be too small, so Elvis' personal system from his bedroom was used. During the session, the light bulbs were changed the match the mood of the song. Elvis loved the setup so much that he wanted to keep it setup after the session.

$1,000 - 1,500

C17 TRUNK LABELS FOR SHOWS

2 sets of four trunk labels with adhesive backs; white with gray stenciling. Lettered with "Elvis," "orchestra," and "girls dressing room." 4 1/8 x 11 inches.

The Colonel always took care of the smallest details when it came to the tours. They were always well organized, even placing labels on trunks so the movers knew where to place them.

$1,300 - 1,500

C7

C8
C10

C11
C12

C18 CHECK SIGNED BY ELVIS FOR A MERCURY

Light green check from the account of E.A. Presley dated September 25, 1970 made out to Palm Springs Lincoln Mercury for $3,957.29. Check is signed by Elvis Presley. 3 x 8 1/4 inches.

While spending the weekend in Palm Springs, Elvis decided to buy a gift for Colonel Parker. That gift was a 1970 Mercury Cougar, and this was the check Elvis used to buy it. $3,000 - 3,500

C19 COLONEL PARKER'S TROPHY

Silver Cup trophy on black base. Engraved silver plaque on base reads, "Elvis Summer Festival."

Indisputably, Colonel Parker was one of the greatest promoters Hollywood has ever seen. His tireless work and commitment to Elvis helped to make Elvis the "King." Engraved on the cup is, "To Colonel Parker in recognition of supreme promotional effort unequaled even in lustrous Las Vegas, for Elvis 1970 Summer Festival, September 7, 1970, from Alex Shoofely & Staff."

$800 - 1,200

C20 ELVIS PRESLEY STORAGE RECEIPT

Receipt from Beverly Hills Transfer/Storage, dated May 15, 1970, in the name of Elvis Presley. Signed in blue ink by Joe Esposito. Bill for the storage of 37 furniture and household items. 13 1/2 x 8 1/2"

Elvis and Priscilla bought a house in Palm Springs on April 2, 1970. This receipt for storage of furniture waiting to be moved into the Palm Springs house.
$2,000 - 2,500

C21 ELVIS PRESLEY CHECKS TO LINDA THOMPSON AND SHEILA RYAN

Four "E.A. Presley" personal checks, each personally signed "E. A. Presley." One check dated December 22, 1975 is written to Sheila Ryan for $1,500. Check dated June 29, 1975 is written to Ryan for $1,000. Check dated July 16, 1975 is written to Linda Thompson for $250. Check dated September 20, 1975 is written to Thompson for $3,000. 2 3/4 x 6".

Thompson and Ryan were girlfriends of Elvis' during the mid-Seventies. $800 - 1,200

C22 TCB, ELVIS, AND VERNON STATIONERY

Two sheets of cream stationery with a gold TCB over a lightening bolt above "Elvis." "Taking Care of Business" printed in gold across the top of the page. One sheet of official cream-colored gold-lettered "Taking Care of Business" stationery with TCB and lightning bolt logo. Printed with Col. Tom Parker. Two sheets of white stationery with Elvis Presley's name and address at 3764 Elvis Presley Blvd. printed in black across the top of the page. Two sheets of white stationery with Vernon Presley's name and address at 3764 Elvis Presley Blvd. printed in black across the top of the page. Two sheets of pink stationery with Elvis' black-and-white photo in top left-hand corner; one sheet has a vertical black rule down left-hand side. One sheet pink Elvis Presley Music, Inc., stationery with New York address and photo of Elvis; bottom has box with Elvis Presley Fan Club Hollywood address. One sheet cream-colored Elvis Music, Inc. stationery with NY address and one cream-colored sheet White Haven Music, Inc. with NY address; envelopes included. One envelope with Graceland return address (Highway 51 south) stamped on back. One sheet gray stationery with letterhead "The Elvis Presley Show, Memphis, Tennessee." Four small stacks of E. A. Presley personalized name stickers (approximately 100), adorned with pasted inside a small folder, compliments of the Disabled American Veterans. The labels bear the name and address of E. A. Presley, Graceland, Memphis, Tenn. 38116. Photograph included. 10 1/2 x 7 1/4 inches TCB. 11 x 8 1/2 inches other stationery. 10 x 8 inches pink stationery. 4

x 9 1/2 inches envelopes. 5 3/4 x 9 3/4 inches Graceland envelope. 2 3/4 x 7 1/2 inches folder for stickers. 5/8 x 1 3/4 inches stickers.

"Taking Care of Business in a Flash" was Elvis' business motto. Vernon did not actually live at Graceland in 1972; however, he did maintain an office there and took care of most of Elvis' personal business.

$2,000 - 2,500

22

22

24

23

C23 VERNON PRESLEY'S ADDRESS BOOK

Vernon Presley's address book from the 1970's. Cover is a olive green with a gold colored border. Cover is well worn and taped together. Photograph included. 8 x 5 1/4 inches. While Colonel Parker managed the business affairs of Elvis, Vernon Presley managed Elvis' personal affairs, from paying the bills, to taking care of Graceland. Vernon's address book includes contact information on friends and family such as Priscilla's

phone number in California, Dee Presley's, Joe Esposito, Vester Presley, and Col. Thomas A. Parker among others. The book also lists contact information for employees and local businesses. Listed on the back, inside cover is Elvis', Vernon's, Minnie Presley's, and Jesse Dee Presley's social security numbers.

$4,500 - 5,000

C24 PERSONAL NOTE FROM ELVIS TO COLONEL PARKER

Handwritten note to Colonel Parker from Elvis Presley. Letter read, "Hello Colonel... I used your phone... Hope you don't mind... Respectfully E.P.... P.S. Also stole your black panther... will replace it later."

$800 - 1,000

C25 ELVIS TOUR TRUNK

Large black wheeled trunk. 43 inches tall x 22 inches wide x 11 inches deep.

This tour trunk was used in the late Seventies, when Elvis resumed a vigorous touring schedule after a decade off the road. These trunks were used to transport sound equipment or wardrobe items.

$3,000 - 4,000

C26 "ELVIS COUNTRY" ALBUM PHOTO SLICK AND AD

Black-and-white front and back cover slicks for "Elvis Country" album. Copy of advertisement for "Elvis Country" album with note on bottom regarding Elvis' appearance in Las Vegas at the International Hotel now through February 23, 1971. 7 x 7 3/8 inches cover slicks. 11 1/4 x 7 7/8 inches ad.

Elvis recorded many of the songs for this album during his Nashville recording sessions in early June 1970. The album was released in early January 1971, entering Billboard's album chart at number 143, then peaked at number 12 and stayed on the list for 21 weeks.

$650 - 750

C27 COLOR SEPARATION PROTOTYPE AND MENU FROM THE SUMMER FESTIVAL

Color separation prototype for the back page of the menu from the Summer Festival. Advertising prototype is done in red, white, and blue promoting Elvis at Madison Square Gardens, "at your favorite theatre," and on tapes and records. Menu is kept between a reddish/brown folder that folds over from the top. Inside is a two page menu. Cover is a photograph of Elvis in a white jump suite holding his guitar and mike. The background behind Elvis is black, however, there are red, white, and blue lines drawn around the picture with stars on top and bottom. The name "Elvis" is on the bottom in white and on each bottom corner is the Hilton logo with the words "Las Vegas Hilton." Bottom is cut in an inverted "V" shape. Inside is the menu done in beige and light brown. Back cover is the advertising prototype described above. 14 x 7 inches Phototype and Menu. 14 1/4 x 7 inches cover.

This Annual Summer Festival took place in 1972. During opening show Elvis had a headache and only performed for forty-five minutes. Two positive things happened during this show; he added to his repertoire "What Now My Love?," and "My Way." It was now known that Elvis and Priscilla were separated. During the opening show Elvis announced:

"Hang on, baby, I'll get to you later, I'm free, you know..." The day after his closing, Elvis held a press conference at the Hilton where he announced that he would be the first artist in the world to hold a show which was going to be directly transmitted via

26

27

satellite to a number of countries, and the show would take place in Hawaii.

$1,300 - 1,500

C28 LETTER TO ELVIS PRESLEY CONCERNING SEPTEMBER 1970 TOUR

Two-page letter to Elvis Presley from Roger H. Davis on "William Morris Agency" letterhead dated August 14, 1970. The letter discusses the agreement for Elvis Presley's September 1970 tour. The word "COPY" is stamped in red on page one, however, page two has original signatures from Roger

H. Davis in black ink, and Elvis Presley in blue ink. Flyer showing Sold Out shows, and advertising his film "That's the Way It Was," and his new single "You Don't Have to Say You Love Me." 11 x 8 1/2 inches letter. 13 x 9 3/4 inches flyer.

The September 1970 tour--his first extended tour since 1957--took him to Phoenix, St. Louis, Detroit, Miami Beach, Tampa, and Mobile. Colonel Parker arranged the last four dates of the tour with Management III and its promoters, Jerry Weintraub and Tom Hulett. The St. Louis show on September 10 was the first time Elvis had an up-to-date sound system and on-stage monitors. The last show took place in Mobile, Alabama, where he and his group were booked at a hotel without air-conditioning. When they tried to find other accommodations, they were told nothing else was available, followed by the comment, "Don't you know Elvis Presley's in town?"

$5,000 - 6,000

C29 CONTRACTS FOR MUSICIANS AND BACKUP SINGERS FOR NOVEMBER 1970 TOUR

Six William Morris contracts for James Burton and his musicians--John Wilkinson, Ronnie Tutt, Glen Hardin, Jerry Scheff, and Joe Guercio-- dated October, 9, 1970 and signed by the individuals and Tom Diskin AGVA Contract dated October 9, 1970 for Kathy Westmoreland--signed by Westmoreland and Diskin. AGVA contract dated October 9, 1970 for The Imperials Photograph included. 11 x 8 1/2 inches each.

The backup singers and musicians were contracted for November 10-17, 1970--a tour that would take them in three chartered jets to eight cities: Oakland, Portland, Seattle, San Francisco, Inglewood (2 shows), San Diego, Oklahoma City, and Denver.

$7,000 - 8,000

C30 JEWELRY INVOICES SIGNED BY ELVIS PRESLEY

Original invoice dated November 4, 1970, from Maurice & Son for twelve pendants. Bill is white lined, with Maurice & Son letterhead printed in blue, and signed by Elvis. Second invoice, dated November 5, 1970, is from Billi Cheatwood for two necklaces. Bill is white lined with Billi Cheatwood letterhead printed in black, and signed by Elvis in red ink. Original check signed by Vernon Presley. 7 3/4 x 7 1//2 inches Maurice Invoice. 8 1/2 x 5 1/2 inches Billi Invoice.

Elvis made these purchases several days before leaving for an engagement in Oakland, California.

$6,000 - 8,000

C31 TELEGRAM FROM COLONEL TOM PARKER REGARDING TICKET ACCESSIBILITY FOR ELVIS PRESLEY FANS

Western Union Telegram from the Colonel to Jerry Weintraub of Management III Limited. Telegram is dated October 12, 1970. The Colonel discusses making sure that Elvis Presley concert tickets are available, accessible and affordable to the Elvis fans who have "made Elvis what he is today." Blue promotional poster with red and white print reading "Elvis Concert Tickets" down the middle and "On Sale Now" down each side. 10 x 8 1/4 inches telegram. 8 x 22 inches poster.

The Colonel writes: WE WANT OUR FANS TO BE TAKEN CARE OF. WHEN THEY WAIT IN LINE FOR HOURS AND HOURS THEY ARE PRIVILEGED CUSTOMERS. THEY COME FIRST.

$400 - 500

C32 ELVIS PRESLEY RECEIPTS - 1970

Five receipts from December 1970, all with original carbon signatures by Elvis Presley. One receipt dated December 26 from Taylor Gun Show for the purchase of a "Python." One receipt dated December 11 from Ramon Drug for the purchase of Vitamin E. Three receipts dated December 20 from American Airlines, one for a passenger named "J.

33

30

32

Carpenter." Photograph included. 3 1/4 x 7 1/2 inches.

Elvis played "Dr. John Carpenter" in his 1969 film "Change of Habit" and often used the name as an alias. The three plane tickets here are for a flight from Los Angeles to Washington on December 20, 1970. This was the trip in which Elvis met President Richard Nixon and received a badge from the narcotics bureau.

$2,000 - 3,000

C33 ELVIS PRESLEY'S INVOICE AND STATEMENT FOR A PRIVATE SCREENING OF "THAT'S THE WAY IT IS"

An invoice, dated December 21, 1970, and an itemized statement billed to Elvis Presley from MGM studios. The invoice is for the private screening of "That's the Way It Is" on December 16, 1970 and totals $47.53. Editor's Portfolio from MGM Publicity; kit includes information and black-and-white publicity photos. 7 3/4 x 8 1/2 inches invoice, 8 1/2 x 7 inches statement, 11 1/2 x 9 inches portfolio.

The documentary "Elvis-- That's the Way It Is" opened in November 1970. The film recorded his appearances at the International Hotel in Las Vegas

$500 - 750

C34 ELVIS DO-IT-YOURSELF ADVERTISING KIT

Two Elvis Do-It-Yourself Advertising Kits put out by RCA Records and Tapes. Includes suggested ad layouts, suggested ad headlines, and stickers of Elvis' RCA records. 11 x 8 1/2 inches (folded) or 33 x 25 1/2" (unfolded).

Colonel Parker sent these kits to record stores in order to guide them in creating Elvis promotions and displays.

$750 - 850

C35 CORRESPONDENCE TO ELVIS PRESLEY REGARDING CHARITY EVENTS

Original, typewritten, letter with envelope, from Johnny Carson to Elvis dated April 7, 1970. Letter on Johnny Carson stationery was sent as a reminder of Elvis' invitation to the 33rd Anniversary Benefit of the Wiltwyck School for Boys. Signed in brown by Johnny Carson. Original invitation included with return envelope and a list of suggested contribution amounts. Yellow order form for Souvenir Journal. One page letter, typed on "The Dick Cavett Show" stationery and dated March 25, 1971. Sent to Elvis Presley as an invitation to the Johnny Carson Tribute Dinner. Signed in brown marker by Cavett. With envelope. Tribute dinner invitation with return envelope and enclosures. Letter on Jack Hylton letterhead addressed to Elvis dated February 26, 1960. Letter invites Elvis to perform for Queen Elizabeth and other Royal in a charity even. Letter dated October 26, 1967 to Elvis Presley from Robert O'Brien on MGM letterhead. The letter invites Elvis to join Variety Club International's Honorary Committee which was planning to honor Jack Valenti with a testimonial dinner on January 16, 1968. O'Brien hoped Elvis would join them in honoring Valenti. Signed in blue, "Bob." Copy of a letter dated November 3, 1967 from Tom Diskin on behalf of Elvis Presley. Letter is addressed to O'Brien and declines the invitation and expresses appreciation for considering Elvis. Two letters from Madame Tussaud's addressed to Elvis and the Colonel regarding a request Elvis to spare an hour of his time for their sculptor to "make the necessary observations for a portrait." Letter from Lawrence Spivak on Meet the Press letterhead dated November 21, 1956. Letter addressed to Colonel Parker invites Elvis to appear on "Meet the Press." 10 1/2 x 7 1/4 inches Carson Letter. 5 1/2 x 7 1/2 inches Envelope. 7 1/4 x 5 1/4 inches Invitation. 5 x 7 inches Return envelope. 6 1/2 x 4 3/4 inches Contribution list. 9 1/2 x 7 journal order form. 10 1/2 x 7 1/4 inches Cavett letter. 7 5/8 x 5 1/4 inches invitation sent by Cavett. 9 5/8 x 8 inches Hylton letter. 11 x 8 1/2 O'Brien, Diskin, Tussaud's letters 10 1/4 x 7 1/4.

Elvis was known for his generosity and was frequently asked to donate money to charities. As with most such invitations to public events, Elvis did not attend. $400 - 600

C36

C36 JUNGLE ROOM CHAIR

Chair with carved wooden frame. Carving depicts open mouthed dragons on the arms of the chair. Cushion is brown and white striped fur. 30 x 38 inches.

This chair, which was given to Colonel Parker by Elvis, is identical to a chair that remains in the Jungle Room at Graceland today.

$5,000 - 7,000

C37 JUNGLE ROOM FURNITURE AND RECEIPT

One high back chair with hand carved pine frame and legs. The back rest and the seat are crushed orange velvet. The top of the chair back has a crown carved in the pine. Hanging lamp made of dark stained white pine. A brass chain connects to a top piece and four pieces of pine connect the top to the base. A large white glass ball sits in the center of the lamp. Two, yellow receipts from Donald Furniture Company at 405 No. Cleveland in Memphis, Tennessee. One is dated July 11, 1974 and includes a phone, end tables, swag lamp, spread, and base and desk. Bill totals $2031.75. Second receipt is dated July 9, 1974 and includes a bench, sofa, two chairs, and one ottoman. Receipts totals $1795.95 Adding machine tape stapled to each receipt. 10 x 8 1/4 inches receipt. 3 3/4 x 2 3/4 inches adding machine tape.

It was love at first sight for Elvis and the Jungle Room furniture. Elvis purchased almost the entire set within 30 minutes of laying his eyes on it. This pine lamp purchased at Donald Furniture Company cost Elvis $279. A similar lamp still hangs in the Jungle Room today.

$7,000 - 9,000

C38 PERTINENT FACTS REGARDING HOUSTON LIVESTOCK SHOW & RODEO

Five light blue, typed pages of "Pertinent Facts" regarding the 1970 Houston Livestock Show & Rodeo. Elvis performed at show February 27, 28, and March 1, 1970. Photograph included. 11 x 8 1/2 inches.

After Elvis' Las Vegas comeback in 1969, this show was the first live appearance of Elvis.

$300 - 350

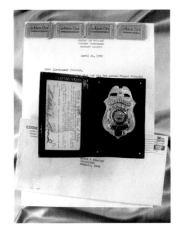

C39
EDDIE BOND LETTER AND BADGE

C40 ELVIS PRESLEY'S PERSONAL VIDEO TAPES AND VIDEO CASSETTE RECORDER.

Elvis Presley's personal collection of three video tapes, and one video cassette recorder. Video tapes are in 3/4" black plastic cases, and each tape is in excellent condition. Two of the black cases have a label that reads "JVC Video cassette," and an orange rectangular sticker with handwritten notes that say "Monty Python & The Holy Grail. 1 of 2 hr.," and "Monty Python & The Holy Grail . 2 of 2 30 min." The third case has an orange rectangular sticker that reads "Memorex Cromex U60." One video cassette recorder. Front side of recorder is silver and blue with the letters "JVC" on the bottom left, and on the bottom right is a clock/timer. Top of recorder, in silver letters on a red back-

sticker in silver with black letters is a list with manufacturer, serial number, and model number. Next to this list is a white tag with red lettering that says "Caution Connection for remote control use only." Listed under the model number are FCC rules, and another caution regarding electrical shock. In back of VCR, across the bottom, are six jacks that read "Dx VH Local F," Video In Audio Tv," Ant. Out," "Video In," VIdeo Out," and "Audio." There is one gray electrical cord with a three prong safety cord. 7.5 in height x 24 inches wide Video Cassette Player

Elvis loved films and spent many hours at home watching them. In the above collection are the movies "The Godfather" (Part one), and "Monty Python & The Holy Grail." The video cassette player was used by Elvis Presley to play his favorite films which he viewed in his bedroom where he spent much of his time when he was at Graceland.

$4,000 - 6,000

C39   C40

Letter dated April 21, 1972 to "Lieutenant Presley" from Eddie Bond, Chief of Police for Finger, Tennessee. The letter is on Bond's business letterhead. Bond urges Elvis to donate $10 for 10 tickets to the 2nd Annual Finger Friendly Festival. Also included are 10 yellow tickets. 11 x 8 1/2 inches letter. 1 x 2 inches tickets.

Though at this point comfortably ensconced in small town government, Eddie Bond had earlier been a figure of some infamy within Elvis legend. In 1954 Bond was a 21-year old veteran of the local Memphis music scene, and his band was looking for a singer. On May 15, 1954 Elvis joined Bond's group at the Hi Hat on South Third Street in Memphis for an audition. Elvis went to the audition with then girlfriend Dixie Locke and sang two songs with the band...but didn't get the job. Elvis later revealed that Bond told him to stick with driving a truck, because he would "never make it as a singer." Less than two months later Elvis' recorded his first Sun single, "That's All Right." Bond would later joke that he'd been "the only person to ever fire Elvis." A couple of years after the rejection, on route to Hollywood to film "Jailhouse Rock," Elvis reportedly said to confidant George Klein, "I wonder what Eddie Bond thinks now. Man, that sonofabitch broke my heart."

$800 - 1,000

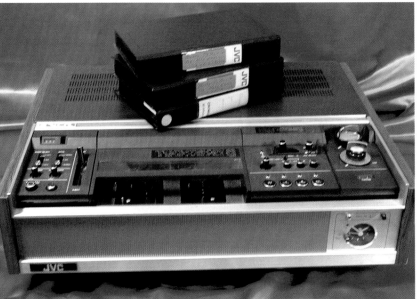

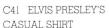

ground, are the letters "VCR"; and in silver letters on a blue background are the words "Video Cassette Recording System Model #CR-63006/Recorder." In the control area on left side is a counter reader, and control knobs that read "Audio Select," Auto Repeat," "tracking," and the power on and off switch. All lettering in this area is white on a black background. Right side of VCR controls has tuning knobs, fast forward, play, stop, rewind and record. On the backside of the recorder on the left is a green and black sticker that reads "UL Listed 277C Video Equipment." To the right of this

C41 ELVIS PRESLEY'S CASUAL SHIRT

Polyester two-tone green shirt in a camouflage-type design; high collar and elastic at the wrists. Five plastic green buttons with raised squares in center of each. Label reads: "I. C. Costume Co. Hollywood, California."

This is one of the many casual shirts Elvis bought from Bill Belew and his I. C. Costume Company in the early 1970s. The design symbolized his interest in a more showy taste in clothing; however, it was not out of character for the decade. $2,000 - 3,000

C41

C42 ELVIS PRESLEY'S PERSONAL COLLECTION OF RECORDS

One set of records containing: 45 rpm of "Way Down" / "Pledging My Love" 45 rpm of "Ain't That Loving You Baby" / "Ask Me" 45 rpm of "One Broken Heart for Sale" / "They Remind Me Too Much of You" 45 rpm of "High Heel Sneaker" / "Guitar Man" 45 rpm extended play "If you Think I Don't Need You," "I Need Somebody to Lean On," "C'mon Everybody," and "Today, Tomorrow, & Forever." "Elvis Is Back" Album "It Happened at the World's Fair" Album "Elvis' Gold Records Volume. 4."

This enticing set of albums and singles came directly from Elvis' bedroom at Graceland. His personal record collection shows the signs of wear and tear, indicating that Elvis did not allow them to sit in the corner and gather dust.

$6,000 - 8,000

C43 ELVIS PRESLEY'S KARATE GI

Bear Brand black cotton karate jacket with four ties at front closure. Yellow embroidering on front reads: "Tiger" and "Elvis Presley," with a crown icon. Patch on left front is red/silver and navy. Design is a fist with Japanese characters and the word "Pasawon." Patch on back of jacket is red/white and black with Japanese characters and the name "Kang Rhee." Label reads: "Sampson Trade Manufacture Seoul Made in Republic of Korea." 44 inches high x 21 inches wide.

Elvis began karate instruction during his time in the Army. He took lessons from many instructors, including Ed Parker and Kang Rhee, and eventually reached 8th degree belts in both Kenpo and Tae

Kwon Do. His karate name was "Tiger."

$20,000 - 30,000

C44 ELVIS PRESLEY'S COPY OF "THE LEGEND OF BRUCE LEE"

Elvis' personal copy of "The Legend of Bruce Lee," a 176-page paperback book. Elvis made notes inside the front cover and underlined passages throughout the book. 7 x 4 1/4 inches.

C42

Elvis was an avid fan and participant in the sport of karate for almost two decades during which time he achieved 8th degree black belt. In "The Legend of Bruce Lee," a biography of the "Kind of Kung Fu," Elvis has marked several passages written about one of his karate instructors, Ed Parker. Elvis himself is mentioned on page 99 when it states that Bruce Lee turned down and MGM offer to do a film with Elvis.

$8,000 - 10,000

C45 "LOVIN' FEELIN'" CONCERT ARRANGEMENTS

Concert arrangements for "Lovin' Feelin'," with charts for each instrument. There are handwritten notes in pencil on most sheets. Encased in black folder with with raised red tape reading "Lovin' Feelin'" and with a gold "Elvis Presley" sticker on the inside cover. 14 x 12 inches folder.

This packet of arrangements was used by Elvis and his band during concerts in the Seventies. There are arrangement sheets for every musician who would play on the song. The Phil Spector-produced classic "You've Lost That Lovin' Feelin'" was a huge hit for the Righteous Brothers, of course, but Elvis frequently performed the song during his Seventies concerts. A rehearsal performance of the song at the International Hotel in Las Vegas can be seen on the 1970 "Elvis—That's the Way It Is" documentary.

$3,000 - 4,000

C46 "PATCH IT UP" CONCERT ARRANGEMENTS

Concert arrangements for "Patch it Up," with charts for each instrument. There are handwritten notes in pencil on most sheets. Encased in black folder with with raised red tape reading "Patch it Up" and with a gold "Elvis Presley" sticker on the inside cover. 14 x 12 inches folder.

This packet of arrangements was used by Elvis and his band during concerts in the Seventies. There are arrangement sheets for every musician who would play on the song. Elvis sang "Patch it Up" at the International Hotel in Las Vegas in 1970, a performance captured in his "Elvis—That's the Way It Is" documentary. $2,000 - 3,000

C47 COLONEL PARKER'S PROMOTIONAL WARDROBE

Consisting of: a short sleeved shirt, "Elvis Presley" Coveralls, two "Elvis in Concert" tour Jackets, one "In Person Elvis" jacket, a black cotton kimono, one RCA Jacket, one "This Is Elvis" Jacket, and a Lab Coat.

1) Man's short sleeved, white shirt with turquoise and black lettering. Sleeves have the words "RCA Records" on them, and written on the front and back are the words "Elvis," "International Hotel," "Las Vegas, Nevada, " and "Summer Festival." There are five clear buttons down the front of the shirt. 24 inches long x 24 inches wide.

2) One red jacket with black nylon sleeves. Logo on left side of front reads, "Elvis In Concert." Left sleeve carries the logo "TCB." Collar, cuffs and waistband are in white, black, and red stripes. 28 inches long x 23 inches wide.

3) Red cotton and nylon zippered jacket with white stripes on the collar, cuffs, and waistband. "Elvis In Concert" patch on chest with gold and white "T.C.B." lightning bolt logo on shoulder. 31 inches long x 23 inches wide.

4) Pink, nylon suit-style jacket with belted back. There are three buttons and three front pockets. A black circle on the back has the words "In Person Elvis" printed in white. This "In Person" jacket worn by Colonel Parker was a walking advertisement for Elvis. The Colonel often wore Elvis gear as he walked around selling Elvis pictures, handing out balloons and promoting Elvis.

5) One black, long sleeved cotton kimono with white vertical Japanese lettering in the front, and a red and white RCA Victrola and dog logo on the back. Bottom of jacket has the same logo (in black and white) stretching from front to back. 32 inches long x 23 inches wide.

6) Red cotton and nylon button-up jacket with white stripes on the collar, cuffs, and waistband, and white "RCA Records" logo on the chest. 29 inches long x 24 inches wide.

7) Pink satin button-up jacket with gray and black collar, cuffs, and waistband. The name "Colonel" is stitched on the chest in back with a "T.C.B." logo on the right arm. Back side reads "This Is Elvis" with a black and white rendering of Elvis. 26 1/2 inches long x 22 1/2 inches wide.

8) Long Sleeved, off-white lab coat with two front pockets and a pink "Elvis Now" patch. 40 inches long x 20 inches wide .

1) This shirt was worn by Colonel Parker, and was one of many different shirts and jackets promoting Elvis.

2/3)Elvis' band members and entourage received these jackets to indicate they were part of his group. It allowed them easy access to the backstage area.

4) This "In Person" jacket, worn by Col. Parker, was a walking advertisement for Elvis. The Col. often wore Elvis gear as he walked around selling Elvis pictures, handing out balloons and promoting Elvis. 5) Kimono RCA jacket was given to Colonel Parker who often worked and received credit on

many RCA projects.

6) "RCA Records" jacket belonged to the Colonel whose relationship with RCA pre-dated Elvis through his management of RCA artists Hank Snow and Eddy Arnold.

7) "This Is Elvis" was a theatrical film that opened in 1981 and was made with full Graceland cooperation. Colonel Parker served as a "Technical Advisor" for the film.

8) The Colonel would wear this coat with Elvis promotional items to public events. He was known for going to outrageous lengths to promote Elvis; his above creative wardrobe choices were only part of the package.

$10,000 - 15,000

C48 VERNON PRESLEY INTERNATIONAL HOTEL BILLS

Twelve sheet stapled packet of bills from the International Hotel in Las Vegas, charged to Vernon Presley for the dates January 25 - February 25, 1970. Bill includes a room charge of $125.03. With green "Elvis Presley Payroll and Expense Fund" check in the amount made out to the International Hotel and signed in blue ink by Vernon Presley. 10 x 6 1/2 inches bills. 3 x 8 1/4 inches check.

These bills date from Elvis' second engagement at the International Hotel in Las Vegas.

$250 - 300

C49 GOOD LUCK TELEFAXES TO ELVIS PRESLEY CONCERNING 1970 SHOW IN LAS VEGAS

Western Union Telefaxes to Elvis Presley dated January 26, 1970 wishing him well for his opening show in Las Vegas. Telefaxes are from Cilla and Lisa; The Imperials; Chet; Donna Lewis; Sam, Knox, and Jimmy Phillips; Herb Omell, Alann Richard, and Ronnie Milsap; George Hamilton; Hal and Martha Wallis; and Lance Legault (double for Elvis). A telefax from Tom Jones dated February 5, 1970 bids Elvis to "keep rocking." Summer Festival postcard Two scarves--one white, one blue--with corner printing "Elvis Presley" and the Hilton "H." Blue scarf has some discoloration. Photograph included. 4 1/2 x 6 1/2 inches telefaxes. 24 1/2 x 23 1/2 inches scarves.

After a successful Las Vegas return in 1969, Elvis returned to the city 6 months later--January 26 - February 23, 1970, playing the Showroom at the International Hotel. He was definitely the headliner in Vegas at the time, with stars and fans coming from around the country to get tickets to his appearances. Even Lisa Marie had her second birthday celebration at his February 1st show.

$1,200 - 1,500

C50 ELVIS PRESLEY STAGEHAND COVERALLS

One pair of blue cotton coveralls with short sleeves, belted front, and zipper closure. Embroidered on the back in gold are the letters "EP."

This style of coverall was worn by Elvis Presley's personal crew of stage hands for the many phases of location preparation for Elvis' live performances. This particular pair belonged to Colonel Parker who was an ever-present supervising figure on location.

$3,000 - 4,000

C51 ELVIS PRESLEY'S JUMPSUIT FROM 1971, AND SOUVENIR BOOK

Black, moderate weight, long sleeved jumpsuit. Collar is pointed, and suit is partially lined in black satin. Tag inside suit reads "IC Costume Co. Hollywood, California." Jumpsuit has green painted leather addition to collar and yoke, and green vinyl inserts at legs. Studs are in a starburst design extending on both sides from the underarm seam to the cuff. One souvenir book with a photograph of Graceland's front porch area on the front cover. At top of cover in purple letters are the words "Elvis Presley's Graceland", and at the bottom in gold lettering are the words "The Official Guidebook." At very bottom in black letters are the words "Updated and expanded second edition."

Back cover of book has an upper body portrait of Elvis wearing a white shirt. First page opens up to a two page full color page of Graceland. Some pages include pictures of Priscilla and Lisa "Now and Then", and a photograph of Elvis in his military uniform with Vernon and Gladys. Book contains information on Elvis' early years, Army years, life at Graceland, Elvis' generosity, Elvis' Movie career, Elvis and Priscilla, the 1968 Television Special, Elvis in 1969 - '70, Elvis' jewelry, Elvis' Jaycees Award, Elvis' Guns and Badges, Citizen Elvis, Elvis in 1971 - '72, Aloha from Hawaii, Elvis from 1975 - '77, Elvis and his fans, Elvis' legend lives on at Graceland 1977 - , pictures of the automobile museum, airplanes, Christmas at Graceland, and many photographs. 11 x 8 inches Souvenir book cover.

Elvis wore this jumpsuit for his Las Vegas engagement at the Hilton Hotel in 1971. This show marked a change in Elvis' show in that a dramatic instrumental commonly known as the theme from "2001: A Space Odyssey" was performed by the full orchestra in the middle of the show to give Elvis a short break. He dropped most of the country tunes, ending several of his performances with "The Impossible Dream" while he accompanied himself on piano.

$70,000 - 90,000

C52 ELVIS PRESLEY'S PEACOCK BELT AND COSTUME RECEIPTS

Elvis Presley's white leather belt. Brass discs around the belt picture flying birds. Blue and gold embroidery decorates the belt in the shape of peacock feathers. Hanging brass chains. Original invoice paid on August 2, 1973, from Bill Belew to Elvis on brown Bill Belew stationary. Includes costs for designer fee, ten belts - five for show use and five for personal use, stones and buckles purchased in Europe, and fabric from Europe for personal shirts. Invoice totals $3,500. 10 1/2 x 7 1/4 inches.

This belt went with Elvis' peacock jumpsuit. The feather pattern on the belt matches the feathers on the chest and legs of the jumpsuit.

$23,000 - 25,000

C33A ELVIS PRESLEY'S BLUE NAIL CAPE

Light blue waist length cape. Decorated with flat, round, gold studs in a circular patterns.

One of Elvis' trademarks was his flashy stage costumes, namely his jumpsuits and capes. Elvis wore this cape with the Blue Nail jumpsuit. It was called this because the studs, unlike many of the vividly colored studs decorating other jumpsuits, were simply flat and round which made them look like nailheads. Elvis wore this ensemble when he performed at the Fair Grounds Coliseum in Indianapolis, Indiana, and at the Swing Auditorium in San Bernadino, California.

$40,000 - 60,000

C34A LANSKY BROTHERS HAT WITH RECEIPT

Black velvet Oleg Cassini fedora with silver metallic band. Inside band contains a "Lansky Memphis, Tenn." logo. Pink receipt stamped "Lansky Bros. Men's Shop, 126 Beale, Memphis, Tenn." dated December 22, 1972 and signed in blue ink by Elvis Presley. Bill for a $262.50 purchase of one hat and two coats by Elvis Presley. 7 x 4 1/4 inches receipt.

The Lansky Brothers Men's Shop holds a special place in Elvis lore. The shop, once located at 126 Beale Street, was opened by Guy and Bernard Lansky after World War II and served a mostly black clientele. The store specialized in bold, flashy clothes and was a favorite of performers who played in clubs on the street, including rhythm and blues stars Rufus Thomas and Junior Parker. As an adolescent, Elvis would peer into the Lansky's display window, enraptured by the style he would later claim as his own. In an interview with Elvis biographer Peter Guralnick, Guy Lansky said, "He came down and looked through the windows before he had any money—we knew him strictly by face." Elvis began shopping at Lansky's as a teenager and bought many of his stage clothes there, including his trademark pink and black suits. As this 1972 receipt attests, Elvis continued to patronize Lansky's throughout his life. The original Lansky's building on Beale now houses "Elvis Presley's Memphis" restaurant and club.

$13,000 - 15,000

C35A COLONEL PARKER'S CADILLAC

Colonel Parker's 1975 Cadillac Seville. Blue with
blue interior. Tennessee license plate reads,
"Admiral." Elvis often gave gifts to express his
appreciation, and nothing says "Thank You" like a
Caddie. Elvis purchased this Cadillac for Colonel
Parker at Jack Kent Cadillac in Denver.

$30,000 - 40,000

C36A SLEEVELESS JUMPSUIT WITH JACKET AND BELT

Matching jacket, belt and sleeveless jumpsuit with "I.C. Costume Co. Hollywood, California" tags. Navy blue with silver and blue rhinestones. Bell-bottom legs.

Elvis wore this jumpsuit on stage during his April 1975 tour, including at a performance in Macon, Georgia. All of Elvis' stage attire from this period, including his trademark jumpsuits, were designed by Bill Belew at I.C. Costumes.

$50,000 - 70,000

C37A ELVIS PRESLEY'S YELLOW SHIRT

Yellow button-down shirt with long, full sleeves. Cuff is elastic with ruffle.

This shirt was part of Elvis' more casual wardrobe in the late 60's and early 70's. He liked this style so much that he had multiple shirts in different colors made at once.

$2,000 - 3,000

C38A ELVIS PRESLEY'S GREEN SHIRT

Green button-down shirt with long, full sleeves. Cuff is elastic with ruffle.

In the late 1960's and early 1970s, Elvis wore this shirt while lounging around. This style shirt was a staple of Elvis' wardrobe, so much so, that he would order several at a time in an array of colors.

$2,000 - 3,000

C39A ELVIS PRESLEY'S BLACK JACKET WITH RED LEATHER POCKET FLAPS

Black, long sleeved jacket with a pointed collar. There are two inside pockets with a yellow, brown, and white geometric designed lining. The front has two pocket flaps that are red with leather material.

Each flap has a fabric covered black button. There are six buttons on each sleeve. On the back is a "kick" panel with a red leather piece, and two fabric covered black buttons.

This jacket belonged to Elvis' casual wardrobe. Elvis loved to dress different from his peers, and would often start trends of his own. He loved flashy, flamboyant clothing that would set him apart for others.

$15,000 - 20,000

C40A ELVIS PRESLEY'S PLAID SHIRT

One long sleeved, plaid shirt made from heavy jacket material. Shirt has a blue, white, and yellow geometric pattern, a belt , and squared off edges. The plaid shirt was one of many items from Elvis' casual wardrobe. He loved to dress contrary to the current trends, and during his life time set many trends of his own.

$2,000 - 3,000

C41A COLONEL PARKER'S MOODY BLUE PARTY CHRISTMAS ALBUM

One side of album is green with one picture of Colonel Parker dressed up as Santa Clause. Other side is cream with seven pictures of the Colonel dressed as Santa with employees at an RCA Christmas party. Encased in clear plastic display case with black base. Gold plaque on base reads, " Colonel, Thanks for arranging to have Santa Clause come down from the North Pole to be with your RCA Records family during Christmas 1978. Only you could do that. Bill Graham." 12 1/2 x 12 1/2 album.

This record was given by RCA to some of its executives as a Christmas gift. However, during production every single one of the albums made was cracked - except for one. Colonel Parker's album was the only one made that did not have a crack.

$600 - 800

C42A ELVIS PRESLEY'S WHITE SHIRT

One lightweight cotton/polyester blend long-sleeved white casual shirt; elastic above elbows and on cuffs--resulting in a puffy effect at the top of sleeve and a ruffle at the wrist. Four buttons.

One of the casual shirts with puffy sleeves that Elvis would order in large quantities in various colors. He usually wore a shirt like this with suits.

$1,800 - 2,400

C44A ELVIS PRESLEY'S VELVET JACKET, PANTS, AND CAPE

One heavy, long sleeved, brown velvet jacket with a pointed collar, and a brown and white spotted lining. The buttons are velvet covered, and there are two false front pockets. Jacket has wide lapels, six buttons for each cuff, and a Velcro strip on the back of the collar for a cape. Pants are moderate weight, brown velvet bell-bottoms. Inseam is 13 inches, with elastic at the waistband. Tag inside pants reads "I C Costume Co. Hollywood, Calif."

GOLDWYN-MAYER STUDIO, 10202 Washington Boulevard, Culver City, California 90230." On the panel beneath the handle is a red sticker that reads "ELVIS PRESLEY SHOW," partially covered by a return address label identical to the one on the lid. Attached to the handle is a red tag, handwritten "These are to go to Long Beach. Arrangements to Tahoe." 19 inches wide x 16 inches long x 8 1/2 inches deep.

This trunk, used for Elvis-related business by Colonel Parker, comes with a large selection of

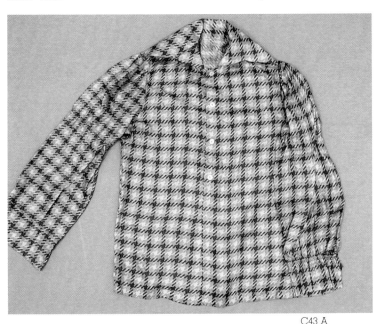

C43 A   C44A

C42A ELVIS PRESLEY'S PLAID SHIRT

Long-sleeved Houndstooth plaid silk shirt in orange, brown, and tan. Elastic above elbow and elastic cuffs--resulting in a puffy effect at top of sleeve and ruffle at the wrist. French-cut fit with pointed collar; 6 mother-of-pearl buttons.

Elvis enjoyed a casual wardrobe for his days off when he was not performing. He probably wore this plaid shirt with a brown suit.

$2,000 - 3,000

One light weight, brown velvet cape that is fully lined in brown satin. These items were a part of Elvis' casual clothes wardrobe. Elvis loved to dress extravagantly, and many of his casual clothes were made by the I.C. Costume company, the company that also made his costumes.

$30,000 - 40,000

C45A COLONEL PARKER'S MEMORABILIA TRUNK

Heavy black cardboard trunk with metal corners, two black strap buckles and handle. Lid has a "Thomas A. Parker" mailing label reading: "To Mr. Tom Diskin, Elvis Exploitation Office, METRO-

Elvis memorabilia, including: Ten 1968 RCA-Victor wallet calendars with color Elvis photo; five 1974 RCA-Victor wallet calendars with "Elvis: Aloha From Hawaii" photo; five 1972 RCA-Victor wallet calendars with "Elvis—That's the Way It Is" photo; two 1969 RCA-Victor wallet calendars with photo of Elvis in his gold lame suit; one 1981 fan club calendar with black and white Elvis image; eleven 1956 "Love Me Tender" hologram buttons in the shape of a 45 rpm single—one red, six orange, four light orange and yellow; one 1971 advertisement for both Elvis' Las Vegas Hilton "Summer Festival" and stuffed "hound dog" merchandise; three 1975 posters of Elvis in "peacock" jumpsuit; three "All Star Shows" posters of Elvis in white jumpsuit. The above represents only represents a small percentage of the contents of the trunk.

$20,000 - 30,000

C46A MEMPHIS MAFIA CHECKS SIGNED BY ELVIS PRESLEY

Checks from the account of E.A. Presley made out to members of the Memphis Mafia including Lamar Fike, Dick Grob, Red West, Sonny West, Billy or Jo Smith, Marty Lacker, Larry Geller, Joe Esposito, Marvin Gambill, George Klein, Jerry Schilling, Gene Smith, Richard Davis, James Caughley, and Dave Hebler. All checks are signed by Elvis Presley. Range from 2 3/4 x 6 to 3 x 8 1/4 inches.

Checks are for various payments to many of the members of the Memphis Mafia. Payments are for expenses, plane tickets for girlfriend, services rendered, personal loans and gifts. Elvis made personal loans to Marty Lacker for $10,000, Red West for $20,000, Lamar Fike for $26,5000 for a home, and Dave Hebler for $7,700 for a karate school.

$25,000 - 30,000

C47A "HOW GREAT THOU ART" GRAMMY NOMINATION WITH RECORD

One page typed notification letter from the National Academy of Recording Arts & Sciences, dated January 1975. Nomination certificate stating that "Elvis Presley has been nominated in the Seventeenth Annual Grammy Awards for "How Great Thou Art" in the category of Best Inspirational Performance." With unreturned RSVP card and envelope and the original mailing envelope, sent to "Mr. Vernon Presley % Graceland." With unopened copy of "Elvis Recorded Live on Stage in Memphis," which includes the nominated performance. 11 x 8 1/2 inches letter. 5 1/8 x 7 7/8 nomination. 12 inches diameter record.

Elvis' original single version of the classic hymn never charted, but this live version from 1974 won Elvis his third and final Grammy. All three of Elvis' Grammys were awarded in religious categories, and, as was his common practice, he didn't accept any of them in person.

$3,500 - 4,000

C48A ACETATE OF FOUR SONGS

Dated 3/18/71 pink receipt from RCA Records with acetate sent to Felton Jarvis marked 3rd of 5. Acetate with songs recorded on one side; speed 33.3; songs are "Amazing Grace," "Early Morning Rain," "That's What You Get," and "First Time I Saw Your Face." Acetate in brown record sleeve. 5 1/2 x 8 1/2 inches receipt. 12-inch diameter acetate.

C46A

This recording session was held in Nashville at RCA's Studio B on March 15, 1971. RCA, the Colonel, and Jarvis had a different agenda for the session than Elvis, who got his inspiration from contemporary folk music. Both "Early Morning Rain" and "That's What You Get" were written by Gordon Lightfoot

and "The First Time. . ." by Ewan McColl. This song was once recorded by Peter, Paul, and Mary. Folk singer Judy Collins had recently sung "Amazing Grace." "Elvis was feeling bad the day of the session, and the next day landed in the hospital with secondary glaucoma.

$650 - 750

C49A ACETATE OF EIGHT SONGS BY ELVIS PRESLEY

Acetate of eight songs by Elvis Presley. Side one contains; "You Don't Have To Say You Love Me," "Just Pretend," "Twenty Days and Twenty Nights," and "Bridge Over Troubled Water." Side two contains; "Patch It Up," "Cabin On The Hill," Cindy, Cindy," and "Strangers In The Crowd." 12 x 12 inches.

Elvis recorded "You Don't Have To Say You Love Me," and "Just Pretend" on June 6, 1970, at RCA's Nashville studios. "You Don't Have to Say You Love Me" spent ten weeks on "Billboards" Hot 100 Chart peaking at #11. "Twenty Days and Twenty Nights" was recorded by Elvis on June 4,1970, and "Bridge Over Troubled Water" was recorded by Elvis on June 5, 1970; both at RCA's Nashville Studios. "Patch It Up," was recorded by Elvis on June 8, 1970, in Nashville. "Cindy, Cindy," was recorded by Elvis On June 4, 1970, and "Stranger In The Crowd," was recorded by Elvis on June 5, 1970; both in Nashville.

$650 - 750

C50A ELVIS PRESLEY'S CORDUROY JACKET AND PANTS

Matching brown corduroy jacket and pants. Jacket lining is brown with lavender squares. There are six fabric covered buttons on each cuff. The tag reads, "IC Costume."

This outfit was designed by Elvis' costume designer, Bill Belew, who designed Elvis' stage costumes. Elvis, a fashion guru in his own right, was not content to save the fabulous and flamboyant outfits just for his performances, so he had Belew design his casual wear as well.

$15,000 - 20,000

C51A ELVIS' BLUE PAJAMAS

One Munsing Wear pajama top, navy blue with red piping around collar, front panels, cuffs, and front pocket on left-hand side. Four front button closures with large white buttons. Designer tag reads: "Diplomat, 100% nylon, large." One Munsing Wear pajama bottom, navy blue with red piping around bottom; elastic waist band; straight-leg pants.

Elvis regularly wore sleepwear. Often he gave overnight guests pajamas if they needed them. Blue was Elvis' favorite color--even for his choice of sleepwear.

$8,000 - 12,000

C52A ELVIS PRESLEY'S MICROPHONE

Microphone by Shure in original red and blue box. Gold and black, Unidyne III Dynamic, model number 545G. Engraved in white, "Elvis Presley." 10 inches.

This was Elvis' personal microphone, made expressly for him.

$15,000 - 20,000

C53 NOTE TO ELVIS PRESLEY FROM JOAN RIVERS

Handwritten note to Elvis Presley from Joan Rivers on the inside of a yellow table card from International Hotel printed with, "Minimum Charge $15 per person." Rivers told Elvis that he was "tip-top". She signed it "XXXXX Joan Rivers." Under her signature is a smiley face. International Hotel Souvenir Menu. Cover shows a picture of Elvis singing, inside shows menu selection. 6 x 6 inches table card. 12 x 9 inches menu. Joan Rivers was a big fan of Elvis. Their daughters, Lisa Marie Presley and Melissa Rivers, went to school together at one time.

$750 - 850

C54 NOTES TO COLONEL TOM PARKER FROM BARRON HILTON

Handwritten notes from Barron Hilton (on his letterhead) to the Colonel: "We have a great logo and when it is identified with Elvis and you it is even greater" and "I like your letter to Hank Greenspan. I also like the comment that Elvis will be staying at Hilton Hotels." Elvis Las Vegas Hilton Souvenir Menu (blue, gold, and black on a white background): front has Hilton logo and rendering of Elvis singing, inside is the food and beverage items, and the back promotes Elvis' latest albums. 8 x 5 inches notes. 7 x 14 inches menu.

Barron Hilton at one time had the Colonel on salary to promote Hilton Hotels. $500 - 600

C55 ELVIS PRESLEY'S CONTRACT FOR THE HOUSTON LIVESTOCK SHOW & RODEO

Seven page agreement between Elvis Presley and the Houston Livestock Show & Rodeo bound in a black folder. Includes a cover sheet and a two

page letter dated January 7, 1970 from Roger H. Davis of the William Morris Agency which details Elvis Presley's compensation of $150,000. Included is a four-page agreement signed in blue ink by Elvis Presley, Col. Tom Parker, and M.C. Buddy Bray, President of the Houston Livestock Show & Rodeo. Photograph included. 11 1/2 x 9 1/4 inches folder. 11 x 8 1/2 inches pages.

Elvis' touring appearances at the Houston Livestock Show and Rodeo took place February 27, 28, and March 1, 1970 at the Houston Astrodome. This was the first show the Colonel lined up for Elvis outside Las Vegas. The audiences during his six

C54

C53

appearances turned out in record numbers at the "Dome." The only drawback of the event was that Elvis was somewhat bothered by the sound system, where he could hear his echo when he sang. Elvis held press conferences before the first performance and again on March 1, after the final show. At the final one, he was honored at a banquet where he was given several gold records from some of his recent hits.

$12,000 - 15,000

C56 PHOTO BOOK AGREEMENT BETWEEN RCA AND ELVIS PRESLEY

Original, typewritten agreement, dated April 17, 1970, between Elvis Presley and RCA Records. Agreement is typed on RCA letterhead, and is signed by Harry E. Jenkins, Col. Thomas A. Parker, and Elvis Presley. Contract covers both the United States and Canada. Elvis Presley photo book included. 11 x 8 1/2 inches agreement. 11 x 8 1/2 inches photo book.

This was one of many side deals that the Colonel worked out. All Star Shows received a flat payment of $50,000 for the unlimited use of this book for up to two years. The book features 16 pages of photographs of Elvis performing.

$5,000 - 6,000

C57 "ELVIS INTRO" SONG ARRANGEMENTS

Concert arrangements for "Also Sprach Zarathustra," with charts for each instrument. Handwritten arrangements credited to "Tommy Check." Encased in black folder with with raised red tape reading "Elvis Intro 2001" and with a gold "Elvis Presley" sticker on the inside cover. 14 x 12 inches folder.

This packet of arrangements was used by Elvis and his band during concerts in the Seventies. There are arrangement sheets for every musician who would play on the song. "Also Sprach Zarathustra" is a 19th century classical piece composed by Richard Strauss. It was used as the theme song to Stanley Kubrick's classic 1968 film "2001, A Space Odyssey." For Elvis it became dramatic entrance music for his concerts starting in 1972.

$3,000 - 4,000

C58 ELVIS PRESLEY'S PERSONAL KARATE EQUIPMENT

One pair of white foot pads with "Safe T Kick" printed on the toe. One pair of white, padded karate gloves with "Safe T Chop" printed on them. One pair of red knee pads. All of these belonged to Elvis Presley. Copy of invoice dated April 13, 1971 from the Martial Arts Supplies Company to Elvis for a list of karate items. Total bill is for $437.43. Original check included. 11 x 8 1/2 inches.

Elvis bought karate supplies at this Los Angeles store when he had a renewed interest in karate during the 1970's.

$2,000 - 2,500

C58

C59 LUGGAGE, CONTENTS AND RECEIPT FROM BEVERLY HILLS LUGGAGE & GIFT SHOPPE

Brown leather 12-inch-high overnight bag: two zipper pockets on one side; one large pocket on opposite side; silver metal locks and zippers. Statement dated 2/1/70 for Mr. Elvis Presley for merchandise purchased on 1/14 for $596.93. Attached receipt, signed by Elvis, shows the purchase of three nofold 8 suitors luggage. Signed by Elvis. Green check made out to Beverly Hills Luggage and Gift Shoppe for $596.93. Written on Elvis Presley Payroll and Expense Fund and signed by Joseph Hanks, one of the accountants. 8 1/2 x 5 1/2 inches statement. 7 x 4 1/4 inches receipt. 3 x 8 inches check .

The luggage is packed with Elvis' clothing and personal items: blue Munsing Wear pajamas with white trim, white shirt with elastic above elbows

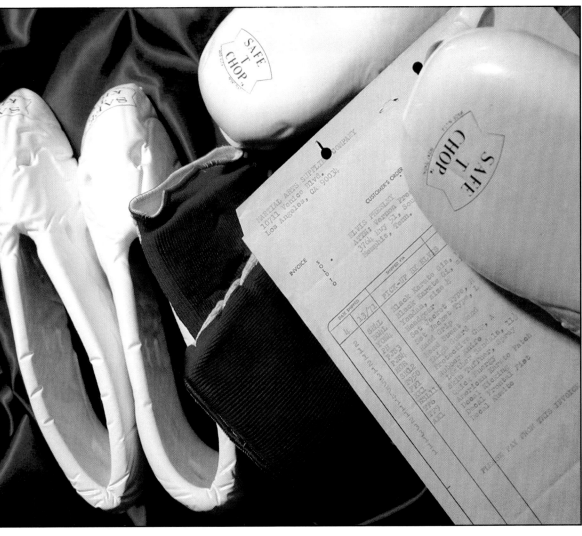

and at wrist, dark blue Pierre Cardin tie with his initials in light blue, black socks with gold toes, tie tack, cuff links, and brown zipper toiletry case made in Germany (containing cuticle scissors, mirror, nail file, plastic comb, silver toothbrush holder, soap holder, hairbrush, cologne bottle, and another large container).

$18,000 - 20,000

C60 ELVIS PRESLEY'S PATENT LEATHER BOOTS

One pair of Elvis' patent leather boots made with side zippers. Boots are size eleven, and on the inside are the words, "Made by Renegrades - made in Italy" - "Man made insole." They are burgundy red with a dark brown wood heel, and are in excellent condition.

Elvis loved these type of boots that had the side zippers, and had many pairs made throughout the sixties and seventies.

$6,000 - 8,000

C61 CORRESPONDENCE REGARDING ELVIS SUMMER FESTIVAL PROMOTION ITEMS

Three page letter dated July 8, 1970 to Bill Lucas from George Parkhill on MGM Studios letterhead. Letter details the Elvis Summer Festival promotion items and shipping and billing instructions. Items include scarves and rings, pennants, lighters, material, and catalogs. Signed by George L. Parkhill. Yellow souvenir scarf with rendering of Elvis' portrait and name on the four corners and Summer Festival and International Hotel imprinted in center. Wallet-size 1970 calendar with a signed color photograph of Elvis on front. Two triangular felt pennants; one yellow, one blue, with words "Elvis Summer Festival, International Hotel, (a Hilton Hotel) RCA Records" printed on them and a rendering of Elvis in concert. 11 x 8 1/2 inches letter. 24 x 24 inches scarf. 4 x 2 1/4 inches calendar. 12 x 29 inches pennant.

Summer Festival 1970 took place August 10 - September 8 at the International Hotel. Besides many celebrities attending the performances, Elvis' grandma, Minnie Mae, joined Priscilla in the booth. It was one of the few times she saw Elvis live on stage.

$800 - 1,000

C62 PROMOTIONAL OF ELVIS PRESLEY'S INTERNATIONAL HOTEL SHOW 1970

One page list of novelty items to be used in the promotion of the Elvis Presley Show at the International Hotel for August, 1970. Lists includes pennants, scarves, tote bags, and straw hats. "Elvis: The Other Sides - Worldside Gold Award Hits, Volume 2" box set in original shrink wrap. One plastic tote bag "Compliments of Elvis and the Colonel." Black, gold and red print Three scarves with "Elvis Presley" signature printed on them. One white, one light blue, and one dark blue. 11 x 8 1/2 inches list. 17 x 15" bag. 34 x 34" scarves.

Colonel Parker made certain that there was never a shortage of promotional items on hand at Elvis shows. This unopened box set includes four records. The records contain both sides of three singles, the A sides of two singles, and tracks from six EP's. Also included in the box set is an envelope containing a swatch of Elvis' clothing, and a large color portrait of Elvis. "Elvis: The Other Sides - Worldside Gold Award Hits, Volume 2" stayed on "Billboard's" Top LP's chart for seven weeks.

$1,500 - 2,800

C61   C62   C63

C63 LETTER AND RECORDINGS FROM JOSE FELICIANO

Letter dated August 3, 1970, to Elvis in Culver City, California, from Jose Feliciano on Feliciano's stationery and signed by the entertainer. Jose sends Elvis lead sheets and demo records for "Once There Was a Love" and "Destiny." Jose continues "Hopefully you can take time out of your busy schedule to listen to my songs which I believe you could do one heck of a job with. These songs have

both soul and inspiration which will appeal to you." 78 rpm acetate of "Destiny" 33 1/3 rpm of "Once There Was a Love" 11 x 8 1/2 inches.

Elvis did not record either of these songs suggested by Feliciano.

$750 - 850

C64 "AMERICAN TRILOGY" CONCERT ARRANGEMENTS

Concert arrangements for "American Trilogy," with charts for each instrument. Piano player Glen Hardin is listed as arranger. Package includes a "revised ending" and has handwritten pencil notes on most sheets. Encased in black folder with with raised red tape reading "American Trilogy With Strings" and with a gold "Elvis Presley" sticker on the inside cover. 14 x 12 inches folder.

This packet of arrangements was used by Elvis and his band during concerts in the Seventies. There are arrangement sheets for every musician who would play on the song. "American Trilogy" is a medley of Civil War-era songs: the Confederate theme "Dixie," the abolitionist anthem "The Battle Hymn of the Republic" and the slave song "All My Trials." The "American Trilogy" was a highlight of Elvis concerts in the Seventies. Performances of the trilogy were featured on the 1972 tour documentary "Elvis in Concert" and the 1973 television special "Elvis: Aloha From Hawaii."

$5,000 - 6,000

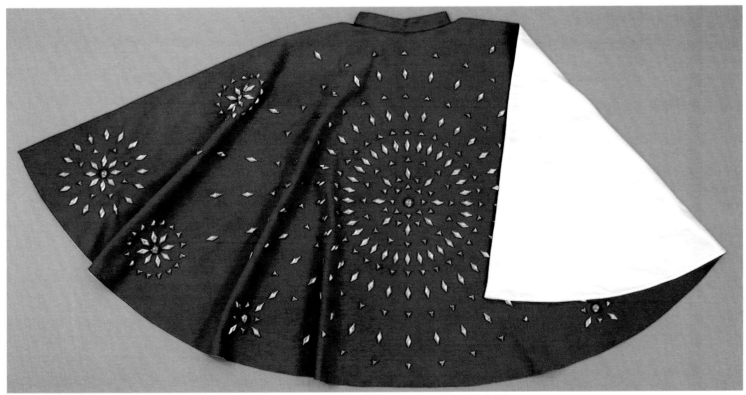

C65

C65 ELVIS PRESLEY'S "BURNING LOVE" CAPE

Red cape in fingertip length; fully lined in cream-colored synthetic material. Decorated with gold studs in a starburst design; cape attaches to back of jumpsuit with hooks and eyes and Velcro fasteners; studs are in various shapes. Center of cape has large starburst design, spreading to smaller starburst designs.

In April 1972, Elvis performed "Burning Love" at his concerts in Richmond, Virginia; Little Rock, Arkansas; and El Paso, Texas. He wore this cape with a bright-red jumpsuit. The concert was shown on the "Elvis on Tour" documentary. In the same year, the song "Burning Love" made it to number 2 on the pop charts.

$50,000 - 70,000

C66 PROTOTYPE FOR THE FORTY-FIVE SLEEVE OF ELVIS PRESLEY'S SINGLE "BURNING LOVE," AND "IT'S A MATTER OF TIME"

Prototype for the sleeve of Elvis' single "Burning Love," and "It's A Matter Of Time." Side one and side two are identical with a photograph of Elvis standing in a red jump suit with a gold belt and a red/white cape. He is holding a microphone in his left hand. At the top of each side is the name "Elvis" in yellow. At the bottom is a red 1/2" strip with the words "Now Available" in white and "Elvis As Recorded At Madison Square Garden Album" in black lettering. The only difference in the two sides is that one side has "Burning Love" listed first, and below that "It's A Matter Of TIme," - the other side is reversed with "It's A Matter Of Time" on the top. On the right hand corner on both sides is "RCA 74-0760 Victor." 7 X 7 Inches.

"Burning Love was recorded by Elvis On March 28, 1972, at RCA Hollywood studios. Dennis Linde who composed the song played guitar on the recording. It reached #2 during a 15-week stay on "Billboards" Hot 100 chart. "It's A Matter of Time" was recorded by Elvis on March 29, 1972, at RCA's Hollywood studios. The single had a thirteen week stay on "Billboards" country chart, peaking at #36; it reached #9 on the Easy-Listening chart.

$3,000 - 3,500

C67 NOTEBOOK FILLED WITH CONTRACTS, INVOICES, CORRESPONDENCE, POSTERS, AND CONTRACTS SIGNED BY ELVIS PRESLEY

Notebook of contracts, invoices, correspondence, and posters broken into twelve categories: Elvis, Colonel, Rinaldi (printing), Miscellaneous, RCA Camden Agreement, RCA agreement for Volume. II Gold, Wardrobe info/RCA Volume. II Project, RCA Promotional Income, Camden Royalty, Camden - 1973, Satellite Agreement, and Satellite LP. A few documents contain original Elvis Presley signatures. Pages vary in size from invoices to letters, and are contained within a hard bound, three hole punch, green notebook. A number of pages are covered with a clear plastic. Varies from 11 x 8 1/2 to 7 x 8 1/2 inches Pages. 11 1/2 x 11 1/2 inches Notebook.

Book includes an itemized wardrobe list of the clothing that was cut into swatches for a promotional giveaway for RCA. This notebook shows the extensive merchandising that the Colonel was known for. $13,000 - 15,000

C68 SIGNED AGREEMENT FOR "ELVIS' WORLD-WIDE GOLD AWARD HITS, VOLUME I"

Letter to Colonel T. A. Parker from Harry E. Jenkins dated February 6, 1970 on RCA letterhead. Letter details the conditions and terms related to the release of "Elvis World-Wide Award Hits, Volume I." This original agreement is signed by Harry E. Jenkins, Colonel T. A. Parker, and Elvis Presley. Box set of 8-track tapes; "Worldwide 50 Gold Award Hits, Volume. 1"; box set holds Special Bonus of New Photo Book. 11 x 8 1/2 inches letter. 12 1/4 x 12 1/4 inches box set.

This unopened 8-track set highlights Elvis' gold record awards. The cover shows each recording and the month and year in which Elvis recorded the song. $7,000 - 8,000

C69 PHOTOS AND MEMORABILIA FROM 1971 SUMMER FESTIVAL

Four black-and-white photographs, including 1 photo of Elvis Presley artwork by June Kelly and 3 photos of "That's the Way It Is" promotional materials. Four trunks-- green, blue, pink, and red-- stuffed with memorabilia of the time period 8 x 10 inches photographs.

C67

C68

Every time Elvis appeared in Las Vegas, the Colonel did a huge promotional for the appearance. Photography for "That's the Way It Is" took place at the International Hotel in August 1970, when the star was touring there during his third season.

$1,300 - 1,500

C70 "CHILD OF THE UNIVERSE" CONCERT ARRANGEMENTS

Concert arrangements for "Child of the Universe," with charts for each instrument. Includes a vocal arrangement sheet with lyrics. Encased in black folder with with raised red tape reading "Child of the Universe" and with a gold "Elvis Presley" sticker on the inside cover. 14 x 12 inches folder.

This packet of arrangements was used by Elvis and his band during concerts in the Seventies. There are arrangement sheets for every musician who would play on the song.

$2,000 - 3,000

C71 MEMPHIS MAFIA PLANE TICKETS

Seven American Airlines Jet Express first class tickets for January 3, 1971, flight #261 from Memphis to Dallas. Each ticket paid by credit card and signed in blue ink by Charles Hodge. Tickets in the name of : "Dr. J. Carpenter," R. Davis, B. Morris, S. West, C. Hodge, R. West, and R. Stanley. Photograph included. 3 1/4 x 8 1/2 inches.

"Dr. John Carpenter" is an alias for Elvis Presley; it springs from his character name in the 1969 movie Change of Habit. During this trip Elvis' registered at the Royal Coach Motor Hotel under yet another favorite pseudonym, "Jon Burrows." The other names are those of "Memphis Mafia" members Richard Davis, Bill Morris, Sonny West, Charlie Hodge, Red West and Richard Stanley. "Memphis Mafia" was a media-created term for Elvis' entourage of friends, employees and associates; the label sprang up in the early Sixties, after Elvis' return from the Army, and it stuck.

$3,500 - 4,000

C72 RACQUETBALL EQUIPMENT AND RECEIPTS FOR RACQUET BALL BUILDING

Elvis Presley's racquetball and racquet. Brown cover printed in gold with "Elvis." Dated 1/20/76 2-page statement of 38 different expenses incurred during the project of building the Racquet Ball Building by Homes by Tomlinson, Inc. in Memphis. Billed to Elvis Presley in the total amount of $34,164.45. Some items include Tri State Tile & Marble Co. for $5,582.60 and Whitehaven Plumbing for $3,551.55. Pink receipt dated July 30, 1975 addressed to Elvis Presley from Game Sales Company, Inc. Red Ink indicates a purchase of 1 New Bally "Knockout" pin game for $945. 8 1/2 x 5 1/2 inches statement from Homes. 10 1/2 x 8 1/2 inches Game Sales receipt.

After one of Elvis' hospitalizations, his physician, Dr. Nick, encouraged Elvis to exercise. Elvis not only took up racquetball, he built an entire racquetball building complete with a court, two lounges - upper and lower, and a private dressing room for Elvis with shower, bath, jacuzzi, massage table, and a dressing area for friends.

$3,500 - 4,000

C73. TEN OUTSTANDING YOUNG MEN AWARD DOCUMENTS

One program for The United States Jaycees 33rd Annual Congress of America's Ten Outstanding Young Men ceremony, held January 15-16, 1971 in Memphis. Seventy-one page booklet, blue cover with gold print. Receipt from Memphis Junior Chamber of Commerce, dated January 12, 1971 and billed to Elvis Presley, for 50 Award Ceremony tickets, eight Prayer Breakfast tickets, eight Keynote luncheon tickets and two registration tickets ($416.00). Receipt from Harry Levitch Jewelers in Memphis dated January 15, 1971 for the purchase by Elvis of 25 men's watches ($1,938.75). Receipt from Tony Barrasso Entertainment Agency in Memphis, dated January 18, 1971 and billed to Vernon Presley, for two violin players for January 16, 1971 ($125.00). Receipt from Pepperite in Memphis, dated January 15 and billed to Vernon Presley, for printed cards ($201.30). Bill from Pinkerton's, Inc. in Memphis, dated January 18, 1971

and billed to Vernon Presley, for the hire of a guard on January 16. Bill from Four Flames restaurant in Memphis, dated January 20, 1971 and billed to Elvis Presley, for dinner and bar charges on January 16, 1971 for 100 guests ($2,155.51). Copy of one-page invoice from IC Costume Company in Hollywood, California addressed to Vernon Presley. Invoice dated January 25, 1971 lists a tuxedo, silk ruffled shirt, five jumpsuits, four belts, and the repair of two suits purchased for Elvis Presley totaling $4,860. Elvis' personal copy of the award press kit. 9 x 7 inches program. 7 x 8 1/2 inches tickets receipt. 7 1/4 x 8 1/2 inches jewelry receipt. 8 x 8 1/2 inches violin receipt. 7 x 8 1/2 inches card receipt. 11 x 8 1/2 inches guard receipt. 7 1/2 x 7 1/4 inches restaurant receipt. 11 x 8 1/2 inches tuxedo invoice. 11 5/8 x 9 inches press kit.

This particular honor was the only award that Elvis ever received in person. It was very special to Elvis, because he felt that it was a rare recognition of him as a man rather than a performer, and the trophy he received was taken along during all of his subsequent travels. Elvis was nominated for the award by former Shelby County sheriff and "Memphis Mafia" member Bill Morris. The keynote speaker at the awards ceremony was future president and then United Nations Ambassador appointee George Bush. As these receipts attest, Elvis bought a watch for each of the other honorees and held a private party for them after the awards ceremony.

$6,500 - 7,500

C74 THE COMPLETE RCA RECORD AND TAPE CATALOG 1971 WITH CAMDEN RECORDS ALBUM

A copy of the 172 page RCA catalog from 1971. One white, heavy cardboard Camden Records

C72
C73

record album containing ten LPs. 8 1/2 x 11 1/4 inches catalog. 12 3/4 x 14 1/2 inches record album.

Record album includes: "Singer Presents Elvis Singing Flaming Star and Others," "Let's Be Friends," "Elvis' Christmas Album," Almost in Love," "Elvis," "C'mon Everybody," "I Got Lucky," "Elvis Sings Hits From His Movies," "Burning Love," and "Separate Ways." Camden was an RCA subsidiary that released Elvis' discount albums. "Burning Love," included here, was Camden's only gold record.

$800 - 1,000

C75 PROTOTYPE ARTWORK OF FABRIC SWATCH FOR 1971 ELVIS PRESLEY ALBUM. "ELVIS: THE OTHER SIDES - WORLDWIDE GOLD AWARD HITS, VOLUME 2"

Four page photographic layout on heavy black card stock, tracing paper, mylar and heavy mat board, each page including technical notes. On first page center includes 4" x 5 " black and white negative of "something from Elvis' wardrobe for you" framed fabric swatch and right corner is "Peter E. George" label. Third page includes actual fabric swatch; third and fourth pages include artwork. Original box set of "Elvis: The Other Sides - Worldwide Gold Award Hits, Volume 2." Ten envelopes with clear window displaying a swatch of fabric. Printed with "Something from Elvis' wardrobe for you." 4 x 5 inches Negative. 13 1/8 x 15 1/4 inches Pages. 1 1/2 x 1/2 inches Swatch. 1 3/4 x 2 1/2 inches Artwork/Frame.

The first batch of this album sold included a swatch of fabric from Elvis' wardrobe, a large full color portrait of Elvis, and four albums. All of the original items are included. "Elvis: The Other Sides - Worldside Gold Award Hits, Volume 2" stayed on "Billboard's" Top LP's chart for seven weeks.

$8,000 - 10,000

C76 BANNER FOR ELVIS:THAT'S THE WAY IT IS,

Fabulous satin banner with hot pink background and orange, white, blue, yellow, and black in the lettering. Banner reads: "A Personal Appearance Film ELVIS THAT'S THE WAY IT IS, an MGM Film Coming Soon. Approximately 9 x 15 feet

This giant banner served as a promotional item for the movie "Elvis: That's the Way It Is," which premiered in November of 1970 as a documentary on Elvis' appearance at the Las Vegas International Hotel. Every time Elvis entertained in Las Vegas, the Colonel did a huge promotional for the appearance. Photography for That's the Way It Is took place at the International Hotel in August 1970, when the star was touring there during his third season.

$15,000 - 20,000

C75

C77

C77 THREE AIRLINE TICKETS FOR ELVIS PRESLEY AND FAMILY

American Airlines ticket for Elvis, traveling under the name of Dr. J. Carpenter, round trip Los Angeles to Memphis for March 24, 1970. Continental Airlines ticket and boarding pass for Elvis, traveling under the name of Dr. J. Carpenter, round trip Los Angeles to Denver, dated April 16, 1971.

American Airlines ticket for Elvis, Priscilla and Lisa, traveling under the names of Mr. and Mrs. J. Carpenter and Lisa, round trip Los Angeles to Philadelphia dated April 19, 1971. 3 1/4 x 8 inches Two American Airline tickets. 7 1/2 x 8 3/4 inches Two jackets for tickets. 3 1/4 x 8 inches Continental Airline tickets. 8 x 8 inches Jacket for ticket. 5 x 2 1/2 inches Boarding pass.

The trip to Philadelphia was to visit Priscilla's brother Don. Dr. John Carpenter was a false name that Elvis used frequently. It was the name of the character he played in "Change of Habit."

$2,000 - 2,500

C78 ELVIS PRESLEY HANDWRITTEN NOTE AND ACETATE

Note from 1971, in Elvis Presley's handwriting, written on back of torn out magazine page. Cursive note: ""The first time I saw your face' using last cut." And a printed note: " 'Help me make it thru the night.' " Acetate of "The First Time Ever I Saw Your Face." 3 x 2 1/2 inches.

These two songs were on a list of possibilities that Elvis brought to a recording session on March 15, 1971. He did record "The First Time . . ." (a Ewan McColl song) on that date, and then recorded "Help Me Make It . . ." on May 17, 1971 (a Kris Kristofferson song).

$2,500 - 3,000

C79 SCOUT WITH AUTO PARTS RECEIPT

1974 yellow Scout Jeep. Pink invoice from Mac's
Auto Parts on Elvis Presley Blvd, dated July 12,
1977. For "1 set of Ignition wires for Scout Jeep."
Cost: $7.37. 5 1/2 x 8 1/2 inches invoice.

Elvis purchased the Scout for use on the grounds of
Graceland.

$13,000 - 15,000

C80 ELVIS PRESLEY TELEPROMPTER LYRIC
BOOK

Heavy blue four ring binder, dated January 16,
1976. Spine reads "lyrics" and has the handwritten
initials "EP." 14 3/4 x 11 x 3 inches.

Includes mimeographed lyrics to over 200 songs
Elvis performed in concert. This was used by Elvis
during concerts in the late Seventies.

$13,000 - 15,000

C81 · ELVIS PRESLEY ON TOUR—NOVEMBER 1971

Black binder containing information relating to Elvis Presley tour dates from November 5-16, 1971. Includes original, five page typed contract, dated September 1, 1971 and signed in blue ink by Elvis Presley and in black marker by Colonel Tom Parker. Two page typed contract between Elvis Presley and Colonel Parker's All Star Shows, dated October 13, 1971 and signed in blue ink by Elvis Presley and Colonel Tom Parker. Also includes other signed contracts and itinerary information. With a 16-page photo booklet from the tour. 11 1/2 x 9 1/4" binder. 10 7/8 x 8 1/2" photo booklet.

This strenuous 14-show/12-day tour was one of firsts for Elvis. It was on this tour that J.D. Sumner and the Stamps replaced the Imperials as Elvis' vocal back-up group and comedian Jackie Kahane became a regular part of the show. This tour also marked Elvis' first appearance in a matching cape and jumpsuit and was when Al Dvorin became the regular concert announcer, coining the phrase "Elvis has left the building."

$16,000 - 18,000

C82 ELVIS' PERSONAL FILM OF "THAT'S THE WAY IT IS" AND ACETATES

One film case holding 16 mm 1970 film of "That's the Way It Is": from Colonel Parker's collection. Side note reads "2,000 feet, 3 reels." Red label with raised white letters reads: "That's the Way It Is" 1970, #32. Cases are brown with metal corners, a handle on one end, and a horizontal and vertical buckled strap. 15 1/4 x 15 3/4 inches.

Produced by MGM in 1970,That's the Way It Is premiered in November of that year as a documentary

C81

on Elvis' appearance at the Las Vegas International Hotel.

ESTIMATE

C83 "ELVIS - THAT'S THE WAY IT IS" DOCUMENTS

Colonel Parker's copy of the MGM contract, dated May 7, 1970, for production of a movie consisting of photography and sound recordings from Elvis' appearances at the International Hotel. Includes copies of agreements with Elvis Presley and with the International Hotel, a rider dated May 26, 1970, and a letter to James Aubrey of MGM from Colonel Parker dated September 24, 1970. Original two-page agreement written on William Morris letterhead. Outlines the payment arrangement between Elvis, the Colonel and MGM. Original and copy are signed in blue ink by Elvis Presley.

Documents are bound by a black folder. Elvis Presley's album, "On Stage February 1970." 11 x 8 1/2 inches Contract. 11 1/2 x 9 inches Folder. 12 1/4 x 12 1/4 inches album.

Elvis received $270,000 plus $50,000 for expenses from MGM for "Elvis - That's the Way It Is." Colonel Parker received $90,000 plus $50,000 for expenses.

$8,000 - 10,000

C84 PUBLICITY PORTFOLIO AND REHEARSAL REQUIREMENTS FOR "THAT'S THE WAY IT IS"

Tom Diskin letter, written on MGM letterhead, explaining what is needed for an Elvis Presley rehearsal. Items include dress (dark pants, white long sleeved shirt), piano (will be tuned prior to rehearsal), and tymphani<sic>. Another sheet on rehearsal needs asks for one kitchen-type stool (30 to 36 inches high), sound engineer, and stage monitoring system, among other items. Photographs included. Editor's publicity portfolio for "That's the Way It Is." From MGM. Includes photographs, lists of credits, information about the documentary, and information about the star. 11 x 8 1/2 inches letters. 11 1/2 x 9 inches portfolio.

"That's the Way It Is," a documentary filmed by MGM, opened nationally on November 11, 1970. The film highlighted Elvis as a performer, showing his energy and enthusiasm on stage and the reactions of his fans. The film documented several concerts, as well as the annual Elvis Presley convention held in Luxembourg.

$650 - 750

C85 BRIEFCASE FILLED WITH PERSONAL ITEMS

Black leather briefcase with "EAP," "TCB," and "PVT" stickers by the handle and a combination lock bearing the inscription of the manufacturer "CORBIN SESAMEE." "EAP" stands for "Elvis Aaron Presley." Briefcase filled with Elvis' personal items. With receipt dated July 18, 1971 from Bon Voyage Bazaar in Beverly Hills for the purchase of two briefcases. Bill totaling $393.75 with "Briefcases for Elvis" written in blue ink. Joe Esposito's American Express credit card receipt for the purchase, signed in blue ink by Esposito. 18 1/2 x 12 x 4 1/2 inches deep briefcase. 7 x 4 1/4 inches receipt. 3 1/4 x 4 7/8 inches credit card receipt.

Briefcase includes: One "Cross" pen and mechanical pencil set inside a black and gold case. Both writing instruments have "Elvis Presley" engraved on the barrel. One gold-colored "Swank" cigarette

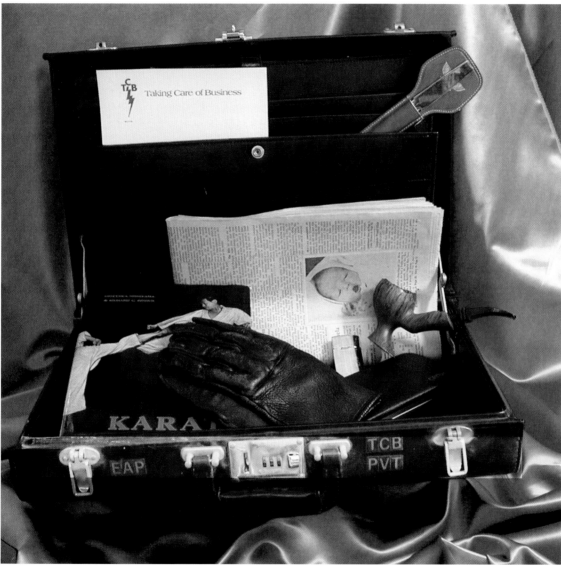

lighter with "EP" engraved on the front and "To Someone Special Pat" engraved on the side panel. Found upstairs at Graceland. One brown and black pipe. Elvis' personal hardcover copy of the book "Karate—The Art of 'Empty Hands' Fighting,'" written by Hidetaka Nishyama and Richard C. Brown. Book dated 1974 lists cover price of $11.50 and contains black and

white photos of karate moves with instructions. One pair of well-worn black leather motorcycle gloves, found upstairs at Graceland. One silver letter opener with brown leather holder. Holder has logo reading "Jack Adams, Aircraft Sales, Twinkletown Airport, Walls, MS." Three sheets of white personal stationery with gold "TCB-Elvis" lightning bolt logo and "Taking Care of Business" written in gold across the top. One complete copy of the Memphis "Commercial Appeal" daily newspaper dated Tuesday, February 6, 1968. This was the day after Elvis and Priscilla's newborn daughter Lisa Marie was brought home from the hospital. Picture of Lisa Marie appears on the bottom right corner of the front page with a caption reading "Song or Yawn? Four day old Lisa Marie Presley was either bored to yawns or she had a Presley song in her heart yesterday as her parents, Mr. and Mrs. Elvis Presley, took her home from Baptist Hospital. Born Thursday, the baby weighed 6 pounds, 15 ounces." There is a color picture on page 32 and a story on page 7.

$20,000 - 30,000

C86 CONTRACTS FOR INTERNATIONAL HOTEL APPEARANCE, AUGUST 4 - SEPTEMBER 6, 1971

AGVA Standard Form of Artists Engagement Contract dated June 7, 1971, between Elvis Presley and the International Hotel. Contract for performance dates beginning on August 9, 1971 through September 6, 1971. Stamped in red with "Members Copy." Signed in blue ink by Elvis Presley. AGVA Standard Form of Artists Engagement Contract dated June 10, 1971, for the Imperials. Contract signed by Joe Moscheo, manager of the Imperials. AGVA Standard Form of Artists Engagement Contract dated June 10, 1971, for Kathy Westmoreland. Contract is signed by Kathy Westmoreland and for Elvis by Tom Diskin. AGVA Standard Form of Artists Engagement Contract for the Sweet Inspirations, dated June 15, 1971. "Elvis Presley" signature by Tom Diskin in blue ink. "Sweet Inspirations" signature by Eddie Harris, their agent, in blue ink. William Morris Agency contract dated June 10, 1971 for James Burton and 5 musicians. Signed in black ink by Elvis Presley and James Burton. William Morris Agency contract dated June 10, 1971 for John Wilkinson. "Elvis Presley" signature by Tom Diskin in blue ink. Signed by John Wilkinson. William Morris Agency contract dated June 10, 1971 for Glen D. Hardin. "Elvis Presley" signature by Tom Diskin in blue ink. Signed by Glen Hardin. William Morris Agency contract dated June 10, 1971 for Jerry Scheff and five musicians. "Elvis Presley" signature by Tom Diskin in blue ink. Signed by Jerry Scheff. William Morris Agency contract dated June 10, 1971 for . Signed in black ink by Elvis Presley and Ronnie Tutt. Contract for the hire of five musicians led by drummer Tutt. Complimentary Souvenir Menu from the Elvis' appearance at the International Hotel in 1971. Yellow and black on front with Elvis singing, pink and white menu inside, and ad on back for record box set. 14 x 8 1/2" each contract. 12 x 9 "menu.

During this 1971 engagement at the International Hotel, Elvis broke his own record of attendance when he played for a crowd of 4,428. Also during this engagement, Elvis was awarded a lifetime achievement award from the National Academy of Recording Arts and Sciences.Elvis asked the Jordanaires to back him; however, they already were quite busy with their careers, so they signed the Imperials as his backup group. Kathy Westmoreland began with Elvis' show on August 16, 1970, when she replaced Millie Kirkham as a soprano backup singer. Elvis asked The Sweet Inspirations to sing backup for him after he heard

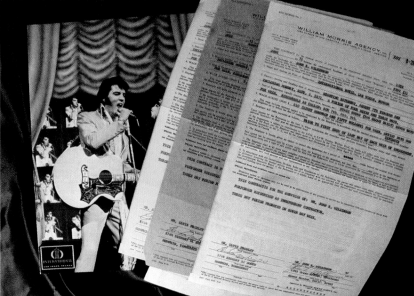

C86

their record and their soul hit, "Sweet Inspiration." They originally sang with Aretha Franklin. James Burton was the lead guitarist of Elvis' touring band from 1969 to 1977 and also played on some of Elvis' later recording sessions. Generally considered to be one of the very best early rock and roll guitar players, Burton did celebrated work with Dale Hawkins ("Suzie-Q") and Ricky Nelson ("Hello Mary Lou") in the late fifties and sixties before joining Elvis' band. John Wilkinson played rhythm guitar for the TCB Band that Elvis put together in 1969. Glen Hardin was the piano player for the same band. Hardin also did some arranging for Elvis.

Jerry Scheff, a bass player, was a member of the TCB Band between 1969 and 1976. Scheff was "blown away" by Elvis upon first meeting him and said of him, "He loved to sing for people, he loved to knock people out." Scheff had previously been a member of the Doors headed by Jim Morrison. The drummer Ronnie Tutt joined Elvis' band before his first Vegas engagement in the summer of 1969.
$8,000 - 10,000

C87   JOHN F. KENNEDY CENTER PROMO BOOKLET AND INVITATION TO PERFORM

Two-page letter dated January 13, 1971, to Elvis from Roger Stevens and Julius Rudel at the John F. Kennedy Center for the Performing Arts and a 16-page promotional booklet about the Center. The Center is asking performers to donate their time to help promote it. A handwritten note says: "Elvis, Read this and we can talk about it. We will have to handle this very carefully. Col." 11 x 8 1/2 inches letter and booklet.

Elvis was asked to perform at the Kennedy Center as a Founding Artist, during the opening season, 1971-72. He did not accept the offer.
$800 - 1,000

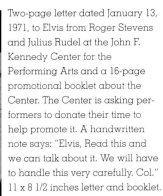

C88 PRELIMINARY PRODUCTION NOTES FOR ELVIS

Presley's Documentary "That's The Way It Is" Three pages of preliminary production notes for a documentary of Elvis which was released November 11, 1970.   "Elvis: That's the Way It Is" album included. 11 x 8 1/2 inches notes. 12 1/4 x 12 1/4 inches album.

The notes discuss Elvis' movies, recordings, and that the project will be guided by Denis Sanders.
$800 - 1,000

C89 ELVIS' ALOHA CAPE

Cream colored cape with large American eagle with full wing span. Eagle made with red, blue, and gold stones and studs. Calf-length cape is fully lined with blue synthetic fabric. 64 x 64 inches.

This was the cape originally designed for Elvis to wear during the "Elvis, Aloha From Hawaii" special. However, with its calf length design and enormous amount of studs and stones, the cape proved to be too heavy. After trying this on, Elvis had his designer Bill Belew make a waist length version of the cape which is the now famous cape he actually wore during the telecast. "Elvis - Aloha from Hawaii" was seen via satellite around the world by one billion people in 40 different countries.

$50,000 - 70,000

C90 LETTER AND CONTRACT FOR ELVIS - ALOHA FROM HAWAII

Copy of letter dated December 4, 1972 from Elvis to the Colonel, giving the Colonel authority to sign the contracts for him for the Hawaii Satellite Show and for the Aloha from Hawaii Album. Copy of Overall Costs and Income for Elvis - Aloha from Hawaii Show. Copy of 3-page contract for Elvis - Aloha from Hawaii Show with original signatures of George L. Parkhill of RCA Record Tours and Colonel Parker. Contract states payment of $900,000, with break down of pay to Elvis, the Colonel, All Star Shows, Diskin, and William Morris Agency. Photograph included. 11 x 8 1/2 inches

RCA Record Tours was a special branch that Colonel Parker had RCA create in order to facilitate and fund Elvis' tours. "Elvis - Aloha from Hawaii" was seen via satellite around the world by one billion people in 40 different countries.

$5,000 - 6,000

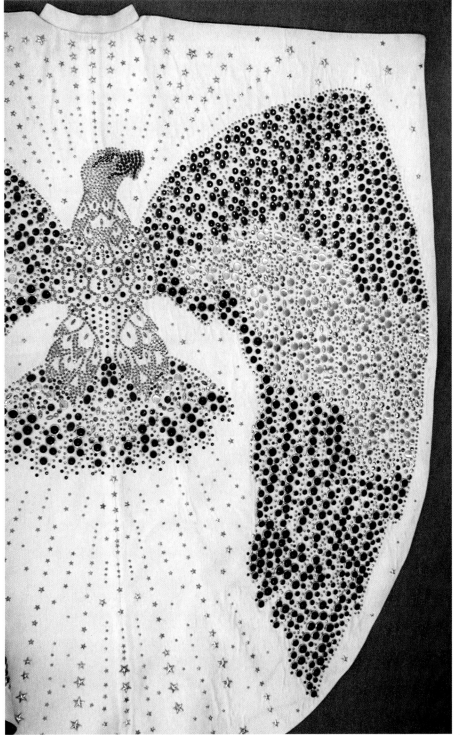

C91 "JAILHOUSE ROCK" SONG ARRANGEMENTS

Concert arrangements for "Jailhouse Rock," with charts for each instrument. Handwritten notes in pencil and red ink on most sheets. Encased in black folder with with raised red tape reading "Jailhouse Rock Arena" and with a gold "Elvis Presley" sticker on the inside cover. 14 x 12 inches folder.

This packet of arrangements was used by Elvis and his band during the 1968 Special. There are arrangement sheets for every musician who would play on the song. The Leiber- and Stoller-penned "Jailhouse Rock" was one of Elvis' most popular records and the title song from one of his most successful films. The song remained a popular component of Elvis' live shows throughout the Seventies. An Elvis performance of the song can be seen in his posthumous "Elvis in Concert" television special.

$4,000 - 5,000

C92 "HOUND DOG" CONCERT ARRANGEMENTS

Concert arrangements for "Hound Dog," with charts for each instrument. Copies of published sheet music also included, with sections crossed out. Don Hannah is listed as the arranger. Encased in black folder with with raised blue tape reading "Hound Dog" and with a gold "Elvis Presley" sticker on the inside cover. 14 x 12 inches folder.

This packet of arrangements was used by Elvis and his band during concerts in the Seventies. There are arrangement sheets for every musician who would play on the song. The Leiber- and Stoller-

penned R&B classic is one of Elvis' most famous and successful songs. The 1956 song remained a popular concert staple throughout Elvis' career, and live performances of the song can be seen in Elvis' "Aloha From Hawaii" and "Elvis in Concert" television specials, both from the Seventies. A large, scrawled pencil note on the "tenor sax" arrangement sheet reads "Turn Over Quick." The

C93

"3rd trumpet" arrangement sheet has the "H" in "Hound Dog" crossed out and replaced with a "Gr" to read "Ground Dog," with "One of my favorites" written below the title. The "4th trumpet" arrangement sheet has the "Dog" in "Hound Dog" crossed out and replaced with "Geek." Elvis' horn players, apparently, had a surfeit of free time.

$5,000 - 7,000

C93 SYMPHONIZER AND BENCH

Lowrey brass-and-string symphonizer: wooden with base covered in red cloth. Numerous controls, including those for a tape recorder, rhythms, octaves, and chorus. Wooden maple bench with hinged top. Organ sheet music by Lowrey inside lid. 24 inches high by 13 x 14 inches wide bench.

This symphonizer and bench are originally from Elvis' single-story, white stucco home on Chino Canyon Drive in Palm Springs. Two songs--"I Miss You" and "Are You Sincere"-- were recorded in this home. This symphonizer is similar to one now found in Elvis' Graceland upstairs office.

$15,000 - 20,000

C94 ELVIS PRESLEY ACETATES AND ALBUM

Acetates of Elvis Presley's "He Touched Me" and "Bosom of Abraham." Album of "He Touched Me." 12 1/2 x 12 1/2 inches.

Both of these were gospel songs that Elvis recorded in 1971.

$800 - 1,000

C95 BANK AMERICARD RECEIPT

Bank Americard Receipt dated January 22, 1971, from a sporting goods store in Sahara, Las Vegas. Receipt is for Elvis Presley's card and signed by him. Sale is for guns and ammo and totals $725.44. Photograph included. Ammunition 3 1/4 x 7 3/8 inches.

From the time he was a young boy, Elvis loved guns. He eventually collected and carried quite an assortment of them.

$1,300 - 1,500

C96 LETTER, PROOF, AND ACETATE FOR "MAMA LIKED THE ROSES"

Typed letter dated March 17, 1970 to Col. Parker from Harry Jenkins' on personalized RCA stationery. States that he has enclosed a color first proof of a single cover for Col. Parker's review. Included is the four-color proof which pictures Elvis Presley dressed in a white jacket against a traditional background including an arrangement of roses, candle, and painting of the Last Supper. This first proof is marked with handwritten notes to the printer in black ink . Acetate for "Mama Liked the Roses" and "The Wonder of You." 11 x 8 1/2 inches Paper. 15 x 15 inches Proof.

This pictures was for the cover of "Mama Liked the Roses" which was released in May, 1970. This song was written for Elvis by Johnny Christopher and stayed on "Billboard's" top 100 chart for 12 weeks.

$2,000 - 2,500

C97 "C.C. RIDER" CONCERT ARRANGEMENTS

Concert arrangements for "C.C. Rider," with charts for each instrument. There are handwritten notes in pencil on most sheets. Encased in black folder with with raised red tape reading "C.C. Rider" and with a gold "Elvis Presley" sticker on the inside cover. 14 x 12 inches folder.

This packet of arrangements was used by Elvis and his band during concerts in the Seventies. There are arrangement sheets for every musician who would play on the song. "C.C. Rider," also known as "See See Rider," is a rhythm and blues song written by Big Bill Broonzy that was an Elvis concert staple in the Seventies, frequently serving as his opening number. The song appeared on numerous Elvis albums, including the live soundtrack albums to his "Aloha From Hawaii" and

"Elvis in Concert" television specials. Pencil doodles on the back of the "4th trumpet" arrangement sheet includes an elaborate drawing of the band playing and the audience. The arrangement sheet for "baritone sax," has the name "Nixon" written twice in pencil with the "X" drawn as a swastika and Soviet hammer and sickle respectively. Apparently the baritone sax player was no great fan of the embattled president.

$3,000 - 4,000

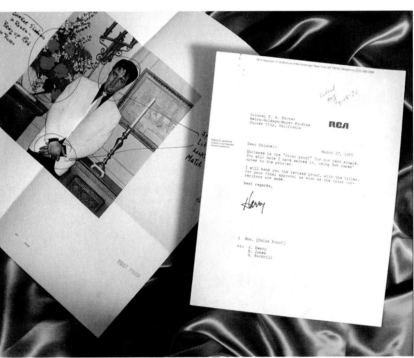

C96

C98 ELVIS AND NIXON OVER THE YEARS

 One page typed letter, dated December 23, 1974, sent from Richard Nixon to Elvis Presley and signed in black ink by Nixon. Original note to Elvis from Lt. Michael R. Nazarawh of the White House Security Services, dated January 24, 1971. The note, written on plain white paper, was in reference to Elvis' visit to President Nixon. Photograph included. 8 x 5" security letter. 10 1/2 x 7 1/4" Nixon letter.

Elvis visited President Nixon in the White House on December 21, 1970, where he received an official agents badge from the narcotics bureau. During the visit Elvis met some of the White House security guards, including Nazarawh, who writes: "Recalling how much you admired the E.P.S. collar insignia on our uniforms - when you arrived quite early in the morning at the Main Gate of the White House several weeks ago, I was able to obtain a set for you (off the record)." The letter from Nixon extends gratitude to Elvis for calling the President while he was hospitalized. The top left hand corner of this letter has been torn.

$2,000 - 2,500

C99 HANDWRITTEN CONTRACT WITH CAMDEN RECORDS

Five-page handwritten contract between the RCA Camden Records and the Colonel and All Star Show and Elvis Presley. Written on tan parchment paper and dated June 29, 1970. Signed by the Colonel for he and Elvis and by Harry Jenkins. Handwritten note included From the Desk of TOM DISKIN: "Mary, put this with the Colonel's personal contract records." 16 3/4 x 14 inches contract. 6 x 4 inches note.

Camden Records was the budget division of RCA. The Colonel did not want to use Camden because the royalty payments would be less, but he finally changed his mind. He felt contracts should be simple and straightforward, so he and Jenkins sat down and composed this one as he wrote the specifics by hand.

$8,000 - 10,000

C100 COLT PISTOL BILL

One page typed bill from Luxury Rental and Leasing in Las Vegas, dated January 30, 1971. Sold to Elvis Presley, for the engraving of one Colt Python pistol, for a balance of $569.25. 11 x 8 1/2"

Bills lists instructions for the engraving of an American Eagle, initials "as per sketch," and, written on the bill in blue ink, "TCB and lightening bolt." $1,000 - 1,200

C101 ELVIS PRESLEY FAN LETTER WITH POLICE EMBLEM

One page, double-sided handwritten letter on orange stationery. Dated February 14, 1972 and sent to Elvis from a fan in Broomall, Pennsylvania. With envelope. Blue cloth emblem from Marple (Penn.) Police with Sgt.'s stripes patch. 7 7/8 x 5 7/8 inches letter. 4 1/8 x 6 inches envelope. 4 1/8 x 4 1/8 inches emblem. 3 3/4 x 3 inches stripes.

The letter writer sends Elvis the police patches after reading about his receiving a "narcotics badge" from President Nixon and about his collection of police paraphernalia. The fan also mentions seeing an Elvis concert in Philadelphia the previous fall.
$400 - 500

C102 ITEMS RELATED TO ELVIS' STUTZ BLACK HAWK

Two keys on black leather key chain with Stutz metal emblem in black and gold. Letter dated September 1, 1971, from George Barris, of Barris Kustom Industries (automobile customizers). Letter on Barris Kustom Industries, Inc. orange-yellow letterhead with brown print, vertical lines down left margin, and a Barris crest superimposed over a custom car in the upper right corner. Barris sends note of grievance in regards to Elvis' Stutz Black Hawk being wrecked. Copy of a letter dated December 29, 1971 on Montedonico, Heiskell, Davis & Glankler Law Offices letterhead. Letter is from Charles Davis, Elvis' lawyer, to the President of

Johnson's Super Service. Letter asks about the missing accessories on the Stutz that Elvis was trying to recover. He believes a man named Julius Lewis may have something to do with the missing parts. Letter indicates a copy of the letter was sent to Vernon Presley. Envelope addressed to Vernon included. Letter dated July 3, 1972 on Stutz Motor Car of America letterhead. Letter is from Jules Meyers, president of Stutz Motor Car of America, to Vernon. "Mr. Sakajian from Johnson's 'Super' Service seems to have dreamed up a 'Super' story, '90%'

C103

C101

of his letter to your representatives is fiction and not the facts. Please call me at your earliest possible convenience and I will be happy to go over the 'true' situation that took place." Certified mail envelope included addressed to Vernon Presley. Copy of a letter dated July 7, 1972, from Charles Davis to Johnson's Super Service regarding Jules Meyers' letter. Letter indicates copy of letter was sent to Elvis Presley. Special delivery envelope to Elvis included. Special delivery envelopes included, one to Elvis and one to Vernon at Graceland. Original invoice, dated January 23, 1971, from KHM Communications to Elvis. Invoice for the installation of an 11 channel mobile telephone with decoder to be installed

in Elvis' Stutz Black Hawk. Invitation to the "Auto Expo '73 in Los Angeles on May 24, 1973, sent to Elvis Presley in Beverly Hills, postmarked May 17, 1973. Also includes gold embossed card from Stutz with envelope. Two light green checks from the account of Elvis Presley made out to Jules Meyers for $9,000 and $17,618.00. One signed by Vernon Presley, one signed by Elvis Presley. Photograph included. 2 1/2 x 1 keys. 11 x 8 1/2 inches letters. 4 1/8 x 9 1/2 inches envelopes. 7 x 8 1/2 inches mobile phone invoice. 4 7/8 x 5 3/4 inches invitation. 3 3/8 x 4 3/8 inches Stutz card. 5 x 6 inches envelope. 3 x 8 1/4 inches checks.

This was the first of a number of Stutz's that Elvis owned. It was wrecked on its way to get it washed. After the accident, the Stutz was shipped to Memphis where it remained for over ten years before it was finally restored. It is now in the Automobile Museum at Graceland. Elvis got a new gadget as soon as it hit the market. This mobile phone set Elvis back $1,467.50, considerably more than a mobile phone would cost today. $4,500 - 5,000

C103. RECEIPT FOR FIREWORKS

Invoice and order sheet from Atomic Fireworks Inc, in West Memphis, Arkansas, on July 3, 1971, billed to Elvis. Total order was for $324.04, which included a 50% discount, and bill was invoiced on July 14, 1971 and paid on July 16, 1971 by ck.# 9612. Order includes 10-ball Roman candles, assorted cone fountains, buzz bomb/helicopters, and Stars and Booms. Check made out to Atomic Fireworks Inc. for $324.04; written on green check from Elvis Presley Payroll and Expense Fund; signed by Vernon Presley. 8 1/2 x 8 1/2 inches invoice. 16 3/4 x 10 5/8 inches order form. 3 18 X 8 1/4" check.

When Elvis was in town over the Fourth of July, he would always order a large amount of fireworks for his grand display at Graceland.

$1,000 - 1,200

C104 ELVIS PRESLEY'S 1967 FORD RANCHERO-FAIRLANE 500
Blue Ranchero with the Serial # 7K48C158168. Purchased from Oakley Motor Company in Memphis on February 14, 1967.
Other than that all info should be the same as the red ranchero-both used at Circle G, both bought for the same price.

This classic 1967 Ford 5L500 Ranchero was purchased on February 15, 1967.
Elvis bought the automobile from the Oakley Motor Company in Memphis. On February 8, 1967 Elvis put down a deposit on a 160 acre cattle ranch called Twinkletown Farm which was located outside of Walls, Mississippi in a town called Horn Lake. Elvis purchased the property from Jack Adams in order to house the numerous horses he recently acquired. Apparently, Graceland was becoming too small to hold all of his horses. Within one week after the purchase of the ranch which Elvis called the "Circle G Ranch", Elvis bought this Ford Ranchero to use for everyday tasks around the property.

ESTIMATE UPON REQUEST

C105 SALES DRAFT COPIES FROM ELVIS PRESLEY'S BANK AMERICARD PLUS CARD

Original statement and sales draft copies from September to October of 1971 of purchases made by Elvis and Priscilla. Draft copies have carbon copy signatures by Elvis and Priscilla. Bank Americard included. 3 1/4 x 7 1/2 inches September charges (7 pages). 3 1/4 x 7 1/2 inches October charges (4 pages).

One sales draft reads: "Hi Elvis - remember me - keypunch operator from Tenn." $6,500 - 7,500

C106. "JON BURROWS" HOTEL WASHINGTON BILL

Three page bill from Hotel Washington in Washington, D.C., dated November 1-2, 1971, with each page signed "Jon Burrows" in blue ink. Invoice from Liberty Limousine Service in Arlington, Virginia, dated November 4, 1971 and billed to Vernon Presley in Memphis. Bill in amount of $449.28 for "Limousine Service for Mr. Elvis Presley." 8 1/8 x 5 1/2 inches hotel bill. 7 x 8 1/2 inches limousine invoice.

"Jon Burrows" was a frequent Elvis alias. Though signing with the alias, Elvis still lists the Graceland address of "3764 Highway 51, South" in Memphis. $4,500 - 5,000

C107 CORRESPONDENCE FROM THE INTERNATIONAL HOTEL IN LAS VEGAS REGARDING ELVIS PRESLEY'S OPENING

Copy of inter-department correspondence from Nick Naff of the International Hotel in Las Vegas, dated January 19, 1971. The memo outlines the arrangements that need to be made for Elvis' opening night on January 26th. Souvenir menu for Elvis' performance. One side features black and white close-up photograph of Elvis, and the other side features the menu selection. 11 x 8 1/2 inches.

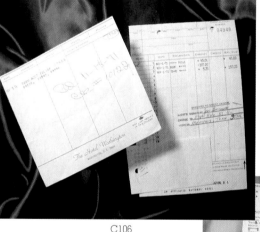

C106

C105

An article from "Fabulous Las Vegas" described Elvis' engagement: "Looking the ultimate in a white jumpsuit with beads and fringe, he's all man, top cat, the true king of the musical jungle. Females of all ages begin squealing ecstatically with his first song note and bit of body English, and their euphoria never flags throughout the show." $600 - 750

C108 RECEIPT FROM WILLIAMS COSTUME RENTAL FOR ONE GORILLA HEAD

Copy of receipt dated January 26, 1971, from Williams Costume Rental leased to Joe Esposito for one gorilla head for the Elvis show. Return date is January 29, 1971, and total due is $21.91. Photograph included. 7 1/2 x 6 1/4 inches

Elvis loved to pull stunts and pranks during his performances. During his January 26, 1971 performance, Elvis turned to face his musicians and slowly turned back toward the audience wearing a gorilla mask.

$1,200 - 1,500

C109 LETTER FROM J.D. SUMNER TO COLONEL TOM PARKER

Original typewritten letter signed by J.D. Sumner to Colonel Tom Parker dated November 30, 1971. Letter on black and orange Sumar Talent Agency letterhead expresses thanks for allowing J.D. Sumner and The Stamps Quartet to appear on Elvis' 1971 tour. Black and white promotional poster with photograph of Elvis singing. Photograph included. 11 x 8 1/2 inches letter. 12 x 8 inches poster.

The Stamps Quartet first appeared with Elvis in November of 1971, replacing the Imperials who had been Elvis backup group. Elvis knew J.D. Sumner when Sumner played with the Blackwoods. $600 - 700

C110 ELVIS PRESLEY CHRISTMAS ADVERTISEMENT

Full page advertisement in the "Las Vegas Sun" and the "Las Vegas Review" for December 25, 1971. Advertisement is a season's greeting from Elvis and the Colonel which lists radio stations and times the Christmas show was playing, and displays covers of three Elvis' albums. Elvis Presley Christmas card. 23 x 14 3/4 inches ad.

Colonel Parker paid to put on radio shows as a Christmas present to Elvis' fans. $150 - 200

C111 ELVIS PRESLEY PORTRAIT PRINTS WITH RECEIPT

Fifty prints of an Elvis Presley portrait done by artist Loxie Sibley. Receipt dated August 5, 1972 on Las Vegas Hilton letterhead indicating Colonel Parker's Office's receipt of the portraits. 11 x 8 1/2" receipt. 27 3/4 x 21 5/8" print.

Portrait of Elvis in his "Madison Square Garden" suit, which he wore during his three day stand at the storied New York City venue in June 1972. $350 - 400

C112 ELVIS' "TCB" SUNGLASSES AND RECEIPT FROM OPTIQUE BOUTIQUE

Original receipt, dated April 19, 1971 from Dennis R. Roberts (Optique Boutique) to Elvis for 2 pair of prescription, solid gold TCB eyeglasses, and one pair of non-prescription eyeglasses. Total bill is for $580.13. Large frame glasses with purple tinted lenses. Gold TCB with lightening bolt on either side of the frame. Glasses are broken at the bridge. Photograph included. 6 3/4 x 6 1/4 inches.

Elvis ordered a number of pairs of these glasses during the seventies; in fact, they became one of his trademarks.

$13,000 - 15,000

C113 ELVIS PRESLEY SCARVES WITH RECEIPT

Four scarves—red, white, gold and blue— with imprinted "Elvis Presley" signature. Handwritten receipt from "Mr. Guy" in Las Vegas, dated November 11, 1972 and charged to Elvis Presley in the amount of $654.64. Bill for 115 scarves. 34.5 x 34.5 inches each scarf. 8 1/2 x 5 1/2 inches receipt.

During concert performances in the Seventies Elvis would commonly throw scarves out to the crowd. This bulk purchase of scarves was for that purpose.

$1,000 - 1,200

C114 ELVIS PRESLEY JUMPSUIT INVOICE

One page invoice on brown paper from Bill Belew in Hollywood. Dated March 3, 1973 and in the amount of $1,550 for "eagle belts and belts for new jumpsuits, plus stones for new capes and jumpsuits." Photograph included. 10 3/8 x 7 1/4 inches.

Elvis was known to give away items from his stage wardrobe, including capes and belts. When he did this, Belew would have to make replacements for him.

$2,000 - 2,500

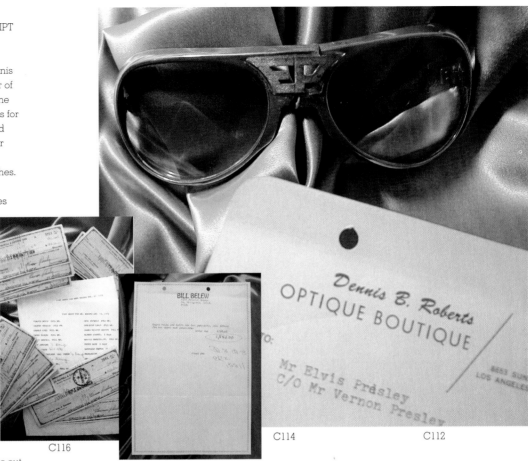

C116

C114   C112

C115 RECEIPTS FOR JEWELRY

Letters and invoices from Schwartz & Ableser jewelers, dated between September 6 and November 30, 1974. One invoice totals $10,600--with five follow up letters asking for payment. The other receipt totals 307.40. Original light green check from the account of E.A. Presley made out to Schwartz and Ableser for $10,907.40. Signed by Vernon Presley. 8 1/2 x 5 1/2 inches bills and letters. 6 x 4 inches invoices. 3 x 8 1/4 inches check.

On September 6, 1974, Elvis purchased a platinum, diamond, and emerald bracelet for $10,600. His other purchase on November 15, 1974 was for for two TCB necklaces.

$800 - 1,000

C116 GRACELAND TIME SHEETS AND CHECKS

Two one-page typed employee lists and time sheets from Graceland for week ending August 18, 1972 and August 25, 1972, respectively. With 40 Graceland paychecks for employees on the lists. 11 x 8 1/2 inches lists 3 3/8 x 8 3/8 inches checks List of employees includes Memphis Mafia members Joe Esposito, Charles Hodge and Bobby West. It also includes Elvis' aunt Delta Biggs, Vernon's sister, who lived at Graceland until her death in 1993.

$2,500 - 3,000

C117 ELVIS PRESLEY'S RED COAT WITH BLACK FUR CAPE

One heavy-weight wool-blend red coat, fully lined with red satin. Made by International. Detachable black fur cape attaches at the high collar. Black fur also trims the collar, 3 buttons, 2 fake pockets, and cuffs. Length is just below the knee.

The design of Elvis' casual clothing imitated the style of his performance clothing--leaning toward a sense of flamboyancy and even many caped items. Elvis wore this coat for casual occasions during 1974-75.

$15,000 - 20,000

C118 ELVIS PRESLEY SHOW BACKSTAGE PASSES AND PASSENGER LIST—1972

Twenty backstage pass buttons assigned to specific members of the show, orange buttons reading "ELVIS SHOW MEMBER" with white name tags. Two page typed "Elvis Presley Show, Show Plane Manifest - April Tour 1972," dated March 8, 1972. Passenger list of 53 names. 2 1/2 inches diameter buttons. 11 x 8 1/2 inches list.

The April, 1972 tour was Elvis' longest road trip since returning to the stage in the late Sixties. Among the included backstage buttons are those assigned to: Vernon Presley, producer Felton Jarvis, guitarist James Burton, guitarist and "Memphis Mafia" member Charlie Hodge, and comedian Jackie Kahane.

$2,500 - 3,000

C119 COLONEL PARKER'S BOOKLET OF ADVERTISING FOR ELVIS PRESLEY'S SUMMER 1972 CONCERT TOUR

Colonel Parker's sixty-eight page booklet of advertising for Elvis' summer concert tour in 1972. Also includes correspondence between Colonel Parker

and Clanton Ross Advertising. Booklet contains advertising expenses for concerts held in Chicago, Evansville, Fort Wayne, Fort Worth, Milwaukee, New York, Tulsa, and Wichita. Pages contained within a dark blue folder. Blue flyer announcing Elvis' performance in Madison Square Garden on June 9 and 10, 1972. 11 x 8 1/2 inches pages. 11 1/2 x 9 1/4 inches folder. 11 x 8 1/2 inches flyer.

C118

C119

Prior to this tour, Elvis had never played live in New York except during his television appearances. Elvis played four sold-out shows in Madison Square Garden. $4,000 - 4,500

C120 SIGNED ELVIS PRESLEY JEWELRY RECEIPT

Receipt from Schwartz & Ableser Fine Jewelry in Beverly Hills, dated September 29, 1971 and made out to Elvis Presley. Signed by Elvis Presley in blue ink. Bill totaling $1,075.90 for seven pieces of jewelry with a description reading "T.C.B." 6 x 4 inches.

"T.C.B." stands for "Taking Care of Business," a motto Elvis was fond of and used frequently during the Seventies. Elvis would often have "T.C.B." jewelry made for him and his friends, and this receipt documents some of the earliest "T.C.B." items Elvis had made. $600 - 700

C121 SONGS SUBMITTED TO ELVIS PRESLEY FOR POSSIBLE RECORDING AND CHRISTMAS ALBUM ACETATE

Eight original pages containing songs submitted to Elvis for possible recording. Four original pages containing Christmas and religious songs submitted for possible recording. Both are for a March-June 1971 session.. Elvis' acetate and LP of "Elvis Sings The Wonderful World of Christmas." Album cover has Christmas artwork with Elvis' picture on the head of Santa and a snowman. 11 x 8 1/2 inches.

Hill and Range would submit demos and song lists for upcoming recording sessions. They were always concerned that Elvis retained publishing royalties on the songs. The album, "Elvis Sings the Wonderful World of Christmas" was certified as a Gold Record on November 4, 1977, and then certified Platinum 27 days later.

$3,000 - 3,500

C122 MISCELLANEOUS RECEIPTS FROM OCTOBER 1971

Fifteen receipts in parchment envelope with silver embossed return address reading "E.A.P. Graceland Memphis." Various cash register tapes and receipts. Receipts are for fast food, grocery, shoes, and curtain rods.

$400 - 500

C123 ELVIS PRESLEY'S
1970 MERCEDES BENZ 600 LIMOUSINE

Elvis Presley's four-door 1970 metallic blue Mercedes 600 "Pullman" Limousine. The automobile has black leather upholstery with wood trim on inside doors, dashboard, glove compartment, and front console. Blue/gray curtains hang from the back window, and along back side windows. The automobile is equipped with special hydraulic suspension. The 600 Pullman was considered Mercedes Benz's finest effort of the period, a dignified machine created for heads of state and notable celebrities.

On January 16, 1971 Elvis used the limo to drive himself and Priscilla to the Memphis Memorial Auditorium to accept the "Ten Outstanding Young Men Of America" award. It was presented to him by the Jaycees, and was the only award Elvis ever received in person. Elvis loved the limo so much that when he sold it he had another one custom made.

ESTIMATE UPON REQUEST

C124 SKETCH, DESIGN, ARTWORK AND FABRICATION OF PROMOTIONAL ROBOTS

Typewritten page from Quasar Industries regarding the fabrication of four SPA-1 robots, and one SPA-7 Robot totaling $2486.00. One page of the artwork for a SPA-1 robot, and a handwritten, two page promotional schedule of the robots for January 26 through February 23, 1973. Photograph included. 11 x 8 1/2 inches Quasar Letter. 11 x 8 1/2 inches Costume Letter. 12 inches Artwork 11 x 8 1/2 inches promotional schedule.

These robots were used in the lobby outside Elvis' Hawaii performance. There were nine robots with flamboyant costumes including blue-silver satin body suits with studded belts and sunburst belt buckles, studded capes, and metallic silver guitars. One robot was a seven-foot Hawaiian-inspired robot with a Hawaiian skirt, floral head-dress, seven-foot spear, and traditional neck lei.

$2,500 - 3,000

C125

C124

C125 LETTER FROM MCDONALD'S TO ELVIS PRESLEY REGARDING GIFT CERTIFICATES

Original, typed letter from McDonald's to Elvis, dated January 5, 1972. Correspondence is from Saul Kaplan thanking Elvis for purchasing gift certificates for his friends. "I am happy that you felt that even though the value of these certificates was only .50 cents each, the quality of the product was good enough for your closest friends." Letter is typed on McDonald's letterhead and signed by Saul Kaplan. Original envelope with McDonald's logo is included. 11 x 8 1/2 inches.

Elvis' friends and family had grown accustomed to receiving fabulous Christmas gifts from Elvis. This year he played a joke on them giving them all 50 cent gift certificates to McDonald's. After letting them sweat it out for a bit, Elvis gave them their real gifts.

$2,500 - 3,000

C126 LETTER TO COLONEL PARKER FROM ELVIS PRESLEY

Original typewritten letter from Elvis to the Colonel dated March 23, 1971. Elvis was unable to be on the West Coast due to an eye infection, however, the letter gives the Colonel authorization to sign the contract on an impeding RCA merchandising deal. Signed by Elvis Presley in blue ink. 11 x 8 1/2 inches.

On March 15, 1971 Elvis went to Nashville, Tennessee for a recording session at RCA's studio. The session was cut short when Elvis complained of increasing discomfort in his eye. On March 16, Elvis was hospitalized in Nashville's Baptist Hospital for iritis and secondary glaucoma. Actress Barbara Leigh flew in to Nashville to be with Elvis while he was hospitalized. Tennessee Governor Winfield Dunn paid Elvis a visit in the hospital. During this time, Elvis had Colonel Parker sign his contracts. Elvis was released from the hospital on March 19. $3,000 - 3,500

C127 CORRESPONDENCE BETWEEN ELVIS PRESLEY AND THE UNITED STATES DEPARTMENT OF JUSTICE/BUREAU OF NARCOTICS AND DANGEROUS DRUGS

Rough draft and copy of letter dated March 8, 1971, from Elvis to Mr. Finlator of the United States Department of Justice. Letter discusses Elvis' involvement with the department, and his beliefs regarding the nation's drug problem. An original signed typewritten letter to Elvis from Mr. Finlator dated October 8, 1971, regarding an upcoming Baltimore concert. Correspondence requests tickets to the concert, and again mentions Finlator's desire for Elvis to get involved with an anti-drug program. Original typewritten and signed letter dated December 1, 1971, to Elvis from John Finlator thanking him for the tickets to the Baltimore concert and praising the show. 11 x 8 1/2 inches Letter from Elvis. 10 1/2 x 8 inches Letter from Finlator. 10 1/2 x 7 1/4 inches Letter from Finlator.

Elvis originally requested a BNDD badge from Mr. Finlator, but was denied. He later met with President Nixon - requested and received the badge. Later Mr. Finlator and Elvis developed a mutual friendship. $6,000 - 7,000

C128 ELVIS PRESLEY BILLBOARD PAINTING

Two panels of a painted Elvis Presley billboard. With four black and white photographs of the billboard. 18 x 9 feet billboard panels.

In a marketing blitz preceding every Elvis Presley performance in Las Vegas, the Colonel would erect billboards, signs, and advertisements throughout the city, trumpeting the coming of the King of Rock n' Roll. From bus stops to marquis, Elvis' name and fame covered every available space of the Vegas scene. This billboard, an original painting of Elvis Presley done by Jim Reber in 1972 for Colonel Parker, was displayed in Las Vegas announcing his latest performances.

$25,000 - 30,000

C129 ELVIS PRESLEY' POLICE BLUE LIGHT AND RECEIPT

Invoice from Mid-South Police Supply for two purchases made by Elvis--blue light on 7/16/73 for $31.45 and 4 aces pistol on 9/26/73 for $37.80. Elvis' blue light with red cord that plugs into a car cigarette lighter. Original check from the account of Elvis Presley included 5 x 6 3/8 inches.

Pictured above are *photographs* of this massive and handsomely painted full color billboard.

Elvis loved to play policeman and pull over cars. Unsuspecting drivers were shocked to find out that they had been pulled over by none other than Elvis Presley, who would usually let them off with a warning and an autograph. $2,500 - 3,000

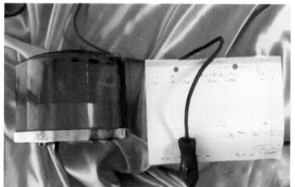

C129

C130 LETTER AND MEMBERSHIP CARD SENT TO ELVIS PRESLEY FROM THE INTERNATIONAL KENPO KARATE ASSOCIATION

Letter to Elvis, dated April 26, 1971, on International Kenpo Karate Association letterhead. The letter is from Ed Parker, President. He enclosed Elvis' membership card with his new rank: 4th Degree Black. The card is dated February 18, 1971, the night Parker witnessed Elvis' performance in Pasadena, California. 11 x 8 1/2 inches letter. 2 x 3 5/8 inches card.

Elvis first became interested in karate while he was serving in the Army. He obtained his black belt in 1960 and went on to eventually achieve an 8th degree black belt. Elvis used his karate skills in several of his movies and frequently demonstrated his prowess on stage during performances. During one performance, Elvis used a karate move to knock an overzealous fan off the stage. Elvis was extremely dedicated to the sport, and encouraged his friends and Priscilla to get involved in karate with him. He trained under Ed Parker and Kang Rhee among others, sometimes taking them on the road with him so as to be able to continue training. During their stay following an engagement, Elvis had Kang Rhee join him in Las Vegas to study. During their training, Elvis used some of the furniture in the suite to demonstrate his expertise, breaking it to pieces. Elvis' Karate name was Master Tiger, a name for which he was very proud.

$8,000 - 10,000

C131 POSTER FOR 1972 LAS VEGAS "YEAR OF THE STAR"

Poster for the 1972 "Year Of The Stars." Print is gold and blue on white paper. Holes punched in the left margin. 11 x 8 /2 inches. Poster reads, "Elvis says see these great stars in person. Johnny Cash, Red Skelton, Tony Bennett, Glen Campbell, Bill Cosby/Diahann Carrol , Liberace, Charley Pride, and Perry Como."

$100 - 150

C132 HANDWRITTEN NOTE FROM ELVIS PRESLEY REGARDING CHRISTMAS GIFTS DECEMBER, 1972

Elvis listing two Christmas gifts for Mr. Campbell, and Mr. Davis. Note is on white paper with a "2001 Space Odyssey" logo on the upper left corner. Photograph included. 8 x 5 inches.

Both Mr. Campbell and Mr. Davis worked at Memphian where Elvis frequently saw movies.

$1,400 - 1,600

C133 LETTER TO ELVIS PRESLEY FROM BARRON HILTON

Hilton Hotels Corporation cream colored stationery with gold logo, dated August 30, 1973 and addressed to Elvis Presley regarding payment and a gift for August 1973 performances in Las Vegas. Signed by Barron Hilton. With two black and white "Elvis in Person" promotional posters. 11 x 8 1/2 inches letter. 10 1/2 x 11 1/2 inches poster.

Barron Hilton was the owner of the Hilton Hotel Chain, which bought the International Hotel in Las Vegas in 1971. Elvis became a regular fixture at the International beginning in the summer of 1969, and he continued to perform there after it became a Hilton Hotel. $400 - 500

C134. INVOICE AND NOTE FROM T-BIRD JEWELS IN LAS VEGAS

Invoice from T-Bird Jewels in Las Vegas dated August 31, 1971. Taped to the itemized invoice are the silver price tags from the jewelry. The total is $7,970.00. Attached is a handwritten note on T-Bird stationary to Mr. Presley stating that they are for-

warding the invoices. Another invoice indicates that the balance of $7,970.00 was added to the account, leaving a balance of $0. 6 x 4 " invoices. 8 1/2 x 5 1/2" notes. 1/2 x 7/8 and 2 x 1/2 " tags.

Included are the original silver price tags that were on the jewelry when it was purchased.

$2,000 - 2,500

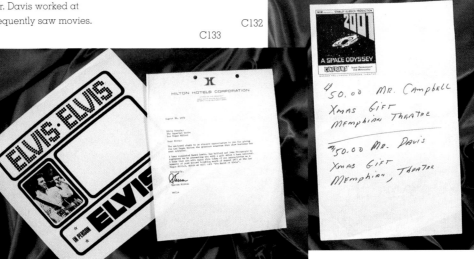

C132

C133

C135 ELVIS PRESLEY NEW YORK STATE SHERIFFS' DEPUTIES ASSOCIATION MEMBERSHIP

One page typed letter on New York State Sheriffs' Deputies Association letterhead, dated February 3, 1972 and sent to Elvis Presley. With envelope. White cardboard 1972 "Honorary Member" card from the Sheriffs' Deputies Association, issued to Elvis Presley. Sheriff's Deputies Association insignia patch. 11 x 8 1/2 inches letter. 4 1/4 x 9 1/2 inches envelope. 2 1/2 x 4 inches membership card. 3 5/8 x 4 inches insignia.

This document is a prime example of Elvis' intense interest in police work and paraphernalia. The envelope is addressed only to "Elvis Presley, Memphis, Tennessee[sic] 38101" and Association director James J. Darmos writes "I do hope that this letter and enclosures reach you as we do not have a mailing address for you." Darmos concludes by

writing "I and the association were very happy to hear of your support for Law Enforcement in these very troubled times." $800 - 1,000

C136 FILM OF ELVIS ON TOUR IN 1972

One movie case with one 16mm film from Colonel Parker's collection: "Elvis on Tour 1972." Black ink on side reads "2,000 feet 3 reels." Cases are brown with metal corners, a handle on one end, and a horizontal and vertical buckled strap. 15 1/4 x 15 3/4 inches film case.

Cinema Associated produced Elvis on Tour, a film from some of his concerts in 1972. Release took place in November 1972. The film focuses mostly on Elvis' tour in April during this year, which began in Buffalo, NY, and ended in Albuquerque, NM.

$1,500 - 2,000

C137 ARTWORK FOR AD FROM CAMDEN RECORDS

Black-and-white pasted-up ad from Camden on tracing paper highlighting "You'll Never Walk Alone" album, but also showing three others: "Let's Be Friends," "Elvis' Christmas Album," and "Almost in Love." Only "Now" and "Order" are in red marker. Artwork is stapled to heavier white paper. 16 7/8 x 13 7/8 inches.

RCA's Camden records division released "You'll Never Walk Alone" on March 5, 1971. Title to album is only on back. Front side carries a photograph in concert and only the word "Elvis."

$1,400 - 1,600

C138 ELVIS: ALOHA FROM HAWAII PREPARATION FOLDER

Black three ring binder with title "Elvis Satellite Show Jan. 1972," filled with documents related to the satellite broadcast show that occurred January 14, 1973. With full color Elvis poster of the event. 11 3/4 x 10 1/2 x 3 inches binder. 28 x 22 inches poster.

The "2" on the cover of the binder is covered by a handwritten "3." The show was broadcast live to countries in the Far East and South Pacific on January 14, 1973, and to 28 nations in Europe the next day. The concert was finally broadcast in the U.S. on April 4, 1973. "Elvis: Aloha From Hawaii" was the King's first television appearance since the '68 Special. It has been estimated that more than one billion people in forty countries saw "Aloha From Hawaii."

$8,000 - 10,000

C138   C139

C139 CONTRACTS FOR MUSICIANS TO PLAY ON THE ELVIS PRESLEY SHOW TOUR

Five original contracts for the band members of Elvis Presley's stage show beginning April 22 through April 30, 1973. The contracts, which are on William Morris letterhead, are dated February 17, 1973, and include James Burton, Glen D. Hardin, John R. Wilkinson, Joe Guercio, and Ronnie Tutt. Contracts are signed in blue ink by Elvis Presley. 15 3/4 x 8 1/2 inches.

A number of the performances on this tour were used for the film, "That's the Way It Is."

$15,000 - 20,000

C140 CLOTHING RECEIPTS FROM SISTER JOHN AND KING FURS

Bill of Sale for Mr. Elvis Presley dated December 29, 1971 from King Furs. Bill is for 1 natural mink 3/4 coat, 1 natural mink coat with dyed fox suede, and 1 red fox purse. Total bill $3,500.63. Attached account statement dated Feb. 26, 1973 shows account paid by ck #12138. Original, typewritten statement from Sister John, Inc. to Patsy at Graceland, dated July 30, 1973. Attached to statement are four invoices for clothes bought by Linda Thompson. Invoices are on light yellow paper with dull orange lettering and lines. All invoices are handwritten. One typewritten invoice from Nolan's addressed to the Elvis Presley Home for equipment

C139 (partial lot pictured)

repair for an RCA 16 millimeter projector. Total bill is for $79.07. Original check from Elvis Presley's account signed by Vernon Presley. Letter from Sister John's Boutique to Patsy regarding Linda Thompson's charges. Two American Express receipts plus carbons from Sister John, Inc. and Vicki's Love Boutiques totaling $1,100.40 and $161.70. Receipt from Sister John's for a $227.50 purple velvet suit for Elvis. Original light green check from the account of Elvis Presley made out to Sister John, Inc. for $1,500.98. Signed by Vernon Presley. Photograph included. 8 1/2 x 5 1/2 inches King Furs bill. 3 1/2 x 5 1/4 inches account statement. 11 x 8 1/2 inches Sister John Statement. 8 x 5 1/2 inches Sister John Invoices. 7 x 8 1/2 inches Nolan's Invoice. 11 x 8 1/2 inches Sister John's statement. 7 3/4 x 5 1/2 inches and 3 1/2 x 4 3/4 inches receipts. 3 x 8 1/4 inches check.

Linda Thompson, a Tennessee beauty queen and third runner-up in the Miss USA Pageant, was Elvis' girlfriend and companion in the 1970's. She lived at Graceland from 1972 to 1976 and frequently travelled with Elvis on tour. It is estimated that Elvis spent $1 million on jewelry for Thompson. For Christmas 1971, Elvis gave Linda Thompson a mink coat. $1,800 - 2,000

C141 LAS VEGAS SHOW NEWSPAPER ADVERTISEMENT—1972

Four newsprint copies of prototype for a full two-page newspaper advertisement for 1972 Las Vegas Hilton show, with photos of J.D. Sumner and The Stamps, The Sweet Inspirations and comedian Jackie Kahane, and mentions of other performers. Advertisement reads "LET US BE YOUR VALENTINES THRU FEB. 23." Two copies of ad in altered form in Las Vegas newspapers, one from the Las Vegas Review Journal and one from the Las Vegas Sun, both dated Sunday, February 13, 1972. 23 x 30 inches,

RCA recorded these performances for an intended live album, "Standing Room Only," that was never released. Jackie Kahane had previously worked with Wayne Newton but was hired by the Colonel in 1971 to open Elvis' Vegas shows. It was Kahane who would often close Elvis concerts by announcing "Ladies and gentlemen, Elvis has left the building." Kahane would go on to deliver Elvis' eulogy.

$400 - 500

C142 ELVIS PRESLEY ADVERTISING AND PROMOTIONAL DOCUMENTS

Circa 1972 mock-up of a thank you note from Elvis and the Colonel. Also included is one handwritten letter, dated July 29, 1972, to George Parkhill regarding changes to be made on the mock-up. Copy of a letter dated August 5, 1972, on Las Vegas Hilton stationery to Bruce Banke from the Colonel: "Please see that one of the attached ad slicks are received by the Entertainment Director or Publicity Department of each of the hotels involved." Proof of large red and blue advertisement. One sheet yellow flyer advertising Elvis Presley tour dates on April 8 in Knoxville, April 13 in Charlotte, North Carolina and April 14 in Greensboro, North Carolina. With an 8-page black and white "Elvis on Tour" press book, sent to movie theaters to help in the promotion of the film. 10 1/2 x 8 inches letter to Parkhill. 10 x8 inches mock-up. 11 x 8 1/2 letter to Banke. 21 1/2 x 30 inches advertisement. 14 x 8 1/2 inches flyer. 13 1/4 x 8 1/2 inches press book.

Thank you reads, "Thanks To Everyone 4 Everything - Elvis and the Colonel." The large red and blue advertisement produced by the Colonel and Elvis paid tribute to all the Las Vegas shows and stars at that time, including Wayne Newton, Bobby Gentry, Paul Anka, and "Sammy." Elvis and the Colonel often showed their appreciation to fans and other celebrities.

$2,000 - 2,500

C143 ELVIS PRESLEY'S TOUR SCHEDULE FOR AUGUST/SEPTEMBER, 1972

Four copies of Elvis' tour schedule for August 4 through September 4, 1972. Tour covers New York, Fort Wayne, Evansville, Milwaukee, Chicago, Fort Worth, Wichita, and Tulsa. Two schedules area blue in color, and two are yellow.14 x 8 1/2 inches.

During this tour, Elvis' first tour which included New York City, he sold out all four of his performances in Madison Square Garden.

$400 - 600

C145

C143

C144

C144 REHEARSAL SCHEDULE FOR LAS VEGAS HILTON

Schedule for the Elvis Presley Show at the Las Vegas Hilton Hotel (August 4 - September 4, 1972) shows rehearsal dates, rooms, times, and list of those to be present. Two-page Summer Festival Souvenir Menu from the Las Vegas Hilton; red, white, and blue with color photo of Elvis in concert on front, food and beverage list inside, and Elvis ads on

back. 11 x 8 1/2" schedule. 14 x 7" menu. Summer Festival 1972 was Elvis' seventh season in Las Vegas. He performed 64 shows over a period of one month at the Las Vegas Hilton. He was ill his opening show and only appeared for 45 minutes; however, he sang "What Now My Love?" and "My Way," which thrilled the audience. Before his show on August 18, he learned that his divorce from Priscilla had become final. It was at the last show of this tour that he announced his upcoming satellite show, Elvis Aloha from Hawaii, which would be transmitted internationally. $750 - 850

C145 DOCUMENTS RELATED TO ELVIS' 7TH LAS VEGAS ENGAGEMENT—SUMMER 1972

One page Musician's Work Dues Report on blue paper. One page typed copy of the rehearsal schedule for this engagement. One page typed note from on Las Vegas Hilton letterhead. With string of six banners used at the hotel. 11 x 8 1/2 inches all documents. 27 x 11 1/2" each banner.

This engagement at the Las Vegas Hilton lasted from August 4 - September 4. The Musician's Report lists the musicians who played with the Elvis Presley Show, their weekly earnings, and their union dues. The note reads "TCB Thanks...For helping make this another great Elvis summer festival. Elvis and the Colonel."

$3,000 - 3,500

C145A BILL TO ELVIS PRESLEY FROM THE MEMPHIS FEDERATION OF MUSICIANS

White bill with blue print dated January 15, 1973 from the Memphis Federation of Musicians to Elvis for yearly dues. 7 x 6 inches Elvis always stayed true to his Memphis roots. Yearly dues in 1973 was $24.00.

$400 - 450

C146 GRACELAND DINING ROOM CHAIRS

Two red velvet chairs with wood legs, silver stud accents and diamond-pattern stitching. One chair has wood arm rests, the other doesn't. 60 inches high x 26.5 inches wide.

These chairs were used in the Dining Room of Graceland from 1974 until Elvis' death in 1977. Diner at Graceland was a relatively formal affair, and Elvis preferred to eat late, usually around 9 p.m.

$10,000 - 12,000

C147 RED VELVET CHAIR, FLORAL LAMP, AND MERMAID TABLE

One chair with crushed red velvet seat and back; heart-shaped back; carved wooden arms and legs, painted gold. Chair originally made by S. Miller Inc. in Brooklyn, NY. One gold electric lamp with twelve flowers forming the shade portion (red, white, and green). Eighteen prisms cascade off the top; three light fixtures resemble candles. Four tall and four short flowers (red, white, and green) adorn the lamp pole. Gold metal base sits on a small marble base. One mermaid end table; ornate carved wooden legs and top, painted gold. Top covered with glass. Three legs are carved to resemble mermaids with seashell on head. The tails of the mermaids curl up and hold a small table, shaped like a fish. Small table holds a bowl of faux flowers in orange, yellow, blue, and pink flowers, and green leaf foliage. 48 x 21 inches chair. 39 x 16" lamp. 24 x 30" table.

In 1974, Elvis and Linda Thompson redecorated Graceland's living room, dining room, and entry in red, gold, and white. These items, bought at Donald's Furniture on July 8, 1974, once adorned the living room. The red decor lasted from 1974-1977.

$15,000 - 20,000

C148 ELVIS PRESLEY'S SELF-REALIZATION MATERIALS

Elvis' personal copies of Self-Realization materials. Two "Self-Realization Fellowship Lessons" entitled "God is Everything - Part One" and "God is Everything - Part Two." Each is three double-sided pages. The letterhead reads, "Thy Self-realization will blossom forth from thy soulful study." Also attached is a one two-sided page list of the lessons in Volume 3. Sixty-four page book entitled "Self-Realization: Founded by Paramahansa Yoganada" Cover is blue with a silver snowflake. Christmas card with handwritten note from Brahma Chari Josef. Letter offers friendship and prayers to Elvis. 11 x 8 1/2 inches lessons. 7 3/4 x 5 1/4 inches book. 5 3/4 x 8 1/4 inches envelope.

The Self-Realization Fellowship was founded in 1920 by Paramahansa Yoganada, an Indian holy man and author of "Autobiography of a Yogi." Several years after Yoganada's death in 1952, Sri Daya Mata became president of the Fellowship. Daya Mata had been a follower of Yoganada for over twenty years when she became president. During the filming of "Harem Scarum" in spring of 1965, Elvis began going to the Self-Realization Fellowship's Lake Shrine retreat in Pacific Palisades, thus embarking on a journey of spiritual enlightenment. It was in this retreat that he met Brahma Chari Josef, a monk with whom he frequently conversed and who ultimately arranged for Elvis to meet Sri Daya Mata. Elvis went to the Fellowship's headquarters on Mt. Washington to meet Daya Mata. Elvis was able to open up to Daya Mata, whose manner reminded Elvis of his mother, and share with her fears, doubts, and thoughts that he was unable to express to anyone else. During the course of their relationship, Daya Mata urged Elvis to "take time for himself and his spiritual well-being, but he was very much pulled toward his following, he wished to please them, they gave him love." Elvis continued to visit and confide in Daya Mata into the early 1970's.

$3,000 - 3,500

C149 LETTER AND POSTER HANGING LOCATIONS

Signed letter of August 10, 1972, to Elvis from the Colonel on Las Vegas Hilton letterhead, regarding locations of poster placement. "Everyone at these addresses will know you are in town," he writes. Included are two sheets showing the locations posters were to hang in Palm Springs and Las Vegas. Photograph included. 11 x 8 1/2 inches.

Poster locations were for the Summer Festival of 1972 in Las Vegas. $750 - 850

C150 JEWELRY PURCHASE BILLS

Statement from Sol Schwartz, Lee Ableser jewelers in Beverly Hills, California, dated December 1, 1970, for $2,184.31. Seven invoices from individual purchases from 10/2/70-11/27/70. One invoice signed by Elvis. Two invoices signed by Priscilla Presley. Two adding machine receipts included. 8 1/2 x 5 1/2 inches statement. 6 x 4 inches invoices. 3 3/4 x 2 3/4 inches and 3 1/8 x 2 3/4 inches adding machine receipts.

Jewelry purchases included TCB pendants, atomizers, engraved handles on a Beretta, and ID bracelets for friends. $800 - 1,000

C151 LETTER FROM BARRON HILTON

Signed letter--on Hilton letterhead--dated September 11, 1972, to Colonel from Barron Hilton, President of Hilton Hotels Corporation. Thanking him for photo album commemorating Elvis' recent engagement at Las Vegas Hilton. "The worldwide telecast from Hawaii will unquestionably be one of the milestones of your and Elvis' careers, and will spread more good will throughout the world than any other feat I can recall." 10 1/2 x 7 1/2 inches.

Barron Hilton, owner of the Hilton Hotel chain, became a great personal admirer of Elvis and benefitted greatly from his appearances at the Hiltons in Las Vegas and from him being the largest draw in that entertainment city. To this day, Elvis still holds the record for the largest draws there. $250 - 300

C152 ELVIS PRESLEY'S FAMILY CADILLAC
STATION WAGON

1972 Cadillac station wagon. Cream with black
vinyl top, four doors, luggage rack, leather interior,
and olive a wood paneled dashboard. Small gold
plaque on passenger side door engraved with,
"TCB." Gold Cadillac hood ornament.

Elvis may have been the King of Rock and Roll, but
he was also a family man, and every family man
needs a family car. Never one to sacrifice style,
Elvis' family car of choice was a Cadillac.

ESTIMATE UPON REQUEST

C153. WOODEN WAGON

Model wooden wagon built like a stage coaches.
Hitch included. 16 1/2 x 23 inches wagon

Colonel Parker collected model wagons and people often gave them to him as gifts. For him it was a
reminder of his days working in the carnival.

$1,500 - 2,000

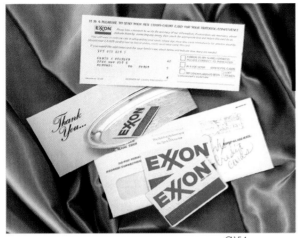

C154

C154 EXXON CARDS

Two red, white and blue plastic credit cards with raised lettering "Elvis A. Presley." With original mailing envelope postmarked May 20, 1976. 2 1/8 x 3 3/8 inches. Each card with expiration date of May, 1978.

$4,500 - 5,000

C155 MOBIL CREDIT CARD ISSUED TO ELVIS PRESLEY

Mobil credit card issued to Elvis. Logo is blue and red with raised black lettering, and Joe Esposito's signature on the back. 2 1/8 x 3 3/8 inches Card Credit card expiration date was March, 1976.

$2,000 - 2,500

C156 EXXON, SHELL, AND MEXICAN INSURANCE CREDIT CARDS ISSUED TO ELVIS PRESLEY AND MILO HIGH

Two blue, white, and red Exxon credit cards issued to Elvis Presley with expiration dates of July 1976 and 1977. One gold and white Shell Credit Card issued to Elvis with an expiration date of August, 1976. Copy of Shell receipt from Des Moines Fly Service dated May 28, 1976, for $669.98, signed by Elvis' pilot Elwood David. One Mexicard credit card issued to both Elvis and Milo High. Original envelope, credit card plan, and verification card from Exxon. 2 x 3 1/2" Credit cards. 3 1/4 x 4 3/4" Shell Invoice. 3 1/2 x 8" Envelope. 3 1/4 x 7 1/2" Credit Card. Plan 3 1/4 x 7 1/2" Verification Card.

1977 Exxon and Shell Credit cards are signed by Elvis' pilot, Milo B. High.

$8,000 - 10,000

C157 ELVIS PRESLEY'S SHELL CREDIT CARD

White and gold plastic credit card in Elvis Presley's name with red and yellow Shell logo and raised black lettering. Includes Business Reply Mail with Elvis Presley's name and address. 2 1/8 x 3 3/8 " card. 3 1/4 x 7 3/8 inches BRM.

This credit card expired April, 1978.

$2,500 - 3,000

C155

C158 ELVIS PRESLEY'S UNION 76 CREDIT CARD

Plastic credit card with a dark orange globe with the number "76" in blue on a orange and yellow background with a green palm leaf in the foreground. White paper insert with blue text for return to Union 76 company. A color brochure of the "Arrow Portable Radio" for sale by Union 76. Original envelope dated October 28, 1976. 2 1/8 x 3 3/8" Card. 6 3/4 x 3 1/4" Brochure. 3 1/2 x 7 3/8" Insert. 3 3/4 x 8 1/4 " Envelope.

Expiration date for card was November, 1979. Card shows that Elvis had been a customer since 1968.

$3,000 - 3,500

C157

C156

C159 ELVIS PRESLEY'S
SIGNED TEXACO CREDIT
CARD

White and gold Texaco credit
card issued to Elvis Presley
with white raised lettering.
Back is signed by Elvis
Presley in blue ink. 2 x 3 1/2

This card shows wear.

$8,000 - 10,000

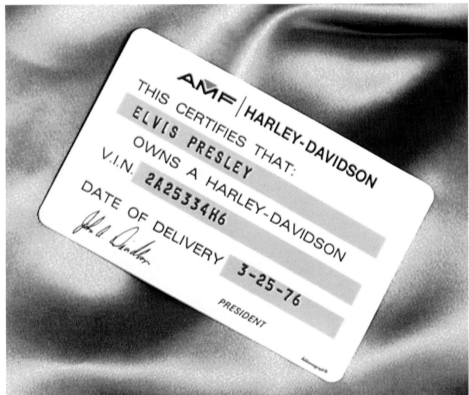

C160 HARLEY-DAVIDSON OWNERSHIP CARD

White plastic card dated March 25, 1976 with raised
lettering "Elvis Presley." 2 1/8 x 3 3/8.

Elvis received this card with his purchase of a red,
white and blue "bicentennial edition" Harley-
Davidson motorcycle.

$8,000 - 10,000

C161 CERTIFICATE OF TITLE AND REGISTRATION
FOR LINCOLN CONTINENTAL MARK IV

Dated July 28, 1975, State of Tennessee, Department
of Revenue carbon copy of application for certificate of title and registration for silver 1975
Continental Mark IV Coupe. Carbon copy of signature by Elvis A. Presley. Attached 1975 City of
Memphis auto tag receipt #255369 in small clear

bag. Paper and receipt
inside Car Papers folder
from Foxgate Lincoln
Mercury in Memphis.
Folder has handwritten note
indication delivery to David
A. Hebler. 8 x 5 1/8 inches
certificate. 1 1/4 x 2 1/2 inches receipt. 4 1/2 x 2 3/4 inches bag. 10 1/8 x 6, opening
to 10 1/8 x 11 1/2" folder.

This car was a gift from Elvis
to David Hebler, one of his
body guards. The day
before this, Elvis spent
$140,000 for thirteen Cadillacs that he gave away to
family, friends, and a woman named Menni Person
who happened to be window shopping for a
Cadillac at the dealership when Elvis arrived.

$750 - 850

C162 ORDER FROM FLASHBACKS INC.

Handwritten notes (on yellow lined notebook paper) and statement for Flashbacks, Inc, in Fountain Valley, California. Order was price quote for Elvis Promotional materials, including large Elvis 4-color banners and Elvis 3-color posters. Delivery date 12/29/72. One three-piece banner for International Hotel appearance: heavy paper, brown and ochre background with black letters that reads "Elvis"; head shot of Elvis on left-hand side; blue Hilton logo at end of banner. 11 x 8 1/2 inches notes and statement. 23 x 111 inches banner.

This order from Flashbacks was for promotional material ordered from Tom Askew for Elvis' January 1973 opening at the Las Vegas Hilton. The shows took place from January 26 to February 23.

$1,600 - 1,800

C163 THANK YOU LETTER FROM JOHN FINLATOR.

One page typed on personalized stationery, dated January 3, 1972. Sent to Elvis Presley and signed "John" in black marker. With envelope. Photograph included. 10 1/2 x 7 1/4 inches letter 4 x 7 1/2 inches envelope John Finlator was deputy director of the Narcotics Bureau when Elvis received his narcotics-agent badge from President Nixon on December 21, 1970. In this letter, Finlator thanks Elvis for a radio Elvis gave him for his retirement.

$300 - 350

C164. EDDIE BOND LETTER AND BADGE

Letter dated April 21, 1972 to "Lieutenant Presley" from Eddie Bond, Chief of Police for Finger, Tennessee. The letter is on Bond's business letterhead. Bond urges Elvis to donate $10 for 10 tickets to the 2nd Annual Finger Friendly Festival. With a gold and silver Finger, Tenn. Police Lieutenant badge, held in a black vinyl case with a card signed by Eddie Bond dated September 16, 1971 that names Elvis a lieutenant in the Finger Police Department. Also included are 10 yellow tickets to the Finger Friendly Festival. 11 x 8 1/2 inches letter. 1 x 2 inches tickets. 4 3/8 x 3 1/4 inches badge case.

Though at this point comfortably ensconced in small town government, Eddie Bond had earlier been a figure of some infamy within Elvis legend. In 1954 Bond was a 21-year old veteran of the local Memphis music scene, and his band was looking for a singer. On May 15, 1954 Elvis joined Bond's group at the Hi Hat on South Third Street in Memphis for an audition. Elvis went to the audition with then girlfriend Dixie Locke and sang two songs with the band...but didn't get the job. Elvis later revealed that Bond told him to stick with driving a truck, because he would "never make it as a singer." Less than two months later Elvis' recorded his first Sun single, "That's All Right." Bond would later joke that he'd been "the only person to ever fire Elvis." A couple of years after the rejection, on route to Hollywood to film "Jailhouse Rock," Elvis reportedly said to confidant George Klein, "I wonder what Eddie Bond thinks now. Man, that sono-fabitch broke my heart."

$800 - 1,000

C165 GRACELAND CHRISTMAS INVOICE

Invoice from H.M. Phipps in Memphis, dated December 20, 1968 and billed to "Graceland-Elvis Presley Home." Bill for $1,522.54 for the rental of a large nativity scene and garland trees. With envelope and "Elvis Presley Payroll & Expense Fund" check to Phipps in same amount, signed by Vernon Presley. Photograph included. 5 1/2 x 8 1/2 inches invoice. 4 x 9 1/2 inches envelope. 3 x 8 1/4 inches check.

This nativity scene was later purchased by the Elvis Presley estate and is still displayed at Graceland every Christmas.

$1,000 - 1,200

C166 "ELVIS ON TOUR" PRODUCTION NOTES AND MENU

Twelve pages typed with production credits, commentary and tour dates. One menu stamped "This menu for Maitre'D and Captain's use only." Gold, purple and red, round menu is image of a record with black and white Elvis photo in middle and title "Elvis-Las Vegas Hilton Summer Festival." Opens to menu. 11 x 8 1/2 inches credits. 18 inches diameter menu.

This 1972 tour documentary was Elvis' thirty-third and final film. Among those listed in the production credits is future "Taxi Driver" and "Raging Bull" director Martin Scorsese, who is listed as "Montage Supervisor." $1,300 - 1,500

C167 ELVIS PRESLEY'S RECEIPTS FROM SCHWARTZ & ABLESER FINE JEWELRY

Yellow receipt for Elvis Presley dated October 14, 1970 from Sol Schwartz, Lee Ableser Fine Jewelry - Diamonds in Beverly Hills, California. Elvis purchased eight T.C.B. necklaces totaling $759.60. Yellow receipt for Elvis Presley dated April 6, 1973 from Schwartz and Ableser Fine Jewelry. Elvis purchased one Karate diamond and ruby pin, six T.C.B. pendants, three T.L.C. pendants, and two additional items totaling $2546.25. Both receipts bear a carbon copy signature by Elvis Presley. 6 x 4 inches.

Elvis gave away T.C.B. jewelry to many of his friends.

$450 - 500

C168 ELVIS PRESLEY SCREEN ACTORS GUILD EARNINGS CARD

White card from the Screen Actors Guild issued to Elvis Presley. Shows earnings from 1973 of $150.00, from 1972 of $147,500 and no screen earnings from 1971. With envelope postmarked September 13, 1974. 3 1/2 x 6 1/4 inches card. 4 x 7 1/2 inches envelope.

This earnings statement from the Screen Actors Guild dates from a period after Elvis had ceased making feature films. The earnings from 1972 are for the tour documentary "Elvis on Tour."

$550 - 650

C169 HOTEL BILLS, AIRLINE TICKETS AND MOBILE RELATED TO "ELVIS, ALOHA FROM HAWAII"

Fifty-four pages of itemized hotel receipts from the Hilton Hawaiian Village during the month of January, 1973 for Elvis and his entourage. Copy of three American Airlines tickets issued in the month of January, 1973. Twelve copies of United Air Lines tickets issued to Elvis and his group for the month of January, 1973. Copy of statement for Airline tickets. Mobile in the shape of a record advertising "Elvis, Aloha From Hawaii." 11 x 8 1/2 inches Invoices. 8 x 5 1/2 inches Hotel receipts. 3 1/2 x 7 1/2 inches Airline tickets. 7 1/4 x 8 1/2 inches Airline statement. 30 x 30 inches mobile.

"Elvis, Aloha from Hawaii" marked the first time that a program was telecast around the world by satellite. It was seen by a record one billion people in 40 countries around the world.

$5,000 - 7,000

1977 with check marks next to three calls to Memphis and one call to Palm Springs made from the Hilton by Elvis Presley. Also attached are 44 pages of individual receipts from the Hilton Hawaiian Village and a piece of adding machine tape. Original envelope included. Eight-page book entitled "The Last Vacation, Hawaii March 1977." Tells the story of Elvis' Hawaiian vacation and shows pictures. Photograph included. 11 x 8 1/2 inches statement. 14 x 8 1/2 inches ledger. 11 x 8 1/2 inches phone bill.

C170

C170 DOCUMENTS FROM HILTON HAWAIIAN VILLAGE

Statement on white paper addressed to Elvis Presley from Hilton Hawaiian Village plus blue carbon copy. Statement dated April 1, 1977 from dates in March totals $16,931.48. Copy of a two-page detailed ledger for Elvis Presley and 18 other guests under the name, "Esposito Group." Copy of a bill from Hawaiian Telephone dated March 28,

7 1/2 x 6 1/4 inches individual receipts. 6 1/4 x 2" adding tape. 7 1/2 x 10 1/2 inches envelope. 11 x 8 1/2 inches "The Last Vacation."

Hawaii was a favorite vacation spot of Elvis'. He wanted to show Hawaii to Ginger Alden, his girl-friend, so he planned a two-week Hawaiian vacation. It began as a romantic getaway for two, however, it quickly escalated into a travelling crowd of 30 family and friends, with Ginger's family being

among the first to be added to the guest list. They all arrived in Hawaii the morning of March 4 settling in at the Hilton Rainbow Tower. After two days, Elvis, the Alden sisters, and a couple of the guys moved to a beach house at Kailua while everyone else remained at the Hilton. They spent their time playing touch football on the beach, playing ping-pong, and relaxing. While everyone seemed to be having a good time, it was was tainted by the fact that Elvis' physical condition was clearly declining. On March 12, an excursion to the U.S.S. Arizona was cancelled when Elvis got sand in his eye. Dr. Nick was afraid that Elvis may have scratched his cornea and wanted him to have several days in Memphis to recover prior to going on out tour later in the month. This meant the end of the vacation and Elvis and the rest of the party returned home, but not before Elvis purchased a gift for everyone in the party as a souvenir of the trip. Elvis later told Larry Geller that the trip cost him around, $100,000, but "What profiteth it to gain the world if you couldn't share your good fortune with your friends?" This was Elvis' last vacation.

$4,500 - 5,000

C171 - C179 No Lot

263

C180 HANDWRITTEN NOTES FROM SATELLITE SHOW

Colonel Parker's handwritten notes prior to Satellite Show in Hawaii (January 14, 1973). His notes refer to costs show would accrue--backup musicians and rehearsal room--with some questions, such as "RCA makes contracts with talent or do we?" Photograph included. Black double-set LP album of "Elvis--Aloha from Hawaii via Satellite" Button: "The Colonel Says: 'How Much Does It Cost If It's Free'" 6 5/8 x 8 1/2 inches notes. 12 3/8 x 12 3/8 inches album.

While the Colonel was in Las Vegas at the International Hotel, he began forming his thoughts about Elvis' worldwide telecast from Hawaii. He wrote his notes on a torn-off piece of International stationery. His significant handwritten notes show the thinking processes he performed before a project and the formation of his to-do list.

$1,800 - 2,000

C181 SNOWMEN'S LEAGUE ITEMS AND LETTER FROM BARRON HILTON

Letter dated February 6, 1973, to "Colonel of the Snows" from Snowball (Barron) Hilton. "Thanks for your latest snow-a-gram which we dutifully thawed out and read dated January 31st . . . In defrosting the lines . . . I made use of a magic two-way mirror." Copy of letter welcoming new snow members and signed, "Potentially, Potentate." Two samples of Snowmen's League of America certificate with two blank lines for "Temporary Member" and "Lifetime Member - Maybe?" Official membership card with a snowman in the upper left corner and a picture off Colonel Parker in the upper right corner. Snowmen's League booklet with chapter titles, but no actual information on pages. 11 x 8 1/2 inches letters. 7 1/8 x 9 1/4 inches certificates. 2 1/4 x 4 inches official card. 6 x 3 1/2 inches booklet.

Colonel Parker was the master of his own universe, and that universe included the creation of his own club, the Snowmen's League. The League was a take-off of the Showmen's League, a group of circus and carnival operators to which the Colonel had previously belonged. The Snowmen had no meetings and no real tangible purpose except to cele-

brate and further the art of "snowing" (an art that falls somewhere between conning and selling) through techniques such as the "melt and disappear" technique. However, it did have a membership list that boasted some of the most powerful and well-known names in Hollywood, including executives, agents, journalists, actors, and musicians. Membership to the club became somewhat of a coo among the Hollywood elite, and although the club cost nothing to join, it cost $10,000 to leave. The Colonel often bragged, "We've never lost a member." The Snowmen's League booklet is a classic Snowmen's item. The Colonel obviously knew that it would be, because the inside cover reads, "This is already a collectors item so buy several copies." Chapter titles include such topics as, "Snowing as Related to Hypnosis," "What Snowing Does for Your Income," "Snowing as a Status Symbol," and "Snowing and Sociability."

$650 - 750

C182 INTERNAL CORRESPONDENCE FROM RCA RECORDS TO GEORGE PARKHILL REGARDING LACQUERS, AND MOCK-UPS FOR "STEAMROLLER BLUES" AND "FOOL"; PLUS MOCK-UPS FOR THE SINGLES

Typewritten letter, dated February 20, 1973, from Joan Deary, of RCA Records New York, to George Parkhill. Internal correspondence is regarding the lacquers and mock-ups for "Steamroller Blues" and "Fool." There is also mention of a "definite difference in (the) sound between the 2 sides." Included are the mock-ups for both singles: front of "Fool" shows Elvis singing, dresses in a white jumpsuit with a red and white lei around his neck; flip side is for "Steamroller Blues" which is green, yellow, and red with an outline of a steamroller. A third mock-up shows a picture of an old steamroller engine with an engineer on the back. The words "Steamroller Blues" are written on multiple colors of green, yellow, orange, red, blue, and maroon. 11 x 8 1/2 inches Correspondence. 7 x 7 inches Mock-ups.

"Steamroller Blues" was a single release from the "Aloha From Hawaii" recorded on January 12, 1973. "Fool" was recorded in July of 1973.

$4,500 - 5,000

C183 THANK YOU LETTERS FOR MEMPHIS CHARITY CONTRIBUTIONS

Letter dated January 3, 1973, from Memphis Boys' Town, thanking Elvis for his contribution. Letter dated January 10, 1973, from Beale Street Elks, thanking Elvis for contributing to their scholarship fund. Letter dated January 12, 1973, from YWCA, thanking Elvis for the contribution that will "enable us to improve our youth program." Original check from the account of Elvis Presley included. 11 x 8 1/2 inches letters.

Elvis was known for his generosity, donating thousands of dollars to charities every year. $400 - 600

C184 THANK YOU LETTER FROM JOHN FINLATOR.

One page typed on personalized stationery, dated January 3, 1972. Sent to Elvis Presley and signed "John" in black marker. With envelope. Photograph included. 10 1/2 x 7 1/4 inches letter 4 x 7 1/2 inches envelope John Finlator was deputy director of the Narcotics Bureau when Elvis received his narcotics-agent badge from President Nixon on December 21, 1970. In this letter, Finlator thanks Elvis for a radio Elvis gave him for his retirement.
$300 - 350

C185 LETTER REGARDING NAME CHANGE OF TUPELO STREET

Letter, on official City of Tupelo letterhead, dated November 7, 1973, from mayor Clyde Whitaker to Elvis Presley. "Please find attached excerpt from the minutes of the Board Meeting of September 4, 1973. I thought perhaps you might be interested in the recent change of Old Saltillo Road to Elvis Presley Drive." Document from the meeting is attached and signed by Whitaker and Temple, City Clerk. Mailable fold-out packet of 14 color photographs including his home in Tupelo, Sun Records, Graceland, and Elvis performing. Photograph included 11 x 8 1/2 inches letters. 4 x 6 inches photo packet.

Elvis was born in a shotgun house that his father built on Old Saltillo Road in Tupelo, Mississippi. This house is still standing and is now a museum.
$650 - 750

C186 ELVIS PRESLEY'S BIBLE

One copy of "The Living Bible" Paraphrased. By Tyndale House Publishers. Blue leather bound Bible with gold letters on front that read: "Elvis Presley." 8 x 5 inches.

Elvis kept this Bible in his bedroom. It was a cherished gift from a loyal fan. A letter found inside the Bible (but not included with it) explained the reason for the gift. The young woman had traveled 700 miles to deliver it-- a purpose God had given her. She told Elvis she prayed for him and asked him to allow God to lead in his life.
$15,000 - 20,000

C186A ELVIS PRESLEY'S PERSONAL TCB NECKLACE

Pendant-necklace featuring a 14k yellow gold pendant designed as a lightning
bolt surrounded by the letters "TCB," designed by Elvis Presley, attached to a
yellow gold neck-chain. 1 3/4 inch pendant, 24 inch chain.

Elvis Presley designed this style pendant as a symbol of his motto
"Takin' Care of Business" for himself and for members of the
"Memphis Mafia." This signature TCB necklace, worn by Elvis
personally, was a gift of appreciation from Elvis to Gee Gee
Gambill. Gee Gee, the husband of Patsy Presley, Elvis'
cousin, retuned to work for Elvis Presley in 1970.
When Gee Gee rejoined Elvis
and his staff, Elvis removed this very necklace
from his neck and placed it on Gee Gee.

$40,000 - 50,000

C186B ELVIS
PRESLEY'S
PERSONAL
HANDGUN

Walther handgun, model PPk/s
9mm Kurz. West German. Silver
barrel with ornate decorative engraving along with an engraving of "Elvis."
Wooden stock with a silver medallion "TCB"
(*Takin' Care of Business*) and lightning bolt.
With case.

$40,000 - 50,000

C187 CONTRACT, PURCHASE, FINANCIAL PLAN, BLUEPRINT, PROMOTIONAL PAGE, AND PLANE SPECIFICATIONS FOR THE "LISA MARIE"

Copy of contract between Elvis Presley and the First National Bank of Memphis listing the cost of plane ($924,411.84), and the terms of payment; $9,629.29 per month for 96 months. Contract is on blue contract paper, attached is a handwritten copy of the financial breakdown, and on back of contract is Elvis Presley's signature. One color, promotional page on thick paper stock, showing photos of the inside of a Convair 880. One customized layout and blue print of "Lisa Marie" sketched on white paper. Thirty-two pages of interior specifications for plane bound within a blue folder. Photograph included. 7 x 7 3/4 inches Contract: Front page. 14 x 8 inches Back page. 11 x 8 1/2 inches Handwritten page. 10 x 8 inches Promotional page. 10 x 13 3/4 inches Layout/blue print. 11 x 8 1/2 inches Pages of specifications. 11 1/2 x 9 inches Folder.

Elvis' "Lisa Marie" was a custom blue and white Convair 880 jet purchased in November of 1975. It cost $750,000 for remodeling, which was done in Fort Worth, Texas. The jet was named after his daughter, and required a crew of four, including a stewardess. Its emblem has the letters TCB (Taking Care of Business) and a lightning bolt in gold on the tail section, under an American flag. Elwood David was the captain, Ron Strauss the copilot, and Jim Manning the flight engineer. The plane was equipped with a $14,000 queen-size bed, a conference room, four TV sets, a bar, leather swivel chairs, and a pair of couches.

$18,000 - 20,000

C188 LISA MARIE AIRPLANE LOG BOOK
Black binder with log sheets from the Lisa Marie airplane dating from January 1 - August 19, 1977. Photograph included. 11 1/2 x 10 x 1 inches.

The last two flights documented are round trips from Memphis to Los Angeles on August 17 and August 19, 1977, the days after Elvis' death and funeral, respectively. The former flight was to pick up Priscilla and others for the funeral and the latter was to return Priscilla and Lisa Marie to California afterwards.

$13,000 - 15,000

C189 FLIGHT CREW ON DUTY EXPENSE REPORT

Flight Crew on Duty Expense Report for eight flights during August and September 1977. Logs flights made between Denver and Memphis on an American Airlines flight, and between Los Angeles and Memphis on the Lisa Marie. A flight was made from Memphis to Los Angeles on August 16, and from Los Angeles to Memphis on August 17. Elwood Davis was the Captain. Expenses total $76.50. Photograph included. 11 x 8 1/2.

After Elvis' death, Joe Esposito sent the "Lisa Marie" to California to pick up Priscilla, Jerry Schilling, Joe's girlfriend Shirley Dieu, Joe's former wife Joanie, and Priscilla's immediate family. This is the last logged entry of Lisa Marie Airplane.

$3,000 - 3,500

C190 CONTRACT, STAGE LAYOUT AND POSTCARD FOR ELVIS PRESLEY'S LAKE TAHOE PERFORMANCE

Elvis Presley's copy of American Guild of Variety Artists Standard Form of Artists Engagement Contract date March 16, 1973. The contract concerns Elvis' show at the Sahara Tahoe beginning May 4, 1973. Signed in blue ink by Elvis Presley and M. Hundley, AGVA Vice President. Layout of the stage arrangement for the Elvis Presley Show at Lake Tahoe, Nevada. Postcard with black and white photograph of Elvis singing on one side, and red and black printed announcement of Elvis' Tahoe engagement on the other side. 17 x 9 1/4 inches contract. 8 1/2 x 13 inches layout. 3 1/2 x 5 1/2 inches postcard.

The Sahara Tahoe overbooked Elvis' May 1973 engagement and many disappointed ticket holders were turned away at the door. The High Sierra Theatre in the Sahara Tahoe was crammed wall to wall with people for Elvis' shows. Unfortunately, Elvis was under the weather and was finally forced to cancel the end of the engagement. Elvis was to receive a two-week salary of $300,000 and the Colonel was to receive $100,000 for the Tahoe engagement, however, when Elvis cancelled the last four days of his show, Colonel Parker forfeited his $100,000 payment.

$7,000 - 8,000

C191 ELVIS PRESLEY'S SCREEN ACTORS GUILD CARD

Elvis Presley's Original Screen Actors Guild card and receipt. Card is white with yellow and black lettering, dated June 26, 1976. Receipt is attached to card in the amount of $20.00, and includes the original envelope. Photograph included. 4 x 7 1/2 inches Card/Receipt. 4 1/2 x 8 inches Envelope.

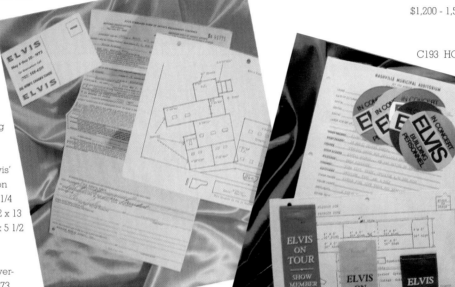

C190

C192

The cards list Elvis' address at Graceland although he was living in California. Elvis always considered Memphis his home. $2,000 - 2,500

C192 NASHVILLE CONCERT PREPARATION

Five page document packet showing preparation for an Elvis Presley concert at the Nashville Municipal Auditorium on July 1, 1973. Includes: a stage diagram, expense report and stage requirements list. With four backstage pass ribbons reading "Elvis on Tour-Show Member" in yellow, green,

red and purple. Six circular "building personnel" patches multiple colors. One white ribbon with red print reading "ELVIS." 11 x 8 1/2 inches documents. 6 1/4 x 2 inches backstage ribbons. 3 1/4 inches diameter "building personnel" patches. 7 5/8 x 1 1/2 inches "Elvis" ribbon.

These items document Elvis' first show in Nashville since appearing on the Grand Ole Opry on October 2, 1954.

$1,200 - 1,500

C193 HOTEL BILLS FOR ELVIS PRESLEY AND OTHERS FROM THE LAS VEGAS HILTON IN MARCH 1973

Invoice dated March 14, 1973 addressed to Vernon Presley from the Las Vegas Hilton totaling $6034.11. Attached are individual invoices for Elvis Presley, Vernon Presley, J.B. Beaulieu, James Coughley, Joe Esposito, Sonny West, Jerry Schilling, Homer Gilleland, Charlie Hodge, Kenneth Hicks, and Red West. Also listed are guests of Joe Esposito: Kany [sic] Rhee, Marty Lacker, Dick Grof, Lamar Fike, and Ed Parker. 11 x 8 1/2"

After closing his tour at the Hilton on February 23, 1973, Elvis and many in his entourage remained as guests at the Hilton until early March. Elvis and Linda Thompson were seen at Ann-Margaret's opening performance which was the night following Elvis' closing performance. His karate instructor, Kang Rhee, was in Las Vegas with him so Elvis was able to maintain his studies.

$800 - 1,000

C194 ONE PAIR OF ELVIS PRESLEY'S BOOTS

Original, handwritten letter from Richard, of Richard's Shoes, to Elvis. Correspondence is thanking Elvis for his business. In appreciation Richard mentions that he is sending two pair of boots to Elvis as a gift. Letter and envelope are light brown in color with dark brown letterhead. One pair of Elvis Presley's white patent leather stage boots. 11 x 8 1/2 inches Letter. 4 1/4 x 9 1/2 inches Envelope.

Elvis was a long-time customer of Richard's Shoes. As Richard explains in his letter, the style of boots that Elvis preferred was becoming increasingly difficult to get and Richard may not carry them any longer. In appreciation of Elvis' business over the previous ten years, Richard sent Elvis the last two pairs of boots he had in Elvis' size, one black and one white pair. $6,500 - 7,500

C195 ELVIS PRESLEY'S JOGGING SUIT AND RECEIPT

Black, nylon, two-piece jogging suit with a red and white stipe on sleeve cuffs and down the side of the legs. White zipper on jacket and on pant cuffs. Two-page receipt from Forty Love, tennis shoppe, in Memphis dated 12/1/73 for such items as warm ups, socks, and glove--total of $384.98. Signed by Joe Esposito. 7 x 4 1/4 inches Forty Love. Elvis often wore warm-up suits around the house. $6,500 - 7,500

C196 ELVIS PRESLEY'S WARDROBE DOCUMENTS INCLUDING MUHAMMAD ALI'S ROBE

Copies of two invoices with attached Airland bills from IC Costume Company in Hollywood, California, dated January 23 and February 19, 1973. Total of two bills is $14,125.91. Among other items was a "Custom-made robe - heavily embroidered w/ "People's Choice" for $900. Orders sent from Ice Capades (from costume designer Bill Belew), with one going to Marvin Gambit in Memphis and the other to Elvis at the Las Vegas Hilton. Adding machine receipt attached with total. Two original invoices from IC Costume Company, dated March 18 and April 21, 1975. Both billed to Vernon Presley. March invoice for total of $7,028.91 for four jump

suits and 11 jumpsuit repairs. April invoice for total of $5,853.86 includes three jumpsuits. Note to Elvis Presley on brown Bill Belew letterhead concerning costumes for Las Vegas. Elvis was billed $3,575 for four jeweled belts with gold and silver medallions, and one and a half dozen elastic undershorts. Original, light green check to Bill Belew for $3,575 signed by Vernon Presley. Invoice addressed to Vernon Presley from IC Costume Company in Hollywood, California dated January 21, 1974. Invoice total is $3,280 for repairs and refurbishments to 16 of Elvis' jumpsuits and reimbursement

for cleaning. Attached is a copy of a dry cleaning bill from Malone Studio Service for $480. Original, light green check to I.C. Costume for $3,280 signed by Joseph Hanks, Elvis' accountant. Invoice addressed to Vernon Presley from IC Costume Company in Hollywood, California dated February 26, 1974. Invoice total is $1,420 for repairs and refurbishments of five capes and nine jumpsuits, and reimbursement for cleaning. Attached is a copy of a dry cleaning bill from Malone Studio Service for $250.00 Original checks from the account of Elvis Presley. 11 x 8 1/2" invoices and Airland bills. 2 1/2 x 2 3/4" adding machine receipt. 11 x 8 1/2" IC invoice. 10 3/8 x 7 1/4" Bill Belew note. 11 x 8 1/2" other invoices. 3 x 8 1/4" checks.

Elvis, a big fan of Muhammad Ali, had an embroidered robe custom made for him. Ali wore the robe on March 31, 1973 in his fight against Ken Norton. It appears that the IC Costume invoice is misprinted, as it states that the robe was embroidered with "People's Choice." In contrast, newspaper clippings from the fight describe the robe as being embroidered with "People's Champion." Regardless, Ali considered the robe to be bad luck after he lost the fight to Norton. He never wore the robe again. $3,500 - 4,000

C197 ELVIS PRESLEY'S JEWELRY RECEIPTS FROM 1103 IMPORTS AND T-BIRDS

Two jewelry receipts for Elvis Presley handwritten in blue ink dated February 20, 1973 and February 21, 1973.

Receipts are from 1103 Imports and total $11,490 for 13 items, and $1,734 for four items. Attached is adding machine tape totaling the purchases. Two receipts for Elvis Presley from T-Bird jewelers in Las Vegas. One receipt, dated February 16, 1973, is for one item and totals$336.40. A second receipt, dated February 19, 1973, is for seven items and totals $7,501. A handwritten statement on blue T-bird Jewels letterhead is addressed to Elvis Presley c/o Vernon Presley in Memphis. This statement is for $7,837.60, the total of the two receipts. 6 x 4 inches 1103 receipts. 3 1/4 x 2 3/4 inches and 5 3/4 x 2 3/4 inches adding tape. 6 x 4 inches T-Bird receipts. 8 3/8 x 5 1/2 inches T-Bird statements.

These receipts are toward the end of Elvis' engagement in Las Vegas. He often bought thank you gifts for people that had worked with him on his engagements. Elvis may have been especially grateful to his friends and employees after this engagement due to the incident at the midnight show on February 18. Four men from the audience rushed the stage. Elvis used a karate move to knock one of them back into the audience and the other three were taken care of by Elvis' staff. $400 - 600

C198 ORIGINAL FORM LETTER SIGNED BY ELVIS PRESLEY

Around 1977, original form letter written from Elvis to thank fans for the "thoughtfulness you expressed in your get well message . . . hopefully, I will be performing for my fans in the very near future. Letter is addressed, "Dear" followed by a blank space. Signed by Elvis in blue ink. 11 x 8 1/2"

Elvis was not one to take the loyalty and love his fans showed him for granted. Elvis sent this form letters to fans who remembered him with cards, flowers, and well wishes while he was ill.

$4,000 - 4,500

C199 ELVIS PRESLEY SHOW DATE AND COSTUME ITINERARY— SUMMER 1973

One page typed itinerary for the Elvis Presley Show, for shows from June 20 - July 3, 1973. Includes dates, locations and times for the shows. In black handwritten notes above each city are the outfits Elvis was to wear for the show. With six-page, full color souvenir photo album from the same summer. 11 x 8 1/2 inches itinerary. 11 x 11 inches photo album.

The name "Charlie Hodge," Elvis' rhythm guitar player and close friend, is scrawled twice on the back side in black marker. It is likely that he made the notations about costumes as well.

$3,000 - 4,000

C200 LETTER AND NEWS PAPER CLIPPING REGARDING STOLEN SUPPLIES FROM YOUTH CAMP

Original June 20, 1973 news clipping regarding supplies, stolen from the Louisiana State Police, that were donated to build a summer camp for needy boys. Copy of letter dated June 20, from Colonel Parker to the Louisiana Police, confirming that a check from Elvis, in the amount of $1000 was received. Original check included. 3 1/2 x 3 inches News clipping. 1 1/2 x 8 inches Newspaper banner. 11 x 8 1/2 inches Letter.

C198   C200
C199

On June 20, 1973 Elvis was performing of Mobile, Alabama. After hearing about this story, Elvis and the Colonel decided to send them a donation to replace the stolen supplies.

$1,400 - 1,600

C201 CORRESPONDENCE BETWEEN CHRYSALIS PROMOTIONS AND COLONEL TOM PARKER

Two typed letters dated July 3 and 9, 1973 addressed to Colonel Parker on green Chrysalis Promotions letterhead with butterfly cut-out in upper right corner. Included with letters is a list of acts promoted by Chrysalis. Copy of letter dated July 13, 1973 written on MGM letterhead to Chrisalis Artistes Services in London from Tom Diskin. 11 3/4 x 8 1/4 inches Chrysalis letter. 11 3/4 x 8 1/4 inches List of acts. 11 x 8 1/2 inches Diskin letter.

Correspondence from Chrysalis is in regards to the possibility of Elvis playing at Wembley Stadium on the 25th and 26th of August, 1973. The list of acts promoted by Chrysalis includes Black Sabbath, Johnny Cash, Liza Minnelli, Van Morrison, and Yes among others. Tom Diskin declined their offer. Elvis never played in England during his entire career.

$1,400 - 1,600

C202 ELVIS PRESLEY'S MEMBERSHIP CARD

Membership card from the Alabama Peace Officers Association. Yellow card with gold shield and blue print. 2 3/8 x 3 7/8 inches.

The Alabama Peace Officers Association made Elvis an honorary member in 1973.

$800 - 1,000

C203 TOUR BONUS CHECKS—1975

Twenty checks from Elvis' personal checking account, each check signed "E.A. Presley" by Elvis in black ink. Checks listed as "Bonus on July 25 Road Tour." 3 x 8 1/4 inches.

Checks are bonus payments for members of Elvis' July 8-24, 1975 tour. Checks for: Jackie Kahane, Charlie Hodge, Dean Nichouplos, Lamar Fike, Vernon Presley, Dave Hebler, Joe Esposito, Red West, Sonny West, Felton Jarvis, Dick Grob, Jerry Scheff, Ronnie Tutt, Glen Hardin, Voice (singing group), Kathy Westmoreland, Joe Guerico, The Sweet Inspirations and J.D. Sumner and the Stamps(x2).

$20,000 - 25,000

C204 ELVIS PRESLEY MUSICIAN CONTRACTS

Six contracts on William Morris Agency letterhead, all dated February 19, 1973 and signed in blue ink by Elvis Presley. Contract with musicians Joe Guercio, Emory Gordy, Glen D. Hardin, Ronnie Tutt, James Burton and John Wilkinson for Elvis Presley Show performances at the Sahara-Tahoe Hotel in Stateline, Nevada from May 3-20, 1973. 14 1/2 x 8"

During this ill-fated two week engagement Elvis was forced to cancel shows due to illness and was briefly hospitalized.

$5,500 - 6,500

C205 MEMPHIS MAFIA AMERICAN EXPRESS CARDS

Four white, green and black plastic credit cards with raised lettering: "Delbert B. West Jr.," "Charles F. Hodge," "Alfred D. Strada," and "Joe Esposito." Photograph included. 2 1/8 x 3 3/8".

All cards signed on back by each cardholder.

$2,000 - 2,500

C206 LABOR COSTS AND MEMBER PASSES FOR THE ELVIS PRESLEY SHOW

Labor costs for the 1973 Elvis Presley Show for the cities of Pittsburgh, Cincinnati, St. Louis, Atlanta, Nashville, and Oklahoma CIty. Costs include stage hands, loading, unloading of truck, rigger, electrician, sound man, and light man. List is typewritten on green and yellow Holiday Inn letterhead. 4 vertical Elvis tour ribbons reading "Show Member" and six round Elvis tour ribbons reading "Building Personnel." Ribbons are of various colors. 11 x 8 1/2 inches.

Those working backstage at Elvis' shows wore these ribbons to indicate that they were in fact members of the crew.

$800 - 1,000

C207 LAS VEGAS HILTON BILLS FOR ELVIS PRESLEY AND OTHERS, AND HOTEL TOWEL

Invoice dated March 14, 1973 addressed to Vernon Presley from the Las Vegas Hilton totaling $6034.11. Attached are individual invoices for Elvis Presley, Vernon Presley, J.B. Beaulieu, James Coughley, Joe Esposito, Sonny West, Jerry Schilling, Homer Gilleland, Charlie Hodge, Kenneth Hicks, and Red West. Also listed are guests of Joe Esposito: Kany [sic] Rhee, Marty Lacker, Dick Grof, Lamar Fike, and Ed Parker. One white towel with Hilton logo shaved into the terry surface of the towel. 11 x 8 1/2 inches invoice. 27 1/2 x 17 1/2 inches towel.

After closing his tour at the Hilton on February 23, 1973, Elvis and many in his entourage remained as guests at the Hilton until early March. Elvis and Linda Thompson were seen at Ann-Margaret's opening performance which was the night following Elvis' closing performance. His karate instructor, Kang Rhee, was in Las Vegas with him so Elvis was able to maintain his studies.This Hilton towel, found in Graceland, must have been smuggled out by Elvis or a member of his entourage.

$800 - 1,000

C208 CORRESPONDENCE BETWEEN J.D. SUMNER AND TOM DISKIN REGARDING LODGING IN LAS VEGAS

Two page typed letter on "The Stamps" letterhead, dated July 17, 1973 and sent by J.D. Sumner to Tom Diskin, signed in black ink by J.D. Sumner. Copy of one page typed reply from Diskin, dated July 30, 1973. 11 x 8 1/2 inches.

Sumner inquires about the chance of getting complimentary hotel rooms for his group, The Stamps, for an upcoming Vegas performance. Diskin writes back to decline this request. The Stamps were a gospel vocal group that sang back-up for Elvis Presley during concerts from 1972-1977.

$300 - 350

C209 ELVIS PRESLEY IS ASKED TO PLAY THE FIRST SHOW AT MARKET SQUARE ARENA

One page typed letter on Market Square Associates letterhead, dated September 14, 1973 and sent to Colonel Parker in Culver City, California. Letter asks for Elvis to perform a concert opening Market Square Arena in Indianapolis in September, 1974. One page typed reply to Market

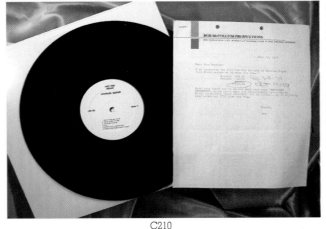

C210
C209

Square Associates from Tom Diskin declining the offer, dated September 28, 1973. With original shrink-wrapped copy of "Elvis in Concert" LP. Photograph included. 11 x 8 1/2 inches letters. 12 x 12 inches record.

The Colonel declines this offer, but Elvis would eventually play Market Square Arena on June 26,

1977—his final public performance. "Elvis in Concert," released in October, 1977, is a soundtrack album from a CBS concert special that aired after Elvis' death. The performances are taken from earlier shows from Elvis final tour in June, 1977.

$400 - 600

C210 LETTER AND POLICE BADGES SENT TO ELVIS PRESLEY FROM HIS FANS

Original typewritten letter, to Vernon Presley from Ed Bonja on MGM letterhead, dated October 19, 1973. Regards three police badges that were sent to MGM for Elvis' collection. Also included are the three police badges. Original envelope included. 11 x 8 1/2 inches Letter. 2 x 1 3/4 inches New Guinea badge. 2 1/2 x 1 3/4 inches Ohio badge. 2 3/4 x 1 3/4 inches Number 13 badge. 7 x 10 inches envelope.

Elvis loved to collect police badges and sometimes received them as gifts from law enforcement officers. The first badge is from New Guinea sporting a silver bird on a red background, and in silver lettering are the words "Royal Papua & New Guinea Constabulary" on a dark blue background. A silver outline of a crown rests on top. The second badge is silver with an eagle on top. In the middle is a carved mountain range with a rising sun, and a fruitful field in the foreground. Above this scene is the word Reserve, and below is the word Stow and Ohio. Third badge is silver with an eagle on top and the word Police under the eagle. In the middle of the badge is a carved mountain range with a rising sun, and a fruitful field in the foreground. Below this scene is the word Stow and the number thirteen.

$1,200 - 1,500

C211 AGREEMENT FOR ELVIS PRESLEY'S NEW YEAR'S EVE SHOW AT PONTIAC, MICHIGAN

Original contract agreement, dated December 1, 1975, for Elvis' New Year's Eve Show in Pontiac, Michigan. Agreement contains terms of the agreement and compensation. Original signature by Elvis Presley and Colonel Tom Parker. Also included is a copy of an itemized cost estimate for the New Year's Eve Show in Pontiac. The estimate of expenses totals $155,000. Black and white concert poster Green and white original ticket. Ticket cost $15. 14 x 8 1/2 inches contract. 11 x 8 1/2 inches estimate. 22 1/2 x 15 1/2 inches poster. 6 x 2 inches ticket.

The Pontiac, Michigan concert was a record breaker. Every one of the 60,500 seats was sold making it the biggest audience of a single artist in an indoor concert. The performance grossed over $800,000, making it the largest sum ever earned for a one-night performance by a single artist. The show, however, was not without its problems. A threat on Elvis' life prior to the performance called for heightened security. No incident took place, but following the show, a man found to be carrying a gun was arrested. The weather was frigid and the sound quality was lacking. As if that weren't enough, Elvis ripped the seat of his pants early in the show. Despite the problems, Elvis and the Colonel took home over $300,000 to divide after expenses. Following the show, Elvis and his entourage including Lisa Marie, Vernon, T.G. Sheppard and his wife, and Linda Thompson flew back to Memphis on the "Lisa Marie." They rung in the new year watching old tapes of "Monty Python" shows in Elvis' bedroom.
$13,000 - 15,000

C211

C212 HOUSTON LIVESTOCK SHOW AND RODEO—1974

Two letters typed on Houston Livestock Show and Rodeo letterhead. Letterhead with black and orange print lists show dates of February 20 -

March 3, 1974 and describes the event as the "world's wildest and largest rodeo. One letter dated December 1, 1973 and sent to show members outlines the show's line-up, which included The Jackson Five, Sonny & Cher and Charlie Rich, along with Elvis Presley. With envelope. Other letter dated April 26, 1974 and sent to Colonel Parker from Show and Rodeo president Tommie Vaughn thanking him for his participation in the event. 11 x 8 1/2 inches letters. 4 x 7 1/2 inches envelope.

Elvis performed two shows on March 3, the last day of festival. As Elvis performed the R&B staple "Fever" during one performance the Colonel came onto the stage riding a small donkey led by Vernon Presley. As Elvis segued into "Let Me Be There" Vernon mounted the donkey as well and he and the Colonel road off the stage.

$1,200 - 1,500

C213 STAGE DIAGRAM FOR 1975 ELVIS PRESLEY SHOW

Original, one-page, typed stage diagram for Elvis Presley Show in June of 1975. The stage was 40 feet wide and 34 feet deep. Photograph included. 11 x 8 1/2.

This diagram was used as a model for the ideal stage set-up for an Elvis performance for many of his shows in the 1970's. The orchestra was in the back, Elvis' band was in the middle, and Elvis was in front.

$350 - 450

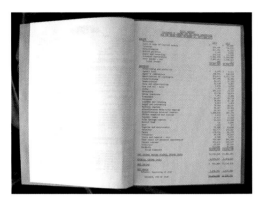
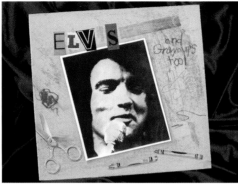

C214   C216   C215

C214 ELVIS PRESLEY'S PERSONAL BALANCE SHEET FROM 1972 AND 1973

Elvis Presley's personal balance sheet from his accountants, Spain and Fisher, for the year 1973. Balance sheet also includes figures form 1972, and lists his assets, liabilities, securities, items of depreciation, income, expenses, taxes, and net worth. Report contains five pages, on white bonded paper, and is in a dark beige folder. 11 x 8 1/2 inches Paper. 11 1/4 x 9 inches Folder.

Elvis' main income changed from being primarily from films in the 1960's, to being primarily from live performances and records in the 1970's. Elvis' gross income in 1973 was $8,607,065.

$2,000 - 2,500

C215 COLOR SEPARATIONS FOR SOUVENIR MENU

Three color transparencies--black, blue, and red--for the front of the Las Vegas Hilton Souvenir Menu in 1974. Photograph used was from the Aloha Special in 1973. Cardboard cover with transparencies marked "Approved 1-14-74, Scott." Las Vegas Hilton Souvenir Menu included with final photograph on front, food and beverage listings inside, and map showing Elvis' sold-out concerts on the back. 12 1/2 x 9 3/4 inches transparencies. 11 x 8 1/2 inches menu.

In 1974, Elvis performed at the Las Vegas Hilton beginning on January 26 for a two-week engagement and then again beginning on August 19 for his two-week Summer Festival engagement.

$600 - 800

C216 ARTWORK FOR ELVIS PRESLEY'S ALBUM

"Elvis Sings For Children and Grownups Too" Original artwork (glued to a KISS album) for Elvis Presley's album "Elvis Sings For Children and Grownups Too." Front cover has a head shot of Elvis with a microphone below his mouth, and his eyes are closed. Above the photo is the name "Elvis" done with letters cut and pasted from various sources (the letter I is missing). The cover looks as if a child composed it with a drawing of a scissors on the left side, a blue and green crayon at the bottom, and on the right side a child's drawing of a tree in the colors red, yellow, and blue. Above the tree are the words "and Grownups too!" Inside cover lists the title of each song, and uses a "phony text" to indicate the correct word placement. Back cover lists side A and side B with a child's drawing of an elephant traced in blue, a red crayon, and a brown drawing of a man. 12 1/2 x 12 1/2 inches.

Except for "Big Boots" all songs on this album had been previously released. A removable bonus greeting card was attached to the albums back cover. The album reached #130 on "Billboards" Top LP's during its 11 weeks on the chart.

3,000 - 3,500

C217 SONG LIST FOR REHEARSALS AND LAS VEGAS HILTON SHOW AND ACETATES

One handwritten song list for January 17, 1974, rehearsal session at RCA Studios, Hollywood. Lists 35 songs on yellow notebook paper. Written in blue ink by Elvis Presley. One-page typed copy of song list for "Elvis Presley Rehearsal Session - RCA Studios, Hollywood Thursday January 17, 1974. Acetates for "You Gave Me A Mountain" and "I'll Remember You." 14 x 8 1/2 inches rehearsal lists.

Elvis rehearsed for over a week in Los Angeles to prepare for his Las Vegas opening on January 26, 1974. Some of the songs Elvis used in this show were Neil Diamond's "Sweet Caroline," Olivia Newton-John's "Let Me Be There," and "Help Me," a song that Elvis released several months later.

$1,400 - 1,600

C218 ELVIS SEES "THE EXORCIST"

One page invoice from Metro-Goldwyn-Mayer for a personal screening of "The Exorcist" on January 19, 1974. Invoice dated January 26, 1974 billed to Elvis Presley in the amount of $350. With check in that amount from the "Elvis Presley Payroll & Expense Fund," made out to M.G.M. and signed by Vernon Presley. 11 x 8 1/2" invoice. 3 x 9 1/4" check.

Elvis was an avid movie watcher and often set up special screenings for himself and his friends. This particular screening was clearly a case of one national phenomenon watching another.

$400 - 500

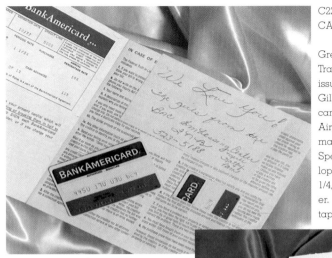

C221 INTERNATIONAL AIR TRAVEL CARD

Green and white International Air Travel Card with raised black letters; issued to Elvis Presley and H. M. Gilleland; expiration 10/77. Green cardholder pamphlet, American Airlines letter to subscribers, adding machine receipt entitled "Total Miss Spent for Month of July," and envelope. 2 x 3 3/8 inches card. 8 1/2 x 4 1/4, opening to 8 1/2 x 7 1/2" cardholder. 11 x 8 1/2" letter. 3 x 2 1/4" adding tape. 5 x 10" envelope.

C223 ELVIS PRESLEY'S AMERICAN FEDERATION OF TELEVISION & RADIO ARTISTS MEMBERSHIP CARD

Elvis Presley's American Federation of Television & Radio Artists Membership card. Receipt for $5 membership. With original envelope. 2 1/4 x 3 1/2 inches card. 3 1/2 x 6 3/8 inches receipt. 3 3/4 x 6 3/4 inches envelope.

This gold colored card is printed with Elvis' name and the address is c/o Col. Tom Parker at All Star Shows. The card's expiration date is November 1, 1977. $800 - 1,000

C224 ATTENDANCE RECORDS FOR ELVIS PRESLEY'S 1974 TOUR

Three page record of the attendance records for Elvis' 1974 Tour. Tour covered 15 cities, 25 shows, and 18 days for the months of March, May and June. Pages are bound within a red folder. Every show on this tour was sold out.

$2,000 - 2,500

C219 INTERNATIONAL AIR TRAVEL CARD ISSUED TO ELVIS PRESLEY

Green plastic credit card with a white and gold globe partially cover by a black sketched plane. In white are the letters "Air Travel Card", and in black is the word "International." Card is issued to Elvis Presley and P. Presley. Original, green two page card holder included.

Date of expiration for card was October, 1977. $3,000 - 3,500

C220 TWO ELVIS PRESLEY BANK AMERICARD CREDIT CARDS

C220
C223
C221

Two blue, white and gold plastic Bank Americard credit cards with raised metallic gold lettering, contained in a two page information brochure. Brochure includes account information, company policies and a handwritten note stapled to the second page from Merle, Kathy and Pam of BAC Embossing center. Original mailing envelope included. 2 1/8 x 3 3/8 inches cards. 7 1/4 x 7 1/4 inches brochure. 4 1/4 x 8 1/8 inches envelope.

Handwritten note reads: "We Love You! The girls from the BAC Embossing Center."

$8,000 - 10,000

Homer Gilleland was Elvis' personal hairdresser in Memphis. He frequently flew to Las Vegas and California to do Elvis' hair. $2,500 - 3,000

C222 BULLOCK'S CREDIT CARD ISSUED TO ELVIS PRESLEY

Beige and brown Bullock's credit card issued to Mr. Elvis A. Presley. Original cream colored two page card holder included. On the front cover of the holder is the Bullock's coat of arms; instructions on inside page opposite a drawing of a light brown purse; back page lists: "The Bullock Ideal" creed. Bullock's is an upscale California clothing store.

$3,000 - 3,500

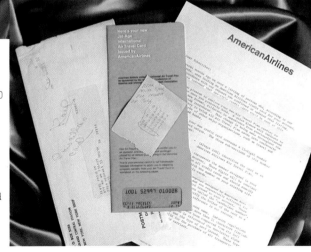

C225 GRACELAND PILLOWS, CARPET AND INVOICES

Two white ostrich feather pillows and framed piece of original quilt style kitchen carpet, all from Elvis' Graceland home. Yellow carbon copies of two invoices dated July 25, 1974 from Engel's Interiors in Memphis. Bills are for furniture and accessories for Graceland. Both invoices have carbon copy signature of Vernon Presley. Totals equal $9,119.77 and $5,692.10. Invoice and statement dated August 22, 1974 from Duck's Carpets to Elvis Presley. Invoice includes one royal vacuum cleaner and a Friendship quilt for the kitchen. Also includes deep blue, vista red, and island green carpet throughout many of the rooms in Graceland, including several walls, ceilings, and doors. Total amount of bill is $9730.83. White and green invoice from Duck's is included. Adding machine tape attached. Original light green check from the account of E.A. Presley made out to Duck's Carpets for $9,730.83. Signed by Vernon Presley. Invoice from Laukhuff Stained Glass Inc. in Memphis, dated October 23, 1974 and billed to Elvis Presley. Invoice for peacock panels. 8 1/2 x 11 inches Engle's invoices. 11 x 8 1/2 inches Duck's invoice. 9 1/2 x 5 1/2 inches Duck's statement. 18 1/2 x 21 inches kitchen carpet. 3 x 8 1/4 inches check. 8 1/2 x 8 1/4 inches Laukhuff invoice.

These are some of the items that were purchased when Elvis and Linda Thompson redecorated Graceland in 1974. Many of the items purchased at Engles remain in Graceland today including: white/mirrored pillows, buffalo horns, crystal ball, white lamp, fur pillows and crystal obelisk. Elvis had the floor, walls, and ceiling of the den in Graceland, also known as the Jungle Room, carpeted with Island Green carpet. Minnie Mae, Elvis' grandmother who lived in Graceland, had red shag carpet on her door. The peacock and rose stained glass designs listed in this invoice were for installation at Graceland, and remain in the house to this day. $4,500 - 5,000

C226 BOX CAR ENTERPRISES CORPORATE CHECKBOOK AND ALBUM

Green corporate checkbook for the account of Box Car Enterprises. Twenty checks have been torn

out, handwritten detailed check stubs remain. Attached to one stub is a a handwritten not indicating the numbers of checks that were mailed to Colonel Parker. Also attached are two voided checks, one to All Star Shows and one to Elvis Presley, both for $25,587.05. The bottom right corners, where the signatures would be, are ripped off. "Having Fun With Elvis on Stage" album. 9 1/2 x 13 1/2" check book. 3 1/4 x 5" note. 3 x 8 1/4" voided checks. 12 1/2 x 12 1/2"album.

Box Car Enterprises was Elvis Presley and Colonel Parker's management company. It was established in 1974 and oversaw the merchandising of non-performance Elvis products. The name was taken either from the gambling term for double sixes in the game of craps, or because it was said that Elvis would sound good even if he recorded in a box car. The checks to All Star Shows and to Elvis are royalty checks for the album, "Having Fun with Elvis on Stage," released by Boxcar Records. The album was an all talking album made up of comments made by Elvis during performances. Colonel Parker and Elvis received the same amount of royalty money. $4,500 - 5,000

C225

C227 COPIES OF COMMENTARIES MADE BY ELVIS PRESLEY

Fourteen copied pages of commentaries and monologues made by Elvis Presley during his performances at the Sahara Tahoe in May 1974 and from taped shows during his March 1974 Tour. "Elvis Recorded Live on Stage in Memphis" album included 11 x 8 1/2 inches.

Elvis' shows were sometimes taped to record the songs for possible release. These are the conversations Elvis had between takes. Some of the transcriptions can be heard on the album, "Elvis Recorded Live on Stage in Memphis." $650 - 750

C226

C228 ELVIS PRESLEY'S GLOBAL BAR

Unique gentleman's bar in the shape of a globe with ornate inlaid features. Four page yellow receipt and contract dated May 27, 1975. Receipt is for Elvis Presley's belongings at 144 Monovale in Beverly Hills, to be moved and stored at 1919 Third Avenue in Los Angeles. Receipt details all of Elvis' belongings that were being stored. Globe in wooden globe stand. 13 1/4 x 8 1/2 inches receipt. 39 x 28 inches globe.

This two-story house sat on two acres of lawns and orange groves in Holmy Hills, California. Elvis and Priscilla lived here beginning in late 1967. Some of the amenities of the home included a pool table, a projection room, and a soda fountain. Priscilla continued to live here for a couple of years after the divorce. On June 18, 1975, Elvis sold the house for $625,000 to Telly Savalas. This globe was in Elvis' Monovale home and is on page one of the moving receipt.

$4,500 - 5,000

C229 ELVIS PRESLEY'S SHIRT

Long sleeve, poly blend shirt. Brown, blue, black and white flower design, with butterfly collar and elastic at elbows and wrists. No tag.

This particular shirt is a casual piece Elvis' wardrobe of the 1970's, a style of which he often seen wearing during his off-stage moments.

$2,000 - 3,000

C230 ELVIS PRESLEY'S YELLOW CHAIR

Dark wood chair with yellow cloth upholstery, with gold etchings within the wood. Engravings of a woman on each arm. 38 x 20 x 21 inches.

This chair was a fixture in Elvis Presley's Chino Canyon Residence located in Palm Springs California.

$4,000 - 6,000

C231 "DON'T CRY DADDY" SINGLE SILVER RECORD

Mounted and framed award, connotating one million records sold. Plaque reads: "To Colonel Parker in Appreciation of his Contribution Toward Making Don't Cry Daddy a Million Dollar Seller 1970" From Colonel Parker's personal collection. 22 x 19 inches framed award.

$800 - 1,200

C232 ELVIS PRESLEY "DEAR ABBY" CORRESPONDENCE

Four one-page typed letters, all from the summer of 1976. 10 3/8 x 7 1/8 inches "Dear Abby" letter. 11 x 8 1/2 inches other letters.

One letter, dated June 11, 1976, sent to "Dear Abby" from Alicia Lester in Benton, West Virginia. Lester encloses a photo of Elvis given to her in West Germany as a child by Vernon Presley. She wants Abby to return this photo to the Presleys and asks for an autographed Elvis photo in return. One letter on "Dear Abby" stationery (with a photo of "Abby" inside of a valentine at top of page), dated June 21, 1976 and sent from Abigail Van Buren to Elvis Presley. Signed "Abby" in black marker. Letter relates the Alicia Lester message to Elvis. Copy of letter on "Vernon Presley" letterhead, dated July 15, 1976 and sent from Vernon Presley to Abigail Van Buren. Vernon thanks "Abby" and writes that he's responded to Alicia. Copy letter, dated July 15, 1976 and sent to Alicia Lester from Vernon Presley. Vernon thanks Alicia for returning the photo and encloses a personally autographed Elvis photo.

$550 - 650

C233 RADIO SPOTS FOR THE 1974 SUMMER FESTIVAL

Check to Bill Cosby Typed memo on Las Vegas Hilton letterhead from Colonel Parker's Office. Dated August 16, 1974 and lists the radio spots for the 1974 Summer Festival, August 18 through September 2, 1974. Original light green check typed out to Bill Cosby for $10,000. Signed by Elvis Presley. Endorsed on back by Bill Cosby. 11 x 8 1/2 inches memo. 3 x 8 1/4 inches check.

During the first week of Elvis Summer Festival, Elvis set a new Las Vegas one-week record by playing for an unprecedented 28,000 fans. Elvis was ill on August 26 and was unable to perform, so Bill Cosby filled in for him.

$4,500 - 5,000

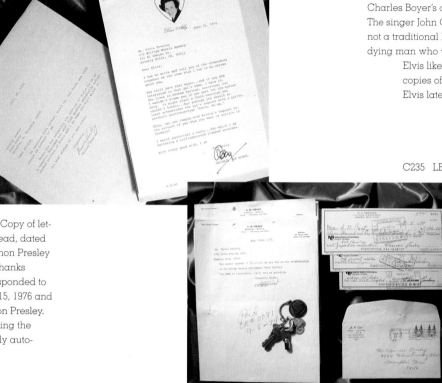

C232

C234 LETTER AND INVOICES FROM BOB MCCOLLUM PRODUCTIONS TO ELVIS PRESLEY

C236

Original, typewritten letter from Bob McCollum to Elvis, dated June 17, 1974. Correspondence is in regards to a bill for records of Charles Boyer requested by Elvis. Letter reads, " Make your check out to me and mark your stub 'SERVICES RENDERED', as we don't want any relationship connected to Elvis concerning these records. (It is illegal, so if anything ever comes up, I'll take the

rap)." Attached are two invoices from Superior Records for album cost and freight. Elvis purchased $489 worth of the album. A copy of the original freight bill is also included. Two Charles Boyer albums in original shrink wrap. Album covers are blank. 11 x 8 1/2 inches Letter. 8 3/4 x 6 1/4 inches Invoices & Freight bill. 12 1/2 x 12 1/2 inches album.

Elvis first heard the song, "Softly as I Leave You" on Charles Boyer's album, "Where Does Love Go." The singer John Gary told Elvis that the song was not a traditional love song, but a song about a dying man who was telling his wife good-bye.

Elvis liked the song so much that he bought copies of the album for many of his friends. Elvis later recorded the song himself.

$300 - 350

C235 LETTER AND ITEMIZED LIST FOR RENOVATIONS ON CHINO CANYON ROAD HOUSE

Letter dated November 12, 1974, from Builder/Designer A.B. Crist in Palm Springs, California. Letter is a bill for extras on Elvis' house at 845 Chino Canyon Road. Total due to date: $12,239.18. Attached list shows services to be completed--such as paneling in the recreation room and red tile in two bathrooms--with costs. Photograph included. 11 x 8 1/2 inches letter. 14 x 8 1/4 inches listing.

Elvis and Priscilla bought this fifteen-room, single-story house in Palm Springs in 1965 with a down payment of $13,187.83 and a $85,000 mortgage. It is located at 845 Chino Canyon Road on two acres of land. On September 22 and 23, 1973, Elvis recorded "I Miss You" and "Are You Sincere" in the living room of this house. In 1979, the house was bought by singer Franki Valli.

$1,000 - 1,500

C236 BILLS FROM A.B. CRIST DESIGNS TO VERNON PRESLEY REGARDING HOMES IN PALM SPRINGS

Four typewritten bills to Vernon Presley from A. B. Crist regarding the building of Elvis Presley's home in Palm Springs, and the redecoration of Col. Parkers home. First bill is dated August 22, 1974, requesting a $7,126.00 payment. Envelope is also included. Second bill is dated September 16, 1974 requesting another $7,126.00 for construction of house. Updates on the progress of the house is noted in each bill. Third bill is dated September 20, 1974, regarding Colonel Parker's Palm Springs home. As per a previous agreement, Elvis is to pay $10,000 toward the renovation of Mr. Parker's home. Fourth bill is dated October 10, 1974, requesting a payment of $7,126.00. Letter mentions that "Work is nearing completion and should be finished in the next two or three weeks". Original envelope addressed to Vernon Presley. Includes a Polaroid picture of house under construction. Three original light green checks from the account of E.A. Presley made out to A.B. Crist and signed by Vernon Presley. One set of original keys to this Palm Springs home. 11 x 8 1/2 inches Bills. 3 x 6 1/2 inches Envelope. 4 1/4 x 3 1/2 inches Picture.

Elvis and Priscilla purchased this Palm Springs house at 845 Chino Canyon Road in 1965. They immediately had a swimming pool installed and in 1974 did major renovations. The house was sold in 1979 to singer, Franki Valli.

$4,500 - 5,000

C237 CERTIFICATE FOR COLONEL PARKER FROM THE INTERNATIONAL KENPO KARATE ASSOCIATION

Certificate of 10th Degree Feather Belt awarded to Col. Parker from the International Kenpo Karate Association on September 3, 1974. Certificate is dark beige in color with black lettering, and is signed by Elvis Presley and Colonel Parker. Photo incl..

Elvis had just recently received his 8th degree black

C237
C239

belt. Because of his fervor for the sport, Elvis liked to give his friends gifts related to karate. This certificate was a joke as Colonel Parker did not do karate. $2,000 - 2,500

C238. ELVIS PRESLEY INTERNATIONAL KARATE CHAMPIONSHIPS INVITATION

White cardboard invitation to the 1974 International Karate Championships in Long Beach, California on August 11, 1974. Sent to Elvis Presley by Ed Parker. With envelope postmarked July 25, 1974. Photograph included. 4 1/4 x 5 1/2 inches invitation. 4 3/8 x 5 5/8 inches.
Ed Parker served as Elvis' bodyguard and personal karate instructor starting in 1972.

$650 - 750

C239 "ELVIS IN CONCERT" PROTOTYPE WITH ACETATE

Prototype album jacket cover for "Elvis in Concert"; photographs of Elvis on front, back, and on insides of both covers. Front cover states name of album; back cover has phony type to show placement of descriptions. Acetate--in cardboard sleeve with writing "Final Concert Album #2; recorded on both sides; labeled with stereo and date 9/2/77. 12 1/2 x 12 1/4 inches album. 12-inch diameter acetate.

Release of "Elvis in Concert" took place in October 1977. The songs on the album were recorded in live concerts in Omaha, Nebraska, and Rapid City, South Dakota, the previous June. The recordings were originally for an upcoming CBS special, but when Elvis passed away in August, RCA quickly released the set of two records. $3,000 - 3,500

C240 INTERNATIONAL BROTHERHOOD OF POLICE OFFICERS LETTER

One page typed letter on International Brotherhood of Police Officers letterhead, dated August 8, 1975 and signed in black ink by organization president Kenneth T. Lyons. Sent to Elvis Presley in Memphis awarding him honorary membership in the organization. With original mailing envelope addressed "Elvis Presley Memphis, Tennessee." Photograph included. 11 x 8 1/2 inches.

This document is an example of Elvis' intense interest in police work and paraphernalia, as well as the high regard the law enforcement community had for him. $300 - 350

C241 ELVIS PRESLEY'S COPY OF "THEY'VE KILLED THE PRESIDENT"

Elvis' personal copy of "They've Killed the President!", a 414-page paperback book written by Robert Sam Anson. A number of passages and words in the book have been underlined by Elvis. A small article from the Commercial Appeal newspaper inside book relates a case of charges being dropped against a local Memphis service station owner. 7 x 4 1/4 inches.

Elvis was fascinated by Kennedy's assassination and the mystery that surrounded it, as evidenced by the large number of passages that are marked throughout this book. Beyond just Kennedy, Elvis was interested in the study of history. He was known to memorize speeches made by Martin Luther King.

$8,000 - 10,000

C242 NEWS RELEASE FROM THE LAS VEGAS HILTON

March, 1975 news release from the Las Vegas Hilton. Included in release are dates of Elvis' upcoming appearance at the Las Vegas Hilton beginning March 18th and closing April 1st. Also announces Elvis' new RCA album "Promised Land" which was "Coming Soon!" Gold Box Concert Album included. 14 x 8 1/2 inches.

This performance marked Elvis' 12th engagement at the plush resort. His opening coincides with opening of the 30 story, 620 room addition of the Hilton which made it the largest resort and convention hotel in the world. During his stay there, Elvis stayed in a five bedroom, 6,000 square foot suite with a sauna.

$400 - 500

C243 LETTER TO ELVIS PRESLEY FROM COLONEL TOM PARKER

Letter dated June 15, 1976 to Elvis Presley from The Colonel. Letter on Thomas Parker wagon letterhead. Letter concerns an upcoming tour and the fact that Elvis' staff has not been in contact with The Colonel. Typed note to Mr. Presley from Jim asking

C243

him to see that Elvis got the enclosed letter. Envelope addressed to Vernon Presley at 3764 Elvis Presley Blvd. with blue handwritten note in blue ink that states, "Give to Elvis." 11 x 8 1/2 inches letters. 4 1/8 x 9 1/2 inches envelope.

In the last several years of his life, Elvis became more and more reclusive, making it increasingly difficult to maintain contact with him. Colonel Parker usually contacted Elvis through Joe Esposito or Marty Lacker, but sometimes had difficulty getting him on the phone. Frustrated, the Colonel made an attempt to contact Elvis directly via Vernon.

$550 - 650

C244 WESTERN UNION TELEFAX'S TO ELVIS PRESLEY

Telefax dated March, 1975 from Bobby Gentry to Elvis Presley regarding Elvis' opening at the Hilton Hotel in Las Vegas. Telefax dated March 19, 1975 from Mac Davis to Elvis, "Congratulations you've given birth to a headliner. I'll see you when I get there. God bless." Telefax from Paul and Linda McCartney to Elvis inviting him to be a guest for a private party on board the Queen Mary on March 24, 1975. Telefax dated March 18, 1975 from George and Barbara Klein to Elvis, "We know you'll have another great opening. Good luck." Telefax's are on a light olive page with Western Union Telefax done in grey lettering. 4 1/2 x 6 1/2 inches Telefax (4). Elvis received these well-wishes regarding his Las Vegas engagement opening June 18, 1975.

$450 - 500

C245 LETTER FROM J.D. SUMNER REGARDING STAMPS BUS PURCHASE

One page typed letter from J.D. Sumner to Vernon Presley, on "The Stamps" cream-colored stationery. Dated September 4, 1975 and signed in black ink by Sumner. Letter is to return the balance of a $21,000.00 check Elvis' wrote to pay for The Stamps' tour bus. With copy of refund check in amount of $552.91 written to Elvis Presley from J.D. Sumner. With gas station and bus charter receipts. Photograph included. 11 x 8 1/2 inches letter. 5 3/8 x 8 1/2 inches check copy.

The Stamps were Elvis' vocal backup group for live performances from 1972 to 1977.

$350 - 400

C246 COMPILATION OF ELVIS PRESLEY'S RECORDINGS

Compilation of Elvis Presley's recordings from the 1950's, 1960's, and 1970's. Book is divided into the categories of; Sessions, Motion Pictures, Song List and How Used, Singles, Extended Play Albums, Long Play Albums, and Compact 33 double. Pages are kept in clear plastic page covers. Book is a black, hard back, three ring binder. 11 x 8 1/2 inches Pages. 11 3/4 x 11 inches Folder.

This mammoth book found in Colonel Parker's office is a testament to the mammoth musical career of Elvis Presley. Without a doubt, Elvis changed the face of music forever, earning his title, "The King of Rock and Roll."

$4,500 - 5,000

C247 RECORD ALBUM CONTAINING ELVIS PRESLEY'S 45 RPM RECORDS

One red, hard cover binder containing fifteen Elvis Presley 45 RPM extended play albums. Cover is red with a four sided embossed design that forms a square on the front. In the middle are the words "Record Album" in gold lettering. Inside are pages of beige record jackets containing the albums. 8 x 9 inches Binder

Records contained in album are:
EPA-830 titled "Elvis Presley": "Shake Rattle & Roll," "I Love You Because," "Blue Moon," "Laudy Miss Clawdy," "Anyway You Want Me," "I'm Left, You're Right," "She's Gone,""I Don't Care If The Sun Don't Shine," "Mystery Train."
EPA-993 titled "Any Way You Want Me": "So Glad You're Mine," "Old Shep," "Reddy Teddy," "Anyplace is Paradise."
EPA -994 titled "Strickly Elvis" : "Long Tall Sally," "First In LIne," "How Do You Think I Feel," "How's

The World Treating You."
EPA-4006 titled "Love Me Tender" : "Love Me Tender," "Let Me," "Poor Boy," "We're Gonner Move."
EPA-4041 titled "Just For You": "I Need You So," "Have I Told You Lately That I Love You," "Blueberry Hill," "Is It So Strange."

EPA-4108 titled "Elvis Sings Christmas Songs": "Santa Bring My Baby Back (To Me)," "Blue Christmas," "Santa Clause Is Back In Town," "I'll Be Home For Christmas."
EPA-4114 "Jailhouse Rock": "Jailhouse Rock," "Young and Beautiful," "I Want To be Free," "Don't Leave Me Know," "(You're So Square) Baby I Don't Care."

EPA-940 titled "The Real Elvis": "Don't Be Cruel," "I Want You, I Need You, I Love You," "Hound Dog," "My Baby Left Me."
EPA-4319 titled "King Creole" : "King Creole," "New Orleans," "As Long As I Have You," "Lover Doll."
EPA-1-1515 titled "Loving You": "Teddy Bear," "Party," "True Love."
EPA-4321 titled "Vol. II King Creole": "Trouble," "Young Dreams," "Crawfish," "Dixieland Rock."
EPA-4382 titled "VIva Las Vegas": "If You think I Don't Need You," "I Need Somebody To Lean On," "C'mon Everybody,"Today, Tomorrow, and Forever."
EPA-4368 titled "Follow That Dream": "Follow That Dream," "Angel," "What A Wonderful Life," "I'm Not the Marrying Kind."
EPA-5141 titled "A Touch Of Gold Vol. 3": "Too Much," "All Shook Up," "Don't Ask Me Why," "Blue Moon of Kentucky."

$1,500 - 2,000

C248 "LAST FAREWELL" CONCERT ARRANGEMENTS

Concert arrangements for "Last Farewell," with charts for each instrument. Charts list piano player Glen Hardin as arranger and include a lyric sheet. There are handwritten notes in pencil on most sheets. Encased in black folder with with raised red tape reading "Last Farewell." 14 x 12 inches folder.

This packet of arrangements was used by Elvis and his band during concerts in the Seventies. There are arrangement sheets for every musician who would play on the song. A Roger Whittaker song originally, Elvis recorded "The Last Farewell" for his 1976 album "From ELvis Presley Boulevard, Memphis, Tennessee."

$3,000 - 4,000

C249 DOCUMENTS RELATED TO ELVIS PRESLEY'S TRAFFIC CITATION

Original pink carbon copy of Elvis Presley's notice of warrant, dated July 1, 1975. The warrant for his arrest was issued duo to his failure to appear in court on a traffic citation on December 18, 1974. Attached is a photocopy of the notice of warrant issuance. Typewritten note to Mr. Presley dated July 30, 1975, from Mary K. Sholty of Hookstratten & Irwin stating that they were able to reduce the bail from $20 to $5, so he didn't have to worry about it anymore. Photocopy of check #1553, and check stub dated July 21, 1975 from the account of E. Gregory Hookstratten for $5 payment of bail. 7 x 8 5/8 inches notice of warrant issuance. 8 x 8 1/2 inches photocopy of notice. 7 x 3 note 7 x 8 1/2 copy of check and stub.

Elvis originally received a citation when his Mercedes was illegally parked near 500 World Way in Los Angeles.

$1,400 - 1,600

C250 RECORDING SESSION AGENDA FOR "MOODY BLUE" ALBUM

Two-page recording session lineup for an Elvis Presley recording session held at Graceland on February 2-7, 1976. Album and photograph included. 11 x 8 1/2 inches.

In later years, Elvis became increasingly adverse to going into the recording studio, despite the recording obligations in his RCA contract. An alternative was to bring the studio to him. In February of 1976, RCA did this by setting up a recording session at Graceland. The red RCA recording van backed up to the jungle room. The ceiling was already carpeted which helped the acoustics, but to further help them, the walls were covered with moving blankets. The speakers that were brought to be used proved to be too small, so Elvis' personal system from his bedroom was used. During the ses-

sion, the light bulbs were changed the match the mood of the song. Elvis loved the setup so much that he wanted to keep it setup after the session. The songs recorded appeared on the albums "From Elvis Presley Boulevard, Memphis Tennessee" and "Moody Blue."

$800 - 1,000

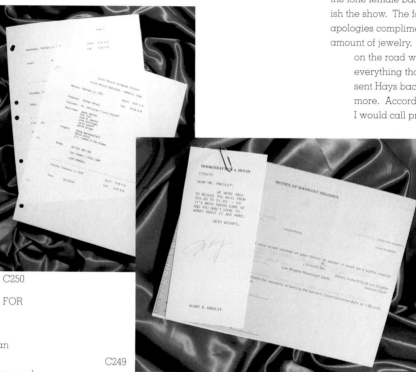

C250

C249

C251 VARIOUS PURCHASES FROM ELVIS PRESLEY'S 1975 TOUR

Lowell Hays Jewelers in Memphis--6 receipts, totaling $85,680, for jewelry purchases on July 25, 1975, and a statement with a balance of $88,481.25 (bought for a crew that he insulted). Bill from Rodeway Inn in Asheville, North Carolina, sent to Elvis from Charlene Nobbett, general manager. Bill, dated 7-24-75, was for one RCA television that Elvis had shot. Bill totals $367.68 for TV he shot out). Original check from the account of E.A. Presley made out to Rodeway Inn for $367.68. Signed by Elvis Presley. 6 1/2 x 4 1/4 inches receipts. 6 5/8 x 5

5/8 inches statement. 9 x 6 inches Rodeway bill.

Joking with his band and back-up singers was common for Elvis on stage. Sometimes, however, it went to far. July 20, 1975 was one of those times. During a performance in Asheville, North Carolina, Kathy Westmoreland and two of the Sweet Inspirations back-up singers walked off stage after an over-the-top insult from Elvis. Myrna Smith was the lone female back-up singer left on stage to finish the show. The following day, Elvis offered apologies complimented by an extravagant amount of jewelry. Lowell Hays, the jeweler, was on the road with Elvis at the time. He bought everything that Hays had with him and then sent Hays back to his store in Memphis for more. According to Hays, "Elvis bought what I would call practically a whole jewelry store! He gave something to everybody in the group. He gave each of the Sweet Inspirations a five-thousand-dollar ring." The Sweet Inspirations returned to the show, however, Kathy Westmoreland did not.

$4,500 - 5,000

C252. SOUTH CAROLINA FANS PETITION TO GET ELVIS TO PERFORM

Petition dated June 23, 1976, contains 121 pages of signatures from Elvis fans in South Carolina asking Elvis to play in the state for the first time. The heading of each page reads "We, the undersigned, pledge our support in bringing Elvis Presley to Columbia, South Carolina." 11 x 8 1/2 inches.

Elvis did play Columbia, South Carolina on February 18, 1977, a show that may have been the result of this petition.

$1,400 - 1,600

C253 ELVIS PRESLEY TOUR BOOK—1977

Yellow card stock, bound book of Elvis Presley's second tour of 1977. Front page is a typed list of each show, location, show times and Elvis' hotel reservations. Book is divided by cities, listing such details as building, box office contact, concessions, security, hotel, transportation, airport and general categories. Some pages include handwritten notes. With promotional poster from the tour. Poster is drawing with large center image of Elvis surrounded by seven smaller images. 11 1/2 x 9 inches tour book.   26 x 20 inches poster.

This item, found in Colonel Parker's collection, documents Elvis' second tour of 1977—one of his last. In erratic heath at this time, Elvis was forced to cancel the last three shows of this tour, in Mobile, Macon and Jacksonville. $1,400 - 1,600

C254 DOCUMENTS REGARDING ELVIS PRESLEY'S 1977 TOURS

Five-page itinerary for Elvis Presley tours from March through August 1977. Itinerary on "Elvis Presley" stationery. Page one is cut shorter than the following pages. One-page itinerary for "Tour Number 5" which includes dates and cities. Tour ends at the Market Square Arena in Indianapolis on June 26.   Copy of a one-page information sheet regarding the details of Elvis Presley's performance in Indianapolis, Indiana on June 26, 1977. Two-page list of musicians, singers, and other personnel on the Elvis Presley Show. Photograph included. 8 5/8 x 8 1/2 inches page 1 of itinerary. 11 x 8 1/2 inches other pages.

These itineraries detail Elvis' last tours. His last performance on June 26, 1977 in Indianapolis, Indiana, is remembered by many to be one of his strongest performances in months. Backstage, Elvis was presented with a special plaque commemorating his 2 billionth record pressed by RCA. According to "The Indianapolis Star," Elvis deliv-

ered "a performance in true Presley style.... The packed Arena was indication enough that Elvis is still as popular as ever. Well, well, well, well!"
$2,000 - 2,500

C254
C253

C255 TOUR CANCELLATION EXPENSES AND ELVIS CONCERT PHOTO ALBUM

Invoice from Management Three in Bellevue, Washington, dated October 6, 1977, sent to Elvis Presley Tour Account, regarding cancellation of

Elvis Presley 1977 Tour #6. Total cancellation amount $166,196.42; Management Three/RCA Record Tours participation expenses, $122,196.42; and Elvis Presley Tour Account participation per contract amounts to $44,000. Gold box with black printing reading "Elvis Concert Photo Album" under a rendering of Elvis. Enclosed in the box is a 64-page album of pictures of Elvis in concert. Four pages in the middle picture Elvis albums. Includes a "Certificate of Authenticity - Elvis Presley Concert Memorabilia." 11 x 8 1/2 inches letter. 11 1/2 x 8 3/4 box. 11 x 8 1/2 album. 5 1/2 x 8 1/2 certificate.

Money had already been spent to set up this upcoming tour when Elvis died on August 16, 1977.

$1,500 - 2,000

C256 MANUAL OF OPERATIONS FOR "THE ELVIS PRESLEY STORY: A FINAL TRIBUTE"

Manual of Operations for the radio program, "The Elvis Presley Story: A Final Tribute." Detailed information concerning the program bound in blue folder. 14 pages of information on white paper, 13 pages of cue sheets on light green paper, 17 pages of music lists on beige paper, and 2 pages of timing sheets on pink paper. Vernon Presley's tape of "The Elvis Presley Story: A Final Tribute." 11 3/4 x 9 inches manual.

"The Elvis Presley Story: A Final Tribute" was 13-hour radio show which included a narrative of Elvis' life and career interspersed with music. $400 - 500

C257 ELVIS PRESLEY RADIO PROMOTIONAL SCRIPTS FOR 1973 TOUR

Four radio ad copy sheets from Clayton-Ross, Public Relations/Marketing firm in Tampa, Florida. Copy announces Elvis performances at the the Arizona Coliseum on April 22, the Fresno Convention Center on April 25, the San Diego Sports Arena on April 26, and the Memorial Coliseum in Portland on April 27. Sixteen-page Elvis pocket edition photo folio. Features photos of Elvis in concert. 11 x 8 1/2 inches copy sheets. 5 3/4 x 5 3/4 inches photo folio.

During this tour, Emory Gordy replaced Jerry Scheff on bass. Elvis did two shows in Fresno with ticket sales that not only broke the previous record, but doubled it.

$450 - 500

C258 ELVIS' DINER'S CLUB CREDIT CARD LETTER, WITH ENVELOPE POSTMARKED JULY 22, 1977

Envelope return address has no name, just a P.O. Box number in Denver. Elvis Presley's Diner's Club card included. 11 x 8 1/2 inches letter. 4 x 9 1/2 inches envelope.

Elvis' fans went to great lengths to obtain souvenirs. The letter from this fan read, "I worked for Diners Club . . . and noticed your check . . . for 24.00 dollar renewal fee for Elvis'<sic> cards. I have kept the check as a souvenir and written my own check to pay the bill, therefore your check . . . will never clear. I hope this won't be too much of an inconvenience to you." The letter closes with a thank you, but has no name.

$4,000 - 4,500

C259 TICKETS AND CBS SCRIPT FOR "ELVIS IN CONCERT"

Five original tickets from "Elvis in Concert." 55-page typed script developed by CBS for its October 1977 "Elvis in Concert," includes songs, interviews, commercials, staff list, and closing credits--with several crossed out items. 1 5/8 x 4 3/8 inches tickets. 11 x 8 1/2 inches script.

The movie, "Elvis in Concert" was filmed during Elvis performances in South Dakota and

C259

C258

Nebraska in June 1977, some of his final performances. The movie did not air until two months after his death.

$750 - 850

C260 BUSINESS CARDS FOR ELVIS PRESLEY'S "SPECIAL DEPUTIES"

Four red business cards. Top left corner has gold embossed "TCB" symbol. Top right corner has gold embossed Star of David superimposed over the Christian cross. Bottom right corner embossed with

black "Elvis Presley." Two cards for James Caughley, one for Mike Keeton, and one for Billy Smith. All were given the title "Special Deputy." 2 x 3 1/2 inches.

Each card is personalized describing what each person did for Elvis: James Caughley - Wardrobe and Details (x2)Mike Keeton - Personal Aide & Wardrobe Billy Smith - Personal Security for Vernon Presley and Graceland $1,500 - 2,000

C261 WESTERN UNION TELEGRAMS TO ELVIS FROM VARIOUS PEOPLE

Western Union telegram dated March 6, 1973, to Elvis from "unsigned." Three Western Union telegrams dated from January 4 through January 8, 1974, to Elvis wishing him a happy birthday. One telegram dated January 4, 1974 from "Jesus" in Baltimore, MD. Telegrams are yellow in color with a brown banner on top of page. 5 1/2 x 8 1/2 inches.

Telegram from "unsigned" is from Centralia, Illinois. Happy birthday telegrams are from Larry Geller; Sweet Inspirations; Joe, Joan, Debbie and Cindy of Los Angeles; and The Beach Boys Brian Wilson, Carl Wilson, Dennis Wilson, Mike Love, and Al Jardine. Telegram dated January 4, 1974 is from Baltimore, MD.

$700 - 900

C262 COLONEL PARKER'S WOODEN COVERED WAGON

Model wooden wagon built like a covered wagon, with hitch and red and white checkered cloth covering. 13 x 17 inches.

Colonel Parker collected model wagons, a nostalgic reminder of the Colonel's past carnival days, and people often gave them to him as gifts

$1,500 - 2,000

C263 PRISCILLA PRESLEY'S RECEIPTS FOR FURNITURE FOR LISA MARIE

Handwritten note to Vernon Presley detailing items purchased for Lisa Marie's room. Signed, "Thank you, Priscilla & Lisa." Attached are the receipts for the purchased items. Receipt dated March 15, 1973 to Priscilla Presley from Grace in Los Angeles. Includes items for Lisa Marie's room totaling $168. Signed by Priscilla Presley. Three receipts from The Antique Guild in Los Angeles. Two are dated March 11 and one is dated March 15, 1973. They total $131.25, $392, and $17. Photograph included 8 x 5 inches note. 7 x 8 1/2 inches Grace receipts. 1 1/2 x 3 1/4 inches and 1 1/2 x 3 1/2 inches and 1 1/2 x 3 7/8 inches Antique Guild receipts.

After Elvis and Priscilla separated, she and Lisa Marie lived in an apartment in Marina del Rey. These are furniture receipts for Lisa Marie's room in this new apartment.

$800 - 1,000

C264 SMITH'S FOOD KING CREDIT CARD ISSUED TO PRISCILLA PRESLEY

Original red, cream, and brown credit card from Smith's Food King. Logo is a drawing of fruits, meats, cheeses, and flowers. Raised gold lettering misspells Priscilla's name as "Priscella". Original goldish/brown paper card holder and envelope addressed to Priscilla Presley dated April 24, 1975. 2 1/8 x 3 3/8 inches Card. 3 1/2 x 8 1/2 inches Insert. 4 1/4 x 9 12 inches Envelope.

Expiration date on card is December, 1976.

$200 - 250

MGM GRAND.
THE CITY OF ENTERTAINMENT.

MGM Grand Hotel/Casino, "The City of Entertainment," in Las Vegas...

is the premiere entertainment destination resort of the world showcasing headline entertainment, signature restaurants owned by world-renowned chefs, major special events and championship boxing. Named a Mobil Guide Book Four-Star Resort three years in a row, MGM Grand is centrally located on the famous Las Vegas Strip.

Diverse accommodations feature four 30-story emerald-green towers with 5,005 guest rooms including 751 suites ranging from 446-square-foot deluxe rooms and mid-range luxurious one-bedroom suites, to the very elaborate and stunning grand class 29th floor two-story, 6,000-square-foot suites reserved for VIP guests and celebrities. The Mansion at the MGM Grand, modeled after a 200-year-old Italian villa, features 29 villas with a Tuscan-Mediterranean influence.

MGM Grand has dedicated more than 171,000 square-feet of the property to gaming facilities. Equal to the size of four football fields, the casino floor offers a full spectrum of table games, slots, race and sports book, baccarat, a poker room, keno lounge and the newest in gaming technology.

Showcasing the world's top performers and special events, MGM Grand has established itself as "The City of Entertainment" featuring the $45 million award-winning stage show, "EFX" starring nine-time Tony Award winner Tommy Tune and nightly headliners in the intimate 650-seat Hollywood Theatre with some of the biggest stars on the Strip including Wayne Newton, Tom Jones and Rodney Dangerfield.

The 17,157-seat MGM Grand Garden Arena is home to major special events including the Barbra Streisand Millennium Concert, the annual Andre Agassi Grand Slam for Children Benefit, the Fox-Billboard Music Awards, ESPY's ESPY Awards and championship boxing. The Grand Garden Arena has also hosted spectacular concerts including The Rolling Stones, Bette Midler, Neil Diamond, Shania Twain, The Artist, 'N Sync, Phil Collins, Elton John, the Bee Gees and more. The reinvention of the legendary nightclub, Studio 54, continues to be an integral part of the entertainment scene at the MGM Grand. The three-story club features state-of-the-art sound, and well as DJ's spinning the hottest selection of chart-topping dance music nightly. Studio 54 is also home to a gallery of black and white celebrity photographs taken at the original Studio 54 in New York City from the 1970's. The nightclub is regularly visited by popular celebrities from around the world.

MGM Grand's 6.6-acre Grand Pool and Spa area sets the precedence of high quality in a stunning complex. The lushly landscaped Grand Pool features five separate pools, 27,000 square feet of swimming space, including a gently flowing lazy river. The 1,000-foot-long river pool is the city's longest ride of its kind.

The Grand Spa is the ultimate experience for the body, mind and soul. The Spa features more than 30 treatment rooms, saunas, steam rooms, whirlpools and relaxation lounges. Services include a variety of facials, aromatherapy treatments and stress relief services. The traditional massage, Shiatsu massage, foot massage and scalp treatments are part of the spa's full slate of services. The Grand Spa, with an enduring reputation for excellence, was named one of the nation's top 15 hotel spas by Fitness Magazine.

An array of culinary choices are offered at the MGM Grand with an impressive celebrity chef line-up. The Studio Walk is home to celebrity chef/author Emeril Lagasse's New Orleans Fish House, Mark Miller's Coyote Cafe and upscale Grill Room featuring modern southwestern hot and spicy cuisine, Italian delights with Tre Visi, exclusive fine dining with La Scala modeled after the famous Opera House in Milan, Italy, and The Hollywood Brown Derby, authentically known since 1926, featuring caricatures of celebrities and specializing in steaks and the

Derby's famous Cobb salad. Neyla, a Mediterranean Grill, is scheduled to open in the fall of '99.

The gourmet restaurant, Gatsby's, features executive chef Terence Fong, where intimate dining fuses a blend of classical cuisine with a Pacific Rim flair. Additional restaurants include Dragon Court highlighting Cantonese and Mandarin specialties, the Wolfgang Puck Cafe, The Rainforest Café, Ricardo's Mexican

Restaurant, MGM Grand Buffet, Stage Deli Express, the 24-hour coffee shop Studio Café, and pool-side dining at the Cabana Grille.

MGM Grand's 5,000-square-foot "Forever Grand Wedding Chapel" makes every bride feel like a star! Fully trained wedding coordinators assist with providing minister services, photography, videography, live piano accompaniment, floral arrangements, themed wedding packages and reception plans.

The Grand Adventures Theme Park, a seasonal outdoor entertainment complex, is home to eight rides, shows, entertainment, casual dining and shops, as well as SkyScreamer, the world's largest Skycoaster.

As a part of the company's $575 million enhancement plan, the new $9 million Lion Habitat showcases live African lions, including Goldie, Metro and Baby Lion, direct descendants of MGM Studios' famous signature marquee lion, Metro. Upon entrance, guests truly experience the surround sound of live lions. A retail outlet is located adjacent to the Lion Habitat.

MGM Grand's 380,000-square-foot state-of-the art Conference Center showcases its tri-level facility with indoor and outdoor meeting space. The contempo-rary-themed Conference Center includes two giant ballrooms and nearly 50,000-square-feet of pre-function space with views of the elegant Grand Pool & Spa complex. The Center features up to 60 meeting rooms for 20 to 6,000 people, as well as two separate loading docks for easy and accessible move-in. The total meeting space at the resort, including existing ballroom space in the hotel and in the Conference Center is approximately 315,000 net square feet.

MGM Grand, "The City of Entertainment," is dedicated to providing the premier entertainment experience. For reservations and information on room packages and entertainment offerings, call MGM Grand Reservations at 1-800-929-1111 or 702-891-7777.

Auctions on the Internet

The Internet has long been used as a global communications tool across a huge range of subjects and products, but in recent years the development of electronic commerce – or e-commerce – has taken the medium into a new and exciting realm, changing the way many people live their lives.

One of the most innovative and enjoyable ways to buy through the Internet is to bid online at auctions.

Online auctions follow the age-old concepts of traditional auctions. Bidders compete against one another to win a lot; there is an estimate, a reserve price and a winning bid; and the lots are delivered as usual at the end of the sale.

So what's the difference? A computer replaces the oak-paneled room; e-mail takes the place of the auctioneer; a mouse click represents a hand signal; and, most importantly, you can bid at your own convenience from anywhere in the world.

There is a wealth of websites now devoted to online auctions offering consumers everything and anything from art, antiques and collectibles to electrical goods, holidays and books. While some unregulated sites allow people to auction their second hand goods directly to other individuals, the other end of the spectrum has seen the rise of a select few premium services which enable established businesses to deal to consumers over the Web.

icollector is pleased to present online the Guernsey's event of 'Elvis Presley: the official auction featuring items from the archives of Graceland' and accept presale bids prior to the auction.

icollector.com

The first to bring the auction industry online in 1994, icollector is now an independent home to over 200 of the world's finest auction houses, dealers and galleries, giving users easy and immediate access to over $1 billion worth of items for sale.

icollector is widely recognized as one of the highest quality services in its field. As a premium company, it can offer potential buyers a high level of trust – all objects offered for sale come from fully professional sellers.

icollector offers a wide range of innovative and exciting products giving amateurs and professionals alike the chance to buy, research, and – above all – enjoy the world of art, antiques and collectibles.

There are two ways you can bid at auction on icollector. Launched in November '98, **Online Auctions** enables users to bid exclusively online for a huge variety of lots across a broad category selection, from rock and pop memorabilia to modern art, Formula 1 to furniture, and silver to ceramics. All of these lots are provided and authenticated by our well-established clients, giving users the trust and confidence to bid safely over the Internet.

We have sold everything from Lord of the Manor titles to signed photographs of Formula 1 racers to Cartier watches and Art Deco figures.

The alternative choice is **Auction Catalogs**, one of the most popular and successful areas of icollector. It enables visitors to search the catalogs of forthcoming auction house sales and submit presale bids to the auction houses. You can browse and shop at your leisure the world's salerooms.

icollector and Elvis Presley:
the official auction featuring
items from the archives of
Graceland

icollector has been chosen to present online the complete Guernsey's catalog of 'Elvis Presley: the official auction featuring items from the archives of Graceland', and to accept presale bids online in the run-up to this historic event.

icollector is pleased to present online Guernsey's catalog of 'Elvis Presley: the official auction featuring items from the archives of Graceland' and accept presale bids in the run-up to the live auction at the MGM Las Vegas.

Surely the most eagerly anticipated auction of the Millennium, the sale's presence online will enable Elvis fans and collectors from all over the world to participate in bidding and to own a part of the life of the King of Rock 'n Roll.

Visitors to icollector can already preview over 1000 lots for sale, and in September will be able to submit presale bids through the site.

icollector also offers a host of information about Elvis Presley and Graceland and gives visitors the chance to participate in a series of exciting competitions.

www.icollector.com

This is the method of sale icollector has selected for the Graceland auction. Visitors can submit presale bids up to five weeks before the sale.

Our clients have seen some of their most successful sales through Auction Catalogs, which attracts a growing bidding market from every corner of the globe.

This year alone British auction house Bearne's have sold a painting for $169,000 and a blue diamond for $49,500 – both to US bidders – while David Lay, also based in the UK, sold three pieces of Troika pottery for $1,650. All thanks to icollector.

But icollector is not just an online market place. The site offers a range of exciting services to entertain and inform users about art, antiques and collectibles.

My Agent is a "lot finder". It will hunt down items that you are looking for among our forthcoming lots offered by the world's markets, and when the items arrive for sale on icollector you will receive an e-mail inviting you to visit icollector to find out more.

Another free service, the **Art Price Guide** allows users to research prices realized at art sales at some 800 auction houses worldwide over the last 11 years.

These are just some of the services offered at icollector. The site is developing all the time in its quest to provide the best possible online environment for professional and amateur collectors alike.

See it all for yourself at www.icollector.com

NOTES

PHOTOGRAPHY CREDITS:
Elvis and Graceland images used by permission, Elvis Presley Enterprises, Inc.
All photographs on pages 26, 27, 28, and 29 courtesy of the Bernard J. Lansky Collection.

NOTES

FOLLOWING ARE THOSE WHO
WERE THRILLED TO HAVE WORKED
WITH GRACELAND:

Arlan Ettinger
Barbara Mintz
Amye Austin
Amanda Kearns
Philip Berne
Becky Porath
Molly Sherden
Richard Herzfeld
Steven Klein
Howard Reece
White Glove/Spartacus
Rubinstein Public Relations
Chip Baldoni
Linda Colley
Scot Knauer
Chris Herrington
Christine Distler
Carol Boker
Leslie Mitchell
The Sunshine Boys
Click Imaging
Interstate Litho.
Rosie Morgan Ettinger

GUERNSEY'S IN THE FUTURE

Entering the new millenium,
Guernsey's has scheduled an exciting array
of exceptional auctions in a wide variety of fields.
Listed below are some of the categories to be covered.
We look forward to hearing from you
should you have interest in these
or other events we will be conducting.

The Private Collections of Several Leading Ladies
The World of Haute Couture Fashion
Historic Jewels
Prominent Collections of Motion Picture Artifacts
Sports Artifacts and Artwork
Fairground Art
Vintage Aircraft
Historic Automobilia

GUERNSEY'S

108 East 73rd Street, New York NY 10021
Telephone: 212-794-2280; Fax 212-744-3638
www.guernseys.com